9/15/93

TEACHING MATHEMATICS TO YOUNG CHILDREN

Also available in the Cassell Education series:

Teaching Mathematics to Young Children

THIRD EDITION

Dennis Thyer
and
John Maggs

CASSELL

Cassell Educational Limited
Villiers House
41/47 Strand
London WC2N 5JE

First edition published in 1971 by Holt, Rinehart and Winston Ltd
Second edition published in 1981 by Holt, Rinehart and Winston Ltd
This edition first published in 1991

Reprinted 1992

British Library Cataloguing in Publication Data
Thyer, Dennis
    Teaching mathematics to young children.—3rd ed.—
    (Cassell education series).
    1. Great Britain. Infant schools. Curriculum subjects:
    Mathematics. Teaching
    I. Title   II. Maggs, John
    372.70440941

ISBN 0-304-32291-1

Typeset by Fakenham Photosetting Ltd., Fakenham, Norfolk
Printed and bound in Great Britain by
Mackays of Chatham PLC, Chatham, Kent

Contents

Preface

The purpose of this book is to describe in detail some of the mathematical ideas which could be introduced to young children. We place great emphasis on language and on non-numerical comparisons in order to build a sure foundation for further mathematical work. We discuss at length various procedures for the comparison of numbers, lengths, times, capacities, surfaces, volumes, areas and masses. Following this, numbers are used to describe attributes and are introduced into the test procedures. Initially lengths, times, capacities, etc. are compared using arbitrary units. Standard units are then gradually introduced according to the readiness of the children for them.

This book is based on the belief that children cannot discover mathematics through the environment alone. Concepts develop from the practical to the theoretical through the medium of language, and for this the teacher is an indispensable element. The role of the teacher is vital to the success of this teaching programme. She, herself, is fully conversant with the concepts she wishes the children to acquire and is also in possession of the correct social language for the various situations presented. The teacher has to show things, talk about and do something with them, and so introduce the language connected with these things together with the mathematical ideas involved. Procedures and techniques are demonstrated, and mathematical terms introduced and explained, before children are given tasks to do.

A chapter is devoted to number which includes notation and place value, and addition, subtraction, multiplication and division. Pictorial representation has been included in order to develop and illustrate numerical ideas, and some attention given to the development of ideas about fractions. The chapters on length, capacity, mass, etc. indicate that numerical ideas and arithmetical techniques can be strengthened by their application to these various fields. A considerable amount of attention is given to time, and to the calendar, both of which are often much neglected. A chapter is devoted to shape and space because geometry is closer to us than other branches of mathematics and its language is much used in everyday conversation. A chapter is also devoted to heaviness and mass, which goes as far as the introduction of kilograms and grams. The final chapter contains further uses of the mathematics introduced in earlier chapters in a variety of questions of the more open-ended type, often requiring investigative approaches, together with additional illustrations from children's literature and integrated projects. Mathematics needs to be presented so that children appreciate that 'the power of mathematics lies in its application'.

This book deals with mathematics and its teaching at Levels 1, 2 and 3 of the National Curriculum in Mathematics, with occasional inclusions at Level 4. It has been written for trainee teachers in departments or faculties of education in colleges of higher education, polytechnics and universities, and teachers of infant and lower junior children. We include details about the preparation of materials needed for demonstrations and activities, and point out some of the main difficulties likely to be encountered in the presentation. We consider it to be very important that there be careful making and selection of materials so that salient facts and ideas may be brought out in a clear manner, and correct conclusions made in the interpretation of the perceptual experiences. The book is specifically designed to aid the preparation and organization of mathematical work for infant and lower junior school children. Each topic is organized and developed as a whole so that the stages are seen in relation to what has preceded it and also what will follow. It does not omit, either, the fundamental ideas and language which may have been missed at home. We try to show clearly the development of each facet of the infant and lower junior mathematics syllabus in complete sequence in one book.

We would like to thank Mr B. S. Pugh, Senior Lecturer, Gwent College of Higher Education, for illustrating this edition. Also our special thanks to Sîan Rees for compiling the index.

Introduction

It is now generally accepted that for mathematics teaching, surer foundations are laid when the child's thinking is closely linked with perceptual experiences acquired by doing things. 'I do and I understand' is a sound principle with which to begin, but one which needs care in application. Children can be quite happily and busily engaged in doing things without the activity leading very far. This may be the result of ill-chosen apparatus, and there may be too many variables involved at once for sound judgements to be made. It may also be that the activity is not part of a progression of work on the topic. This is especially true, as far as mathematical work is concerned, of the activities at the sand tray or water trolley. There often is a lack of direction and the apparatus is not sufficiently well chosen to lead to useful conclusions being drawn. After some free play what is needed is a set of carefully chosen situations which might be engaged in and then discussed so as to lead in a direction which might fruitfully develop the topic.

Theoretical concepts develop out of perceptual experiences partly through the medium of language. With lower and middle infants especially we are trying to provide a foundation for the development of the concepts of number, mass, length, capacity, time and surface but we cannot begin individual work effectively with any of these topics until essential words, key phrases and procedures for comparing attributes have been introduced. General terms like 'bigger' can be developed in the appropriate circumstances to mean 'longer', 'wider', 'thicker', 'taller', etc., if we are dealing with length. In other circumstances it might be developed into 'holds more' or 'covers more'. Teachers can illustrate the meaning by doing things, talking about what is done and seen, and also by arranging activities for individual children to engage in. There is a need, at the early stages especially, for more 'talking time' with groups of children.

As the material contained in the book is intended as a source to which teachers and students can turn for examples of teaching lessons and activities appropriate to the topics dealt with, we have facilitated the development of a topic by breaking it down and analysing the individual steps.

The topics could be developed in the order suggested in each chapter but no significance should be placed on the order of the chapters. Children would work at the levels appropriate to their needs. In practice this would probably mean that most top infants would be working at Level 2 of the National Curriculum in Mathematics, some at Level 3 and a few still at Level 1.

In this work, after an initial qualitative approach, we have used length, time, surface, capacity, volume and mass to provide situations which lead to the formation and growth of number concepts. Most of the activities included require the sorting of items, and from this, number words and operations are developed. It seems fitting that number should be developed by associating it with measuring activities from various fields. Pictures and diagrams are also introduced and used to further develop numerical ideas.

Piaget's work has led us to believe that it is advisable, when displaying objects about which quantitative judgements have to be made, to use fixed procedures and in this to stabilize the configuration of the sets. It is for this reason that the sets of objects are put in rows side by side on card on which a square or rectangular grid has been drawn. The individual items in each set can then be matched in one-to-one correspondence, where that is applicable, and conclusions of 'more than', 'fewer than' or 'same number' be more easily drawn. Number concepts can be enriched by comparing the physical properties of things, e.g. the capacities of two boxes could be compared by filling each one with marbles and comparing rows of marbles. In this case it would be advisable to use a marble channel as described in the later text.

Fig. 1

When presenting articles whose physical properties are to be compared, it is necessary in the early stages to organize and control the shapes and the dimensions of the things to be compared, e.g. when presenting work on mass. At first comparing noticeably different amounts of plasticine, we could compare (a) two pieces which approximate to a cylindrical shape, having the same diameter but markedly different heights, or (b) two balls of plasticine markedly different in diameter (Fig. 1). The amounts are then seen to be different and the heavier is correctly chosen because those variables likely to confuse the senses involved in the judgement are kept to a minimum. Where more variables are allowed later, test procedures are introduced so that reliable judgements may still be made.

In order to compare capacities, initially a pair of cylindrical tins could be selected, one of which is taller and larger in diameter than the other. The tin of larger capacity could be selected by looking. This should have been preceded by free play in the sand tray, with containers amongst which this pair had been included. The choice can then be verified by pouring water from one tin into the other or by placing the one tin inside the other. Had we been considering which of two cylindrical tins holds more and had chosen one which was taller and narrower than the other, then it could have been that we were influenced by only one dimension, particularly if it were prominent. In this case (Fig. 2), the height might be the most arresting feature and so influence the choice in favour of the taller vessel. We have to demonstrate, talk about, discuss and give exercises to show

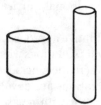

Fig. 2

that our senses may be inadequate in the formation of judgements unless supplemented by procedures designed to overcome the difficulties. We have to show methods which, though based on perception, do not deceive the senses. At first, a method such as filling one with water and pouring it into the other could be used, and a direct comparison made. Bearing in mind the nature of the ultimate tests of comparison which are used, tests could be introduced which are based on the use of a set of like containers against which the original containers are in turn compared. At first such comparisons are made without the use of number, and only when children are ready for it are numbers used in the comparison.

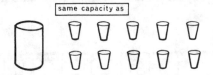

Fig. 3

One tin could be filled with water and then its contents poured, via a jug if necessary, into a set of like plastic beakers (Fig. 3). In this way the capacity is transformed into an equivalent capacity involving measuring units.

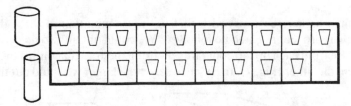

Fig. 4

We now have a means of comparing capacities by comparing the representative sets of measuring units. These can be put side by side on a grid background (Fig. 4). The row with more beakers, the longer row, shows that the tin which provided these units has the larger capacity. In order to reinforce the conclusion drawn, a check could be made by pouring water from one cylinder into the other as in the former test. The use of the grid background facilitates the pairing of respective members of the sets of beakers, and unpartnered members can be quickly seen. The measuring units themselves could also be rearranged and paired off to emphasize these ideas (Fig. 5).

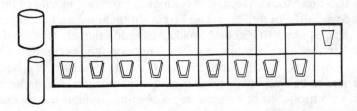

Fig. 5

In the investigation of other properties the units could possibly be displayed in other ways as well as on a grid. Units could be arranged in vertical piles, or placed in rows, side by side, and touching each other, e.g. stacking masses could be formed into vertical columns.

At a later stage the units could not only be displayed and judged for more, or fewer, or as many as, by the lengths of the rows, but could also be described using numbers (Fig. 6). The tins have capacities equivalent to ten and nine beakers respectively, to the nearest beaker. We see that the top row contains more beakers than the bottom row so that ten may be judged to be a bigger number than nine. This concrete representation enables numbers to be compared before they can be dealt with mentally. When children become more certain in their ideas of the ordering of numbers and of the counting sequence, the need to display sets of units to compare their number becomes unnecessary.

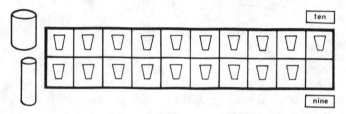

Fig. 6

When comparing surfaces, met with first in the examination of three-dimensional objects, a similar procedure could be followed. We could obtain two boxes and select a rectangular face from each box to compare, choosing them so that one of them is longer and wider than the other (Fig. 7). In trying to select the larger we could put them side by

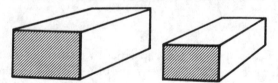

Fig. 7

side at first, and then put one face against the other within its boundary. Our senses will not always tell us what we want to know about the sizes of surfaces and so test procedures have to be adopted. The principles of these procedures can be developed from an early stage. The singular element of the test for surfaces is the fitting of a set of congruent shapes on to the surfaces to be compared. As a preliminary to this we could cut one of the two surfaces into pieces and try to fit them within the boundary of the other. Later, shapes which fit together could be used and the sets compared by putting on a grid as described above, and eventually numbers could be used.

Where standard units are introduced they are the units of the metric system although children still need to be aware of commonly used Imperial units, e.g. gallons, pints and miles. Units are introduced at various stages bearing in mind the mental outlook, numerical attainment and manual dexterity of the children. Work is carried out at first in non-standard units and the children helped to see a need for standard units. These are then introduced, one at a time; a new one not being introduced until the previous one can be used successfully.

These schemes of work have been designed with the view to making them operative within the framework of group organization and individual assignments. At the reception class stage the most convenient group size to take for 'talking-time' would probably be the whole class, but as the schemes progress the group size would be determined by who was ready to proceed to the next stage. This would necessitate the keeping of records of the progress of the children at the various stages, and this basically depends upon the judgement of the teacher. Can the child do the given task unaided? Can he describe the situation that he is involved in adequately?

It is also necessary that children see mathematics in operation. Cross-curricular projects will need to involve mathematics as well as other aspects of the National Curriculum. Projects such as '*Ourselves*' could serve as a vehicle for 'mathematics in action'. To illustrate this point we indicate in succeeding pages some mathematical activities from the four main areas of the National Curriculum which could be included.

OURSELVES

Attainment Targets 2–6: Number/Algebra

1. Sorting ourselves, e.g. sex, age, height, mass, birth months.
2. Sorting our clothing, e.g. sizes, types, colours, purpose, material used, fastenings.
3. Counting in groups using hands and fingers. Sorting ourselves into sets of 2, 3, 5, 10, etc. Even and odd numbers. Growth patterns—2, 4, 6, 8, . . .; 5, 10, 15, 20, . . .; 3, 6, 9, 12, 15, . . .
4. Sharing equally some lemonade, biscuits, Smarties, marbles, or sugar among 2, 3 or 4 children. Halves, thirds, quarters.
5. Birthday dates, and ages in years and months.
6. How much pocket money we get. How we spend it. Savings over a perid of time.
7. Costing a pastime or hobby.
8. Costing our cooking.
9. Cost of keeping a pet.
10. Costing a birthday party.
11. Our day. Times when various events occur. Telling the time and recording it.
12. Our day. How long we spend on various activities during a school day or a Saturday or Sunday.
13. Each child keeps a 'passport', e.g. age, date of birth, family tree, height, mass, waist measurement, shoe size, length of span, length of pace, how far I can jump, etc.

Attainment Target 8: Measures

1. Who are the tallest and shortest children in the class?
   (a) by using silhouettes
   (b) by using non-standard units
   (c) by measuring to the nearest decimetre
   (d) by measuring to the nearest centimetre.

2. Who are the heaviest and lightest children in the class?
   (a) by sight and lifting
   (b) by using a see-saw
   (c) by using bathroom scales.
3. Measuring items using body measures, e.g. spans, feet, paces.
4. Measuring our bodies, and body measures, using standard units, e.g. neck, waist, height, span, foot, digit, yard. Clothes sizes.
5. Who has the longest span, the shortest foot, the longest pace?
6. How far can I jump? How high can I jump? Who can jump the farthest, highest? How far can I throw a bean bag?
7. Whose hand covers most? Whose foot covers most?
8. How much water do we drink at lunch time?
9. How much liquid does a child, or family, drink each day?
10. How much water is used at home daily for washing up?
11. How much water does my family use in a day?
12. How much water is wasted if we leave a tap dripping?
13. How much milk is used at home each week?
14. Measure out the ingredients and make some cakes.
15. Kind, and amount, of food a child, or family, eats on a particular day.
16. Timing activities using
    (a) non-standard measures
    (b) standard measures, e.g. seconds, minutes and seconds, hours and minutes.
17. What can we do in a minute?
18. Time taken to run, hop, walk a specified distance. Fastest and slowest?
19. How far do I live from school? How long does it take to walk or ride to school?
20. Time spent watching television each day.
21. The canteen ladies' day.
22. Birthdays and ages of children. Who are the oldest and youngest children in the class?

Attainment Targets 10 and 11: Shape and Size

1. Opportunities in P.E. and games for geometrical vocabulary, e.g. under, above, next to, behind, left turn, four paces forward, one turn clockwise.
2. Giving instructions for getting from home to school.
3. Shapes of things that we use, or see, at home, school or elsewhere, e.g. a ball, a bicycle, a cream carton, a fruit tin, a house, a church.
4. Patterns we see at home. Tiles, tablecloths, teacloths, pullovers, carpets, wallpapers.
5. Drawing and colouring patterns on squared, triangular and hexagonal ruled papers. Using various geometrical shapes to draw patterns on plain paper.
6. Making pictures of everyday objects using gummed paper circles, squares, oblongs and triangles.
7. Symmetrical things we have at home.
8. Toys we play with. Patterns for making stuffed toys. Scale models of cars, trains,

aeroplanes, ships, doll's house furniture. Spinning tops, yo-yos, kaleidoscopes, gliders, Meccano, Spirograph, gyroscopes.

9. Drawing to scale the classroom, hall and playground. Also teacher's table.
10. Sketching things we use from above and from the side, e.g. a cup, a ball, a toothbrush, a table, a chair.
11. A child sketches his/her house upstairs and downstairs, and a room with furniture in it.
12. Making a cardboard model of the school or our house.
13. Sketching items in 3-D on triangular dotty paper.
14. Congruence—Tracing pictures. Comparing different sizes of photographs of the same children. Looking at things in curved mirrors and lenses—similarity.
15. Making paper serviettes for a birthday party by paper folding and cutting.
16. Making Christmas decorations by folding, cutting and colouring.

Attainment Targets 12, 13 and 14: Handling Data

1. Collecting data
   number of boys and girls in the class
   colours of hair, eyes
   how we come to school
   what food I eat each day
   number of children staying for dinner
   shoe fasteners
2. Pictorial and graphical representation
   shoe sizes
   heights
   masses
   favourite food
   favourite kind of crisps
   shoe colours
   favourite television programme
   favourite reading book or poem
   family sizes
   number of brothers and sisters
   kinds of pets kept
   numbers of each kind of pet
   colours of our cars
   birthmonths
   days of week on which birthdays occur this year
   put our birthdays on a time line
   how far we can jump or throw a bean bag
   times taken to run 100 m by a group of children
   times spent on various subjects during a school day
   pocket money received weekly
   amount of television watched each day
   scores we obtained in a spelling test

how many of each item were sold at the class shop during break
daily takings from the class shop at break time
how I spend my time on Saturday or Sunday
lengths of our feet, spans and paces
my height, each month, over the year
my mass, monthly, over the year

3. Using data bases
4. Probability/chance
   (a) use of words in everyday language, e.g. I will, I might, probably, possibly, impossible.
   (b) ideas about probabilities arising from the playing of games, e.g. obtaining a particular number when throwing a die,
       landing on a particular square when playing snakes and ladders or Monopoly,
       drawing particular cards from a pack.

Other projects which are commonly followed in schools could be analysed in a similar way. These will be mainly cross-curricular because there will be a need to cater for attainment targets from various subject areas. Some of the projects will stem from the desire of the science co-ordinator to see science-oriented projects. Equally well some could stem from the influences of the primary school History Attainment Targets. Some projects may also arise from mathematics itself. Mathematics will thus be seen to have cross-curricular significance and since many of the projects are 'environmental' the mathematics developed will be seen to be useful in the 'real world'.

The following projects would have a considerable potential for mathematical involvement:

Transport	Patterns
Water	Colour and Light
Our Homes	Autumn
Our School	Castles
People who were here before us	Buildings
Change	Our Village
The Neighbourhood	The River
The Supermarket	Tourists
The Biscuit Factory	Birthdays
Shape and Space	Toys
Puzzles	Games we play

Such work as this, whether within or outside the boundaries of a project, should not be confined to aspects of knowledge, skills and understanding. Children should be able to use their mathematics whether in practical everyday situations or within mathematics itself. According to the *Cockcroft Report*, '*problem solving is at the heart of mathematics*', and so some of the applications of knowledge, skills and understanding should be to problem-solving and to the rather more open-ended, and possibly extended, investigations. For this reason the first eight chapters include examples of the uses and applications of mathematics directly related to the subject matter of those chapters. However, since not all mathematical tasks are simply related to one topic area, and since the authors wished to include some examples of problem-solving and investigations, a further chapter has been added to contain these further uses and applications.

In the paragraph headings of this book we have included references to Attainment Targets of the National Curriculum in mathematics. The references given indicate that the content of the paragraph lies within those Attainment Targets at the Levels stated. The method of referencing the National Curriculum is as follows:

(4, 8 L2) means the work is relevant to Attainment Targets 4 and 8 at Level 2;
(3 L2, 3) indicates the topics are included in AT 3 at levels 2 and 3;
(2, 3 L2; 3, 5 L3; 3, 5 L4) means the work is appropriate for ATs 2 and 3 at Level 2, ATs 3 and 5 at Level 3 and ATs 3 and 5 at Level 4.

Some of the work concerning number is pre-Level 1, which we describe as 'working towards Level 1'.

Our hope is that we have provided a source of schemes and activities which will aid the student and the teacher in the preparation of work to meet the needs of the teaching of mathematics in the primary school and in particular those associated with the implementation of the National Curriculum. The content of this book is mainly concerned with Levels 1, 2 and 3 of the National Curriculum.

Chapter 1

Number Including Pictorial Representation

1.1 INITIAL ACTIVITIES (Working towards 2 L1)

Some play activities for children take place at home but many are provided in the nursery or reception class in an infants school. The school often supplies a much wider and more stimulating range of activities involving more expensive materials and equipment than many homes could hope to provide.

The provision of games for pre-number play in which a number of socially identifiable objects may be displayed in a meaningful way by the child and the teacher is highly desirable. For example, some of the play activities could be centred around a garage, a farm, a shop or a Wendy house. Language growth is most important and the development of more precise mathematical language from everyday language should be fostered.

When a child is playing with the garage, for example, the adult might ask what all the cars placed together are doing there. It might be that in the child's game they are waiting for petrol. Talk could proceed about there being many cars waiting for petrol. 'What a lot of cars there are waiting for petrol. There aren't enough pumps. There aren't many cars for repair. There's a petrol pump free so another car can get petrol. Do we have enough garages for the cars? Are there too many cars to go in the garages?'

The familiarization of the children with number names, essential for counting, could take place by the use of nursery rhymes, stories and finger plays. The number names to five might be dealt with by saying

> One, two, three, four, five,
> Once I caught a fish alive.

or by using the finger play,

> Here is the beehive, where are the bees,
> Hiding where nobody sees, etc.

Many other rhymes could be used to familiarize the children with number names in which the names are said in the usual order or the reverse order. A rich source of such rhymes is *This Little Puffin—Nursery Songs and Rhymes*, a Young Puffin original compiled by Elizabeth Matterson.

1.2 SORTING (Working towards 2 L1)

A cardinal number is used to describe how many items there are in a collection. If

10

children are to learn about cardinal numbers we must first ask them to establish sets of things and then talk about the total of the objects in each set. The teacher should provide materials which can be sorted, using sensory experiences, according to size, colour, shape, feel (texture), purpose, and so on.

Some suggestions for sorting activities are listed:

1. Sort Cuisenaire rods according to colour and size.
2. Use assorted beads. Sort by colour, shape or size.
3. Use assorted marbles. Sort into big and small, different colours, blue ones and not blue ones.
4. Use assorted cubes. Sort into big and small, different colours, red ones and not red ones.
5. Use miscellaneous plastic objects, Counting Toys. Find pigs, cats, horses, orange things, yellow things, etc.
6. Use farm animals. Sort into different types, e.g. cows, sheep, pigs, horses. Sort according to large and small, or colour.
7. Use miscellaneous cardboard shapes. Find triangles, rectangles and circles. Find circles the same size as this one. Find a triangle larger than this.
8. Use Poleidoblocs. Sort according to colour. Find more shapes just like this one (a cone). Find the shapes which roll. Find shapes which slide.
9. Use a 'feely' box. Sort things into rough and smooth; also big and small.
10. Use plastic pegs. Sort into various colours.
11. Use zoo animals. Sort into different colours. Find tigers, elephants, giraffes, etc. Find ones with spots. Find those with stripes. Find those which climb trees.
12. Use a collection of buttons. Sort according to colour, shape or size.
13. Use a box of miscellaneous objects in which some are the same. Find the things which are the same.
14. Use the percussion band instruments. Find those which make a 'bang' and those which 'tinkle'.
15. Some sorting may proceed naturally through a play activity, e.g. the vehicles of a model garage. Sort by colour. Find cars, vans and lorries. Possibly some model cars could be sorted into different makes by some children.
16. Collect leaves from trees. Sort into big and small, light and dark green, or rough and smooth.
17. With the children, collect stones from the school grounds. Sort into big and small, rough and smooth, or red stones (pieces of brick) and not red stones.
18. With the children collect twigs from trees. Sort into long and short, or those with black buds (ash) and not black buds.
19. The articles in the class shop could be sorted for type of package, e.g. tins or packets. Find tall tins or boxes. Find shapes like this one (a cylinder).
20. Sort objects for sinking and floating using the water trolley.
21. Use miscellaneous objects. Find objects lighter than a given stone by picking things up or by using a common balance.
22. Use various containers. Find those which hold more water than this bottle. Find the tallest.
23. Use bamboo canes of different lengths. Find sticks longer than this one.
24. The teacher could give a child a marble, a table tennis ball, a tennis ball, a golf ball,

a ball made of plasticine, a bag of sand, a lump of 'Playdoh', a ball bearing. Sort into those which bounce and do not bounce.

25. Sorting could be pursued using Logic Blocks. The teacher could control the variables to make the activity suitable for a particular child, e.g. find red things, yellow triangles, or large blue circles.

The children could also be presented with sets of objects and asked which item does not belong to the set. For example, show 4 apples and 1 orange; an apple, an orange, a banana and a cup; etc.

Children who succeed at sorting with concrete materials could proceed to sorting using pictures of objects. Cards, each with a picture of one item, could be prepared showing:

socks—	1 blue long,	1 brown long,	1 blue short,	1 brown short.
worms—	1 red long,	1 brown long,	1 red short,	1 brown short.
dogs—	1 black long,	1 brown long,	1 black short,	1 brown short.
cars—	1 red long,	1 blue long,	1 red short,	1 blue short.

Find red and not red things; long and short things; dogs and not dogs; blue socks and not blue socks; long dogs; etc.

A set of pictures could be given showing things which fly or do not fly, e.g. a bird, butterfly, aeroplane, kite, bus, motorboat. Ask a child to sort these. A child could form unexpected sets and this is very acceptable provided a valid reason is given, e.g. the aeroplane, bus and motorboat could be put together because they have engines; and the kite, bird and butterfly because they do not.

A set of pictures could be used showing different fruits (apple, orange, pear, banana, lemon); various tools (hammer, saw, pincers, screwdriver), various animals (cat, dog, rabbit, mouse); articles of clothing (shirt, trousers, dress, socks, shoes). These could be sorted.

1.3 MATCHING AND PAIRING (Working towards 2 L1)

Articles or pictures of objects could be paired according to whether they are the same or go together to fulfil a purpose. The following are some suggested activities for individual children:

1. Use objects and pictures of these objects. Sort them by putting each object on its picture.
2. Use shapes and an inset board. Fit each shape into its appropriate compartment.
3. Pictures of objects could be stuck or drawn on cardboard squares, and these put on top of corresponding pictures on a larger master card. (A lotto-like game.)
4. Pictures for the lotto-type game in **3** could be confined to geometrical shapes. Circles, squares, triangles, diamonds, semicircles, T- and H-shapes could be included. These could be of various colours, and large and small. Matching pictures could be selected according to size, colour and shape.
5. Pictures of objects mounted on cards could be paired, e.g. a cup and a saucer, a knife

and a fork, a car with a garage, a bucket and a spade, a cricket bat and a ball, a doll and a doll's pram, etc.

6. Pictures of animals could be paired with their young, e.g. a cow with a calf, a horse and foal, a hen and a chick, a sheep and a lamb, a pig and a piglet, a cat and a kitten, a duck with a duckling, etc.

7. Pictures of objects could also be used, a few of which do not pair off, e.g. a dog, a bone, a hammer, a nail, a goldfish, a fish tank of water, a sausage, a frying pan, a pen, an apple. Which things have no partners?

The exercises mentioned in **5**, **6** and **7** could be done by providing pictures of objects on cyclostyled sheets and asking the children to draw connecting lines between related pairs. A more permanent piece of apparatus could be obtained by sticking or drawing the pictures on a piece of strong cardboard and fixing strings or laces to some of the objects. Each string, or lace, is stretched to its corresponding partner, and put into a lacehole. When completed, all objects are connected in pairs, by strings.

1.4 COMPARING TWO SETS OF ITEMS NON-NUMERICALLY (Working towards 2 L1)

Sets of objects can be compared according to the number of items in each. To compare the number of items in two sets we pair an item in one set with an item in the other set. If the objects pair off exactly the sets have the same number of objects, if not, one set has more objects in it than the other (Fig. 1.1). This is an important mathematical principle and children should have plenty of practice comparing sets for more than, fewer than and the same number.

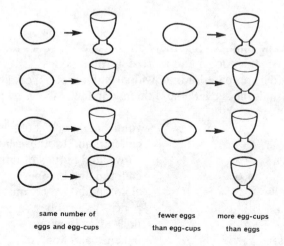

| same number of eggs and egg-cups | fewer eggs than egg-cups | more egg-cups than eggs |

Fig. 1.1

Models

We might begin by using a model of a real situation on which to base our language of comparison, e.g. the model garage. Small boxes could be glued together or put side by side to represent garages for cars and lorries. One vehicle only goes into each garage. Do we have *enough* garages? Have we *too many* cars for the garages? Let us get some *more* garages. Have we *too many* garages for the cars? Some garages are *empty*. We could put in *more* cars. A discussion involving these situations could lead to more formal mathematical language, such as there are *more garages than cars*, or there are *fewer cars than garages*, or possibly that there are the *same number* of cars as garages.

Suppose a group of children are comparing sets of eggs (table tennis balls) and egg-cups, and after the egg-cups are filled there are some eggs left. Explain and discuss the fact that there are fewer egg-cups than eggs and more eggs than egg-cups.

Other activities could be organized with actual objects, such as cups and saucers, knives and forks, straws and bottles of milk, dolls and doll's cots, etc.

Pictures

Pictures of objects could be drawn, or stuck, on cardboard squares of the same size. Prepare no more than 10–15 cards in each set. Suppose eight dog and four bone cards were prepared and put together in an envelope. A child is given the cards and asked if each dog could have a bone. He sorts the cards into pairs and finds there are some dog cards left over. Encourage the children to arrange the cards in pairs, and in rows, as they are being sorted (Fig. 1.2).

Fig. 1.2

Talk with the child and establish that there are not enough bones for the dogs; that is, there are fewer bones than dogs, and more dogs than bones.

Sets of cards could be prepared, for individual children, on the following themes. In each case the child finds the set with more things and fewer things by pairing the cards:

birds and nests;
dogs and kennels;
buckets and spades;
children and bars of chocolate;
cricket bats and balls;
birds and worms;
flowers and vases;
pennies and purses;
dogs and cats;

goldfish and bowls of water;
children and toothbrushes;
straws and bottles of milk;
children and bicycles;
children and ice-creams;
pencils and rubbers;
dolls and prams;
bananas and apples.

Grids

Exercises could be set involving the use of a squared background or grid, to compare sets of objects. A grid is necessary when comparing sets because it ensures that the objects in each set are spaced out in like manner. A longer row of objects on a table does not necessarily contain more items than a shorter row. If a grid is used, and one object is put in each compartment, the longer row always displays the set with the greater number of objects. At first use ten-grids, with two rows, to compare two sets containing no more than ten objects, and proceed to the use of twenty-grids (Fig. 1.3).

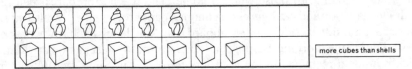

more cubes than shells

Fig. 1.3

Arrange for individual children to do the following activities which involve the use of a grid to compare two sets of items:

1. The teacher puts various sets of items into a box, e.g. shells, beads, marbles, cubes, conkers, acorns, etc. Ask the child if there are more shells than cubes, more acorns than beads, etc. (Fig. 1.3).
2. The teacher puts a selection of objects in a box, such as 6 pigs, 8 cars, 9 vans, 7 cats, 5 dogs, etc. (use Counting Toys). Ask a child if there are more cats than dogs, more vans than cars, more cats than pigs, etc.
3. Use coloured beads of the same size. The teacher puts 10 yellow, 15 red, 8 green, 10 blue and 6 brown beads in a tin. Ask if there are more red beads than blue beads, fewer green beads than yellow beads, etc.
4. The teacher prepares a box containing different coloured cubes of the same size. Ask if there are more red cubes than green cubes, more yellow cubes than blue cubes, etc.
5. The teacher prepares a box containing sets of congruent plastic square counters of different colours. Ask if there are more red than yellow, more blue than green, etc.
6. Two children take some cubes, conkers, etc. from a box. Ask who took more.
7. One child takes cubes from a box and puts them in a row on a grid. Her partner is asked to take out more cubes.
8. One child takes conkers from a bag. Her partner is asked to take out the same number of conkers.

Pegs

Sets of pegs can also be compared using a pegboard:

1. A child puts a row of pegs on a pegboard. Her partner makes a row alongside containing the same number of pegs.

2. A child takes some pegs from a box and puts them in a row on a pegboard. His partner puts a row alongside with more pegs.
3. A child selects red and green pegs so that there are more red pegs.

1.5 COMPARING TWO SETS NON-NUMERICALLY USING PICTOGRAMS
(Working towards 2 L1; 12, 13 L1)

The teacher could arrange, as a class activity, to compare the number of children who stay for school dinner with those who go home. The teacher prepares, beforehand, simple drawings of boy and girl figures on gummed paper rectangles; she also marks two rows of rectangles, side by side, on a cardboard strip, and labels each row with a picture (Fig. 1.4). During the morning ask the children, in turn, to collect a boy or girl drawing and stick it inside a rectangle in the appropriate row. If possible, before sticking the figures on the strip, get the children to print their names on them. When all the children have stuck their figures on the strip the teacher could assemble the class and talk with the children for a few minutes about the pictogram. Which row is longer? Match the 'children' in one row with those in the other. Do more 'children' go home or stay at school for dinner?

Fig. 1.4

A few days later repeat the exercise but present the data differently. Ask each child in turn, during the morning, to stick a boy or girl drawing inside or outside a circle previously drawn on a piece of card, and labelled 'we stay for dinner' (Fig. 1.5). If possible, get the children to print their names on the figures before they stick them on the card. Gather the class together for a few minutes when all the children have stuck their figures on the strip. Ask whether more 'children' stay at school for dinner than do not stay. Explain that it is difficult to say by looking. (We could match figures, or try to, by stretching strings between 'children' inside and outside the circle, but we would have quite a few strings and the situation is likely to be confused.) Then refer to the other way

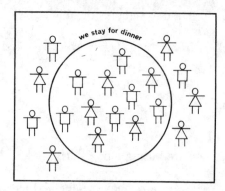

Fig. 1.5

of presenting the same information (Fig. 1.4). Why do you think putting the figures in rows, side by side, is the better way of showing this information? Talk about this.

The class could take part in building pictograms for the following instances using the form of presentation shown in Fig. 1.4. This could be done within a project, e.g. '*Ourselves*'.

1. those who wear glasses and those who do not wear glasses
2. those who have a pet, and those who do not have a pet
3. those who walk to school and those who do not walk to school
4. those who have buckles on their shoes and those who do not have buckles on their shoes
5. those who have a bicycle and those who do not have a bicycle.

Children could, during the morning, each stick a drawing on a squared paper strip and in an appropriate row. When each pictogram is completed, the teacher could ask the class non-numerical questions, and talk with the children about the results.

1.6 COMPARING TWO SETS: NON-NUMERICAL APPLICATIONS (Working towards 2 L1; 8 L2)

Many instances to compare two sets non-numerically arise from the learning activities connected with length, area, capacity, volume, time, money, heaviness and mass. Many of the preliminary activities in these fields concern more than, fewer or less than, the same number as, and so provide excellent opportunities for reinforcement and application. For example, children could be set individual exercises as follows:

1. Find the heavier of two tins of sand by balancing them with metal bolts. The tins are prepared beforehand to balance seven bolts and five bolts. The bolts that are just as heavy as each tin are laid in rows, side by side, on a paper strip with rectangles just large enough to contain a bolt (Fig. 1.6). The top row contains more bolts than the bottom one, so the top tin is heavier.

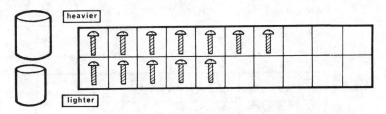

Fig. 1.6

2. Find the heavier of two lumps of plasticine, or two bags of sand, by balancing them with wooden cubes, marbles or pieces of metal (stacking masses). The teacher prepares each item beforehand so that it balances an exact number of cubes, marbles or stacking masses. The child displays the units in rows, side by side, on a squared paper strip (Fig. 1.7). Stacking pieces, and possibly cubes, could be built into two

towers instead, side by side, to be compared. The taller tower would indicate the heavier.

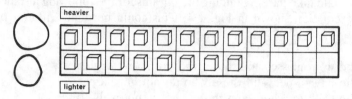

Fig. 1.7

3. The teacher puts two bamboo canes already cut into lengths equivalent to eight Cuisenaire orange rods and six orange rods on different tables well apart. Compare the lengths of these canes by placing the orange rods against each one, and then putting these rods in two rows, side by side. Check the answer by holding the canes together. Repeat this activity using other specially prepared pieces of cane or wooden dowel.

4. Compare the capacities of two small tins or boxes, by filling them as well as possible with marbles or wooden beads. The child places the beads between three thin wooden strips to compare them (Fig. 1.8). (The teacher selects boxes that hold no more than 50 marbles.)

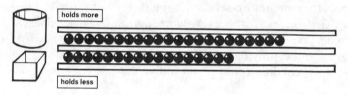

Fig. 1.8

5. Compare the capacities of two bottles or tins, using identical beakers or other small containers. Fill each bottle with beakers of water, and stand the empty beakers in two rows, side by side, on a squared paper strip. Which tin needs more beakers of water to fill it? Which tin holds more water? Which tin has the larger capacity? (Fig. 1.9).

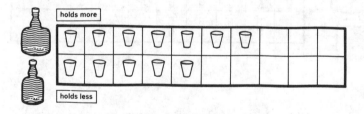

Fig. 1.9

6. Compare the capacities of two boxes or tins, by filling them as well as possible with cubes of a convenient size. Shake the boxes as they are being filled so that the cubes

fit in reasonably well. Put the cubes which fill each tin, touching, in two rows, side by side, and so compare the capacities of the boxes or tins.

7. Provide two rectangles, or other shapes, with straight sides, which have been specially cut so that squares just cover them. The child covers each shape with squares, and fits the squares, end to end, in two rows, side by side, in order to find the row with more squares. The row with more squares covers more. The child checks the result, if possible, by placing one shape on the other and seeing if its boundary lies within the boundary of the other.

8. Repeat **7**, but use two shapes specially cut so that congruent plastic right-angled triangles will just cover them. Any congruent plastic shapes will do providing they just cover the shapes to be compared (Fig. 1.10).

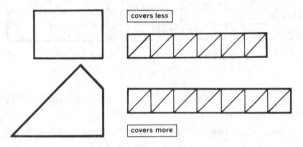

Fig. 1.10

9. A child compares the times taken for two other children, in turn, to build a tower with blocks. The child times each event by taking marbles from a box, one at a time, and at regular intervals, and putting them in a tin. The marbles collected are then compared by arranging them in two rows between three straight sticks. Which row has more marbles? Which row of marbles took longer to collect? Who took the longer time to build a tower, Bill or John? Also compare the times taken for other activities, such as putting on a coat, filling a tin with water, sorting cubes into various colours, etc.

1.7 COMPARING MORE THAN TWO SETS OF ITEMS NON-NUMERICALLY (Working towards 2 L1)

When a child can compare two sets of objects successfully he or she could be given three or more sets of items to compare. The language of comparison in these cases would include the words **most, fewest, more, fewer** and **as many as**.

Children could work individually, or as specified, at the following tasks. Compile work cards and read them to the children or give oral instructions.

1. The teacher puts three or four sets of different objects into a box or plastic bag, e.g. vans, cars, lorries; or cats, dogs, pigs, horses (use Counting Toys). A child sorts the items and places them in rows on a three- or four-row grid. Ask 'Are there more cars than vans; more lorries than cars? Which row contains most vehicles? Name them. Which row has fewest vehicles? Name them.'

2. Use coloured beads of the same size. Put yellow, red, green, blue, orange and brown beads in a tin (less than 20 of each colour). Ask a child to pick out three colours of bead, e.g. red, blue and yellow. Arrange the sets of beads in rows on a three- or four-row twenty-grid. Ask 'Are there more red than blue, more yellow than red? Which colour of bead is there most of? Which row has fewest beads? What colour are they?'
3. Give a child some shells in four bags. Find the bag with most shells, and the bag with fewest shells in it by putting the shells on a four-row twenty-grid (Fig. 1.11). Repeat with cubes in three or four boxes.

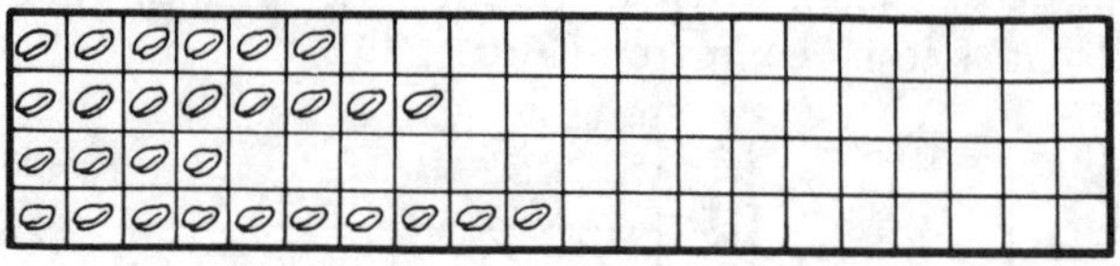

Fig. 1.11

4. Working in threes, each child select shells, acorns or conkers from a bag. Who took most shells? Who took fewest shells?
5. Three children select pegs from a box. Who took most and fewest pegs? Put the pegs in rows, side by side, on a pegboard to find out.

1.8 COMPARING MORE THAN TWO SETS NON-NUMERICALLY USING PICTOGRAMS (Working towards 2 L1)

Now we proceed to pictograms involving more than two categories. As previously described the children could stick drawings or cut-out shapes in labelled rows of squares or rectangles, drawn by the teacher beforehand, on a strip of thin card. The teacher could make cardboard templates for the children to draw around in order to obtain some of the cut-outs or, if the items can be drawn easily, the children could do them on gummed paper rectangles the same size as the rectangles drawn on the prepared strip. Alternatively, bought gummed cut-outs or pictures could be used.

Information could be presented using boy and girl figures arranged in labelled rows, or by sticking cut-outs or pictures of the items in rows (Figs. 1.12 and 1.13).

The class could build a pictogram for each of the situations listed below, some of which could be included in '*Ourselves*'. Each child could, in turn, during the morning, stick a drawing or cut-out onto the strip. The teacher would ask the children questions, and talk with them, about each pictogram as it is completed, paying particular attention to the language used, e.g. **more, fewer, most, fewest, as many as.**

1. Use three categories of socks: grey, white and other colours. Ask the child to draw around a cardboard 'sock' template, colour the sock the appropriate colour and cut it out. Display the 'socks' in rows on a squared background.
2. Let each child choose his or her favourite fruit from an orange, an apple and a banana. Display the information in two different ways using fruit pictures and boy and girl figures (Figs. 1.12 and 1.13).

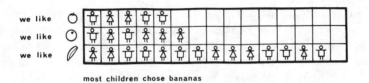

we like ○
we like ◉
we like ∅

most children chose bananas

Fig. 1.12

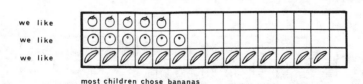

we like
we like
we like

most children chose bananas

Fig. 1.13

3. Use three categories: children with blue eyes, brown eyes, and other colours of eyes. Display boy and girl figures, arranged in rows labelled with a blue eye, a brown eye, and an uncoloured eye.
4. Use three categories: children with brown shoes, black shoes, and other colours of shoes. Display rows of boy and girl stickers, or rows of 'shoe' cut-outs coloured black, brown, and other colours. (The teacher could prepare a 'shoe' template, or use shoe pictures cut from catalogues.)
5. Use three categories: those children who walk to school, come by car or come by bus. Display boy and girl figures, arranged in rows labelled with pictures of a bus, a car and a walking figure.
6. Use three categories: those children who are wearing laced shoes, buckled shoes or slip-on shoes. Display boy and girl figures, or pictures of shoes from catalogues.
7. Sort children into those with fair, black, brown and ginger hair. Display boy and girl figures, arranged in four rows labelled with faces showing dark hair, fair hair, black hair and ginger hair.
8. Use four sets: those children who have a scooter, a two-wheeled bicycle, a three-wheeled bicycle, or none of these. Display boy and girl figures in rows opposite pictures of these items, if appropriate.
9. Use four categories: children who have a cat, a dog, a bird, any other animals. Each child draws a picture of his animal on a gummed paper rectangle and sticks it in the appropriate row.
10. Draw (on cardboard) and cut out three or four purses of different colours and on each purse stick gummed paper pennies (less than 20). The child could cover the pennies in each purse with gummed paper pennies and then stick the pennies from each purse in three or four rows on a squared grid. Ask the children 'Which purse has most pennies in it? Which purse has fewest pennies in it?'

1.9 COMPARING TWO OR MORE SETS: NON-NUMERICAL APPLICATIONS (Working towards 2 L1)

Compile work cards and set individual work. Read the cards to the childen or give oral instructions.

1. Ask a child to compare the capacities of three or four different coloured boxes using cubes of a convenient size. (The teacher should select the boxes, or make them, into which cubes will just fit. Confine the number of cubes needed to below 30.) The cubes could be laid out on a squared paper strip with their respective boxes alongside as shown in Fig. 1.14. (If there are not too many cubes they could be built into towers, side by side.) Ask 'Which box holds most? Which holds least? Does the green box hold more than the yellow one?'

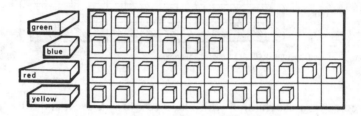

Fig. 1.14

2. Prepare three or four bags of sand so that they balance cubes, nuts and bolts, or large nails. The child can then compare the heaviness of the bags by balancing them with prescribed units using a common balance, and then arrange the units in rows, side by side, to discover which bag is heaviest and which is lightest.
3. Ask the child to compare the amounts in three or four lumps of plasticine, or sand in three or four bags, by balancing them with cubes, marbles, metal bolts or stacking masses. (Prepare the plasticine or bags of sand so that they just balance the units used.)

   The child can place the units needed to balance each lump of plasticine in rows, side by side, and so find the largest and smallest amounts. Cubes or stacking masses could be compared by building towers with them, side by side.
4. Ask the child to compare the surfaces of three or four cardboard shapes by covering them with plastic squares, having first made sure the squares just fit the shapes. Put the squares which cover each shape, touching, in three or four rows, side by side, to find which shape is biggest because it covers most.

   Which row has most squares? Which row of squares covers most? Which shape did these squares fit on? Which shape covers most? Also find which shape covers least.

1.10 GENERAL COMMENTS ABOUT NUMERICAL WORK

All comparisons so far have not involved numbers. The items in the sets concerned were matched, one-to-one, and the greater number associated with the set containing unmatched members. If the elements of one set partner all the elements in another, we said that the sets contained the same number of items. These ideas were developed by placing items in rows, side by side, always on a squared grid, thus ensuring one-to-one correspondence. Because of this layout the number could also be interpreted by the length of the row, the longer the row the greater the number, the shorter the row the smaller the number. Rows of items of the same length indicated sets containing the same number of things.

Before starting school, and at school, children acquire ideas about cardinal numbers, that is, about numbers which quantitatively describe sets of things. When children can use these numbers correctly and arrange them in order of size mentally, they can compare sets of things without having to display them or their representations. The teacher can also ask many more questions about data which have been collected and the units used to measure and compare attributes, e.g. length or capacity.

Pictorial and concrete representation, and cardinal numbers, are complementary. Children learn about numbers, and their relative sizes, by learning number names and symbols; by handling, observing and counting sets of objects; and by observing and counting pictures of items; and from these activities they acquire a facility for dealing with numbers mentally. If a child knows that fifteen is greater than eight, there is no need to represent a child by a coloured square, and to make columns with fifteen and eight squares to show that more boys stay for dinner than girls. If children are uncertain about these numbers, however, this representation serves a useful purpose. When a child is learning number names and is not sure of their relative sizes, a display of rows of pictures or measuring units often helps to clarify a situation and enables sets to be compared. He can see, for example, that fifteen marbles are more than twelve marbles, because when the marbles are arranged in rows, side by side, the former number makes the longer row.

Before children are asked to use numbers to compare lengths or masses they should describe and compare sets of things, e.g. conkers, cubes, animals, or acorns. When children can do this, fairly successfully, numbers could be applied to other fields. If we ask which has the larger capacity, and by how much, the terms **larger** and **smaller** could be interpreted by comparing the number of beads which fill each container. The container which has the larger capacity is judged to be the one which holds more beads. To find how much larger, a child would find the difference between the number of beads needed to fill each container. Similarly, to time events and compare them, the child could collect marbles regularly dropped into two tins, the longer time being determined as the duration of that event in which the greater number of marbles was collected. All comparisons using units of measure and involving the use of pictures and abstracts need numerical ideas in order to be examined, and this is why the development of number is needed before we can proceed far in this field.

Children learn about numbers by handling and looking at sets of items and learning number names, comparing sets of things and learning the counting sequence, and combining and partitioning sets of items in various ways. Counting is often the only way of finding how many items there are in a set, particularly with groups of more than four or five items.

There is a great danger in allowing a child to say the number whilst pointing to a particular item of a collection if he is at all unsure of the meaning of what he is doing. Some children need a lot of experience in counting and the children might be helped by making them transfer the items being counted into a tin-lid as the number names are being said. They need to be closely watched and listened to in order to ensure the next number is said just after the additional item has been put on the lid.

The number of items in small groups can sometimes be recognized, and sometimes a rearrangement of the items helps children to find how many things there are, but as children gain numerical knowledge the need to count could diminish. For example, if a set of items appears to be clustered as three items and two items, a child could say 'three and one is four', and 'one more is five', or just 'three and two more is five'.

Children in earlier activities will have met the word **none** in various ways. The idea of none occurs in some rhymes, through counting backwards, as in *Ten Green Bottles* or *There Were Ten in the Bed*. Children will also have come across it in everyday situations where, for example, sweets are eaten until they are all gone, that is, none are left. Milk bottles are taken from a crate one at a time until it is empty, that is, no bottles are in the crate. None also occurs when looking for sets of objects and finding there are not any, such as there are no blue beads, no children with green eyes, no children have a guinea pig. Situations such as these, where there are no things to count, lead to ideas about nothing and the number **nought**, both spoken and written.

1.11 NUMBER ACTIVITIES UP TO AND INCLUDING TEN (Working towards 2 L1; 12, 13 L1)

With a group of children, put objects on the table one at a time and introduce names associated with these collections developing the counting sequence: **one**, **two**, **three**, **four**, **five**. Removing one item at a time from a set is also valuable. Show also sets of objects and pictures of sets of objects, count them and develop good counting practices. When children are ready, provide individual work. No recording is needed, only oral answers.

1. Give a child pictures of up to five objects. 'How many things are shown in each picture?'
2. Ask the child to put three animals in a field, draw two birds, thread four beads on a string, put five cubes in a bag, etc.
3. Prepare polythene bags containing up to five items. 'How many things are in each bag?'
4. Ask a child to make sets containing one peg, three pegs, four pegs, two pegs and five pegs on a pegboard.
5. Ask a child to arrange two, three, four and five items, such as acorns or shells, in 'grouping in twos' patterns.
6. Use cards showing pictures of items, up to five in number, in various arrangements. Ask the children to find cards showing four things, three things, two things, one thing and five things.

With the aid of the following activities introduce number symbol cards from **1** to **5**:

1. Give a child number symbol cards. Ask him to display the appropriate number of shells, acorns, cubes, etc. next to the card (Fig. 1.15).

Fig. 1.15

2. Ask a child to display cubes in Stern pattern boards with the number symbol cards alongside.
3. Ask a child to make a row on a pegboard containing up to five pegs and label each row.
4. Ask a child to illustrate numbers up to five using Unifix cubes, labelling each set.
5. Ask a child to display up to five items, such as shells, acorns or cubes, in 'grouping in twos' patterns, near number labels.
6. Give the child cards showing pictures of objects, up to five in number. Ask him to sort the cards and put appropriate number labels near them (Fig. 1.16).

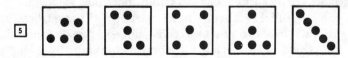

Fig. 1.16

   Now introduce to a group of children numbers from six to ten, by displaying groups of items, showing pictures of collections of objects, and showing Stern pattern boards. Introduce the number labels **6, 7, 8, 9** and **ten** and go through the counting sequence from one to ten. Individual activities could be used to reinforce this. Ask a child to perform the following:

1. Display pattern boards, number pieces or Unifix blocks, in order of size, and learn the sequence one, two, three, etc., up to ten. Which piece is seven? Which is nine? Is seven greater than nine? Put the two pieces side by side or on top of each other to check the answer.
2. Thread eight beads on a string, put seven marbles in a box, put six acorns in a tin, build a tower with nine cubes, etc.
3. Using cards prepared beforehand, showing sets of items no more than ten in number, ask him how many items there are and to put a number label near each picture (Fig. 1.17).

Fig. 1.17

4. Arrange ten, six, eight, nine, seven and five cubes in 'grouping in twos' patterns, and put number labels alongside.
5. Using prepared cards showing pictures of sets of items no more than ten in number, sort the cards and find those with nine things, seven things, etc.
6. Make four different shapes on a pegboard, each containing six pegs (Fig. 1.18). Repeat for seven pegs, eight pegs, nine pegs, and ten pegs.

Fig. 1.18

7. Arrange one, two, three, ..., nine, ten pegs in rows, side by side, on a pegboard. Which row has six pegs? Which row has eight pegs? Is six greater than eight?

8. Answer the following questions: which is the greater number, six or four? which is the smaller number, five or eight, etc.? Check the answers by putting appropriate sets of cubes in rows, side by side, on a squared paper strip.

9. Answer the following questions: which is the greater number, five or six? which is the smaller number, nine or seven? Check the answers by comparing Stern or Unifix number blocks.

10. Use Stern blocks or make number blocks from one to nine with Unifix cubes. Add a one-cube to all the other blocks up to nine, starting with the smallest, and establish that one and one is two, two and one is three, three and one is four, four and one is five, etc., up to nine and one is ten. Give oral answers initially. Later, use number symbol cards and write these results.

    Fit a two-block to all the other blocks up to eight and establish that one and two is three, two and two is four, three and two is five, etc., up to eight and two is ten.

    Repeat with a three-block, a four-block, etc., until the sum is ten, in each case.

11. Find two Stern or Unifix blocks which fit together to make six and describe the results. One and five is six, two and four is six, three and three is six, etc. Repeat this procedure with other numbers up to ten and obtain *addition facts*. Give oral answers, initially. Later, write the results down or use number symbol recording cards.

12. Select any number of cubes up to ten, partition into two groups, and describe the results. That is, the *addition facts*, five and four is nine, four and five is nine; the idea of difference, nine is five more than four, nine is four more than five; and the *subtraction facts*, nine take away five is four, nine take away four is five.

13. Add two sets of items to give a sum no more than ten, e.g. five red cubes and five yellow cubes, seven green pegs and two white pegs, three green counters and five yellow counters, etc.

    Use a group of items, ten or less, partition it into two sets, remove one set and describe the results, e.g. eight take three is five, eight take one is seven, eight take two is six, etc. Give oral answers initially and use recording labels later or write results.

14. Answer the questions: how much greater is six than two? eight than five? nine than six? etc. Put wooden cubes, side by side, on a grid to find out. That is, find the number of cubes to be added to the shorter row to make it just as long as the longer row.

15. Answer the questions: how much greater is eight than six? seven than four? five than two? Find out by representing the numbers with Stern or Unifix blocks and placing them side by side (Fig. 1.19).

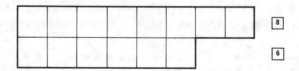

Fig. 1.19

16. Answer the questions: how much larger is ten than seven? eight than six? Find out by putting two rows of pegs, side by side, on a pegboard.

The work done so far on number is considerably reinforced when the children are engaged in various activities concerning measurement. The following examples illustrate how numerical ideas are used, practised and further developed. Set the kind of individual work suggested below and ask children to display their results. Accept oral answers and help children with recording sentences.

1. Use a balance to find the heavier—five marbles or eight cubes, nine cubes or five nuts and bolts, ten cubes or seven metal washers, three nails or seven marbles, etc. (Fig. 1.20).

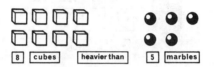

Fig. 1.20

2. Prepare tins of sand which just balance five metal bolts, nine wooden cubes, eight marbles, etc.
3. Using a stick 40 cm long fit Cuisenaire brown rods against the stick to measure its length (Fig. 1.21). With other sticks prepared beforehand, measure a 30-cm stick with yellow rods, a 40-cm stick with orange rods, a 30-cm stick with dark green rods, and a 90-cm stick with blue rods.

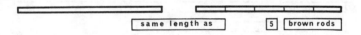

Fig. 1.21

4. With shapes prepared so that plastic squares, or triangles, will just fit on them find out how many squares, or triangles, cover each shape (Fig. 1.22).

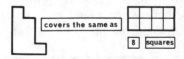

Fig. 1.22

5. The teacher obtains a number of cream and yoghurt cartons, plastic beakers from coffee and vending machines and cuts various plastic containers so that they just hold four plastic beakers, five cream cartons or seven yoghurt cartons of water. Ask a child how many beakers of water are needed to fill this container, etc. Display the measuring units used (Fig. 1.23).

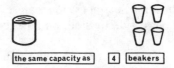

Fig. 1.23

6. Empty eight beakers of water into a large jar, nine egg cups of water into a tin, five Oxo boxes of sand into a dish, etc. At each emptying collect a card showing a picture of a beaker, egg cup or box, and continue the emptying process until the required number of cards is collected. Display the results as shown in Fig. 1.24.

Fig. 1.24

7. The teacher prepares two paper strips equivalent in length to 6 and 9 Cuisenaire blue rods and places them well apart on two tables. Ask a child to look at the strips and say which is longer. He then places blue rods against each strip to copy their lengths, and arranges the rods in straight rows, side by side, and labels each row (Fig. 1.25). Which strip is the longer? Did you estimate correctly? How much longer is one stick than the other? (Discuss this with the child.)

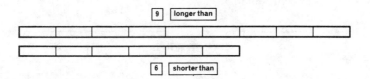

Fig. 1.25

8. Compare the capacities of tins or jars by filling them with water using a small cup, tin or carton. Every time a small cup or tin is emptied into the larger vessel take, as a tally, a gummed paper rectangle with a drawing of a cup or tin on it. (Count as one cup any part-cup needed at the end.) Find the number of cups needed to fill each vessel and stick the 'cups' on the prepared background (Fig. 1.26). (Help the

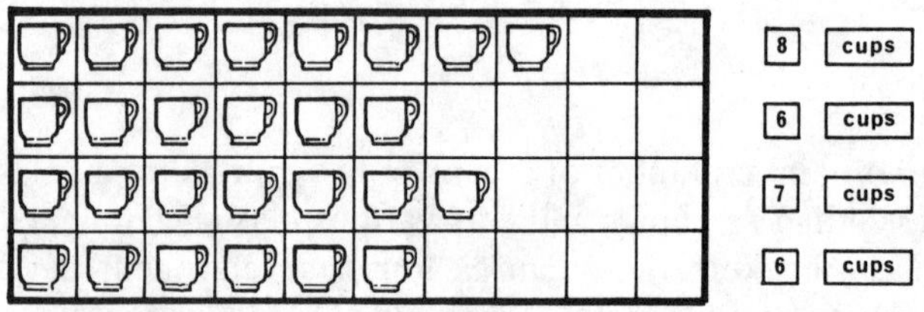

Fig. 1.26

children label the pictogram and talk with them about the results.) Answer the following questions: which vessel holds most water? how much does it hold? which vessel has the smallest capacity? how much does it hold?

9. Obtain two items from the classroom shop each costing no more than ten pence. To find out which item costs more and how much more it is, supposing that the items chosen cost 6p and 9p, arrange 6 pennies and 9 pennies side by side in rows on a grid, together with the items and number labels (Fig. 1.27).

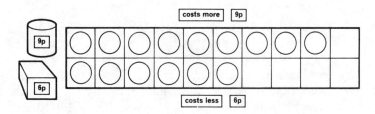

Fig. 1.27

10. A child balances identical tins, or boxes, containing different amounts of sand, using nuts and bolts, bolts, large nails, 100-g stacking masses, etc. (The teacher makes sure the tins balance the measuring units.) Pick up each tin and say which is heavier, then find how many items balance each tin and say which is heavier by comparing the numbers involved. Arrange the measuring units, side by side, on a squared background to check this answer (Fig. 1.28). Answer the questions: how much heavier is one tin than the other? how can we find out? Discuss this with the child.

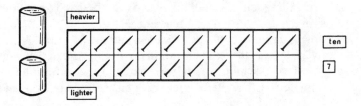

Fig. 1.28

Stacking masses, if used, could be fitted on top of one another to make towers. The heavier tin is the one whose balancing units make the taller tower. Answer the question: how much heavier is one tin than the other? Talk with the child about this.

1.12 NUMBER ACTIVITIES BEYOND TEN (2 L2)

Children can deal with larger sets of items when they can count beyond ten, and are able to group in tens and describe the numbers of tens obtained and the number of single units remaining.

With a group of children introduce larger numbers in this manner. Count a collection

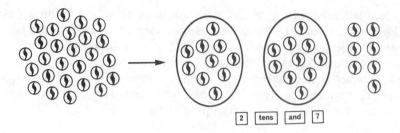

Fig. 1.29

of objects one at a time into a tin lid until ten is reached. Repeat this until a collection of tens is built up with some objects left over. We could for example sort marbles and end up with two sets of ten marbles and seven marbles left over (Fig. 1.29). Recording could be done using number symbol cards and a **tens** label, and the number of marbles recorded as **2 tens** and **7**. When this is written down on paper it could be shortened to **2t 7** and later **27**. The use of labels could also be changed gradually when children are ready, e.g. **4 tens** and **5** could be described as **4 tens 5**, later as **4t 5**, and eventually as **45**. A foundation of understanding for the recording process which involves progression and leads to an appreciation of number notation and place value must be provided. For this reason it is necessary that groups of ten are displayed to the left of ones because our written numbers use this principle. The writing of **6t 7** (six-tee seven) is particularly valuable because it links written symbols with spoken numbers.

Plenty of sorting and oral work is necessary so that children learn the number words for larger groups whilst recording labels are being used, e.g. two tens is called twenty and recorded as **2 tens**; three tens is called thirty and recorded as **3 tens**; three tens and five is called thirty-five and recorded as **3 tens and 5**.

Twenty, thirty, forty, ten, etc. could be recorded initially as **2 tens, 3 tens, 4 tens, 1 ten**, etc. and later by **20, 30, 40, 10**, etc. This would involve the use of two number labels and the introduction of the 0 symbol and label. The 0 in these cases indicates the sets that can be formed into tens with no items left over. Thus, 20 means 2 tens and no more, whereas 24 means 2 tens and 4 more.

Numbers between ten and twenty present a problem with respect to their names because the units are said before the tens, whilst eleven and twelve contain no reference to ten. In order to learn about these numbers Unifix blocks are particularly useful. Display a number staircase made from blocks representing numbers from one to twenty. Point to the blocks, in turn, and teach the counting sequence from one to twenty, examining those numbers beyond ten carefully. Eleven could be restructured as one ten and one; twelve as one ten and two; thirteen as one ten and three; and so on. Put number labels near each set, e.g. near eleven put **1 ten and 1**, near twelve put **1 ten and 2**, and so on. Delay the introduction of proper notation and use a more instructive form initially, e.g. fifteen could be displayed as **1 ten and 5**, and written as **1t 5**, and not **15**. The Stern twenty-tray, or ten-blocks and unit cubes, could also be used to gain insight into these numbers.

When these children are ready, ask them to do the following activities individually. The children would use number labels to record their answers.

1. Put in rows, side by side, on a pegboard, ten, eleven, twelve, . . ., twenty pegs (Fig. 1.30). In each row, leave a gap after ten pegs, before adding more. Label each row, with number words and number labels, and learn the counting sequence ten, eleven, twelve, ..., nineteen, twenty. What number is 1 ten and 3? What number is 1 ten and 6?

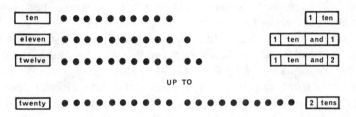

Fig. 1.30

2. Put out Unifix blocks to represent eleven, seventeen, sixteen, twenty, fourteen, eighteen, twelve, nineteen and thirteen. Label each set with word and number labels, e.g. **fourteen** and **1 ten and 4**.
3. By making a ten-group and a smaller group, put out on the table fifteen acorns, sixteen cubes, eleven conkers, thirteen plastic pigs, fourteen plastic cats, etc. Label the sets. (Use Counting Toys.)
4. By counting beyond ten, put twelve acorns in a lid, seventeen marbles in a box, fourteen cubes on the table, etc. Also thread fifteen beads on a string. Label the sets.
5. Using sets of things, up to twenty in number, already placed in polythene envelopes, find how many items are in each envelope.
6. Using a box containing fourteen cats, twelve pigs, eleven racing cars, sixteen rabbits, seventeen dogs, etc. (Counting Toys) sort the items and find how many are in each set.
7. With the aid of a collection of zoo or farm animals, containing no more than twenty of each kind, sort the animals, find the number of each kind and put a number label near them.
8. Using prepared cards showing pictures of sets of objects consisting of no more than twenty items, count the objects on a card. Then check the answer by matching each object with a cube, grouping the cubes in a ten-group and a smaller group, and describing their number.
9. Using a display of cardboard strips with pictures of shells, boys, shoes, cats, pigs, etc., arranged in rows, up to twenty in a row (Fig. 1.31), match each row of pictures

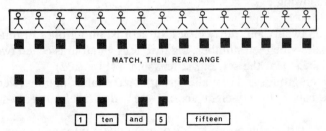

Fig. 1.31

with plastic counters or cubes, and rearrange them into a ten-group and a smaller group to find their number. Count the pictures of items to check the results.

10. Pour fifteen egg-cups of water into a tin. Make a tally of each egg-cup emptied into the tin with a cube or plastic counter, and by arranging the cubes into a ten-group and a smaller group as the tally proceeds, record the fifteen egg-cups of water. Repeat with other numbers up to twenty by emptying a prescribed number of small tins or bottles of water or sand into a larger vessel.

11. Add 6 and 7, 9 and 9, 6 and 8, etc., using number pieces. Describe the results using labels, e.g. **9 and 9 make eighteen**, or **9 and 9 make 1 ten and 8**. Later, the results could be written as $9 + 9 = 18$, or $(9, 9) \overset{+}{\rightarrow} 18$.

12. Subtract nine from seventeen, six from fourteen, seven from fifteen, etc., using Unifix cubes. Record results using labels, e.g. **fifteen take 7 leaves 8**. Later, record the results as $15 - 7 = 8$, or $(15, 7) \overset{-}{\rightarrow} 8$.

13. Using simple multiplication questions (with the results twenty or below) find four threes, seven twos, three fives, six threes, etc. Use Unifix or Stern blocks and cubes to obtain the answers.

14. Answer the questions: which is greater, sixteen or fourteen, twelve or fifteen, sixteen or eighteen, etc.? Represent each number pair with Unifix or Stern blocks, put the blocks side by side in order to obtain the answers.

15. Answer the questions: which is greater, twelve or seventeen, nineteen or sixteen, fourteen or twelve, etc.? Put rows of pegs, side by side, on a pegboard to represent each of the numbers in order to answer these questions.

16. Answer the questions: how much greater is fourteen than seven, fifteen than ten, seventeen than fourteen, etc.? Using Unifix or Stern blocks find what number block must be added to the shorter block to make it as long as the longer block.

17. Answer the questions: how much larger is sixteen than fourteen, fifteen than twelve, sixteen than eleven, etc.? Put two rows of pegs, side by side, on a pegboard to represent the pair of numbers, and find how many pegs must be added to the shorter row to make it just as long as the longer row.

18. Using red counters (up to twenty in number), sort into a ten-group and a smaller group. Exchange ten red counters for a yellow counter. What is a yellow counter worth? What number does a yellow counter represent? Arrange the counters on the table with the yellow one to the left of the red ones. What number is represented by the counters? For example, 1 yellow and 3 red would represent **1 ten and 3**, or **thirteen**. How could sixteen be represented using yellow and red counters?

The activities listed below concern numbers over twenty. Ask individual children to perform the following exercises:

1. Sort between twenty and thirty cubes, or acorns, into groups of ten and a smaller group, and describe their number, e.g. two tens and four is called twenty-four. Put recording labels near the set, e.g. **2 tens and 4** (Fig. 1.32).

2. By making ten-groups and a smaller group, on the table, put out twenty-two shells, twenty-five cubes, twenty-eight acorns, etc. Also thread twenty-six beads on a string.

3. Sort a pile of red counters (up to thirty in number) into ten-groups and a smaller group. Exchange ten red counters for a yellow one. What is a yellow counter worth?

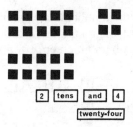

Fig. 1.32

What number does a yellow counter represent? What number is represented by the counters? For example, alongside 2 yellow and 4 red counters would be placed the labels **twenty-four** and **2 tens and 4**. What counters would represent twenty-two, twenty-seven, etc.?

4. Use Stern ten-pattern boards and display one ten, two tens, three tens, etc. up to nine tens. Learn the words for these numbers, and the sequence **ten**, **twenty**, **thirty**, **forty**, **fifty**, **sixty**, **seventy**, **eighty** and **ninety**. Place number names and labels near each group (Fig. 1.33).

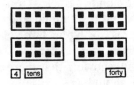

Fig. 1.33

5. Represent thirty-six, forty-five, sixty-two, etc. using Stern pattern boards.
6. Use Unifix or Stern ten-blocks and cubes to represent thirty-seven, twenty-nine, forty-eight, etc.
7. Given a box containing up to a hundred plastic pegs of different colours, sort the pegs and find the number of each colour, by putting them in tens on a pegboard. Describe the results orally and using labels, e.g. say fifty-six and display **5 tens and 6** labels.
8. If a yellow counter has value ten and a red counter has value one, represent these numbers using counters: thirty-four, fifty-three, forty-six, fifty, sixty-two, etc. Label these numbers with symbol cards.

Up to now a child has been recording thirty-two as **3 tens and 2** using labels. When he is ready, however, the child could write his own recording label, **3t 2**, to put near a set of items. A little later he could display two number symbol cards only, e.g. **32**, or write 32 on a slip of paper (Fig. 1.34).

Fig. 1.34

During the process of recording, numbers such as ten, twenty, thirty, etc. will need to be written down. Be prepared to talk about the recording of these numbers. This could be done by considering the numbers nineteen, twenty and twenty-one (Fig. 1.35).

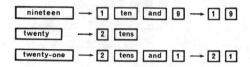

Fig. 1.35

How do we write twenty? We cannot just write 2 or only use a **2** label. Why not? Look at the way nineteen and twenty-one are written. They both have two digits, a tens digit on the left and a digit for units left over on the right. So twenty also needs two digits. The tens digit must be 2, but what will the other digit be? It cannot be 1, 2, etc., up to 9, because we use these when we have something left over to describe. Twenty is 2 tens exactly with no items left over. To show there are no items left over, when we group in tens, we write 0 to the right of the tens. (0 is called nought or zero.) Thus, twenty is recorded as **20**. How would thirty be written? (30). How do we write ten? (10). Link with counting in tens on a Stern number track.

Also, ask a child to sort red counters into tens, and exchange ten red counters for a yellow counter. A yellow counter is worth ten. Two yellow counters and 3 red counters represent twenty-three, which is written as 23. Two yellow counters only represent twenty, which is written 20, the 0 showing that there are no red counters, or ones.

A spike abacus could be used, should one be available, to explain the need for 0 as a space filler, when we write numbers down.

The child could now be given activities involving numbers up to a hundred, the notation used for instructions and recording being the normal one. Children could write their results.

1. Give written instructions: put 26 beads on a string, 32 cubes on the table, 24 acorns in a tin, 16 egg-cups of water in a jar, etc.
2. Sort marbles, beads, cubes, pegs or conkers, less than a hundred of each, into groups of ten. Describe the results orally and write them down, e.g. thirty-five, 35.
3. Fit Unifix cubes together to make ten-blocks. Use ten-blocks and separate cubes to represent 36, 28, 14, 43, etc.
4. The teacher reads out numbers below a hundred, the children write these numbers using symbols, or form them with number symbol cards.
5. A yellow counter is worth ten and a red counter is worth one. What numbers are represented by 2 yellow and 5 red counters? 1 yellow and 8 red counters? 6 yellow counters? 3 yellow and 9 red counters? etc. Give the answers orally and also write them down.
6. Put out counters to represent the numbers 36, 27, 41, 38, 40, 59, etc., a yellow counter being worth ten and a red counter being worth one.

1.13 COMPARING SETS NUMERICALLY USING PICTOGRAMS
(13 L1; 2, 3, 12 L2)

Reinforcement of numerical work could take place through activities where information is collected and displayed in pictorial form. Some of the topics examined briefly at the pre-number stage could be repeated, but on this occasion treated numerically. Questions could be asked about the number of items in various sets and how many more items there are. The rows of pictures displayed could be labelled in a suitable manner for the children. For example, a row with eighteen pictures could be labelled **1 ten and 8**, **1t 8 or 18**. The number of cut-out figures, if over ten, in each category, could be found by arranging them in ten-groups before sticking them on the squared background. The items in each row could then be counted to check the result and give valuable counting practice beyond ten. The compartments on the grid could be marked off in tens, with red lines, to help the children 'see' the numbers of items in each row and the structure of each number.

Arrange for the class to compare the number of children who stay for dinner and those who go home. Give each child the appropriate cut-out figure on which to write his or her name. Let each child stick his cut-out on a previously prepared and labelled squared background (Fig. 1.36).

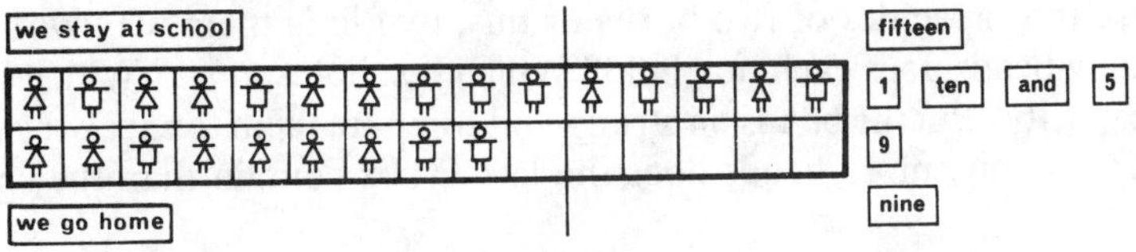

Fig. 1.36

Ask the class questions about the pictogram when it is completed. How many stay at school for dinner? How many go home? Put appropriate number symbols and words near each row. Is fifteen a greater number than nine? Do more children stay at school or go home? How many more go home than stay at school?

Arrange for the class to study other situations. Possibly one pictogram could be done each week. Talk with the class about the number of children in each category after the cut-outs have been collected and sorted, and question the class about the completed pictogram. Allow the children to stick their own cut-outs on the squared background.

Investigate the following, many of which could be included in '*Ourselves*':

1. Colours of shoes. Use three categories: black, brown, not black or brown. (Also use cut-outs of shoes from catalogues.)
2. Colours of socks. Use three categories: grey, white, not grey or white. (Children could draw around a sock template and make sock cut-outs.)
3. Ways of coming to school: walk, bus or car.
4. Shoe fastenings: laces, buckles or slip-on. (Also use cut-outs of shoes with different fastenings from catalogues.)
5. Kinds of houses lived in: detached, semi-detached, terraced, a flat.
6. Colours of eyes: brown, blue, green, grey, hazel.

7. Favourite fruit: select one from peaches, grapes, cherries, pears and plums.
8. Favourite TV programme. Discuss some of the programmes, and then propose five or six programmes. Select one.
9. Things bought in the school shop: crisps, plain biscuits, chocolate biscuits, etc.
10. Reading levels: Book 1, Book 2, Book 3, etc.
11. Kind of pets kept.
12. Favourite toys. Discuss some of the kinds of toys, and then propose about eight categories. Select one.
13. Favourite school activity. Discuss activities, then select one.
14. Types of cars owned by the family.
15. Colours of cars owned by the family.

1.14 COMPARING SETS: NUMERICAL APPLICATIONS (2, 3, 8 L2)

The comparison of sets of units, either concretely or pictorially, is included in all measuring activities in the early stages, and this provides opportunities for using numbers and developing number ideas. The following activities, to be done by individual children, illustrate the involvement of number in measurement:

1. Compare the capacities of two boxes or tins, by filling them with wooden beads. How many beads does each box hold? Which box holds more? Which box has the larger capacity? Put the beads on strings and compare them to check the result (Fig. 1.37). How many more beads does the larger box contain than the smaller?

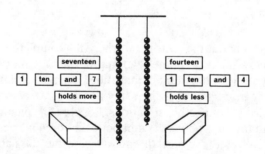

Fig. 1.37

2. Compare the capacities of two boxes or tins, by filling them with Stern cubes. Find the number of cubes needed to fill each box, and say which holds more. Build the cubes into two towers, or put them in two rows, side by side, to check the result.
3. Using two prepared cardboard strips which measure 16 and 12 Cuisenaire yellow rods long find the length of each strip by placing yellow rods against them, and display the rods, end to end, in two rows. Label each row. Which strip is the longer? How much longer? See Fig. 1.38.
4. Given bags of sand (which balance 17 and 11 nails) balance each bag of sand with nails on a common balance, display the nails in rows on a twenty-grid, and put

Fig. 1.38

number labels near each row. Which is the lighter? Which is the heavier? How much heavier?

5. Compare the prices of two items, each less than 20p, from the classroom shop. Display the pennies needed to buy the items in two rows on a twenty-grid and number each row. Which costs more? How much more?

6. Compare the capacities of two small boxes by filling them with marbles. How many marbles fill each box? Which box holds more? Arrange the marbles in two rows, side by side, between three wooden strips, to check the result (Fig. 1.39). How many more marbles does the larger box hold?

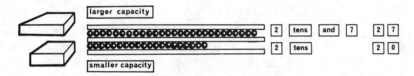

Fig. 1.39

7. Compare the times taken for two children, separately, to build a tower with cubes, or put on their coats, by putting beads or cubes, at regular intervals, from one box into another. One child performs the task after the other has finished. How many beads, or cubes, were collected whilst each child did the task? When were more beads, or cubes, collected? Who took the longer time? (This activity is for three children—one child times while the other two perform the task.)

Thread the beads on strings, and compare them, to check the result. How much longer did John take? (Six beads longer.) If cubes were used, they could be built into two towers, or arranged in two rows, and compared. How much longer did John take? (Six cubes longer.)

8. Using envelopes containing 15 pennies, 12 tenpences, 16 fivepences and 13 two-pences sort the coins and put them in rows with number labels on a four-row twenty-grid. Which row has most coins? What are they and how many are there? Which row has fewest coins? What are they and how many are there? Are there more pennies than tenpences? How many more? Are there fewer tenpences than fivepences? How many fewer?

9. The teacher obtains a large transparent plastic jar or jug, cuts a strip from the edge of a piece of narrow ruled paper, and pencils over the lines in black to make the divisions clearer, sticks the strip on the outside of the jug from top to bottom with a division line coinciding with the bottom edge and covers the strip with transparent PVC to make it waterproof. The children can use this jug to measure, the measuring units being the amounts between adjacent lines on the strip.

Ask a child to compare the capacities of two tins, or jars, by filling them with water, and pouring the water into the empty measuring jug, and marking the levels (Fig. 1.40). Find the amount of water in the jug each time by counting the units in the height of the columns, to the nearest unit. Which is the greater number? Which tin has the larger capacity? Check the result by comparing water levels on the strip, e.g. the water from one tin went up eight divisions, to here; the water from the other tin went up six divisions, to here; so the first tin holds more because the water went to the higher level.

Fig. 1.40

10. Use the graduated jug of activity **9** to compare the volumes of stones or pieces of metal. Find the rise in water level, to the nearest unit, when each stone is put into the jug, compare these numbers, and find which stone takes up more room, e.g. stone A makes the water rise five units, stone B makes the water rise eight units. Which takes up more room? Which stone has the larger volume? Check the result by immersing the stones, separately, in the same water and comparing the distances between the initial and final water levels in each case, non-numerically, e.g. from here to here is farther than from here to here, so this stone takes up more room.
11. A child times two other children doing a certain activity, separately, by collecting water from a dripping tap, or sand from a tin with a hole in it, in a measuring jar, initially empty, and marking the level when each child finishes. (A measuring jar could be made by sticking a strip of narrow ruled paper on the outside of a transparent plastic jar.) How many units of water were collected each time? Which is the greater number? Who took the longer time? Check the answer by comparing the levels on the strip.

1.15 COMPARING SETS NUMERICALLY: CONCRETE AND PICTORIAL REPRESENTATION USING AN ABSTRACT OF THE UNIT (2, 3, 12, 13 L2)

So far the children have displayed information using cut-outs of children, and sometimes with cut-outs of other items under consideration, e.g. cut-outs of shoes. When dealing with lengths, capacities and heaviness, they have displayed the measuring units used, such as nuts and bolts, orange rods and marbles. When the children reach the top infant or lower junior school, however, they could start to represent things using abstract figures, either two- or three-dimensional.

Arrange for colours of eyes to be studied by the class. To collect and display information, each child could, during the morning, place a bead on an appropriate string to indicate the colour of his or her eyes. Three strings could be used, representing **brown, blue** and **other colours**. These could be put on different tables with colour labels near them. In difficult cases the teacher could decide the colour of a child's eyes and help children select the correct string, if necessary. When all the children have put a bead on a string, the strings could be hung up, and the teacher could ask the class questions about the results (Fig. 1.41). Are there more brown-eyed children than

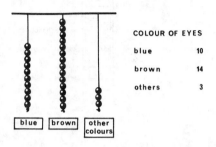

COLOUR OF EYES

blue   10

brown   14

others   3

Fig. 1.41

blue-eyed? How many children have blue eyes? brown eyes? other colours of eyes? Put the number labels near the strings. Which colour is most common in this class? The latter question could lead to an investigation of eye colours in other classes to see if similar findings are obtained. Include in *'Ourselves'*.

Information could be collected about favourite flavours of ice-cream, the results illustrated by each child sticking a gummed paper circle in an appropriate column, on a specially prepared background (Fig. 1.42). The teacher could talk with the class about the complete display and as a result build up and write a summary alongside it (*'Ourselves'*).

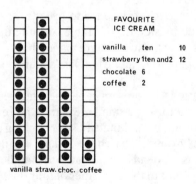

FAVOURITE
ICE CREAM

vanilla   ten   10

strawberry 1ten and 2   12

chocolate 6

coffee   2

vanilla straw. choc. coffee

Fig. 1.42

A number ladder could also be used to represent the same information. The teacher draws the ladder beforehand and numbers the rungs (Fig. 1.43). One category of ice-cream could be dealt with at a time. Those children who prefer strawberry could each move a pink pointer up the ladder, one rung at a time. Label the highest rung reached by strawberry. Repeat this with other categories. (The pointers could be made of a special plastic material which adheres to other surfaces. Different colours of pointer

Fig. 1.43

could be used, e.g. pink for strawberry, brown for chocolate, etc.) When completed, question the class about the results. How many like strawberry best? Which flavour is preferred by most children? How many like chocolate best? Which flavour is not liked very much? What flavour should the ice-cream man carry most of in his van? Possibly, the results could be compared with those from another class.

Other abstracts which the children could use to represent collected information are as follows:

1. matchboxes piled on top of one another in columns
2. cubes piled on top of one another in columns
3. rows of marbles placed side by side
4. rows of cubes placed side by side
5. rows of plastic squares or circles placed side by side
6. beads on strings put side by side on the table or hung up
7. gummed paper shapes, stuck on a square paper background, either in rows or columns, i.e. gummed paper circles, triangles, squares, stars, etc.

Abstracts could also be used to represent capacities, masses or times. When a child is filling a tin or bottle with water using a small measuring jar, each time a unit is emptied into the tin it could be recorded by making a tick, or sticking a gummed paper circle or triangle on a squared background. The child, instead, could collect beads and later thread them on strings. Thus, 15 beads would indicate that the tin holds 15 jars of water. Should a child be asked to compare the capacities of four tins, painted different colours, he could record the results using one of the forms shown in Figs. 1.44, 1.45 and 1.46.

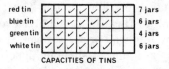

Fig. 1.44

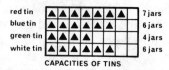

Fig. 1.45

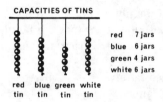

Fig. 1.46

Similarly, masses of tins of sand, found to the nearest 100 g on a compression balance, could be represented by columns of cubes or matchboxes, strings of beads, or rows of gummed paper shapes, each figure representing 1 hundred grams (Fig. 1.47).

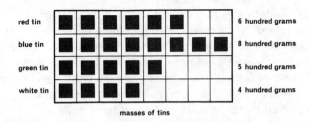

Fig. 1.47

To compare the times for three children to do something separately, such as put on their coats, another child could at regular intervals, drop marbles or beads into a tin whilst each child does the task. Rows of marbles, or strings of beads, could then be compared to see who took the longest time (Fig. 1.48).

Fig. 1.48

The teacher could arrange for the class to build up displays using abstract units and, possibly, one display could be done each week. (These could form part of the 'Ourselves' project.) The teacher would prepare the background beforehand and ask the children to insert their own information. Upon completion the display would be discussed with the class and a title, subtitles and numerical labels added. The following topics are suitable:

1. birthmonths
2. day of the week on which a child's next birthday occurs

3. types of pets kept by each family
4. number of pets of different kinds kept by each family
5. number of children who have travelled in a train, on a large boat, on a hovercraft, in an aeroplane
6. number of brothers in each family
7. number of sisters in each family
8. number of children in each family
9. colours of cars owned by each family
10. kinds of cars owned by each family.

The following activities could be investigated by individual children and the results displayed using beads on strings, rows of cubes, columns of gummed paper circles, etc.:

1. The number of children at school each day last week.
2. The number of children absent from school each day last week.
3. The teacher puts about 60 coloured plastic squares, of five or six colours, in a box, such that no more than 20 squares are the same colour. The child sorts the squares and displays the results using columns or rows of gummed paper stars.
4. Sort out a collection of farm or zoo animals; or find, from the class collection, three or four kinds of animal only, e.g. lions, giraffes and bears; or sheep, cows, pigs and horses. Use gummed paper squares to display the results.
5. Compare the times for three or four other children to do something, such as a jigsaw puzzle, using a timer with a revolving pointer, and matching each turn with a cube, bead, marble or gummed paper shape. How long did each child take? (x turns.) Who took the longest time?
6. Fill three or four tins using a small plastic measure. Match each measure poured into a tin with a gummed paper circle, and stick circles in rows on a squared background. How many measures fill each tin? Which tin has the largest capacity?
7. The teacher prepares cardboard strips of lengths 10, 12, 16 and 18 Cuisenaire yellow rods. The child measures each strip using yellow rods and displays their lengths using beads. One bead represents a yellow rod.
8. The teacher fills some tins with sand. A child finds the masses of these tins, to the nearest 100 g, using a compression balance. He displays the masses of the tins using a gummed square to represent a hundred grams.
9. The teacher puts some pennies, twopences, fivepences and tenpences (no more than twenty of each) in a box. The child sorts the coins and displays the number of each using gummed paper triangles.

1.16 COMPARING SETS NUMERICALLY: BLOCK GRAPHS (2, 12, 13 L2)

Up to now children have used geometrical shapes to represent other things, and put these abstracts on a squared paper background so as to emphasize the discrete nature of the count. Putting six circles, touching, in a row enables six circles to be picked out fairly easily; and four squares in a row, with spaces between them, enables four squares to be seen clearly. Should matchboxes, or cubes of the same colour, be put in columns, or squares of the same colour in rows, their discreteness is not so obvious and it is difficult to see how many there are.

Build a tower with matchboxes (or cubes) of the same size. Discuss with the children how many matchboxes there are in the tower, and demonstrate how to make a matchbox counter. That is, mark off on a cardboard strip divisions equal to the width of a matchbox, and number these divisions from one end. Stand the strip by the side of the tower and read off the number opposite the top of the tower. Does this number agree with the number counted?

As an activity the children could work individually or in pairs and make counting strips which will find the number of cubes in a row or column, the number of marbles in a row, the number of plastic squares in a row, the number of pennies in a row, the number of tenpences in a row. The children could use plain paper strips, about 3 cm wide, to make counting strips. Ask them not to number the smaller divisions marked on the strip, but number them in fives, or tens, up to 50.

The teacher could, as a preparation for block graphs, arrange for the data to be presented in the following ways:

1. Use coloured plastic squares, about 2.5 cm in side. Ask each child to put a square on the table, but place them in rows, side by side, with a space between to represent various categories, e.g. favourite amusement in a park (Fig. 1.49). When the display is complete, ask a child to make a square counter and put it alongside. Put labels beneath the columns and provide a title. Talk with the class about the results. How many like the swing best? How many like the roundabout?

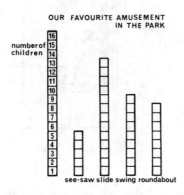

Fig. 1.49

2. Use gummed paper squares of side 2 cm and a 2-cm squared background. Ask each child, during the morning, to stick a square on the paper above various category labels, and build columns of squares, side by side, with a space between, e.g. favourite fruit selected from apple, banana, pear and orange (Fig. 1.50). When this has been done a child could draw a counting strip on the left-hand side of the paper and number it. The teacher could talk with the children about the results and ask numerical questions.

3. Use gummed paper 2-cm squares and a 2-cm squared paper background. Ask the children to do as described in the previous paragraph **2**, but not leave a space

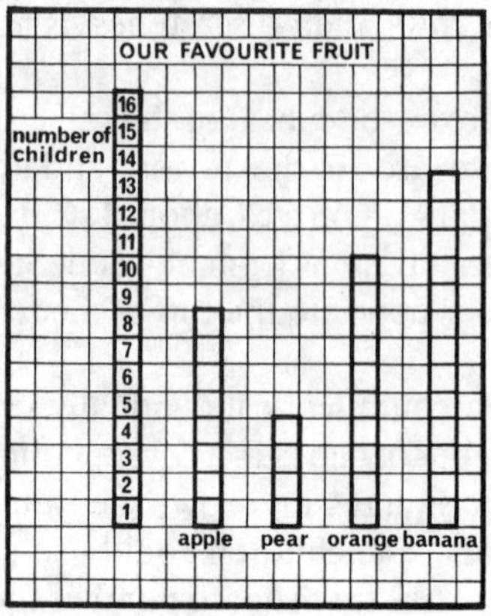

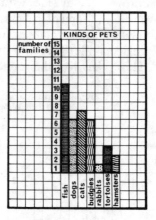

Fig. 1.50

between the columns of squares (Fig. 1.51). Draw a counting strip on the left-hand side of the paper, and ask the class questions about the information collected.

Fig. 1.51

4. Use 2-cm squared paper and draw a line across it near the bottom edge. The children, in turn during the morning, build columns of 2-cm gummed squares on this line (Fig. 1.52). When the graph is complete, the teacher could draw a simplified counting strip on the left-hand side using a single line with divisions marked on it, each interval being numbered. Talk with the children about this counting scale, explaining that it is easier than drawing a counting strip.

The children, as a class, are now ready to compile a block graph. Use 2-cm, or 5-cm, squared paper and build a graph as described in **4** above, each child colouring in a square. Suppose shoe colours were being studied. The categories could be black, brown, red, white, etc. Columns of squares of these colours could be crayoned, side by side, standing on the base line. When completed, draw a counting scale on the graph,

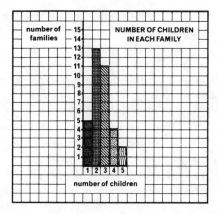

Fig. 1.52

insert a title, label the axes and question children about the results. Tell the children that a block graph must always have a title, a number scale and properly labelled axes.

Other block graphs, some of which may come within the project '*Ourselves*', that could be compiled by the whole class are as follows:

1. favourite school activity
2. favourite dessert at school dinners
3. favourite TV programme
4. number of children in each family
5. the various districts, surrounding the school, where children from a particular class live
6. types of houses lived in: detached, semi-detached, terraced house, or a flat
7. marks obtained in a spelling test or multiplication table test, out of 10 or 20
8. the numbers selected if each child is asked to write a number between 10 and 20 on a piece of paper, that is, one of 11, 12, 13, ..., 18, 19.

Individual children, when they are ready, could also be asked to draw block graphs. Use 2-cm, or 5-cm, squared paper, and make sure initially that the data collected are represented by an equivalent number of squares, even if large sheets of paper have to be used. Select activities, therefore, that will not involve numbers which are too large. (Later in the junior school the need for a scaled representation could be discussed in order to draw graphs involving fairly large numbers on relatively small pieces of paper.) Make sure the children represent the number of items in each category by the lengths of the blocks. Also ensure that the axes are clearly labelled and numbered and the graph has a title.

Give oral instructions about the drawing of a graph, if necessary. Put questions on work cards to be answered by the child when the graph is completed. Children, individually, could draw block graphs on the following situations:

1. daily absences from class for a particular week
2. the numbers of children absent on a particular day from various classes in the school

3. the numbers of children from various classes who stay for dinner on a particular day
4. the class collection of zoo animals
5. the class collection of farm animals
6. a collection of beads of various colours
7. a pile of money sorted into various denominations
8. a collection of Cuisenaire rods
9. a collection of plastic pegs of various colours
10. the number of times each letter is used in a given sentence
11. the first letter of each word in three consecutive sentences from a child's reading book
12. Write on the faces of a wooden cube the numbers 1, 2, 3, 4, 6 and 6. Use it as a die. A child throws it 36 or 48 times, records the results and graphs them. Compare these results with those obtained by other children. Which number is easiest to obtain? Why? Discuss this
13. A child throws an ordinary die 36 times, records the results and illustrates them. Compare the results with those obtained by other pupils. Is it easier to get a 3 or a 5? A 6 or a 4? Discuss this. Throw more times, if necessary
14. Put 3 twopences in a beaker, shake it, and tip the coins on the table. Record the results for 40 throws. Is it easier to get 3 heads or 2 heads? Why? Is it easier to get 3 heads or 3 tails? Discuss this
15. The child throws two dice and adds their scores. Record the totals for 36 throws and graph them. Is it easier to get a total of 7 or a total of 3? Why? Is it more likely to score 8 than 2? Discuss this. How likely is it to score 1? What about 15? (Both impossible to obtain.)

1.17 NUMERICAL WORK: ADDITION (2 L1–3; 3 L1–4)

Sorting exercises provide opportunities for addition should the question 'How many altogether?' be asked. When children realize that addition is the process of combining sets, activities should be introduced from which all the *addition facts* can be derived in an economical and well-ordered fashion. These facts are then learnt by applying them in various situations where concrete materials are still available to aid thinking and supply those answers not yet memorized. The teacher needs to make children aware of laws and structure because memorization and calculation is made easier. (For example, five add three is the same as three add five. Three add nine is better done as nine add three because three can be counted easily on to nine. Six and one, five and two, four and three, etc. all add up to seven. This pattern incorporates the idea that the total number of items in two sets remains the same should items be transferred from one set to the other.) Finally, a stage is reached when addition facts are known, or can be derived without apparatus, and additions can be done economically by bringing the necessary techniques into play.

   The teacher could use two or three sets around which to base the demonstration and discussion with a group, e.g. red and blue counters. They are sorted by colour and the teacher asks how they might find how many counters there are altogether (*all together*). Let one child put *all* of them *together*, and ask all the children to count the items in the combined set. This procedure could be repeated with other sets.

The children should practise adding sets on their own using a recording procedure which the teacher thinks suitable for them. In the initial stages, when dealing with countable items, number symbol cards could be used.

1. Use red and blue beads, yellow and red cubes, blue and yellow marbles, etc. The ·child sorts the items and counts each set. He then finds how many items there are altogether and puts an appropriate number symbol label near the combined set.
2. A child is given a collection of big and small stones. The child sorts them into big and small and puts number labels near each set. Ask the child how many stones there are altogether, and to place a number label near the combined set, then put these items back into their original sets. Look at the sets and the number labels and talk about what was found, e.g. four small stones and three big stones—seven stones altogether. Repeat with red and yellow rods, white and green pegs, blue and yellow marbles, etc.
3. The teacher draws three trees on a card and covers it with transparent plastic film. The child uses pictures or cut-outs and places the blue birds on the first tree and the red birds on the second tree, with appropriate number labels near them. She is then asked to fly all the birds into the third tree and put a number label near it (Fig. 1.53). The child is asked to talk about the number of birds, e.g. five blue birds and three red birds—eight birds altogether.

Fig. 1.53

4. Cards like the one described in **3** could be made using the themes: spiders on webs, fish in pools, boats on lakes, eggs in nests, butterflies on plants, chicks in nests, wasps on jampots, pennies in purses, kittens in baskets. The teacher could indicate by drawings on the card the number of things to be put in the first two sets. The children could match pictures or cut-outs with the drawings, and then combine them to find their total. Recording could be done using number and word labels (Fig. 1.54).
5. The teacher prepares two containers which can just be filled with an integral number of beakers of water. A child fills each container with water, and displays the empty beakers in rows on a grid (Fig. 1.55). How many beakers of water does each

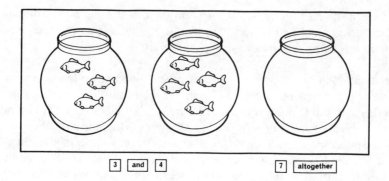

Fig. 1.54

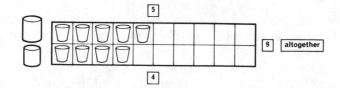

Fig. 1.55

container hold? How many beakers would be needed altogether to fill both containers?

6. The teacher prepares two cardboard shapes so that congruent squares, or right-
   angled triangles, will just cover each. A child finds how many units will fit on each
   shape and displays these units in two rows on a grid. Which shape covers more? How
   much more? How many units would be needed altogether to cover the two shapes?
7. The teacher draws two straight lines measuring an integral number of Cuisenaire
   dark green rods in length. A child measures each line with dark green rods and puts
   the rods, end to end and touching, in two rows, side by side, comparing the lengths of
   each line by comparing the lengths of the rows of rods. How long would the straight
   line be if the two drawn lines were placed end to end? Answer this question by
   finding how many dark green rods were used altogether.
8. The teacher chooses two small boxes and asks the child to fill each one with Stern
   cubes. The volumes of the boxes are compared by displaying the cubes, touching, in
   rows, side by side. Find the volume of each box, and then how much larger one box
   is. How many cubes do the boxes hold altogether?
9. The child obtains two items, each costing 9p or less, from the classroom shop. He
   puts the pennies needed to buy each item in two rows on a ten-grid. How much more
   is one item? How many pennies altogether whould be needed to buy both these
   items?

   Many activities such as those listed from **1** to **9** are needed to enable children to gain
experience in addition procedures and an understanding of the laws involved, together
with a knowledge of the related spoken and written language. The teacher must
carefully control the activities. At first the sum might be confined to five or less,

progressing to ten, to twenty, then to fifty, and so on. The teacher must use careful judgement in deciding when a child is ready to proceed from the informal to the formal method of recording. Practice exercises, on cards, are also needed, and these should be done at first with, and then without, the help of some kind of structural apparatus.

The apparatus could be used in the formation of a number story (Fig. 1.56). Here, Unifix cubes are used in the story of six. A child puts red and yellow cubes together to make a total of six cubes. Initially, he gives an oral description of the blocks, e.g. one and five together make six, two and four together make six, etc. Later symbolic descriptions would be written, e.g. $1 + 5 = 6, 2 + 4 = 6, 3 + 3 = 6, 4 + 2 = 6, 5 + 1 = 6$.

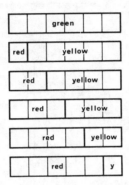

Fig. 1.56

Many interesting, and important, number relationships can be represented using coloured blocks drawn on 1 cm or 2 cm squared paper. Diagrams could be drawn by individual children to illustrate situations obtained when using Unifix cubes or Stern blocks, or they could be compiled independently (e.g. colour in two blocks of squares, end to end, and in various ways, to give a total of seven) and used to obtain the addition facts of seven. Block diagrams could promote the telling and writing of stories by individual children, or the whole class should diagrams be displayed on the classroom wall (Fig. 1.57).

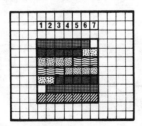

Fig. 1.57

Orally, six and one is seven, five and two is seven, etc. up to one and six is seven. Later, these descriptions could be written, using symbols. That is, $6 + 1 = 7, 5 + 2 = 7$, etc. up to $1 + 6 = 7$, interpreting the diagram a row at a time.

Structural apparatus such as Stern or Unifix blocks could also be used to help children find the answers, if not known, to addition questions presented on a series of ordered work cards. The facts could be arranged so that the sum is 5 or less, then up to 9, then 10, then from 11 to 18 inclusive. The presentation on the cards varies to meet the readiness of the children. Some examples, involving numbers below 10, are:

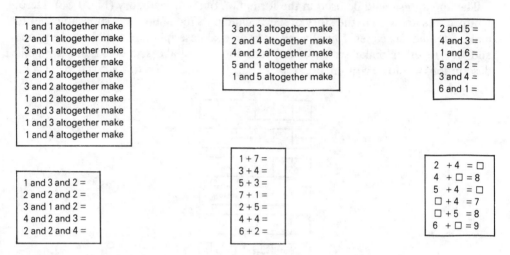

1 and 1 altogether make	3 and 3 altogether make	2 and 5 =
2 and 1 altogether make	2 and 4 altogether make	4 and 3 =
3 and 1 altogether make	4 and 2 altogether make	1 and 6 =
4 and 1 altogether make	5 and 1 altogether make	5 and 2 =
2 and 2 altogether make	1 and 5 altogether make	3 and 4 =
3 and 2 altogether make		6 and 1 =
1 and 2 altogether make		
2 and 3 altogether make		
1 and 3 altogether make		
1 and 4 altogether make		

1 and 3 and 2 =	1 + 7 =	2 + 4 = □
2 and 2 and 2 =	3 + 4 =	4 + □ = 8
3 and 1 and 2 =	5 + 3 =	5 + 4 = □
4 and 2 and 3 =	7 + 1 =	□ + 4 = 7
2 and 2 and 4 =	2 + 5 =	□ + 5 = 8
	4 + 4 =	6 + □ = 9
	6 + 2 =	

When the addition proceeds beyond ten it has to be integrated with the work on notation and place value: that is, the items are arranged in tens to find their number, e.g. 2 tens and 4 is twenty-four. If addition is being done using Unifix a number of single-coloured ten-blocks should be readily available in the Unifix collection. Thus 5 + 6 could be done by putting 5 cubes and 6 cubes together, sorting the cubes into tens and exchanging 10 cubes for 1 ten-block, so giving 1 ten-block and 1 cube. Therefore, 5 + 6 would be seen as 1 ten and 1. If the work being done results from some measuring activity the units used should be collected in tens. Marbles could be put in tens on tin lids, gram cubes could be sorted into tens and each set fitted together to make a 10-g block, pennies could be put in tens and perhaps 10 pennies exchanged for 1 tenpence. Suppose nine beakers and seven beakers of water are needed to fill two tins. The empty beakers used could be displayed with number labels alongside (Fig. 1.58). How many

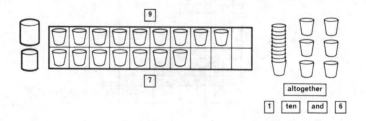

Fig. 1.58

beakers of water would be needed to fill both tins? This question could be answered by combining the empty beakers and arranging them into a ten-group and six others. The 10 beakers could be stacked inside one another. We would need 1 ten and 6 beakers, or 16 beakers, to fill both tins.

Combining larger sets generates the need for, and addition of, larger numbers. The teacher puts 14 plastic dogs and 18 plastic cats in a box, asks individual children from the teaching group to sort the animals, find how many there are of each, and put number labels near each set. Then she asks how many animals there are altogether. This involves putting the cats and dogs together, whilst retaining the ten-groups to save further sorting, and rearranging the ones into tens and ones, if possible. Demonstrate these steps. Ask a child to label the combined set, and then display the number labels to show what happened.

$$\begin{matrix} \text{1 ten and 4} \\ \text{1 ten and 8} \end{matrix} \quad \text{altogether 3 tens and 2}$$

Following this the children, individually, would be given further practice in combining sets of objects.

Unifix ten-blocks and cubes could also be used to imitate the process of addition. That is, at first combine the tens and ones from each set, and after this, if possible, regroup the ones into tens. Finally describe the result, e.g. add 27 (2 tens and 7) and 15 (1 ten and 5) (Fig. 1.59).

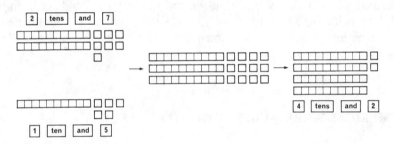

Fig. 1.59

These steps could be recorded as:

$$\begin{matrix} \text{2 tens and 7} \\ \text{1 ten and 5} \\ \hline \text{altogether} \quad \text{4 tens and 2} \end{matrix} \quad \text{or} \quad \begin{matrix} 27 \\ 15 \\ \hline 42 \end{matrix}$$

Such work would lead to a more formal study of addition. The most advantageous way of learning the formal process is to ensure that the manipulation of concrete articles imitates closely the steps involved in the formal process. That is, to combine the sets in two stages. At first, combine the ones, exchange for tens and 'carry' these tens, then add the tens, e.g. add 16 and 17 (Fig. 1.60).

These steps could be recorded, including any tens 'carried', as:

$$\begin{matrix} 1\,6\,+ \\ 1\,7 \\ \hline 3\,3 \\ \hline 1 \end{matrix}$$

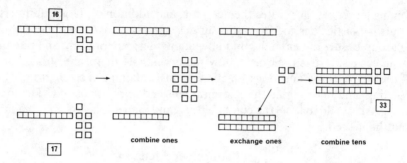

Fig. 1.60

When children become proficient in adding using apparatus, and know the formal method of recording, they could be given examples to do without using concrete aids. If, in the working, tens were formed, these tens 'carried' could be included in the written record. At first, set examples with no carrying, such as 14 + 45, and then with carrying, such as 28 + 13. When children are ready they could be introduced to hundreds by considering an addition, such as 58 + 61. This would generate the need for sorting 10 tens into 1 hundred, and introduce place value and notation for 3-digit numbers.

1.18 NUMERICAL WORK: SUBTRACTION (2 L1–3; 3 L1–4)

When we wish to compare sets of objects and find how much larger one is than the other we are finding the difference between them. We have met this idea in the work on measurement and some discussion on this aspect of subtraction is included in the chapters on Money, and Heaviness and Mass.

A child will encounter the idea of subtracting in various situations. When eating or sharing out sweets he takes them from the bag one or more at a time leaving some behind until eventually none are left. A child involved in the saying and 'acting' of '*Five currant buns in the baker's shop*', sees '*Jimmy*', who '*came with a penny one day. He bought a currant bun and he took it right away*', take a bun and leave the others behind which are then counted by the children. The teacher could refer to the taking away and leaving idea in this activity, e.g. five take away one leaves four, four take away one leaves three, etc.

Children should be encouraged, in appropriate situations, to solve subtraction problems by taking away, e.g. I had eight sweets and ate three of them. How many are left? To solve this, a child could put out eight objects and take away three by counting so leaving five objects. It would not, however, be desirable to work out 31 − 24 by putting out 31 separate objects and removing 24 of them. This is better done by finding what we add to 24 to make 31, or what to take from 31 to obtain 24. Children, particularly the brighter ones, should be encouraged to use their own methods for finding the required difference, perhaps by adding 10 to 24 to make 34, and then seeing this is too large and removing the necessary 3 to get back to 31, so seeing that the difference is 3 less than 10, or 7.

When the subtraction sign is being used the teacher needs to explain that 15 − 7 could mean 15 take away 7 or find the difference between 15 and 7, and that the answer can be found by adding or taking away.

The teacher could, with one or more children, take away objects from a set, talk about the numbers involved and show how to record the results using word and number labels. Individual children, when ready, could be given these activities:

1. The teacher provides a set of marbles of different colours. How many marbles? Pick out the red ones. How many are red? How many marbles are left? Accept oral answers, if necessary.
2. The teacher provides a set of cubes, marbles, wooden beads or plastic squares of two sizes. Pebbles could also be used. How many pebbles are there? Take away the big ones and count them. How many are left? Accept oral answers, or record using labels, e.g. **8 take away 3 leaves 5**.
3. Provide a set of nine nails, six four-inch and three one-inch. How many nails are there? Take away the small nails and count them. How many nails are left? The child could use labels for recording, or draw large and small nails and write a recording sentence alongside.
4. The teacher could prepare taking-away activities using Cuisenaire rods, cubes, pegs, beads, marbles and counters, of different colours. How many are there? How many are green? Pick out the green ones. How many are left? Use labels to record the results.
5. A child uses acorns, conkers, cubes, etc. Give instructions about how many to put out, and how many to take away. Find how many are left.
6. Put out nine pennies. Spend three pennies. How many pennies are left?
7. The teacher provides a set of wooden sticks or cardboard strips of different lengths and colours. A stick is selected from the set. How many sticks are left? Find sticks from the set which are shorter than the selected stick. How many are there? How many sticks are left? Use recording labels, or accept oral answers.
8. Use bags of sand and a stone. How many bags of sand are there? Use a common balance to find those bags heavier than the stone and put them in a group. How many bags were taken away? How many bags are left?
9. Use beads, cubes or counters to find the difference between 8 and 5, 9 and 4, 7 and 3, and so on. Do the questions by putting out the larger number and taking away from it the smaller number. Record as **8 and 5 difference 3**.
10. Use acorns, conkers or cubes to find the difference between 8 and 4, 7 and 2, 9 and 6, and so on. Answer the questions by putting out the larger number and removing items until the smaller is reached.
11. Use cubes or acorns to find the difference between 8 and 3, 7 and 4, 9 and 3, and so on. Answer the questions by adding items to the smaller until it equals the larger number.
12. Questions on differences are catered for in many other chapters of this book where numbers of objects, or measuring units, are being compared. These activities are usually included in the numerical comparison sections.
13. Take away 6 from 9. Find the difference between 12 and 8. Ask children to do

questions like these using structural apparatus such as Stern or Unifix blocks. Initially the recording should follow the physical manipulation. Later both processes can be described using the subtraction sign (Fig. 1.61).

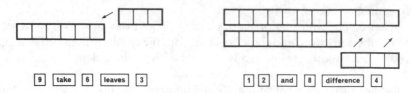

Fig. 1.61

14. Put nine pegs on a pegboard. Take away 1 peg, 2 pegs . . . up to 9 pegs, and record the results by copying and completing, each time, the following sentence: . . . take . . . leaves . . .

> 9 take 1 leaves 8
> 9 take 2 leaves 7
> . . . .
> 9 take 8 leaves 1
> 9 take 9 leaves 0

After the facts have been written down ask the child to read them through and try to memorize them.

15. Put two Stern or Unifix blocks end to end and describe the result. Then take each block away in turn and describe the result. Give spoken and written answers, e.g. four and three make seven; seven take four leaves three; seven take three leaves four; or $4 + 3 = 7, 7 - 4 = 3, 7 - 3 = 4$.

16. Practice work cards on subtraction for use with and without apparatus could be introduced together with a gradual progression to the formal methods of recording. Present the subtraction facts on an ordered set of work cards. That is, subtract from numbers below 10, then 10, then above 10 and up to 18.

5 take 1 leaves
7 take 4 leaves
9 take 6 leaves
8 take 2 leaves
9 take 2 leaves

Take away
$7 - 2 =$
$8 - 4 =$
$9 - 6 =$
$6 - 2 =$
$9 - 4 =$

Find the difference between	
8 and 4	9 and 3
10 and 7	14 and 9
12 and 8	16 and 7

17. Sorting exercises of various kinds, and graphical representations, lead to comparisons of various categories and the finding of differences. Questions arising from these activities should at first involve differences between smaller numbers, that is those usually included in the subtraction facts. Gradually, comparisons between larger numbers, involving tens and units, could be made. At this stage a more formal study of subtraction could be undertaken using Stern or Unifix, after which the subtraction process could be further practised by finding differences, and taking away, in other sorting activities and graphical work.

When subtraction needs to be studied more formally the following could be done:

How much larger is 48 than 16? To answer this we could take 16 from 48.
The teacher demonstrates:
  Put out 48 (that is, 4 ten-blocks and 8 cubes).
  Take away the 16 (1 ten-block and 6 cubes) in two stages:
        First take away the 6 cubes from the 8 cubes leaving 2 cubes;
        then take away the 1 ten from the 4 tens leaving 3 tens.
  This procedure could be recorded as:

	4 tens	8 ones	
take away	1 ten	6 ones	48 is 32 more than 16.
	3 tens	2 ones	left

After more demonstrations, individual exercises of the type 48 − 36, 58 − 32, could be set. A quicker form of recording could also be introduced:

$$
\begin{array}{r}
7\ 5- \\
3\ 2 \\
\hline
4\ 3 \\
\hline
\end{array}
$$

Next ask 'how many more is 62 than 36?'
The teacher demonstrates:
  Put out 62, that is 6 ten-blocks and 2 cubes. (To answer this we could take away 36, that is, 3 ten-blocks and 6 cubes.)
  Firstly take away the cubes. 2 cubes take away 6 cubes we cannot. (We need more cubes, so exchange 1 ten-block for 10 cubes, and put them near the other cubes. We now have 5 ten-blocks and 10 cubes and 2 cubes, or 5 ten-blocks and 12 cubes. Be sure the children appreciate that the 6 tens and 2 ones have been rearranged into 5 tens and 12 ones. That is, sixty-two is the same as fifty-twelve. This step could also be established using a number line.)
  Can we take away the 6 cubes now? Take 6 cubes from the 12 cubes leaving 6 cubes, then take 3 tens from the 5 tens leaving 2 tens.
  This could be recorded as:

6 tens	2 ones		5 tens	12 ones	
3 tens	6 ones	take away	3 tens	6 ones	
			2 tens	6 ones	left

62 is 26 more than 36.

After further demonstrations and individual practice exercises, children could gradually dispense with the apparatus and record formally:

$$
\begin{array}{cc}
7 & 10 \\
\not{8} & 3- \\
4 & 6 \\
\hline
3 & 7 \\
\hline
\end{array}
$$

18. Extra sorting exercises leading to questions on taking away or finding differences are:

   (a) Sort a collection of tins, boxes, bottles, etc. to find rectangular boxes, cylinders and other shapes.
   (b) Sort a collection of cardboard shapes into triangles, four-sided shapes, five-sided shapes, etc.
   (c) Sort a collection of cardboard triangles into congruent isosceles, equilateral and scalene, by matching.
   (d) Count the various birds seen on the school bird table within a specified period.
   (e) Count various types of road vehicles passing the school within a specified period, e.g. cars, vans, bicycles, motor cycles, etc.
   (f) Number of trees of various kinds growing in a particular piece of woodland, or in a hedgerow.
   (g) Compare the capacities of tins, bottles, etc. by filling them with water using a small container.

19. Many of the pictograms and block graphs included in Sections 1.13 and 1.14 lead to questions on finding differences between numbers. Additional topics involving sorting, followed by some kind of graphical representation, which lead to questions on finding differences are now listed. Many of these may be incorporated into the project '*Ourselves*'.

   (a) Shoe sizes
   (b) Number of cousins
   (c) Number of aunts
   (d) Ages of children in years and months
   (e) Kinds of sweets and their prices
   (f) Various items and their prices in pence
   (g) Number of children in various classes in the school
   (h) Number of children who stay at school for dinner from different classes
   (i) Number of children of different heights, grouped in 5 cm intervals
   (j) Number of coins of various denominations, from pennies to pounds, inside a purse
   (k) Years of minting for £1-worth of pennies or twopences
   (l) Birthmonths
   (m) Number of uncles
   (n) Bedtimes (use 15-minute intervals).

1.19 NUMERICAL WORK: MULTIPLICATION (2 L1–3; 3 L1–4)

Children will have already met some examples where the same number is repeated whilst adding sets, or doing additions from work cards, e.g. $3 + 3 + 3$, and multiplication is often introduced by situations like these. A preliminary to the introduction of multiplication would be to practise a variety of repeated addition examples using concrete objects to obtain the answers, if necessary, e.g. $4 + 4 + 4$, $3 + 3 + 3 + 3 + 3$.

The teacher should then, with a teaching group, demonstrate and discuss the idea of repeated addition including the recording and the spoken and written language of the new notational form. She could do examples using sets of objects and structural apparatus such as Stern or Unifix. She could fit Unifix cubes together to make twos and put them on the table. How many twos are there? (Seven twos) Add these together. The two-blocks could be arranged into 1 ten-block and a 4-block. So seven twos make fourteen. Write down what was done using addition. $2 + 2 + 2 + 2 + 2 + 2 + 2 = 14$. Introduce the quicker notation, $2 \times 7 = 14$. (2×7 means 2 multiplied by 7, or seven twos, or seven times two, or two seven times.) She could do more examples and ask children to describe the results in words and by writing down addition and multiplication statements.

Individual children could now do more repeated additions and record them in the new form. A few examples would be given at first to get them used to this procedure and this would be followed by a more systematic study of sets of things which lead to the building up of multiplication tables and ideas about structure. At first any sets of items could be used to obtain answers but later some kind of structural apparatus, preferably with a number track, could be used because results are obtained more easily and quickly, possibly with fewer errors being made. A number line is also particularly valuable to build up repeated additions.

Multiplication notation could be introduced via these activities:

1. The child could work with eight cubes on a lorry and imagine that a crane could lift off two cubes at a time. Take them off in twos and record using addition and multiplication.
2. The teacher chooses three children for a child to work on. They each have two ears so count the ears of the three children. The child draws heads with ears for each of the children and finds the total, recording it using addition and multiplication.
3. The teacher turns up a chair. She asks a child to count the legs and then asks her to find the number of legs on three chairs. Record as $4 + 4 + 4$ and 4×3.

    Also do this exercise by considering the wheels on toy cars, e.g. four cars. How many wheels altogether?
4. The teacher provides some large specimens of clover. How many leaves on one stem? How many leaves on four stems? on five stems? Record using the shortened form.
5. The teacher could prepare cards with drawings on them, or ask the children to draw items in order to find answers to repeated additions, e.g. 6 birds—number of legs, 5 dogs—number of legs, 4 bicycles—number of wheels.

    Twos could be dealt with using wheels on bicycles, pairs of gloves, socks, and shoes, eyes, ears, arms and legs on people, wings on birds, engines on planes, or sycamore seeds.

    Threes could be introduced with wheels on tricycles, legs on three-legged stools, leaves on three-leaf clovers, or corners in triangles.

    Fours could be dealt with using wheels on cars, legs on chairs, dogs and cats, sides on rectangles, engines on planes, or wings on butterflies.

    Other pictures could be five-petalled flowers, fingers on hands, six-legged ants, six-wheeled shunting engines, seven-spotted ladybirds and eight-legged spiders.

A systematic study of *multiplication facts* could be introduced in this manner:

1. A child could learn how to count in twos using pegs and a pegboard. The teacher

makes the first three patterns (Fig. 1.62), and asks the child to make the next, and the next. What numbers of pegs have been used so far? Two, four, six, eight, ten. Without making the pattern, what is the next number? Make the pattern to check the result. What is the next number? Continue counting in twos up to 30.

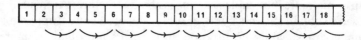

Fig. 1.62

2. Using a paper strip marked from 1 to 100 a child counts in twos, pointing to the numbers on the scale as he does so, starting with 2 (Fig. 1.63).

1	2	3	4	5	6	7	8	9	10	11	12	13	14	15	16	17	18

Fig. 1.63

3. A child uses Stern or Unifix two-blocks and the related number track. Add in twos, recording the results in table form, up to 20.

$$2 \times 1 = 2$$
$$2 \times 2 = 4$$
$$2 \times 3 = 6$$
$$\cdots\cdots\cdots\cdots$$
$$2 \times 9 = 18$$
$$2 \times 10 = 20$$

He then practises writing the table out, and saying it, e.g. one two is two, two twos are four, three twos are six, up to ten twos are twenty. The teacher asks questions on these facts, mixed up, on a work card. The child practises these questions until he can say, and write, the answers quickly.

When this table has been learnt, or nearly so, the teacher could ask the child to build another table using pegs and a pegboard, or Stern or Unifix cubes, and then learn it. Multiples of three, four, five and ten, up to ten threes, ten fours, etc. would be built up and learnt.

To facilitate the learning of multiplication tables a child could:

(a) Write out the particular table.
(b) Say the table, individually, or with the class.
(c) Answer questions from a work card about the table.
(d) Answer oral questions, asked individually or around the class, about the table.
(e) Match multiplication questions from a particular table with their answers. For this the teacher needs to prepare a set of question cards and a set of answer cards (Fig. 1.64).
(f) Match questions, written on squared pieces of card, with their answers, written in squares, on a larger master card. (A lotto-like game).

Fig. 1.64

(g) Repeat these activities but include facts from two tables, then three tables, and so on, until all the tables built up so far have been covered.
4. Work on the remaining tables of six, seven, eight and nine could be tackled in the manner described in paragraph **3** when the teacher considers a particular child is ready. To assist the learning of tables a knowledge of the commutative law of multiplication is extremely valuable.

The teacher could arrange for the multiplication tables derived to be displayed on a multiplication square (Fig. 1.65). Talk with a child, or group, about how the square could be used to find four fives, three eights, seven sixes, etc. Then discuss and explain how it could be used to deal with written questions such as $4 \times 3, 7 \times 6, 8 \times 5$, etc.

NUMBER IN A SET

	1	2	3	4	5	6	7	8	9	10
1	1	2	3	4	5	6	7	8	9	10
2	2	4	6	8	10	12	14	16	18	20
3	3	6	9	12	15	18	21	24	27	30
4	4	8	12	16	20	24	28	32	36	40
5	5	10	15	20	25	30	35	40	45	50
6	6	12	18	24	30	36	42	48	54	60
7	7	14	21	28	35	42	49	56	63	70
8	8	16	24	32	40	48	56	64	72	80
9	9	18	27	36	45	54	63	72	81	90
10	10	20	30	40	50	60	70	80	90	100

NUMBER OF SETS (row labels, left side)

Fig. 1.65

The children then use the square, if necessary, to find answers to four eights and eight fours, seven sixes and six sevens, nine fives and five nines, etc. Talk with the children about the results and also write them down, e.g. four fives and five fours make twenty, $5 \times 4 = 4 \times 5 = 20$. Establish the idea that two numbers when multiplied together provide the same answer no matter what order is used. This idea is valuable because it can help children to learn and remember multiplication facts. If they know that eight fours is thirty-two then they should know what four eights are.

Multiplication facts and their answers, put on cards, could be matched to gain further practice (Fig. 1.66).

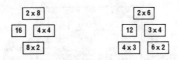

Fig. 1.66

Multiples of numbers could be further extended, and growth patterns studied, as follows:

(a) Use a number square. Colour those squares with numbers on them which are multiples of two (even numbers) up to 50 (Fig. 1.67). What do you notice about the squares you have coloured? Continue the colouring pattern. What numbers from 50 to 60, 60 to 70, 70 to 80, 80 to 90, 90 to 100, do you think are even? Do you think 104, 117, 113, 123, 126, etc. would be even? How can even numbers be detected?

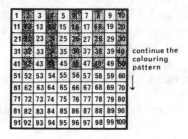

Fig. 1.67

(b) Use Unifix three-blocks or pegs and a pegboard or shade in rows of three squares, side by side, on centimetre squared paper, to obtain multiples of three, up to 48 (Fig. 1.68). Write down the results in order, e.g. 3, 6, 9, 12, ..., 48.

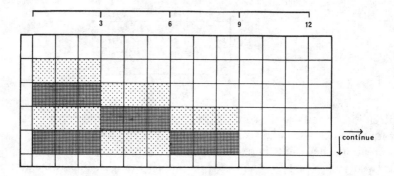

Fig. 1.68

On a number square, shade those squares with numbers on them which are multiples of three, up to 48 (Fig. 1.69). Can you shade any numbers from 50 to 60

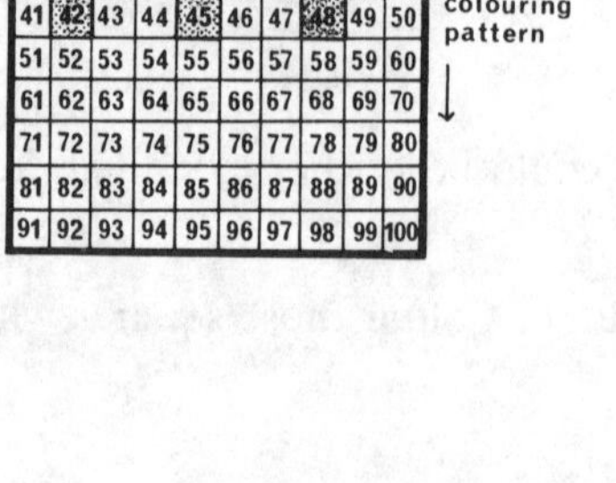

Fig. 1.69

which continue this pattern? Which numbers? Now from 60 to 70; then 70 to 80; then 80 to 90; then 90 to 100. Add threes on to 48, and count in threes on a 1–100 number strip, to check your answers.

(c) Use Unifix four-blocks or pegs on a pegboard, to build the number sequence for multiples of four up to 48. Shade these numbers on a number square (Fig. 1.70). Can you shade and find numbers over 50 which continue to show how fours grow? Check these answers by adding fours on to 48 and by counting in fours on a 1–100 number strip.

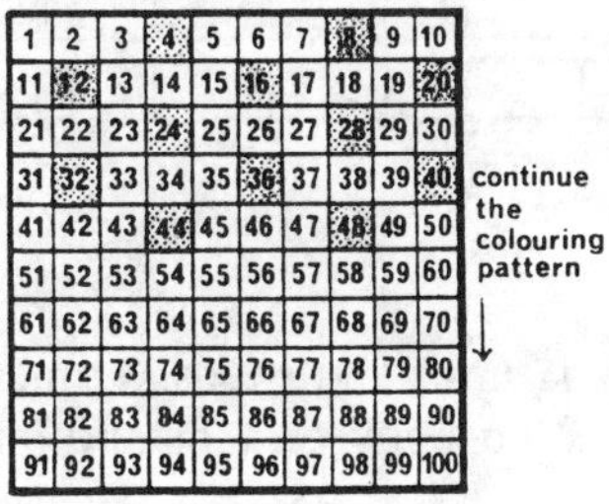

continue the colouring pattern

Fig. 1.70

(d) Collect Unifix five-blocks together to study the growth of fives, and build the sequence 5, 10, 15, 20, ..., to 50. Shade these numbers on a number square, and continue this sequence to 100, by colouring squares to follow the previously shaded pattern (Fig. 1.71). Count in fives on a 1–100 number strip or number line to check these results.

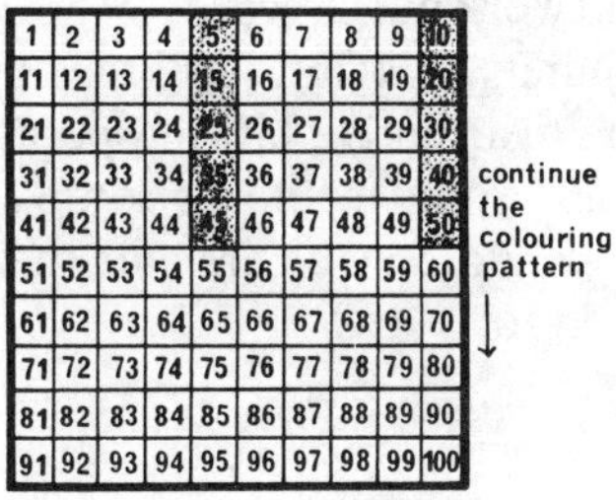

continue the colouring pattern

Fig. 1.71

All the tables should eventually be learnt by those children capable of doing so. When some are known they may be applied in realistic situations, involving problem solving, so that children can see their value. A multiplication square displayed in the classroom can help children in those areas of uncertainty, and assist in recall and memorization. Those children who know all their tables could proceed to the multiplication of larger numbers, and then apply this knowledge in further realistic activities.

In order to proceed to multiplication of the type 27 × 3 a child should have a knowledge of the structure of 27 (2 tens and 7 ones) and appreciate the meaning of multiplication and know the relevant multiplication facts, and be aware of the ideas encompassed by the distributive law. The teacher, therefore, needs to spend some time introducing and developing the latter, as it is the only topic not yet dealt with.

With a group, the teacher could use Stern or Unifix ten-blocks and cubes to illustrate the working of 24 × 3. 24 × 3 means three twenty-fours. 24 can be represented by 2 ten-blocks and 4 cubes. Put this number out three times because we require three twenty-fours (Fig. 1.72). We see that altogether there are 2 tens, 3 times and 4 units, 3

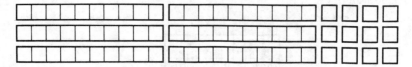

Fig. 1.72

times. Now 4 units, 3 times is 12 units and 2 tens, 3 times is 6 tens. The working so far could, if a reasonable space is left between tens and units headings, be written as:

$$
\begin{array}{cc}
\text{tens} & \text{ones} \\
2 & 4 \times \\
& 3 \\
\hline
6 & 12 \\
\hline
7 & 2 \\
\hline
\end{array}
$$

The ones could then be rearranged into tens and ones and the answer 72 obtained. The teacher could do some more examples, such as 15 × 5 and 16 × 4, and talk with the children about how they would work out 26 × 4, 18 × 5, and so on. That is, 26 × 4 would be done by multiplying the 6 units by 4 and the 2 tens by 4 and adding these answers together. (This is, in fact, the distributive law in operation.)

Set the children, individually, some examples to do from work cards. Be sure the answers are less than 100. The children who are able to cope with these may gradually modify the written layout used to:

$$
\begin{array}{c}
17 \times \\
4 \\
\hline
6 \ 8 \\
\hline
2 \\
\end{array}
$$

Notice that the third row of the original layout has been left out as well as the tens and ones headings. A child could, as the units are exchanged for tens, write down the tens 'carried'.

When children are ready they could proceed to examples such as 26 × 5, 36 × 3 and 43 × 4. These have answers involving hundreds, tens and ones. Following this, multiplications of the type 245 × 3 could be introduced. Some kind of structural apparatus could be used initially in each of these stages to illustrate the procedures involved.

The following activities, arising from measurement, provide practice exercises in multiplication. These could be structured to involve easier or harder multiplications to meet the readiness of particular children.

1. Ask a child to measure the length of a table, to the nearest decimetre, using Cuisenaire orange rods. What would be the length, roughly, if three such tables were placed end to end?
2. The child is asked to measure, in grams, the mass of an egg carton (about 12 g). What would be the mass, roughly, of seven such cartons.
3. Some children are asked to find out from their parents how far the family car travels on a gallon of petrol. They then predict how far the car might go on three gallons.
4. A child is asked to cover a given shape with triangles. This shape is prepared by the teacher so that triangles just fit on it. How many triangles would be needed to fit on six such shapes?
5. A child fills a small box with cubes or marbles. He then finds, roughly, how many cubes would be needed to fill four such boxes.
6. The child is asked to find, from the classroom shop, the cost of a bar of chocolate or box of sweets. He then works out the cost of four bars of chocolate, or three boxes of sweets.
7. A child is timed, in seconds, whilst he walks 50 metres. How long, roughly, would he take to walk this distance four times?
8. A child uses a plastic container graduated in centilitres and puts it under a dripping tap. He then finds how many centilitres of water, to the nearest centilitre, are lost when the tap drips for one hour. How much water, roughly, would be lost if the tap was left to drip for six hours?

It is usually easier to multiply a larger number by a smaller one, and often we reverse the order of multiplication to bring this idea into play. Talk with a child, or group, about this, e.g. 16 tables—how many legs altogether? We have sixteen fours, 4×16, to work out, but we only know our tables up to 10 fours. It could be done by saying sixteen fours is the same as ten fours and six fours added together. Or we could say sixteen fours is the same as four sixteens. Refer to some multiplication facts—seven fours and four sevens make twenty-eight, eight threes and three eights make twenty-four, and so on. So instead of working out sixteen fours we could find four sixteens, because we have learnt to multiply by four. Deal with other instances—32 children, how many eyes? 25 children, how many legs? 16 hands, how many fingers? 14 weeks, how many days?

Set children practice exercises where the order of multiplication could be reversed, e.g. 36 bicycles, how many wheels? 25 clover stems, how many leaves? 16 ants, how many legs? 43 people, how many legs?

As a preliminary set of ideas leading to work on continuous graphs in the upper junior school, growth patterns obtained by multiplying numbers by two, three, four, etc. should be examined. Unifix cubes or Stern blocks could be used at this stage. For example, Fig. 1.73 shows how two equal sets of cubes, or blocks, could be used to multiply by two, and assist in building the sequence 2, 4, 6, 8, etc.

These numbers could be represented on a block graph as shown in Fig. 1.74 and subsequently by the kind of graph shown in Fig. 1.75.

It is important for the teacher to talk with the children about the growth patterns.

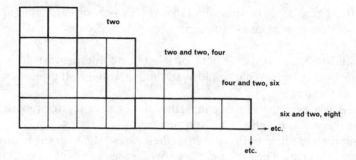

Fig. 1.73

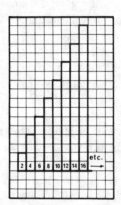

Fig. 1.74

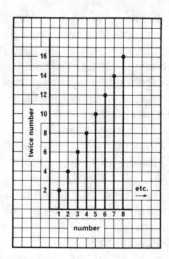

Fig. 1.75

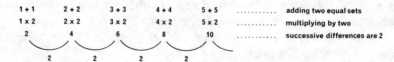

Fig. 1.76

Graphs of numbers being multiplied would show growth in equal steps and this connects with the constant numerical intervals shown in the number patterns of Fig. 1.76.

When children appreciate that twice a number could include fractions they see that more and more points could be entered on the 'twice a number' graph. This leads to the idea that so many points may be put on the graph that a straight line could be drawn, on which they all lie, to represent the growth (Fig. 1.77).

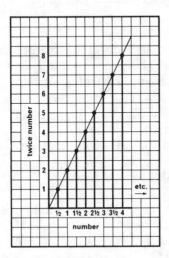

Fig. 1.77

1.20 NUMERICAL WORK: DIVISION (2 L1–2; 3 L1–4)

Children will have come across the idea of sharing out a set of things equally, such as sweets, usually by repeated subtraction in ones. One for you, one for me, etc. The teacher could talk with a child, or group, about this idea, by doing a few examples, e.g. 15 sweets and 3 children. Could the sweets be shared out equally? (Use cubes for sweets.) How many sweets would each child have? This involves putting out the sweets, one at a time, into three sets. After the sharing there would be three sets each containing five sweets. We could record this as 5 + 5 + 5 = 15. We could also write 15 ÷ 3 = 5. Explain that ÷ 3, divide by 3, means sharing equally between 3.

Individual exercises such as those listed below could then be set. After each, talk with the child about the group size, the number of groups, and the recording.

1. 12 cars from the classroom garage are to be taken away in 3 transporters. The child finds, using toy cars and boxes for transporters, whether each transporter could have the same number of cars on it. Record 4 + 4 + 4 = 12 and 12 ÷ 3 = 4.
2. Cattle from the class 'farm' are to be taken to market. The teacher arranges that there are 12 cows and 2 lorries. Could each lorry carry the same number of cows? Record 6 + 6 = 12, 12 ÷ 2 = 6.
3. A crane lifts crates (wooden cubes) from a ship (a model made by the children). The teacher ensures that there is a cargo of, say, 18 cubes. Can the cargo be taken in 3

railway trucks (matchboxes stuck together at the ends) so that each truck has the same number of crates? Record $6 + 6 + 6 = 18$, $18 \div 3 = 6$.
4. A child could investigate the ways in which a cargo of 12 crates could be taken away, equally, in trucks. Could 2 trucks, 3 trucks, 4 trucks, etc. be used?
5. There are 20 marbles. Could these be equally shared between 4 children? between 5 children? between 3 children?
6. Use 24 pennies. Could these be equally shared between 4 children? 6 children? 8 children? 5 children?

More essential to the idea of division is the repeated subtraction of items, more than one at a time, in equal sets. The teacher could demonstrate and discuss whether a number of articles could be arranged in certain sized sets. Could a forklift truck move 12 boxes (cubes), 3 boxes at a time? How many journeys would be needed? Talk about, and write down, the results, e.g. $3 + 3 + 3 + 3 = 12$ and $12 \div 3 = 4$. In this case 12 $\div$ 3 means 12 is to be arranged in sets of 3.

Could the boxes be moved 4 at a time? Illustrate this and record it. $4 + 4 + 4 = 12$, $12 \div 4 = 3$.

Individual children could do these activities:

1. The model ship has 24 boxes (cubes) on it. A child uses a 'crane' to lift off 4 boxes at a time. How many crane loads would be needed? How many fours in twenty-four? Record $4 + 4 + 4 + 4 + 4 + 4 = 24$, $24 \div 4 = 6$.
2. A child has 15 farm animals. Could these animals be put in pens, 5 animals to each pen? How many pens would be needed? How many fives in fifteen? Record $5 + 5 + 5 = 15$, $15 \div 5 = 3$.
3. The child has 12 cars to park in the 'garage'. A parking space has room for 3 cars. How many parking spaces are needed? How many threes in twelve? Record $3 + 3 + 3 + 3 = 12$, $12 \div 3 = 4$.
4. A child is asked to make different rectangles, each with 16 pegs, on a pegboard. She then examines the sets of pegs in the rows, and columns, and describes their number (Fig. 1.78). The teacher, initially, would help with the spoken and written descriptions.

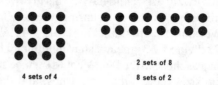

2 sets of 8

8 sets of 2

4 sets of 4

Fig. 1.78

Look at the rows, or columns, of the square. We see four fours are sixteen ($4 \times 4 = 16$) and the number of fours in sixteen is four ($16 \div 4 = 4$). Look at the rows in the oblong. We see two eights are sixteen ($8 \times 2 = 16$) and the number of eights in sixteen is two ($16 \div 8 = 2$). Look at the columns of the oblong. We see eight twos are sixteen ($2 \times 8 = 16$) and the number of twos in sixteen is eight ($16 \div 2 = 8$). If all these statements are put together we have:

$$4 \times 4 = 16 \qquad 16 \div 4 = 4$$
$$8 \times 2 = 16 \qquad 16 \div 8 = 2$$
$$2 \times 8 = 16 \qquad 16 \div 2 = 8$$

5. A child is asked to do the same as in **4** but use 9 pegs, 10 pegs, 14 pegs and 15 pegs. (Only one rectangle can be made in these cases.)

6. A child is asked to make rectangles using 9 pegs, 12 pegs, 18 pegs, 24 pegs, 7 pegs and 11 pegs, and investigate the number of equal sets of pegs needed. (7 pegs could be arranged as 7 sets of 1 peg or 1 set of 7 pegs.)

    This activity could be linked with geometry. Why could 14, 15, 9 and 8 be called **rectangular numbers**? 9 is a special rectangular number called a **square number**. Why? Numbers such as 2, 3, 5, 7, and 11 are not rectangular. Why? A non-rectangular number is also called a **prime number**.

7. The teacher could provide a child, or children, with a multiplication square. Such a square would probably be on display already in the classroom to help children with multiplication activities (Fig. 1.79). A child uses such a square to find whether rectangles could be made with pegs, e.g. 14 pegs. We see 14 in the table twice, and that seven twos and two sevens make 14. So a rectangle 7 pegs long and 2 pegs wide could be made with 14 pegs.

    Could rectangles be made with 25, 27, 36, 45, 49, 56, 63 and 72 pegs? Use the table to find square numbers, and some prime numbers, up to 100.

NUMBER IN A SET

	1	2	3	4	5	6	7	8	9	10
1	1	2	3	4	5	6	7	8	9	10
2	2	4	6	8	10	12	14	16	18	20
3	3	6	9	12	15	18	21	24	27	30
4	4	8	12	16	20	24	28	32	36	40
5	5	10	15	20	25	30	35	40	45	50
6	6	12	18	24	30	36	42	48	54	60
7	7	14	21	28	35	42	49	56	63	70
8	8	16	24	32	40	48	56	64	72	80
9	9	18	27	36	45	54	63	72	81	90
10	10	20	30	40	50	60	70	80	90	100

NUMBER OF SETS

Fig. 1.79

8. Show a child, or group, how to use the multiplication square to find the number of twos in eight, threes in twelve, fives in twenty, etc. (To find the number of fours in thirty-two, go down the '4 in a set' column until 32 is found. Then look left to the end of the row and we see that it is 8.)

    Then talk about finding the missing numbers in written statements such as $10 = 5 \times \square$, $15 = 5 \times \square$, $20 = 4 \times \square$. ($36 = 6 \times \square$ means 36 is so many sixes, how many?)

    Also deal with $7 \times \square = 14$, $5 \times \square = 10$, $4 \times \square = 24$. ($8 \times \square = 16$ reads so many eights make sixteen, how many?) Then set workcard questions on this.

9. Show how the square can be used to find $16 \div 2$, $20 \div 4$, $56 \div 7$, etc. In this case interpret $16 \div 2$ as how many twos in sixteen? Set practice exercises on workcards.

10. Show how the square can be used to share 18 between 2, to share 15 between 3, to share 20 between 4, etc. (To share 35 between 7, go across the '7 sets' row until 35 is found, then look to the top of the column. We see that it is 5.)

Also talk about finding the missing numbers in written statements such as $24 = \square \times 6$, $30 = \square \times 5$, $24 = \square \times 8$. ($42 = \square \times 7$ means 42 is 7 sets of how many?) Then deal with $\square \times 4 = 32$, $\square \times 3 = 27$, etc. ($\square \times 5 = 45$ means 5 sets of how many make 45?) Set practice questions on workcards.

11. Talk with a child, or group, about using the square to find $20 \div 4$, $81 \div 9$, $72 \div 8$, etc. In this case interpret $20 \div 4$ as twenty shared equally between four. Set questions on work cards.

12. Talk with a child, or group, about related multiplication and division facts. From $6 \times 2 = 12$ we have $12 \div 6 = 2$ and $12 \div 2 = 6$. That is, the number of sixes in twelve is two, and 12 shared equally between two is six.

Set a work card on this. Ask questions, such as $8 \times 3 = 24$, so $24 \div 8 = \square$ and $24 \div 3 = \square$.

The children, as well as doing work card questions, could also be using division in measurement exercises. The following activities, amongst others, could be done. Multiplication squares could be consulted, if necessary.

1. The teacher supplies a piece of dowel, or bamboo cane, which is 27 cm long. The child is asked to measure the rod. How many pieces 9 cm long could be cut from this length? He could check his answer using Cuisenaire blue rods.

2. A child is told that 35 pennies are to be shared equally between 7 children. How many pennies would each child get? The child checks his answer by putting 35 pennies into 7 equal sets.

3. A child is told that 32 cl of water is to be shared equally between 4 children. The child finds out how much water each person would have and uses a centilitre measure to put this amount in each of 4 beakers.

4. The teacher prepares a shape which can just be covered with congruent plastic hexagons. She gives the shape to a child and tells her that 6 of these shapes can be covered with 30 hexagons (show one), so how many hexagons would cover the shape? She checks her answer by fitting hexagons, given to her by the teacher, on the shape.

5. A child is asked to measure out, using 1 g centicubes on a common balance, 27 g of sand. This sand is to be put into three equal amounts. How many grams in each amount? The sand is then measured out and put in three tin lids.

The work card exercises on division, up to now, have been done, or could have been, by consulting a multiplication square. As children memorize the multiplication tables, and realize that division and multiplication are related, the work card exercises done previously could be done again without using aids of any kind, together with additional cards.

Those children who can divide numbers successfully using multiplication or division facts could proceed to the dividing of larger numbers, e.g. $64 \div 4$. At first, use of structural apparatus of some kind is necessary to mime the sequence of operations needed in the normal treatment later. $64 \div 4$ is better done by sharing, that is, to divide 64 into 4 equal parts. The other method, finding how many fours in 64, is lengthier and leads to difficulties with language when division is treated formally.

The teacher could, with a group, use Unifix or Stern ten-blocks and cubes to demonstrate and discuss the steps involved in finding 48 ÷ 4. Put out 48, that is 4 ten-blocks and 8 cubes. These blocks and cubes are to be put into 4 equal sets (Fig. 1.80). Four tens ÷ 4 is 1 ten for each set. (□ × 4 = 4 tens.) Arrange this on the table. 8 ones ÷ 4 is 2 ones for each set. (□ × 4 = 8 ones.) Arrange this. We have 12 in each set so 48 ÷ 4 = 12.

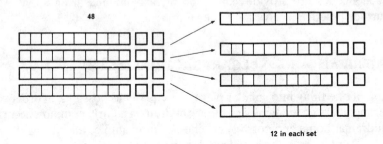

Fig. 1.80

Questions could then be given to individual children. The recording could be:

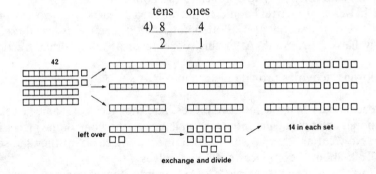

Fig. 1.81

Following this the teacher could demonstrate and discuss 42 ÷ 3 with the group as a whole. Put out 4 ten-blocks and 2 cubes. The blocks and cubes are to be put into 3 equal sets (Fig. 1.81). 4 tens ÷ 3 is 1 ten for each set with 1 ten left over. Arrange this. The 1 ten left can only be divided if it is exchanged for 10 ones. Do this, and put the ones with the 2 ones. Altogether there are now 12 ones. 12 ones ÷ 3 = 4 ones. (□ × 3 = 12) Put 4 ones in each set. We have 14 in each set so 42 ÷ 3 = 14. The written layout could be:

$$
\begin{array}{ccc}
 & \text{tens} & \text{ones} \\
 & & 10 \\
3\overline{)} & 4 & 2 \\
\hline
 & 1 & 4 \\
\hline
\end{array}
$$

After working out more examples the children could be given work card exercises. These could be done at first with apparatus. The tens and ones heading could later be omitted from the written layout.

$$\begin{array}{r} 10 \\ 4\overline{)\ 5\quad 6} \\ \hline 1\quad 4 \end{array}$$

The teacher could also provide realistic problems, and measuring activities, in order to give further practice in dividing larger numbers.

1.21 NUMERICAL WORK: VULGAR FRACTIONS (2 L2–4)

The cutting of one thing into smaller pieces, as equally as possible, in order to share it with other members of the family or other children, is a fairly common occurrence for young children at home and possibly at school. For example, the cutting of a birthday cake into pieces at a party, the cutting and sharing of an apple or cake with a brother or sister, or the breaking of a bar of chocolate into four parts and sharing it. Such experiences, amongst others, could lead to ideas about fractions together with the development of spoken and written language. Written fractions should, however, be delayed until a child is ready to appreciate the notation.

At first halves and quarters could be introduced because the process of dividing things into two or four equal parts is often not difficult, and this is why these fractions, particularly halves, are used. After this, develop ideas about other fractions up to tenths.

The following activities provide ideas about halves:

1. The teacher cuts an apple into two pieces. Are the pieces the same? (Yes) Explain that should an apple be cut into two equal pieces, then one of the pieces is half the apple. Now cut another apple into two unequal pieces. Are they the same size? (No) Talk about these pieces not being halves.
2. A child folds a rectangular piece of paper into halves and crayons each half a different colour. This is repeated with a circular piece and a square piece.
3. A child is given two paper squares. He folds one in half diagonally, and the other by putting two opposite sides together. Crayon each half a different colour. What shapes are the halves?
4. A child is given a paper rectangle to cut into two pieces along a diagonal. What shape is each piece? Are the pieces the same size? What can be said about each triangle? (It is half the rectangle, that is, it covers half as much.)
5. Fold a piece of paper and cut it. Open it out and crayon, in different colours, the parts on each side of the fold. Talk about the shape and its coloured parts. The shape is symmetrical about the fold. The fold divides the shape into halves. Symmetrical shapes made by the children, and coloured, could be displayed.
6. A child uses a piece of string of suitable length. Fold it and cut it into halves. How many pieces of string are there? Are they the same length? Test them. Was the string cut carefully, or not?
7. Provide a cardboard strip about 1 metre long on which a straight road (about 1 cm wide) is painted. Use a toy car. The car drives from one end of the road to the other. Where would the car be if it broke down halfway along the road? The child places

the car on the road to illustrate this. He then uses a stretched string to test its distance from both ends of the road, and changes its position if necessary.

8. The teacher obtains a revolving pointer, and turns it, e.g. a clock with one hand. The children describe the amount of turning. Turn it around once, twice, three times. Turn it halfway around. Turn it around one and a half times, three and a half times, etc.
9. A child is given some sand and a common balance. He is given two bags and asked to put half the sand into each bag. (Balance equal amounts of sand.)
10. Provide two identical transparent vessels and some water in a jug. The child pours half the water into each vessel by putting them near each other and comparing water levels.
11. Provide two identical plastic bottles. Ask a child to half fill each bottle with water. (Fill one bottle and pour water from it into the other. Put the bottles side by side and check water levels to obtain equal amounts.) Use the same method to half fill two beakers with water.
12. A child is given two tin lids and an even number of items, e.g. 12 cubes. Put half the cubes on each lid. What is half of 12? Record, one half of 12 = 6. Repeat with other numbers. Set work card questions, e.g. what is one half of 14? a half of 10? a half of 18? etc.
13. Put two Stern or Unifix blocks together, of the same length, and describe the results, e.g. two 4-blocks. We see from Fig. 1.82 that $4 + 4 = 8$, two fours is eight, and one half of eight is four.

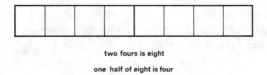

two fours is eight

one half of eight is four

Fig. 1.82

The activities just described provide ideas about halves, many of which can be applied in measurement. At first measurements would be described orally. Later the teacher would introduce the notation ŋ, and written recordings could be made, e.g. $3\frac{1}{2}$ decilitres, $5\frac{1}{2}$ cups.

1. When measuring lengths, with various units, the part unit at one end may sometimes be described as roughly half a unit, e.g. the pencil is about three and a half yellow rods long, the stick is about $3\frac{1}{2}$ dm long, etc.
2. When measuring capacities, using beakers or cups, a partly filled beaker or container could be involved. The amount left may possibly be described as about half a beaker full, e.g. the tin holds about two and a half beakers of water.
3. The idea of half a turn is used in reading the time, e.g. half past three, half past twelve, etc. Half past three means the minute hand has made a half turn since 3 o'clock.
4. Two metal pieces, or bags of sand, which balance each other, and together balance a kilogram mass, each have a mass of half a kilogram. Masses of objects could be

measured using kilograms and half kilograms, e.g. the mass of the parcel is between $1\frac{1}{2}$ kg and 2 kg, the tin has a mass just under $2\frac{1}{2}$ kg, etc.

5. Finding areas by square counting could involve half squares, or the comparing of parts of squares with half squares.

6. The idea of a half is necessary in the reading of number scales, for example when children use compression balances, various timers, graduated jars for liquids and measuring devices for length. Should the pointer, or water level, or end, be roughly midway between two whole numbers, the description 'about a half' could be used, e.g. the tin has a mass about $1\frac{1}{2}$ kg.

7. A knowledge of what a half unit looks like is essential to measure to the nearest unit because parts less than a half unit are not counted and parts a half unit or more are counted as 1 unit. Measuring a length to the nearest centimetre using a centimetre measuring strip, or a mass to the nearest $\frac{1}{2}$ kg using a compression balance, or a capacity to the nearest centilitre using a centilitre measure, all provide practice in the use of halves.

Quarters could be introduced when activities involving halves are underway. Some activities which could be done are:

1. The teacher cuts a cake into four equal parts and talks about one quarter, two quarters, three quarters and four quarters.

2. A child folds a paper rectangle into four equal parts and crayons each part a different colour. Talk with the child about these parts being quarters. How many quarters in the whole? Repeat this with a paper circle, and two paper squares. One square is to be folded diagonally into four equal parts and the other so that opposite sides meet. Talk about the shapes of the quarters. The idea that two quarters and one half cover the same could also be talked about.

3. The teacher obtains a revolving pointer and turns it around once in quarter turns. Ask a child to turn around once on the spot in quarter turns. Then to make three quarters of a turn, two quarters of a turn, one and a quarter turns, etc. Link with reading the time. Deal with quarter past, then the two quarters past or half past position, then the three quarters past or quarter to position.

4. Demonstrate and then ask a child to cut a piece of string into quarters. (Fold it and cut into halves, then fold and cut each half length into halves.)

5. A child uses a quantity of water, two identical transparent plastic jugs and four beakers. The teacher shows her how to put a quarter of the water into each beaker. (Use the identical jugs to divide the water into two equal amounts, and then use them again to divide these quantities into two equal amounts.) The child then practises this.

6. A child puts cubes into four equal sets to find one quarter of 12, one quarter of 20, three quarters of 16, three quarters of 24, and so on. Record as one quarter of $12 = 3$, three quarters of $20 = 15$.

Up to now the children have been introduced to halves and quarters and possibly the notation $\frac{1}{2}$. The teacher should now deal with the notation for fractions in general and illustrate this with particular reference to fractions up to tenths.

1. With a group the teacher could introduce thirds, fourths, fifths, . . ., tenths. Talk

about five and fifths. Illustrate this by showing five things and cutting another into five equal parts, as equally as possible, so comparing five with one fifth. (Slices of bread could be used.) Also talk about two-fifths, three-fifths, and so on. Emphasize that one fifth, or a fifth, is one of the parts should an object be cut into five equal parts.

    When children are ready, set some work card exercises, e.g. find one fifth of 10, one fifth of 25, two fifths of 15, four fifths of 20, and so on. Counters could be shared into five equal sets to answer these questions.

2. On other occasions talk about eighths, tenths, and so on, and illustrate them by cutting and showing slices of bread. Explain that fourths are usually called quarters. Set workcard exercises at each stage.

3. Ask children to count from two to ten and then to say the associated fractional words, in order, e.g. one **half**, one **third**, one **quarter**, one **fifth**, one **sixth**, ... up to one **tenth**. Introduce the notation $\frac{1}{2}, \frac{1}{3}, \frac{1}{4}, \frac{1}{5}, \ldots \frac{1}{10}$ to write these fractions. Talk about the numbers at the top and bottom of these fractions. Set work card questions which use the new notation, e.g. find $\frac{1}{5}$ of 10, $\frac{1}{4}$ of 12, $\frac{1}{6}$ of 18, etc.

4. The teacher could prepare cardboard shapes on which identical units fit. (Less than 10.) A child covers each shape with appropriate units and then writes down what fraction of the shape is covered by one of the units (Fig. 1.83). In this case, one of the smaller pieces covers $\frac{1}{8}$ of the shape.

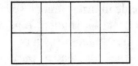

Fig. 1.83

5. Introduce the writing of such fractions as three-fifths, two-thirds, four-sevenths, and so on. Talk about the numbers to be written at the top and bottom of a fraction.

    Show shapes drawn on squared paper, with parts shaded, and ask children to describe, using symbols, the shaded parts (Fig. 1.84). Prepare a work card.

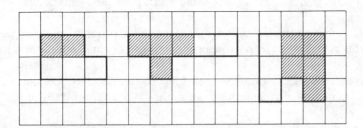

Fig. 1.84

6. A child draws shapes, on squared paper, and shades parts of them to illustrate given fractions, e.g. $\frac{5}{7}$. For this the child would draw a shape which encloses 7 squares and shade any 5 of them.

7. Set work card exercises, e.g. find $\frac{2}{5}$ of 20, $\frac{2}{3}$ of 9, $\frac{4}{5}$ of 15, etc.
8. Talk with the child about the link between fractions and division, e.g. one fifth of 10, or $\frac{1}{5}$ of 10, is the same as $10 \div 5$. ($10 \div 5$ in this case means 10 shared equally into 5 sets.) Set mixed questions on a work card, e.g. find $\frac{1}{5}$ of 15, $18 \div 3$, one quarter of 16, $20 \div 5$, $\frac{1}{8}$ of 32, etc.
9. A child uses Stern or Unifix blocks to illustrate six threes, five sevens, four eights, three nines, and so on, and describes each result using multiplication, division and fraction statements (Fig. 1.85). She would write, in this case, $7 \times 5 = 35, 35 \div 5 = 7, \frac{1}{5}$ of $35 = 7$.

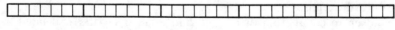

five sevens

Fig. 1.85

In preparing the way for decimal fractions it is particularly important that children have an idea about **tenths**. Some useful activities are:

1. A child draws on centimetre squared paper a rectangle 5 cm long and 2 cm wide and divides it into small squares. What fraction of the rectangle is a small square? How is one-tenth written? How is four-tenths written? Shade in four-tenths of the rectangle. Draw more rectangles and shade in three-tenths, seven-tenths, nine-tenths, of each. Near each diagram write the fraction shaded, e.g. $\frac{7}{10}$.
2. Prepare a work card with various shapes drawn on it, each divided into tenths, with parts shaded. The child describes the shaded parts.
3. The child draws on squared paper various shapes to represent $\frac{2}{10}, \frac{7}{10}, \frac{5}{10}, \frac{4}{10}$ and $\frac{8}{10}$. (None of the shapes are to be rectangles.)
4. Use longs and flats from the Dienes apparatus. Fit longs on a flat and find their relationship, e.g. a long is one-tenth of a flat. Use longs and flats to represent $2\frac{4}{10}$, $1\frac{7}{10}, 3\frac{1}{10}, 1\frac{8}{10}, \frac{9}{10}$ and $\frac{5}{10}$.
   Add together $1\frac{3}{10}$ and $2\frac{4}{10}$, $2\frac{6}{10}$ and $1\frac{2}{10}$, $1\frac{6}{10}$ and $2\frac{7}{10}$, $2\frac{7}{10}$ and $3\frac{4}{10}$, $\frac{7}{10}$ and $\frac{6}{10}$, and $1\frac{7}{10}$ and $\frac{5}{10}$.
5. Represent $3\frac{2}{10}, 2\frac{5}{10}, 1\frac{7}{10}, 1\frac{1}{10}$ and $\frac{7}{10}$ using Stern longs and unit cubes.

Various measuring activities, involving metric units, provide opportunities for using tenths and this in turn could lead to the introduction of decimal notation at a later stage.

1. Lengths and distances could be measured in metres and decimetres, and then expressed in metres, e.g. 5 metres 4 decimetres $= 5\frac{4}{10}$ metres. ($10\,\mathrm{dm} = 1\,\mathrm{m}$, so $1\,\mathrm{dm} = \frac{1}{10}\,\mathrm{m}$)
2. Lengths could be measured in decimetres and centimetres (Cuisenaire orange and white rods), and the results expressed in decimetres, e.g. 8 dm 4 cm $= 8\frac{4}{10}\,\mathrm{dm}$. ($10\,\mathrm{cm} = 1\,\mathrm{dm}$, so $1\,\mathrm{cm} = \frac{1}{10}\,\mathrm{dm}$)
3. Capacities could be found in litres and decilitres, and then expressed in litres, e.g. 3 litres 8 decilitres $= 3\frac{8}{10}$ litres. ($10\,\mathrm{dl} = 1$ litre, so $1\,\mathrm{dl} = \frac{1}{10}$ litre)
4. Capacities could be found in decilitres and centilitres, and then changed to decilitres, e.g. 2 decilitres 7 centilitres $= 2\frac{7}{10}\,\mathrm{dl}$. ($10\,\mathrm{cl} = 1\,\mathrm{dl}$, so $1\,\mathrm{cl} = \frac{1}{10}\,\mathrm{dl}$)

5. Masses could be found on a common balance using kilograms and hectograms, and then changed to kilograms, e.g. 1 kilogram 7 hectograms = $1\frac{7}{10}$ kg. (10 hectograms = 1 kilogram)

The next step could be to introduce the shorter notation 6.3 to represent $6\frac{3}{10}$ and then proceed to develop decimals.

Chapter 2

Money

Money is much more difficult to teach than length or capacity, for example, because the relationship between coins cannot readily be seen. Ten decimetre rods can be put end to end against a metre stick to show equivalence, and ten decilitre measures of water poured into a litre measure, but we cannot show that ten pennies have the same value as a tenpenny bit. Pennies and tenpenny bits are of different metals and the exchange rate between them has to be accepted. It is true that two pennies have the same mass as a twopence coin but the teacher would need an extremely sensitive balance to show this relationship. Should we use more coins the argument becomes difficult for young children. (Suppose we find that 100 pennies balance 50 twopences. Infant school children would not, in all probability, be able to deduce that two pennies balance one twopence.)

With junior school children discussion could be held about the need for money and appropriate mass relationships between different valued coins of the same metal, e.g. one twopence should have the same mass as two pennies and five pennies should have the same mass as a fivepenny piece. The children could balance coins and find mass relationships. For example, balance 50 twopences and 100 pennies and so deduce that one twopence balances two pennies. Stick pennies together with Sellotape and make metal cylinders worth 5p, 10p, 20p and 50p. Would copper coins of these values be suitable? Why not? Suppose we made a cylinder worth 10p from a metal more expensive than copper. Would the cylinders be the same size? Talk about the idea that mass could be reduced by using more expensive metals, as in the case of the 5p, 10p, 20p, 50p and £1 coins. A study of our coins along the lines suggested could be made, but such an investigation is suitable for older children.

With young children the teacher is mainly concerned with the recognition of coins and money relationships between them, and the need to set out different amounts of money using various coins. Children would only use pennies at first in order to gain experience with cardinal numbers. Pennies would also be displayed to show different amounts of money and represent the value of objects. This could continue until the children know addition facts well, otherwise counting on fingers, or counting aloud, would be encouraged. When children know addition facts to five we can use 2p and 1p coins, and when they know addition facts to ten we can use 5p, 2p and 1p coins.

We suggest, however, that the 10p coin is introduced after the penny, but before other coins, because its use depends only on a knowledge of number language and notation, and the latter should precede the learning of addition facts.

Initially, the child uses only pennies to buy things and find total costs. Suppose he buys items for 6p and 8p. Six pennies and eight pennies would be obtained and put together, rearranged into a ten-group and a four-group, and the total 14p is clearly seen and determined without further counting. Should he put 5p and 1p, and 5p, 2p and 1p coins, together on the table, the total 14p is not seen but has to be determined by addition. For this reason we recommend that coins other than pennies, and tenpences, are not used until addition facts are known.

We are mainly concerned with oral work although some recording could be encouraged with lower infants. Written calculation involving tens and units, arising from shopping and giving change, should only be attempted when children can deal with money up to 20p using addition bonds, and handle money using various coins. When children can deal with numbers up to 20 the teacher can introduce shopping which involves larger numbers, firstly up to 50p, and then to 100p. After this, with the more able children, the teacher can make an introduction to pounds and 'decimal' notation.

Calculation involving tens and units can be derived from shopping, but addition and subtraction are the main processes to be considered. Subtraction can be avoided by using complementary addition. Multiplication and division are not used so often and less time should be devoted to them. The latter processes could be introduced incidentally when the need arises.

On no account should money be treated as decimals for calculation purposes until children have been taught decimal fractions. In the lower classes of a junior school any calculation with amounts over £1 needs to be worked in pennies or pounds and pence.

2.1 GENERAL SCHEME

We suggest that money is introduced in these stages:

1. Put out amounts up to 10p using pennies only.
2. Put out amounts up to 20p using pennies only.
3. Introduce the 10p. Represent amounts up to 50p using 10p and 1p coins.
4. Introduce 5p and 2p coins. Deal with amounts up to 50p using 10p, 5p, 2p and 1p coins.
5. Introduce the 20p coin. Deal with amounts up to 100p using 20p, 10p, 5p, 2p and 1p coins.
6. Introduce the 50p coin. Represent amounts up to 100p using 50p, 20p, 10p, 5p, 2p and 1p coins.
7. Introduce simple addition, subtraction, multiplication and division of money derived from the buying of goods and giving change. Only deal with amounts up to 100p.
8. Introduce the pound. Simple conversion of pence to pounds and pence and the notation £2.30 to mean £2 and 30 pence.
9. Addition, subtraction, multiplication and division of money arising from shopping activities involving amounts up to £10 concerning pounds and pence.
10. Introduce the use of £5 and £10 notes in shopping activities up to £100 involving pounds only.

2.2 ORGANIZATION OF ACTIVITIES

We intend the activities concerning money to be arranged on an individual work basis. The teacher could number the activities included in this chapter and put details about them, and questions needed for and arising from them, on numbered sets of work cards of different colours, e.g. blue cards would only involve pennies, pink cards would concern 10p and 1p coins, yellow cards would include 10p, 5p and 1p coins, grey cards would concern 10p, 5p, 2p and 1p coins, green cards would concern 20p, 10p, 5p, 2p and 1p coins, and finally white cards could involve 50p, 20p, 10p, 5p, 2p and 1p coins. Thus, children would use blue, pink, yellow, grey, green and white cards, in that order, as their knowledge of money develops.

Details for the children about what to do, how to set out the coins on the table, how to record results, and what coins are needed, are not often worth writing fully on cards because they are better conveyed orally. These details are difficult to put on cards, and even if they were, would only be useful for children who can read. A few brief notes on the back of each card would enable the teacher to tell the child what to do, what apparatus is needed, and so on. Questions for the child are put on the front of the card in the simplest possible language but using suitable mathematical terms.

The cards, together with appropriate money labels, could be put in polythene envelopes, and arranged in order in a shoe box, or shoe boxes, or put in racks or pockets fitted to the wall. Plastic coins, sorted into various denominations, would be close at hand in plastic or polythene containers, e.g. margarine containers. Items to be bought, such as toys, boxes of sweets and containers of various foodstuffs, with price labels attached, would also be readily available. Work cards, coins and other necessary materials would be collected together and kept near the money 'table' or 'corner'.

Perhaps no more than 3 or 4 children would be allowed to do money cards at the same time, but not necessarily the same activity. (The number of coins available, rather than the classroom organization, would limit the number of children doing money.) Children would work at their own pace but have to devote a prescribed amount of time each week to money cards. Should the cards not contain enough questions to consolidate a point then supplementary questions have to be made up and set by the teacher. Supplementary cards, already prepared, are very useful for these occasions and the teacher would soon find those items on which they are generally required.

The teacher could record the number of the card that each child is doing and so have a list of completed cards and work currently being done. In fact, each child could keep a list of cards that he or she has done in a drawer, the teacher recording on it the number of each new card the child is given. For the activities in Sections 2.3 and 2.4 the teacher could keep the work cards near at hand and communicate the content of the card to the child by reading the card to him, or telling him what to do. The child could display the answers by putting coins, and money labels, side by side, on the table, and also give oral answers to the teacher. Children would also need explanations for, and guidance with, numbers up to 10 and then up to 20.

With the activities of Sections 2.5 and 2.6 the teacher could rely more on the children finding their own work cards, but the teacher would probably still have to read the cards to some children, or tell them what the card says. Again, in appropriate places, the teacher has to provide additional information, particularly about the need for and introduction of 10p, 5p and 2p coins. Some children would be able to give written answers whilst others would still need to display their answers on the desk or communicate answers orally to the teacher.

Questions needed for the activities given in Sections 2.7 to 2.12 are also intended to be put on cards so that children can do individual work. There are still certain questions, however, and details about how and what to do for each activity, that are best given orally. It is possible that children roughly at the same stage could do money cards at the same time so making the task of putting out materials, and the giving of assistance, much easier. Children would be able to collect their own cards, and write down their answers, without so much help from the teacher. Within the scheme the teacher has to introduce and talk about 20p, 50p and £1 coins, and £5 and £10 notes, and explain calculations involving shopping and the giving of change. Instruction is also needed on the use of the calculator to deal with the arithmetic of money. Arithmetic processes can often be explained to groups of children and followed up by individual help where needed. Sometimes, children could do shopping questions from books if they fit the scheme. Often, however, textbooks do not contain appropriate questions so the teacher has to make them up and write them on the blackboard or on work cards.

2.3 ACTIVITIES USING ONLY PENNIES (1, 2, 3, 4 L1)

When children have some appreciation of numbers to ten we can set individual work concerning money to three or four children at a time. Compile work cards based on the following activities:

1. Use a box of plastic pennies. Ask a child to put on the desk four pennies, six pennies, two pennies, five pennies, eight pennies, ten pennies, three pennies, seven pennies and nine pennies.
2. When the child recognizes number symbols from 1 to 9, and the word **ten**, he could display groups of pennies with number symbol cards alongside. Explain that **p** means penny. Thus, **3p** means three pennies, and 3 pennies would be displayed near it. Display amounts up to ten pence.
3. The teacher puts pennies in tins or plastic envelopes. (Put no more than 10 in any envelope.) Ask a child how much is in each envelope, and to display the envelopes, with money labels near them, on the table. (Money labels are pieces of card with **1p**, **2p**, **3p**, . . ., **9p** and **ten pence** written on them.)
4. Use miscellaneous items with price labels on them, such as sweet boxes, toy animals, toy cars, imitation cakes and buns, bags of marbles, etc., having prices less than 10p. A child selects an item and puts alongside it the number of pennies needed to buy it.
5. A child uses pairs of items with price labels on them, each item costing no more than ten pence. Which costs more and by how much? Suppose sweets cost 5p and marbles 7p. The child could display rows of pennies containing 5p and 7p, side by side on a squared background, together with the items and price labels (Fig. 2.1). He can

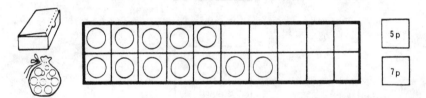

Fig. 2.1

then see which costs more. The teacher directs the activity on the following lines. How much more? How do we solve this problem? Add pennies to the shorter row until the rows are the same length. How many pennies were added? Or, we could remove pennies from the longer row until it is the same length as the shorter row. How many pennies were removed? Record answers by completing sentences written on slips of paper, such as:

> . . . . . costs . . . . . pence more than . . . . .

6. Use items with price labels of 5p or less. Select two things. How much altogether? The child puts out the pennies needed for each item, combines the sets of pennies and counts them. Accept oral answers and/or use money label cards.

2.4 FURTHER ACTIVITIES USING PENNIES (1, 2, 3, 4 L2)

Repeat the activities described in the previous section using only pennies, but extend the numbers used to twenty. (Individual work for two or three children at a time.)

When items have their prices written on them be sure to use both long and short forms, e.g. **1 ten and 7 pence**, and **17p**.

Should an item cost 15p the pennies could be arranged alongside in a ten-group and a five-group. Always put the ten-group, or ten-groups, on the left (Fig. 2.2).

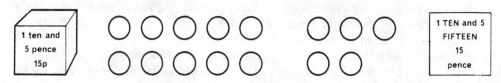

Fig. 2.2

The teacher talks about the need for 0 (nought). 2 tens could not just be written as 2, or 1 ten as 1. But 20 indicates 2 tens and no more, and 10 means 1 ten and no more. Use price cards which describe numbers in words and symbols (Figs. 2.3 and 2.4).

> 1 TEN and 7
> SEVENTEEN
> 17
> pence

Fig. 2.3

> 2 TENS
> TWENTY
> 20
> pence

Fig. 2.4

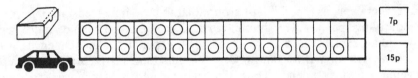

Fig. 2.5

The child obtains pairs of items with price labels on them, each item costing no more than 20p. Ask which costs more and by how much. Supose a model car costs 15p and sweets 7p. The child displays on a squared background, 15 and 7 pennies, and alongside puts the items and price labels (Fig. 2.5). The teacher could develop the subject as follows. We can see that fifteen pennies is a larger number, or larger amount, than seven pennies. The car costs more than the sweets—it is dearer. The sweets cost less than the car—they are cheaper. We could put more pennies on the shorter row so that its length becomes the same as that of the longer row. Eight pennies are needed. Therefore, the car costs eight pennies more than the sweets. We could say that seven pennies and eight pennies make fifteen pennies, that fifteen pennies is eight pennies more than seven pennies, and that the difference between fifteen pennies and seven pennies is eight pennies. These statements could be recorded as **7p + 8p = 15p**, and **15p − 7p = 8p**, so . . . **costs . . . pence more than**. . . .

This activity would help children form addition and subtraction facts and use money at the same time, at a stage when numbers could not be dealt with abstractly.

Use articles costing up to 10p each. The child has to select 2 of them and find their total cost. Suppose the articles have price labels of **8p** and **6p**. The child would obtain 8 pennies and 6 pennies. These coins are put together and arranged in tens and a smaller group, e.g. in this case 1 ten and 4. This would enable the number to be determined without counting for 1 ten and 4 is fourteen, or 14. The total cost is 14p.

The child buys an article from the classroom shop using only pennies. Keep prices less than 20p. (The child finds the price of the item beforehand and puts out the necessary money before going to the shop. He will then not have to wait long when money is handed to, and checked by, the 'shopkeeper'.)

2.5 INTRODUCTION TO 10P COINS (1, 2, 3, 4, 5 L2)

When the child knows the notation and words for numbers up to about fifty he is then ready to start money exchanges involving other coins. Do not introduce 2p, 5p and 10p coins at the same time, but separately as the work progresses and the need arises. We suggest that the 10p coin is introduced first, and 5p and 2p coins are left until the child can deal with addition facts to ten, and when further refinements are necessary in paying for goods and giving change. The 10p is much easier to use than 5p and 2p pieces because only a knowledge of notation is needed. To use 5p and 2p coins intelligently we need addition facts and an understanding of notation. The buying of an article with a 10p coin also provides an opportunity to introduce addition and subtraction bonds of ten.

The following activities would be tackled, on an individual basis:

1. The teacher explains to a child, or group, that to buy an item costing 35p we would need thirty-five pennies. Get the child to put 3 groups of ten pennies, and 5 pennies, on the table. Explain that we have coins worth 10 pennies called tenpences, in order to make it easier to pay for things. Give the child tenpences. Exchange each pile of ten pennies for one tenpence. Thus, 35p is represented by 3 tenpences and 5 pennies. This makes payment much easier and quicker. Now set individual work. Put out the 10p and 1p coins needed to buy items marked 28p, 42p, 32p, 26p, etc. Prepare a work card for the latter.
2. The child finds, by grouping pennies in tens and exchanging each group for a tenpence, that:

   1 tenpence has the same value as ten pennies
   2 tenpences have the same value as twenty pennies
   3 tenpences have the same value as thirty pennies
   4 tenpences have the same value as forty pennies
   5 tenpences have the same value as fifty pennies

   The teacher directs the activity and accepts oral answers.
3. The teacher gives oral instructions. Put out amounts of money to the value of twenty-four pence, thirty-eight pence, forty-two pence, seventeen pence, etc.
4. The child uses cards with prices on them, e.g. 32p. Near the card put out the appropriate amount of money, i.e. three tenpences and two pennies.
5. Give the child boxes of pennies. (Fewer than 50 in each box.) Group the pennies in tens, exchange for tenpenny pieces, and describe the amounts in each box.
6. Buy items from the classroom shop using only 10p and 1p coins, e.g. an item costing 36p would be paid for with three tenpences and six pennies.
7. The child finds the change from a 10p supposing he has bought an article costing 9p or under. Suppose sweets cost 6p, he puts the 10p and the sweets on the table with rows containing 10 pennies and 6 pennies alongside, on a squared background (Fig. 2.6). The teacher talks about this situation, where four pennies added to six pennies

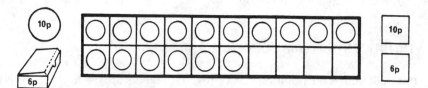

Fig. 2.6

makes a row equivalent in length to that of ten pennies, i.e. six and four is ten. Also, that ten pence is four pence more than six pence, and the difference between ten pence and six pence is four pence. Ask the child to give verbal statements of this kind, and then to write them down, i.e. 6p + 4p = 10p, 10p − 6p = 4p. Recording would be assisted if sentences were completed on specially prepared recording sheets (Fig. 2.7). This activity would help the child find and learn addition and subtraction facts of ten, and amounts of change from a 10p. (The shopkeeper needs to know immediately what change to give, and the buyer needs to know quickly if the change given is correct.)

$$\ldots\ldots \text{costs} \ldots\ldots \text{p}$$
$$\text{change from 10p?}$$
$$\ldots \text{p} + \ldots \text{p} = 10\text{p}$$
$$10\text{p} - \ldots \text{p} = \ldots \text{p}$$

Fig. 2.7

8. When the child is learning addition and subtraction facts for ten the teacher can ask him to buy one article from the shop using a 10p, the shopkeeper giving only pennies for change. Thus, if a 5p item were bought the shopkeeper would give 5 pennies in change.
9. Buy two items with price labels of 20p or less. How much altogether? Suppose the prices were 16p and 18p. The child puts out 1 tenpence and 6 pennies, 1 tenpence and 8 pennies, and combines these amounts. The pennies, if enough, are arranged in tens and ones and the tens exchanged for tenpences. In this case we have 3 tenpences and 4 pennies so the total cost is 34p.

2.6 INTRODUCTION TO 5P AND 2P COINS (13 L1; 1, 2, 3, 4, 5, 12 L2)

After the children can use pennies and tenpences for paying amounts up to 50p, the teacher can introduce 5p and 2p coins, separately, to a child or group of 2 or 3 children. Compile work cards and set individual work based on the following:

1. Explain that a 2p coin could be used instead of giving two pennies. Give the child some pennies, less than 30, to group in twos, and exchange each pair for a twopence. Thus, 16 pennies ≡ 8 twopences, 23 pennies ≡ 11 twopences and 1 penny. Give oral answers, or record as shown in Fig. 2.8.

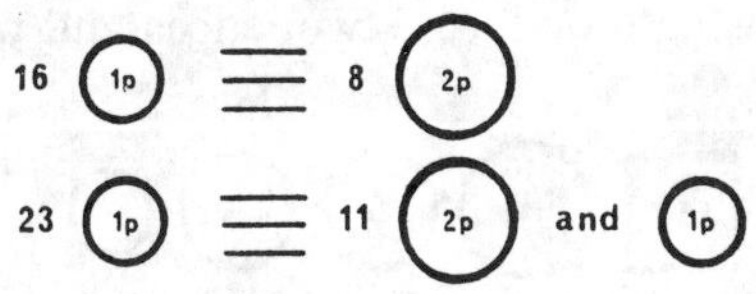

Fig. 2.8

2. Give the child 2p coins, less than twenty, to exchange for pennies (Fig. 2.9). Also, enter the results up to ten twopences in tabular form, or as a mapping, and link with the table of twos (Figs. 2.10 and 2.11).

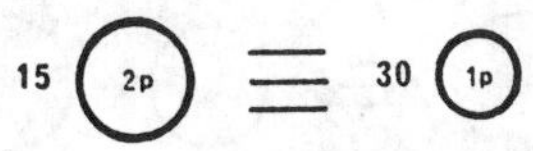

Fig. 2.9

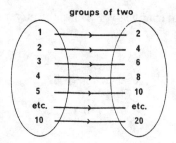

Fig. 2.10

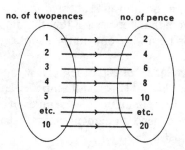

Fig. 2.11

3. The child uses price labels up to 10p. By the side of each label he puts the appropriate amount using 2p and 1p coins (Fig. 2.12). (If necessary put out the required number of pennies at first, and then exchange each pair for a twopence.)

Fig. 2.12

4. Use price labels from **10p** to **20p**. Alongside each label the child displays the appropriate amounts using tenpences, twopences and pennies (Fig. 2.13).

Fig. 2.13

5. Explain to the children that a 5p coin could be used instead of five pennies. Give them some pennies, less than fifty, group the pennies in fives, and exchange each group for a fivepence (Fig. 2.14).

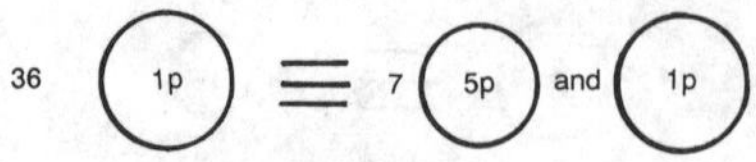

36 (1p) ≡ 7 (5p) and (1p)

Fig. 2.14

6. The child exchanges up to ten 5p coins for pennies. Record the results in tabular form, or as a mapping, and link with the table of fives (Figs. 2.15 and 2.16).

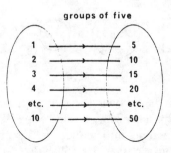

Fig. 2.15

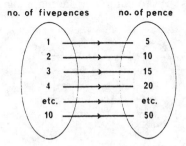

Fig. 2.16

7. Find the change, supposing the child buys an item costing 4p or less, using a 5p. Display the item and the 5p, with corresponding rows of pennies alongside and price labels (Fig. 2.17). The child should then be able to see and find the change needed, and establish and learn addition and subtraction facts of 5, e.g. 2p + 3p = 5p, 5p − 2p = 3p. Prepare a work card for this activity.

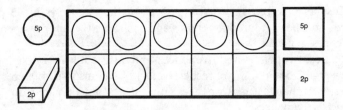

Fig. 2.17

8. Use price labels up to **10p**. By the side of each label the child puts appropriate amounts using 5p, 2p and 1p coins (Fig. 2.18).

Fig. 2.18

9. Use price labels from **10p** to **20p**. The child displays the amounts alongside each card using 10p, 5p, 2p and 1p coins (Fig. 2.19).

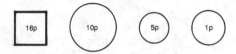

Fig. 2.19

10. Ask the child to make up the following amounts of money using 10p, 5p, 2p and 1p coins: 36p, 47p, 23p, 32p, 44p, 28p, 39p and 35p. (Work card needed.)
11. Ask a child to change 10 pennies into twopences by grouping them in twos, and then into fivepences by grouping in fives. Establish that 10 pennies = 5 twopences = 2 fivepences. (Link with five twos = two fives = ten; $2 \times 5 = 5 \times 2 = 10$.) Exchange more pennies, if necessary, to complete the mapping shown in Fig. 2.20.

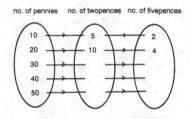

Fig. 2.20

12. Compile a work card of carefully ordered questions: how much altogether is 3 twopences and 2 pennies? 4 twopences and 3 pennies? 5 twopences and 4 pennies? 2 fivepences and 3 pennies? 3 fivepences and 6 pennies? 1 fivepence and 2 two-pences? 4 twopences and 2 fivepences? 2 fivepences, 3 twopences and 4 pennies? 3 fivepences, 4 twopences and 3 pennies? Exchange twopences and fivepences for pennies, if necessary, to obtain answers.
13. Using pennies or twopences find different ways of paying 3p (2 ways) and 4p (3 ways). Display possible answers, e.g. for 3p, the two ways are 3 pennies *or* 1 twopence and 1 penny. Put out pennies and exchange them for twopences, one at a time, if necessary.
14. Using pennies, twopences and fivepences find different ways of paying 5p, 6p and 7p. (Answers: 4, 5 and 6 ways, respectively.) Use coins to display results. Put out pennies and exchange for twopences, one at a time, then put out pennies and exchange for fivepences.
15. Compile investigations like the following with no more than 3 answers, keeping numbers reasonably small.
    (a) Chocolates cost 1p each and toffees, 2p each. I buy some of each and spend 7p altogether. What may I have bought? (3 answers.) Use 7 pennies and group them into ones and twos to explore possibilities.
    (b) Chews cost 2p each and Fruitos 3p each. I spend 12p and buy some of each. What did I buy? Group pennies in twos and threes. (1 answer.)
    (c) Mints cost 2p each and Crunchies 4p each. I spend 10p and buy some of each. What may I have bought? Group 10 pennies in twos and fours. (2 answers.)

2.7 INTRODUCTION TO 20P COINS (13 L1; 1, 2, 3, 4, 12 L2)

When a child can deal successfully with amounts up to 50p using 10p, 5p, 2p and 1p coins the teacher could extend the numbers used to 100 and then introduce the 20p coin.
Set work orally, or from work cards, involving these activities:

1. Ask the child to put out 5, 6, 7, 8, 9 and 10 piles, each containing 10 pennies, and exchange each pile for a 10p coin. Establish orally that

$$
\begin{aligned}
\text{fifty pennies} &\equiv 5 \text{ tenpences} \equiv 50\text{p} \\
\text{sixty pennies} &\equiv 6 \text{ tenpences} \equiv 60\text{p} \\
\text{seventy pennies} &\equiv 7 \text{ tenpences} \equiv 70\text{p} \\
\text{eighty pennies} &\equiv 8 \text{ tenpences} \equiv 80\text{p} \\
\text{ninety pennies} &\equiv 9 \text{ tenpences} \equiv 90\text{p} \\
\text{one hundred pennies} &\equiv 10 \text{ tenpences} \equiv 100\text{p}
\end{aligned}
$$

2. Give oral instructions. Ask the children to make up the following amounts of money using 10p, 5p, 2p and 1p coins: fifty-two pence, sixty-three pence, seventy-five pence, eighty-four pence, ninety-seven pence, fifty-seven pence, sixty-one pence, eighty-six pence, seventy-eight pence and ninety-seven pence.
3. Use price labels from **50p** to **100p**. The child displays alongside each label the appropriate amount of money using 10p, 5p, 2p and 1p coins (Fig. 2.21).

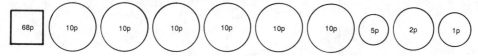

Fig. 2.21

4. Ask a child, or group of children, to put out 20 pennies. Show a 20p coin and explain it can be used to pay more quickly than 20 pennies. Rearrange the pennies into tens and further explain that 20 pennies are worth 2 tenpences. So 20 pennies $\equiv$ 2 tenpences $\equiv$ 1 twentypence. Put out 40, 60, 80 and 100 pennies and exchange them, in turn, for 10p, and then 20p coins. Record the results as a mapping (Fig. 2.22).

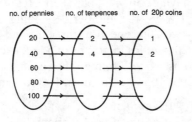

Fig. 2.22

Link also with:

$$
\begin{aligned}
2 \text{ tens} + 2 \text{ tens} &= 4 \text{ tens,} \\
\text{so } 2 \text{ twentypences} &= 4 \text{ tenpences;} \\
2 \text{ tens} + 2 \text{ tens} + 2 \text{ tens} &= 6 \text{ tens,} \\
\text{so } 3 \text{ twentypences} &= 6 \text{ tenpences; etc.}
\end{aligned}
$$

5. Use price labels **20p, 30p, 40p** ..., **100p**. Near each label put out the required amount using 20p and 10p coins. Put out tenpences, group them in twos, and exchange for 20p coins (Fig. 2.23).

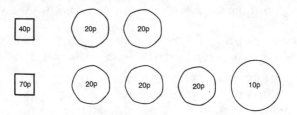

Fig. 2.23

6. Use price labels for any amount from 20p to 100p. Alongside each label display the required amount using 20p, 10p, 5p, 2p and 1p coins. Put out tenpences at first, group them in twos, and exchange for 20p coins. After this deal with the remaining pence.
7. Show collections of 20p, 10p, 5p, 2p and 1p coins totalling less than 100p. How much in each collection? The collections could be put in small sealed transparent plastic envelopes or made with gummed paper coins stuck on cards (Fig. 2.24).

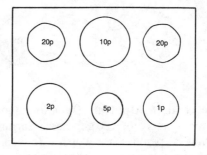

Fig. 2.24

8. Find different ways of paying 35p; 47p; 68p; 83p, etc. using coins 20p or less. Ask for a specific number of ways, the number depending on the ability of the child concerned, e.g. 57p = two 20p, one 10p, three 2p and one 1p.
9. Ask a child to arrange 20 pennies in groups of 5 and exchange them for 5p coins. Establish that four 5p coins = one 20p coin. Then exchange a number of fivepences, no more than 40, for 20p, 10p and 5p coins, by grouping in fours initially, e.g.

        16 fivepences = 4 twentypences;
        23 fivepences = 5 twentypences, 1 tenpence and 1 fivepence.

10. Use items with price labels less than 20p. Buy an item with a 20p coin and find the change. This is best found using coins by addition. Later the process can be worked mentally. Suppose the item costs 14p. The change is put out, a coin at a time, and a running total kept up to 20p. Put down 1p (say 15p), put down 2p (say 17p), put down 2p (say 19p), put down 1p (say 20p). The coins displayed total 6p, which is the change. When addition facts are known a child could think 14 + ? = 20 is the same

as 4 + ? = 10, so the change is 6p. The coins displayed depend on those we can choose from. We could instead, possibly, put down 1p (say 15p), put down 5p (say 20p), the change being 1p + 5p or 6p.

If the amount is less than 10p the change is best worked by adding up to ten, then adding another ten to make 20. Suppose the item costs 3p. A child could put out 2p (say 5p), put out 5p (say 10p), put out 10p (say 20p), the change being 2p + 5p + 10p or 17p.

There are many alternatives when working out change mentally by addition and these require addition facts, particularly those of 10, e.g. 1 + 9 = 10, 2 + 8 = 10, etc. Encourage pupils to work out change mentally and to use the same procedures in later written methods. If addition is used when working mentally it should also be used for written work.

2.8 INTRODUCTION TO 50P COINS (1, 2, 3, 12 L2; 4 L3)

When children can successfully use 20p coins the teacher could introduce the 50p coin through the following activities:

1. The teacher talks about a 50p coin being used instead of 5 tenpences. Ask the child to put out 50p, 60p, 70p, 80p, 90p and 100p using only tenpences. Exchange 5 ten-pences for a 50p coin in each case, and so display the original amounts in terms of 50p and 10p coins. Display the coins on the table near a money label (Fig. 2.25).

Fig. 2.25

2. Repeat activity **1**, above, but exchange 10p coins with 50p, 20p and 10p coins, e.g.

    60p = 1 fiftypence and 1 tenpence;
    80p = 1 fiftypence, 1 twentypence and 1 tenpence.

3. Use price labels from **50p** to **100p**. The child displays near each label the appropriate amounts using 50p, 20p, 10p, 5p, 2p and 1p coins (Fig. 2.26).

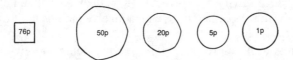

Fig. 2.26

4. Use work cards with gummed paper coins stuck on them showing amounts up to 100p. How much altogether? Record the answers by copying and completing sentences (Fig. 2.27).

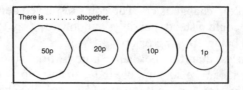

Fig. 2.27

5. Give the child twopences, less than fifty in number. How many coins are there? Sort the twopences into groups of five, exchange each group for a 10p, and then describe the amount of money (Fig. 2.28). Also display the amount using as few coins as possible.

Fig. 2.28

6. Give a child fivepences, fewer than 20 in number. How many coins are there? How much altogether? (Group the fivepences in twos and exchange each pair for a 10p.) Next display the amount using as few coins as possible. Record as shown in Fig. 2.29.

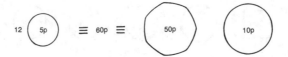

Fig. 2.29

7. Find different ways of paying 58p; 76p; 84p; etc. using 50p coins or less, e.g. 76p = 1 fiftypence, 2 tenpences and 3 twopences. Ask for a definite number of ways.

2.9 MONEY CALCULATIONS (1, 2, 12 L2; 3, 4 L3)

When the children can recognize various coins, put out prescribed amounts up to 100p, and pay for an article by giving the correct money, the teacher can introduce to a child, or a group of children, various activities which involve mainly addition and subtraction of money.

Confine amounts to no more than 100p. Buying items and giving change provide excellent opportunities to develop addition, and possibly subtraction, of tens and units. There is little point in introducing the pound, or going over £1 until children can deal with numbers to a hundred because £1 is defined as the equivalent of 100 pence. Shopping for mother could involve taking a £1 coin to the shop but its true value is not appreciated until activities with 100p have been experienced.

If the children do not know addition facts up to 9 + 9, or are uncertain about them, total costs and the giving of change have to be found by putting out, and sorting, appropriate coins. The children could record the prices of articles bought, find the total cost and change using coins, and then record the answers. As children learn addition facts the need to display and sort coins becomes less, and answers can be written down from memory.

We need to encourage written additions and subtractions because we cannot always calculate in our heads, but the calculations must arise from shopping activities and should be carefully graded.

Use current prices for items bought. Items with prices too high for the child's arithmetical skills should not be displayed or listed. It seems better to do this than use fictitious, artificially low, prices, e.g. a cake costs 1p or an orange costs 2p.

Lists of items, and their prices, could be put on the blackboard, or pictures of items (with prices alongside) mounted on large sheets of paper and displayed. Pictures can be cut from magazine advertisements. Sheets of items can be compiled concerning groceries, vegetables, sweets and toys.

Work cards can also be made showing pictures and prices of items, and questions asked about them, e.g. what is the total cost of a bag of sugar and a pack of margarine? a bottle of milk and a pack of butter? a carton of yoghurt and half a dozen eggs? etc.

Pupils also need calculators to find total costs and change, and sometimes to check mental or written methods. At this stage pupils will be working in pence with totals less than 100 but, later, children need to know how to deal with amounts involving pounds and pence.

Investigative situations are also needed. These involve arithmetic, decision making and the development of strategies and orderly procedures. For example, supply a price list of items and ask a child which two, or three, different things could be bought costing 70p or less. Another example is to ask for ten different ways of paying 82p. These activities involve more thought than definite prescribed situations.

Addition

Compile work cards to cover the following graded activities:

1. Find the total cost of two items, each less than 10p, and display the coins needed to buy them. This activity involves addition facts up to $9 + 9$.
2. Find the total cost of two items, each less than 20p, and display the coins needed to buy them. Initially, do not involve carrying, e.g. $12p + 14p = ?$ Later, involve carrying, e.g. $16p + 17p = ?$ This activity introduces tens and units addition.
3. Find the total cost of two items, each less than 50p, and display the coins needed to buy them. This involves addition of tens and units up to nearly 100, e.g. $37p + 45p = ?$
4. Find the total cost of three, four or five items, each less than 20p, e.g. $12p + 14p + 16p + 5p + 16p = ?$

Some desk-top investigations, such as those below, could also be included:

1. Using coins, less than and including 50p, find eight different ways of paying 68p. Devise similar questions.

2. 48p was paid using eight coins. What may they have been? Can you find three different ways?
3. I bought two things, each costing more than 20p, and spent 76p altogether. Find ten different possible prices, e.g. 42p and 34p, 26p and 50p. (Start with a price more than 20p and add on to this until 76p is reached to find the cost of the second article. Will this do?) Suppose three things were bought instead. Suggest some possible prices.

Multiplication

Multiplication facts up to 10 × 10 can be established, or revised and applied, in shopping activities involving the purchase of up to 10 items costing up to 10p each. Write work cards, e.g. find the cost of two items at 6p; three items at 5p; four items at 4p; three items at 9p; eight items at 3p; etc. Display, in each case, the coins needed to buy the items concerned (Fig. 2.30).

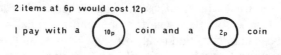

Fig. 2.30

Short multiplication of tens and units could also be introduced keeping answers below 100. For example, find the cost of three tins of beans costing 26p each, four pints of milk costing 28p per pint, five tins of lemonade costing 16p each, four packets of margarine at 19p each. Check results with a calculator.

Subtraction

Plan shopping which involves the buying of an item and the giving of change. Use the complementary addition method for finding differences, e.g. what change will I have if I buy an item for 22p and pay with a 50p piece? Put coins on the table to the value of 22p (Fig. 2.31). Place coins alongside, one at a time, until the total is 50p, whilst saying or

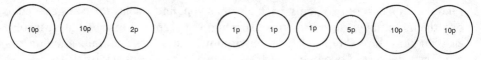

Fig. 2.31

thinking, 22p and 3p is 25p—put 3p down; 25p and 5p is 30p—put 5p down; 30p and 10p is 40p—put 10p down; 40p and 10p is 50p—put 10p down. Altogether we have put 28p alongside. Coins need not be used at a later stage. The change would be calculated by jotting down, and adding, the amounts to be added to 22p in order to obtain 50p (Fig. 2.32), so 50p − 22p = 28p.

The following seven activities provide a carefully graded progression. Compile work cards, or put questions on the blackboard, to cover them.

$$50p - 22p = ?$$

$$
\begin{array}{r}
3 \\
5 \\
10 + \\
10 \\
\hline
28
\end{array}
$$

Fig. 2.32

1. Buy an item with a 5p coin.
2. Buy an item with a 10p coin.
3. Buy an item costing between 5p and 10p using two 5p coins.
4. Buy an item costing between 10p and 20p using two 10p coins, between 20p and 30p using three 10p coins or one 20p and one 10p coin, between 40p and 50p using five 10p coins or two 20p and one 10p.
5. Buy an item costing between 40p and 50p, 30p and 40p, 20p and 30p, 10p and 20p, and up to 10p, using a 50p coin.
6. Buy an item costing between 40p and 60p using three 20p coins, between 60p and 80p using four 20p coins, between 80p and 100p using five 20p coins.
7. Buy an item costing between 50p and 60p, 60p and 70p, 70p and 80p, 80p and 90p, 90p and 100p, using two 50p coins.

Shopping involving the buying of more than one item, giving change and comparing prices could also be dealt with. Put a price list on the blackboard. What is the change from 50p if I buy a bottle of milk and a packet of margarine? What is the change from two 50p coins if I buy a packet of biscuits, a tin of beans and a tin of sardines; three tins of spaghetti; etc.

Orange squash costs 64p and bread 46p. Which costs more and by how much? 64p = 6 tenpences and 4 pennies, while 46p = 4 tenpences and 6 pennies, so squash costs more. How much more involves finding the difference between 64p and 46p and it is best done by thinking 46p + ? = 64p. Should any written account be needed then 4p + 10p + 4p = 18p is sufficient.

There is little reason for teaching subtraction of money using *decomposition* or *equal addition* when *complementary addition* is used in everyday life. The paragraph heading *Subtraction* is misleading, therefore, because addition only has been used.

2.10 INTRODUCTION TO £1 COINS (2, 3 L3; 3 L4)

The more able children, those who can deal with numbers to 100 and money to 100p, could be introduced to larger numbers and make a start with pounds. The following topics could be investigated:

1. A child could be asked to buy goods costing 50p and 60p, using tenpences, and to find the total cost. 50p would be represented by 5 tenpences and 60p by 6 tenpences. Altogether there are 11 tenpences. Sort the tenpences into groups of ten. Explain that 10 tenpences are worth a pound. Show a pound coin--a real one. Then show a

classroom pound. Exchange the 10 tenpences for a pound coin. We now have 1 pound and 1 tenpence, or 1 pound and 10 pence. We write this as £1.10; the dot separates pounds and pence, and £ means pounds.

Find more total costs using tenpences and pennies and exchanging pennies for tenpences and tenpences for pounds. Describe in words and write the total amounts, e.g.

$$28p + 36p + 70p = 13 \text{ tenpences and } 4 \text{ pennies}$$
$$= 1 \text{ pound and } 3 \text{ tenpences and } 4 \text{ pennies.}$$

This is one pound and thirty-four pence which is written £1.34.

Plenty of practice is needed with questions like these. How do we write three pounds and forty-five pence? Write 3 pounds and 16 pence on the blackboard. A child writes this amount a shorter way. Write £4.68 on the blackboard. What amount of money is this?

2. Explain that ten tens grouped together are called one hundred which is written 100. Ten 10p grouped together would be worth one hundred pence, which is written 100p. So one hundred pence could be exchanged for a £1 coin.

Ten 10p could also be exchanged for two 50p coins, and these could be exchanged for £1.

$$5 \text{ tens} + 5 \text{ tens} = 10 \text{ tens} = 1 \text{ hundred,}$$
$$\text{so } 50p + 50p = 100p = £1.$$

Ten 10p could be grouped in twos and exchanged for five 20p coins and these could be exchanged for £1.

$$2 \text{ tens} + 2 \text{ tens} + 2 \text{ tens} + 2 \text{ tens} + 2 \text{ tens} = 10 \text{ tens} = 100,$$
$$\text{so } 20p + 20p + 20p + 20p + 20p = £1.$$

Therefore, one hundred pennies, ten tenpences, five twentypences and two fiftypences, could each be exchanged for £1. These relationships could be displayed on a wall chart (Fig. 2.33).

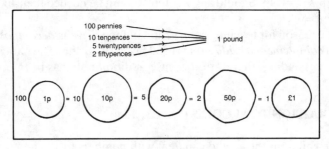

Fig. 2.33

3. When children have some knowledge of number notation involving hundreds, tens and ones, simple conversions of money could be introduced. Write down a number of pence, larger than 100p, and talk about changing it to pounds. Remember that one hundred pence is worth £1, e.g.

$$256p = 2 \text{ hundred and } 56 \text{ pence} = 2 \text{ pounds and } 56 \text{ pence} = £2.56.$$

This form of recording is suggested, and it could be aided by the use of specially prepared recording sheets (Fig. 2.34).

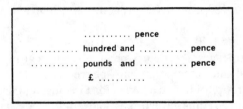

Fig. 2.34

The same slips could be used for changing £ to pence by filling in the bottom line first and then working line by line to the top of the sheet, e.g.

£3.75 = 3 pounds and 75 pence = 3 hundred and 75 pence = 375p.

Individual work for two or three children at a time could follow these explanations and discussions. Make up work cards, put questions on the blackboard and give oral instructions to cover the following activities:

1. Write down using a shorter way, £1 and 30 pence, £2 and 15 pence, £1 and 27 pence, £3 and 60 pence, £2 and 55 pence, and £4 and 15 pence.
2. What are these amounts: £1.30? £2.40? £1.65? £2.33? £4.17? £5.06? £7.00? £5.28? Give oral answers.
3. Use money labels up to **£10**. Alongside each label display the prescribed amount of money using £1 and other coins (Fig. 2.35).

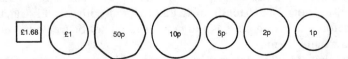

Fig. 2.35

4. Set shopping questions involving the purchase of two or three items, less than 100p each. Use coins, if necessary, to find the total cost of the items in pounds and pence. Display the money and write the amount alongside.
5. Use items each costing less than 100p. Buy one, pay with £1, display and describe the change. For example, a jelly costs 23p; add on to find the change; 23p + ? = 100p; 2p + 5p + 20p + 50p = 77p. Check with a calculator.
6. Find the total cost of two items between 50p and £1 each and display the money needed to buy them. Suppose we pay with two £1 coins. What change would we have? Display the change.
7. Use coins to find the total cost of two or three items each costing between £1 and £2. Check with a calculator.
8. Use a calculator to find the total cost of up to five items priced between £1 and £2 each and display the money required.

9. Make £1 using ten coins. Can you find six different ways?
10. Express 140p, 165p, 120p, 240p, 625p, 592p, 600p, 108p in pounds and pence. Record as 425p = £4.25.
11. Put out 150p, 115p, 180p, 168p, 225p, 340p, 400p, 309p and 520p using £1 and other coins.
12. How many pence in £1.40, £2.30, £1.68, £2.48, £4.15, £5.60 and £2.05?
13. The child sorts tenpences, less than 50 in number, into groups of ten, and expresses the total amount in pounds and pence. Record as 32 tenpences ≡ £3.20.
14. Put 20p coins in groups of five, exchange for £1 coins, and describe the total amount. (Less than 50 coins.) Record as 36 twentypences ≡ £7.20.
15. Arrange 50p coins in pairs, and express the total amount in pounds and pence. (Less than 20 fiftypences.) Record as 15 fiftypence coins ≡ £7.50.

2.11 CALCULATION INVOLVING POUNDS AND PENCE (2 L3; 3 L4)

Calculations, involving sums over £1, can only be justified if they arise from realistic situations. For most adults these involve buying items, checking change, seeking information from price lists, comparing prices, estimating costs, or borrowing and saving money. School work should include these needs. Addition and subtraction are used more than multiplication and division. Less time should be spent on the two latter processes. Pages of mechanical questions serve little purpose.

With lower junior children there is little need to go beyond £10 should pounds and pence be involved. More expensive items could be included if their prices are given in pounds only, or expressed to the nearest pound, and not involve pence, e.g. a bicycle costs £85 or a television set costs £340.

For many junior school children the decimal point in £2.65 would act as a separator and its full mathematical meaning would not be appreciated. £2.65 would indicate £2 and 65 pence, and not £2 and 6 tenths of a £1 and 5 hundredths of a £1. Calculations with money, therefore, involving pounds and pence should not be treated as decimals until children understand them.

We suggest that calculations are worked in pence if amounts over £1 are dealt with before the children know about decimal fractions. This would provide excellent practice in the four rules of number including hundreds, tens and units. We include some specimen questions to illustrate explanations and written layouts.

1. A box of chocolates costs £1.69 and a chocolate gateau £3.20. Find the total cost.

   £1.69 = 1 pound + 69 pence = 1 hundred + 69 pence = 169 pence
   £3.20 = 3 pounds + 20 pence = 3 hundred + 20 pence = 320 pence

$$\begin{array}{r} 169\ + \\ 320 \\ \hline 489 \end{array}$$

   489 pence = 4 hundred + 89 pence = £4 + 89 pence = £4.89

2. A tub of ice-cream costs £1.56. We pay for it with a £5 note. The change could be calculated by working out 156p + ? = 500p.

$$156p + \quad 4p = 160p$$
$$160p + \quad 40p = 200p$$
$$200p + 300p = 500p$$

so $156p + 344p = 500p$

The change is 344p or £3.44.

This question could also be worked in pounds and pence:

$$£1.56 + \quad 4p = £1.60$$
$$£1.60 + \quad 40p = £2.00$$
$$£2 \quad + £3 \quad = £5$$

so $£1.56 + £3.44 = £5$

The change is £3.44.

3. A tin of paint costs £3.39. What would two tins of this paint cost?

$$£3.39 = 339p$$

$$339 \times$$
$$\underline{\quad 2}$$
$$678$$

$678p = 6$ hundred and 78 pence $= £6$ and 78 pence $= £6.78$.

4. If three packets of fish fingers cost £5.55, what does one packet cost?

$$£5.55 = 555p$$

$$3 \overline{)\ 555}$$
$$\overline{\quad 185}$$

$185p = 1$ hundred and 85 pence $= £1$ and 85 pence $= £1.85$.

Pupils should also be given shopping activities in which calculators are used and learn how to add, subtract, multiply and divide amounts of money. Note that the calculation method is sometimes different than the written one. £4.25 − £2.68 is best done by subtraction on a calculator and complementary addition on paper or in one's head. When using a calculator pupils should record intermediate results otherwise, should a mistake be made, all previous calculations have to be repeated.

2.12 INTRODUCTION TO £5 AND £10 NOTES (2 L3; 3 L4)

Talk with the pupils about making cash payments beyond £5, e.g. £60, and so introduce £5 and £10 notes. Show real notes and classroom versions. Ask the children to put out £60 in four different ways using £5 and £10 notes and discuss the advantages of having such notes. Further activities could include:

1. Use money labels, whole pounds less than £100. Near each label display the required amount using £10 and £5 notes and £1 coins, e.g.

    £55 = five £10 notes and one £5 note;
    £48 = four £10 notes, one £5 note and three £1 coins.

2. Use money labels, involving pounds and pence, less than £50. Alongside each display the stated amount using £10 and £5 notes and other coins, e.g.

    £34.65 = three £10 notes, four £1 coins, one 50p, one 10p and one 5p.

3. Use items priced less than £5. Buy an item e.g. costing £2.66. Pay with a £5 note. Work out and display the change then check it using a calculator. The display of change would include two £1, one 20p, one 10p and two 2p coins.
4. Use items priced less than £10. Buy an item. Pay with a £10 note. Work out and display the change. Check it with a calculator.

2.13 SOME INVESTIGATIONS CONCERNING MONEY

We should encourage pupils to use money in everyday situations, school projects and cross-curricular activities. A few suggestions follow, some of which could be included into projects such as '*Ourselves*' or '*The Supermarket*':

1. Choose items from catalogues, price lists and advertisements. What is the total cost, including postage or delivery charge?
2. Find prices of certain items, e.g. a bicycle, a scooter, a portable TV. What is the cheapest and dearest price? What is the price range?
3. Investigate the amount of pocket money received weekly by a group of children. Sort out information and illustrate it with a block graph.
4. Consider the money spent daily at the school shop. Record individual spending and find the total takings. Illustrate graphically.
5. Find the prices of articles at the same shop, daily or weekly, e.g. a lettuce, 6 eggs, 1lb of potatoes or tomatoes. Illustrate price changes graphically—line and block graphs. Why do prices change?
6. Make up small packets and parcels. Find their masses in grams. Find the cost of posting each one. Consult Post Office information sheet for charges.
7. Find out how much your hobby or pastime costs each week, or month, or year?
8. Calculate the cost of keeping a dog, a cat, a gerbil, each week, or month, or year?
9. Calculate the cost of a class visit to a museum, castle, etc. What is the price per pupil?
10. The child wins £500 in a competition and can spend it all. What would he or she buy? List the items. (Choose an amount suitable for the pupil.)
11. The teacher compiles a work sheet using extracts from travel brochures. The child finds the cost of a week's holiday in a prescribed country for a given sized family. Investigate various alternatives.
12. Make a collection of foreign coins. What countries do they come from, where are those countries and how many pennies is each coin worth?
13. Find names of different British coins, e.g. groat, florin, farthing, sovereign. When

were they introduced? What metals were used? What is the value of each now? What could it buy then?

14. What could be bought for 1 shilling in 1600, 1700, 1800 and 1900?
15. Sort out the takings from the classroom shop. How many of each coin? Tabulate results. Illustrate with a block graph.
16. Use the takings from the classroom shop. Find the dates of minting of the coins. Tabulate results and illustrate graphically.

2.14 FUTURE WORK

A decimal treatment for adding, subtracting, multiplying and dividing money would occur in the teaching of the four rules of decimals involving tenths and hundredths. Applications of money would also occur in more complex situations involving larger numbers, vulgar and decimal fractions, ratio and percentage, e.g. saving money, methods of payment, and hire purchase. Calculators would be used to deal with much of the arithmetic. Money activities also provide opportunities for more difficult graphical work, e.g. conversion graphs, ready reckoners, and block and line graphs.

Chapter 3

Length and Distance

There is little need to deal with formal processes involving addition, subtraction, multiplication and division of length, with lower junior children, or even upper juniors. The aim should be an appreciation of units, and the main principles involved in measurement. Any calculations should arise naturally from activities. The latter are selected for their value in mathematics or everyday life and suitability to the previous knowledge and attainment of the children.

3.1 GENERAL SCHEME

Suggested stages are as follows:

1. Introduction to words such as **long**, **short**, **thick**, **thin**, **tall**, **short**, **narrow**, **wide**, etc. (8, 10 L1)
2. Comparisons of lengths and distances to bring out fundamental ideas such as **longer than**, **shorter than**, **taller than**, **same length as**, etc. (1, 8 L1)
3. To describe a length or distance we put a measuring unit against the item, or within a gap, and count the number of times it will fit. (2 L1; 1, 2, 8 L2)
4. In order to communicate the lengths of things it becomes necessary for us all to use the same sized units. We need *standard measures*. We feel that standard measures are best left until the children can see a need for them. The **metre, decimetre** and **centimetre**, introduced in this order is suggested, but not at the same time. As the need for greater accuracy becomes apparent, and the measurement of smaller items becomes necessary, the choice of smaller units becomes clear. Metre and decimetre sticks are also reasonably long for the children to handle. The centimetre is much smaller, and fitting centimetres against items to measure them calls for further motor skills. The millimetre is too small and would only be introduced possibly to upper juniors if the need arose. Units, such as decametres and hectometres, exist in textbooks but these units are rarely used, and should not be taught. The **kilometre** is widely used for measuring longer distances but its appreciation is difficult because of its definition. To say a kilometre is 1000 metres is of little value until the child appreciates 1000 (Attainment Target 2, Level 3). Juniors could mark out 50 m or 100 m on the playing field. Travelling this 'track' the required number of times could lead to some appreciation of a kilometre. (2, 8 L2; 1, 2, 8 L3)
5. Measuring lengths and distances using standard measures, involving simple measuring devices. Note that many manufactured rulers and tapes are complicated for the

learner because they contain many units, and the divisions and numbers are most confusing. It is best for children to use plain sticks to measure with at first and then progress to a graduated stick or paper strip when the advantages are clearly seen. Although the teacher has to cut measuring rods and materials for general use, we suggest that infant and lower junior children should make their own measuring instruments as much as possible, under careful supervision. (1, 8 L3)

3.2 MATERIALS NEEDED

Balls of wool and string
lengths of coloured dressmaking tape up to 2 m
bamboo canes up to 3 m in length
wooden dowel, 1 cm in diameter, up to 2 m in length
wooden strips, section 3 cm by $\frac{1}{2}$ cm, up to 1 m in length
sheets of centimetre squared paper
paper strips 3 cm wide up to 1 m in length, some white and some coloured
6 sets Cuisenaire rods, together with extra orange, yellow and light green rods, if
    needed
6 sets of Stern number lengths, together with extra blue, brown or red rods, if necessary
2 or 3 cases of Stern unit cubes
collection of tins, bottles, jars, etc.
beads
skittles
zoo animals
sheets of cardboard and hardboard to make rectangles
cardboard shapes with straight sides made from art and craft waste

Special sets of these items are also needed:
1 set of rectangles 4 cm wide with lengths ranging from 20 cm to 1 m
1 set of rectangles 40 cm long with widths varying from 2 cm to 30 cm
1 set of rectangles of various sizes ranging from 20–40 cm in length and 2–20 cm in width
1 set of wooden dowels of the same thickness with lengths ranging from 20 cm to 1 m
1 set of wooden rods, dowels, etc., of the same length but different thicknesses

3.3 MEASURING DEVICES TO BE USED

1 m click wheel
1 toothed meccano wheel about 3 cm in diameter, mounted on a short axle, to measure
    curved lines
Cuisenaire rods
Stern rods
bamboo canes
wooden dowels and strings 1 m in length
wooden rods 1 dm long
wooden strips 3 cm by $\frac{1}{2}$ cm, 1 m long, graduated in decimetres, and numbered from
    1 to 10

paper strips 3 cm wide and 1 m long, graduated in orange lengths, not numbered
paper strips 3 cm wide and 1 m long, graduated in yellow lengths, not numbered
paper strips 3 cm by 60 cm long, graduated in light green lengths, not numbered
paper strips 3 cm by 1 m, graduated in orange lengths, and numbered from 1 to 10
paper strips 3 cm wide and 1 m long, graduated in yellow lengths, and numbered from 1 to 20
paper strips 3 cm wide and 60 cm long, graduated in light green lengths, and numbered from 1 to 20
paper strips 3 cm wide and 1 m long, graduated in decimetres, and numbered from 1 to 10
measuring strings 10 m in length
paper strips, 3 cm wide and 30 cm long, graduated in centimetres, and marked from 1 to 30

3.4 INTRODUCTORY WORDS (8, 10 L1)

The following activities are intended to be done individually. The teacher would indicate, where necessary, the particular dimension under consideration by asking the child to run his fingers along the item, to spread out his arms alongside it, or reach up to it.

1. The child is given four or five bamboo canes or wooden rods of the same thickness, with lengths ranging from about 20 cm to 2 m, to sort into big and small. In this case, big and small are used to mean long and short. The words long and short are relative to the child's world.
2. The child uses four cords of the same thickness with lengths ranging from about 20 cm to 2 m, and sorts them into long and short.
3. The child uses four cardboard or hardboard rectangles all 4 cm wide but with lengths varying from 20 cm to 1 m. Sort them into long and short.
4. Ask the child to look at five straight lines drawn on the classroom floor or wall. Which lines are long? Which ones are short? (Oral answers.)
5. The teacher points out to a group of children various doorways, spaces between desks and tables, corridors, etc. Sort into wide and narrow. (Oral answers.)
6. The teacher mentions to a group of children various things in the classroom, e.g. light bulb, light switch, chair seat, window ledge, top shelf of cupboard, the wastepaper basket, etc. Which things are up high? Which ones are down low? (Oral answers.)
7. The teacher asks a child to look at other children in the classroom and find a tall person and a short person. (Oral answers.)
8. The child uses six bamboo canes or dowels of the same length but different thicknesses. Sort into thick and thin.
9. The child uses ropes, cords, strings, of the same length, but different thicknesses. Sort into thick and thin.
10. Use five or six cardboard or hardboard rectangles of the same length (about 40 cm), and widths ranging from 2 cm to about 20 cm. Ask the child to sort them into wide and narrow.

11. The child uses strings, cords, ropes, bamboo canes and wooden dowels of various lengths and thicknesses. Find those which are thick, thin, long, short, long and thin, long and thick, short and thin, and short and thick.
12. Use hardboard rectangles 40 cm by 10 cm, 40 cm by 5 cm, 40 cm by 2 cm, 20 cm by 5 cm, and 10 cm by 2 cm. Find those which are long, short, wide, narrow, long and narrow, long and wide, short and narrow.

With regard to answers, the teacher could mainly accept oral answers. Also, should the items sorted be reasonably small, the different sets can be placed inside hoops or boxes, placed side by side on the table. Larger objects could be placed in two sets on the floor. The teacher can provide labels for describing the content of each set, e.g. **long**, **short**, **wide**, **narrow**, **thick**, **thin** (Fig. 3.1).

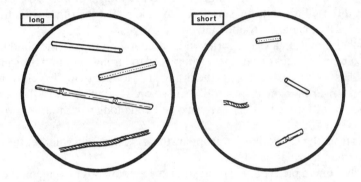

Fig. 3.1

3.5 DIRECT COMPARISONS (8, 9, 10 L1)

The teacher shows a child, or group, on different occasions, various pairs of items and explains in each case how the larger is determined. The two items are always placed or held, side by side, with one end of each together. *Longer*, *shorter* and *the same length as* are then determined by looking at the relative positions of the other ends of each item. When children have been shown test procedures, using different pairs of items, the teacher would set individual work concerning the following tasks. The teacher could make work cards and read them to the children, or read them and tell the children what to do.

1. Use pairs of wooden dowels of different lengths but of the same diameter. Paint each pair a different colour. Compare the two red rods, the two green rods, etc. Which is longer? Which is shorter? Put **longer than** and **shorter than** labels near each rod. Also include pairs of the same length. Display with a **same length as** label.
2. The child puts two rows of pegs, side by side, on a pegboard, with one row longer than the other. He also makes two rows the same length. Put **longer than**, **shorter than** and **same length as** labels alongside.
3. The child puts identical wooden cubes together, touching, to make a straight row,

and then makes a longer row of cubes alongside. He also makes two rows the same length. Put a label near each row.

4. The child puts a row of zoo animals on a squared background, on the table. He then puts a longer row of animals alongside. Label the rows **longer than** and **shorter than**. Which row has more animals?

5. The child builds two towers with identical bricks and makes them different heights. He also builds two towers the same height.

6. Show the child two unequal pieces of tape stretched side by side on the wall. Which is the longer? Also show two pieces the same length. Which is the longer?

7. Show the child two unequal straight lines drawn parallel and side by side on paper. Which is the longer? Also show parallel lines of the same length, side by side. Which is longer?

8. Give the child two pieces of string. Which is the longer piece? How can we tell?

9. Work in threes. Two children stand side by side whilst the other child finds who is the taller. Then change around. Give oral answers.

10. The teacher hangs up a string with beads threaded on it. Ask the child to thread a longer column of beads on another string. Also to thread a column the same length.

11. The child uses Cuisenaire rods. Is the orange rod longer than the yellow rod? Is the black rod longer than the brown rod? And so on. Find two rods of the same length. Find rods of different lengths. Are two red rods longer than a yellow rod? Ask questions like these.

12. Use rods from the Catherine Stern apparatus. Ask the child whether the brown rod is longer than the black rod, etc.

13. The teacher pins a piece of tape or a paper strip, about 50 cm long, on the wall. Ask the child to cut pieces of wool the same length as, longer than and shorter than the tape.

14. Obtain a plain wooden strip with a straight edge. The child draws pairs of straight lines of different lengths, side by side, and also lines the same length, or nearly so.

15. The child is given six pieces of string. He arranges them, side by side, in order of length.

16. Give the child eight or more bottles, boxes or tins. He arranges them in order of height, tallest on the right.

17. Give the child eight or more wooden sticks, some of which are the same length. Find those pieces with the same length, the longest stick and the shortest stick.

18. Use eight or more pieces of string of which two or three pieces are the same length. Ask the child to find pieces of the same length, the longest piece and the shortest.

19. Ask the child to select six different animals from the class collection of zoo animals, and then arrange them in order of height. Which animal is the tallest? (Make sure the animals are made to the same scale.)

20. Give the child one Cuisenaire rod of each colour. Arrange them in order of length. Can you stand the rods on end and make a staircase?

21. Give the child one rod of each colour from the Catherine Stern apparatus. Sort the pieces in order of length. Also stand the rods on end and make a staircase.

22. Give the child wooden rods, ropes and strings. He arranges them in order of thickness on the table, the thickest on the left.

23. Give the child eight rectangles of the same length (about 30 cm) but different widths (from 4 cm to 20 cm). Arrange them in order of width.

24. Give the child tins, bottles, jars and boxes to arrange in a row in order of width, widest on the left.
25. Ask the child to obtain a pair of cylinders from the 'shapes' box such that one is taller and wider than the other. Also find a pair such that one is shorter and wider.
26. The child rolls out two sausage shapes with plasticine so that one piece is longer than the other, thicker than the other, longer and thinner than the other, or shorter and thicker than the other.
27. Give the child hardboard rectangles of which some are the same length, and some the same width. Find those with the same width, and those with the same length. Find two rectangles such that one is wider and longer than the other, longer and narrower than the other, or shorter and wider than the other.
28. Within the class project '*Ourselves*' the teacher asks six or seven children, at different times during the day, to dip the end of a finger in poster paint and reach up and make a mark on a piece of paper on the wall. The teacher labels the marks. Afterwards the class, or group, could spend a few minutes talking about these marks. Which mark is highest? Which mark is lowest? Who has the longest reach? Who has the shortest reach?
29. The teacher asks five or six children to stand in a row facing the rest of the class, in order of height, tallest at this end and shortest at that end. The children arrange themselves initially. Then the teacher asks some of the children watching to make adjustments in the positioning, if necessary. Spend two or three minutes on this, occasionally. (Link with '*Ourselves*')
30. A group of children, with the teacher's help, produce silhouettes of the children in that group. These can be mounted on the wall with the 'feet' touching the floor. A talking session can be conducted around these silhouettes, with them finally being displayed in order from tallest to shortest. ('*Ourselves*')
31. The previous activity, **30**, could be done with children's teddy bears or dolls.

3.6 RECORDING

A set of labelling cards marked **tallest**, **shortest**, **widest**, **longer than**, **same height as**, **narrower than**, **thicker**, and so on, could be useful here. The child could get the appropriate label, with the help of the teacher, and place it near the item concerned. Many answers will also be given orally.

Where appropriate the child could copy descriptive words or phrases from labels, or a wall chart, and make his own recording label or write a sentence in his book.

3.7 INDIRECT COMPARISONS USING A LONGER MEASURING DEVICE (8, 9 L1)

1. The teacher fixes a red strip of paper, about 40 cm long, on one wall of the room and a blue strip, about 50 cm long, on another wall. She then asks a child, or group, which is the longer strip? How can we check our answer? Ask the child to cut a piece of string or wool the same length as each strip. Which string is longer?

Compare the strings by placing them, side by side and as straight as possible, on the table. Which is the longer string? Which is the longer strip? Talk about this.

The children could then work in pairs, one or two pairs at a time. They have to copy lengths and distances using pieces of wool and compare them as just described. Write questions on cards and also ask oral questions. Accept oral answers, and help children to write sentences or make them with labels, e.g. the window is wider than the door.

Ask if the door is wider than the window, the desk longer than the cupboard, the door wider than the width of the table, the desk longer than the width of the corridor, the distance between those two desks shorter than the distance between the table and that chair, etc.

Also use six paper strips of different colours fixed to various walls. Is the red strip longer than the yellow strip? etc.

2. The teacher draws straight lines on opposite walls of the room. Ask a group of children which line is longer. Present this as a problem. How can we tell? (Hint: a bamboo cane which is longer than both lines could be used.) Slide your fingers on the cane so that the distance between them equals the length of a line. Without moving the hands go to the other line and hold the cane before it. See if the length of this line falls within the copied length of the other line between the fingers.

Set individual work based on this method. Is the window wider than the door? the window wider than the sand tray? the cupboard longer than the width of the desk? etc. Also draw seven or eight straight lines of different colours on the walls of the classroom. Is the red line longer than the green line? the blue line longer than the yellow line? the green line the same length as the white line? etc. (Compile work cards.)

3. Use two straight lines drawn on different walls of the room. Which is the longer? Can the children solve this problem using a piece of string which is longer than both lines? Hold a piece of string stretched between the hands against one of the lines and copy its length. Now go to the other line, without moving your hands on the string, and stretch out the string on top of it. Is the string between the hands longer or shorter than this line? Which line is the longer? Discuss this.

Set individual work using this method. Compare straight lines of different colours drawn on the classroom or corridor wall. Is the red line shorter than the green line? etc. (Compile a work card.)

Recording can be done using prepared labels with words such as **door**, **cupboard**, **corridor**, **window**, **desk**, etc. The child could select labels, with the teacher's help, and make a statement with them, e.g. **corridor longer than window**. The child could then copy the sentence into his book. The teacher would also accept oral answers and write down sentences which include these answers for the child to write in his book.

3.8 INDIRECT COMPARISONS USING A SHORTER MEASURING DEVICE (8, 9 L1; 8 L2)

The teacher uses 10 cm Cuisenaire orange rods. She puts a red paper strip, 60 cm long, on a table, and a green paper strip, 80 cm long, on another table some distance away.

Which strip is the longer? The teacher puts orange rods, end to end, on both strips in order to copy their lengths. Then, without mixing up the rods, rebuilds the two lengths, side by side, on another table. Which strip is the longer? Discuss this, explaining that the longer row of rods fits on the longer strip. Check the result by putting the two strips alongside each other.

Make sure that the paper strips are multiples of the measuring unit. The situation would be too complicated if fractions were involved at this stage. Also notice that numbers are not used in this case. Children could use this method of comparison, however, when they have some knowledge of number but not enough to deal with numbers abstractly.

Set individual work for one or two children at a time. Use orange rods to compare pairs of paper strips, about 3 cm wide, each strip being a different colour. Make sure the strips in each pair are placed on tables well apart, and that the child estimates which is longer before doing the test. Make pairs of strips these lengths: 60 cm and 90 cm; 40 cm and 50 cm; 110 cm and 100 cm; 90 cm and 90 cm; 60 cm and 70 cm; 70 cm and 70 cm.

Recording can be done either by putting **longer than** and **shorter than** labels near appropriate strips, with the teacher checking the result, or the child could record, with help from the teacher, that the red strip is **longer than** the blue strip.

3.9 DESCRIBING LENGTHS AND DISTANCES USING NUMBERS (2 L1; 8 L2)

Work prior to this has not needed numbers. From now on, however, numbers play an increasing part in length. At first use numbers up to ten, then between ten and twenty, finally from twenty to a hundred. The work in length must keep pace with the child's number knowledge.

The teacher shows a child, or group, how to measure a paper strip, 60 cm long. Put a row of Cuisenaire orange rods, end to end, along the strip, and count the number needed. We used 6, so we say the strip is 6 orange rods long. Put a label **6 orange rods** near the strip.

Now set measuring activities to be done individually. Compile work cards and read them to the child, or tell the child what to do.

1. Give the child a strip of thin cardboard with straight lines 70 cm, 40 cm, 80 cm, 50 cm, 10 cm, 20 cm and 90 cm drawn on it. Measure each line using orange rods. Say how long each line is, and also put a label near each one, e.g. **7 orange rods**.
2. Use Cuisenaire rods. The child cuts pieces of wool equal in length to 5 orange rods, 8 brown rods, 10 yellow rods, 6 black rods, and 7 blue rods. Write a label to put near each piece of wool.
3. Use Catherine Stern rods. The child cuts pieces of wool equal in length to 7 brown rods, 5 blue rods, 6 red rods, etc. Label each piece of wool.
4. Use milk straws. The child makes straight lines with chalk on the floor of length 5 straws, 8 straws and 4 straws. Label each line.
5. The child builds a tower with bricks so that it is roughly 3 orange rods tall, and then another roughly 5 orange rods tall, etc.
6. The child threads beads on a string until the row is about 3 orange rods long, about 4 black rods long, etc.

7. Use cardboard rectangles 15 cm by 20 cm, 25 cm by 40 cm, 20 cm by 30 cm, 45 cm by 15 cm, 25 cm by 20 cm, 40 cm by 40 cm, etc.
    The child measures the length and breadth of each rectangle using Cuisenaire yellow rods. Record as 5 yellow rods long and 4 yellow rods wide.

To record, use number symbol cards from **0** to **9**, and cards with **orange rods**, **yellow rods**, **blue rods**, **black rods** written on them. The child, with the teacher's help, prepares a label using one card of each type, e.g. **7 yellow rods**. Or the teacher could write the words down on a piece of paper for the child to copy, e.g. 4 yellow rods. This label is placed near the item concerned.

3.10 DESCRIBING LENGTHS AND DISTANCES NUMERICALLY TO THE NEAREST UNIT (2, 8 L2)

Cut paper strips about 3 cm wide with lengths 43 cm, 38 cm and 25 cm. Show a child, or group, how to measure these strips using Cuisenaire orange rods, to the nearest unit.
    With the 43 cm strip, 4 orange rods can be placed alongside, but there is a piece of strip left over. Now place 5 orange rods on the other side of the strip. Which is the better answer, 4 or 5 rods? Look at the end of the strip left over and decide whether it is nearer the end of the row containing 4 orange rods, or the end of the row containing 5 orange rods. In this case it is the former, and we say the strip is 4 orange rods long, to the nearest orange rod.
    Now ask a child to measure the 38 cm strip under your guidance. Three orange rods are shorter and 4 orange rods are longer than the strip. Look at the end of the piece of strip left over. It is nearer the end of the row containing 4 rods so this strip measures 4 orange rods long.
    Now let a child measure the 25 cm strip. When we measure it a difficulty arises because its end is midway between the ends of the rows containing 2 rods and 3 rods respectively. In this case the general rule is to call the piece left over one orange rod. This strip, therefore, measures 3 orange rods.
    Thus, parts less than half the measuring unit in length are ignored, and parts half or more of the measuring unit in length are counted as one unit.
    Now let the child measure strips of length 62 cm, 57 cm, 54 cm and 45 cm, as just described. Put a label near each strip, e.g. **4 orange rods**.
    When the teacher is satisfied that the child can measure to the nearest unit, she would then set the following activities. (Compile work cards and give oral instructions.) Rows of rods are placed on, or against, the items concerned and the number required described to the nearest unit. Give oral answers and make a label to put near each item.

1. The child uses Cuisenaire yellow rods to measure the length and width of an exercise book, length of a pencil and a milk straw, the length, breadth and height of a chalk box, a cornflakes packet and a washing powder packet.
2. The child uses Catherine Stern blue rods to find the length and breadth of a table.
3. Using Cuisenaire orange rods the child finds the width of the door, the width of the window, the length and breadth of the desk.

4. Give the child cardboard shapes with straight sides. (These shapes can be made from art and craft waste.) Measure the sides of each shape using Cuisenaire yellow rods.
5. The child needs bamboo canes, each 1 m long, to measure the length and breadth of the classroom in bamboo canes.
6. The child finds the height, diameter and circumference of each of the following cylindrical tins using Cuisenaire yellow rods: large drinking chocolate tin, powdered milk tin, bean tin, detergent bottle, large instant coffee tin, fruit tin, etc. (Wrap a piece of wool round each cylinder once, and cut it in order to show and measure the circumference.)
7. The child measures the lengths of curved lines, presented as worms or snakes, less than 10 cm long, drawn on a work card. Cuisenaire unit cubes are placed, just touching, along the snakes or worms to measure them.

3.11 MEASURING ITEMS TO THE NEAREST UNIT USING ONE MEASURING DEVICE (1, 2, 8 L2)

Can we make things easier when we measure lengths or distances? Discuss this with a child or group. Previously we have been measuring things by placing rows of units along them and counting the number. This is rather inconvenient because we would often need lots of units. A corridor would need a row containing hundreds of orange rods to measure it, far more rods probably than we have. Suggest the use of one rod, or other item, to measure with.

Ask a child to measure the length and breadth of the table in spans. Start with your thumb on the edge of the table. Use one hand only, open it to its fullest reach, then close it moving thumb to little finger each time, so 'walking' along the path to be measured, counting the spans needed. Demonstrate, if necessary.

Next discuss how to use one orange rod to measure a bamboo cane. Start at the end of the cane, place the rod alongside, and mark the position of its end along the cane by placing a matchstick on the desk. Then move the rod along the cane so that one end coincides with the matchstick, and mark the position of the other end of the rod using another matchstick. This process is repeated until we arrive at the end, or nearly at the end, of the cane (Fig. 3.2). The length of the cane is determined by counting the numbers of times the rod fits, together with an adjustment for any remaining piece, if required. The cane is 9 rods long to the nearest rod.

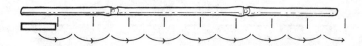

Fig. 3.2

Now set individual work. Compile work cards. Find the width of the door in spans, the length and breadth of the room using a one-metre bamboo cane, in bamboo canes, the length and breadth of an exercise book using one Cuisenaire yellow rod, and the length and breadth of the table using one Catherine Stern blue rod.

The child places two zoo animals on the floor 6 spans apart, two tins in the corridor 4 bamboo canes apart, two model cars 7 yellow rods apart, and two cars 8 Stern blue rods apart using only one measuring unit in each case.

3.12 MEASURING ITEMS TO THE NEAREST UNIT USING TWO MEASURING DEVICES (1, 2, 8 L2)

Explain to a child, or group, that sometimes we use two items of the same kind in order to measure things. Demonstrate how to measure with both feet (walking heel to toe), both hands (widths), both thumbs (widths) and both legs (pacing). Compile work cards and set individual work on the following activities.

1. Find, in feet, the width of the corridor, and the length and breadth of the room. Place two tins 7 feet apart in the corridor.
2. Find, in paces, the length of the corridor, the length and breadth of the room, the length, breadth and perimeter of the playground. Place two skittles 10 paces apart.
3. Find, using both hands, the length and breadth of the desk, the length and breadth of a table, the length of a bamboo cane, or the length of a piece of string. Put two tins 14 hands apart, etc.
4. Using both thumbs, find the length and breadth of your exercise book, the length of a stick, or the length of a piece of string. Put two animals on the table 15 thumbs apart, etc.

3.13 MEASURING ITEMS TO THE NEAREST UNIT USING A GRADUATED STRIP WHICH IS NOT NUMBERED (1, 2, 8 L2)

We can measure things by placing units against them, and make this easier by only using one or two measuring devices, but this way of measuring is still awkward and often takes a considerable time. Can we use a quicker way? Discuss with the children the idea of using a measuring strip and demonstrate how to make one. Use a paper strip 3 cm wide and 1 m long. Put a row of Cuisenaire yellow rods, end to end, against the longer side of the strip. Mark the positions of the ends of the rods on the strip with a pencil, near to the edge. When the rods are taken away the strip is divided into lengths equal to that of a yellow rod. We will print **yellow rods** on the strip to tell us what the divisions are (Fig. 3.3).

Fig. 3.3

Obtain a string or stick less than 1 m long, and ask the child how we can measure its length using the paper strip. Discuss how we put the measuring strip alongside the stick with one end of each together and then we count the number of yellow rods contained in the length of the stick. Count from where the ends are together to the opposite end of the stick.

For individual work, let each child make measuring strips by marking off:

1. a 1 m length using Cuisenaire yellow rods and label it **yellow rods**
2. a 1 m length using Cuisenaire orange rods and label it **orange rods**
3. a 60 cm length using Cuisenaire light green rods and label it **green rods**.

(Compile work cards.) Use the strips to measure the length and breadth of the desk in yellow rods and orange rods, the length and breadth of an exercise book in green rods, and the lengths, breadths and heights of cereal, detergent and food boxes in green rods. Record answers in notebooks, or place labels near the items concerned.

3.14 MEASURING ITEMS TO THE NEAREST UNIT USING A NUMBERED GRADUATED STRIP (1, 2, 8 L2)

The teacher asks a child, or group of children, how the measuring strips described in the previous section could be improved. We have to count every time we measure something with them. What can we do to save time? Number the rod-lengths on the strips, starting at one end.

Ask each child to do this with their own strips, marking each interval centrally (Fig. 3.4). The strip marked off in orange lengths is numbered from 1 to 10. The strip marked off in yellow rods is numbered from 1 to 20, and the strip marked off in green rods is numbered from 1 to 20.

Fig. 3.4

Set individual work, which concerns the use of these measuring strips, by means of work cards. Write answers in a notebook, or write labels to place near each item.

1. Measure the lengths of a pencil and milk straw, and the lengths, breadths and heights of boxes, in green rods.
2. Measure the lengths, breadths and heights of boxes, and the heights and diameters of tins and plastic bottles, in yellow rods.
3. Measure the lengths and breadths of a small table, and a sheet of newspaper, in orange rods.
4. The child draws straight lines on paper, or on the floor with chalk, the same lengths as 5 yellow rods, 4 orange rods, 14 green rods, 8 yellow rods and 11 green rods. (Draw along the edge of a straight wooden strip, 50 cm long, mark out the required length of line and then rub out the remainder.)
5. Cut pieces of wool, or strips of paper, with lengths the same as 9 orange rods, 18 green rods, 15 yellow rods, etc.
6. Place two zoo animals on the table 15 green rods apart, or 5 orange rods apart, or 17 yellow rods apart, etc.

3.15 MEASURING LONGER ITEMS TO THE NEAREST UNIT USING A NUMBERED GRADUATED STRIP (1, 2, 8 L2)

Cut a piece of wool between 1 m and 2 m in length. Tell the child, or group of children, that we wish to measure the wool using the paper measuring strip marked orange rods. Now demonstrate that when we place the strip alongside the wool we notice that the strip is not long enough.

To solve this we then put a matchstick across the wool, or near it, to show how far the strip has reached, and using this matchstick as a marker we put the strip against the wool again. This time the strip extends to the end, but, how long is the wool? Supposing we use one whole strip of 10 orange lengths, and a further 6 orange. Altogether the wool stretches 10 + 6, or 16 orange lengths.

Measure other pieces of wool, if necessary, and then set individual work.

1. Use the measuring strip marked orange rods to find the length of a desk, the height and width of a door, the width of the corridor, and the lengths of various pieces of string (up to 4 metres long).
2. Place two bricks on the floor 16 orange rods apart, or 24 orange rods apart, or 36 orange rods apart.
3. Cut four pieces of wool the same lengths as 15 orange rods, 23 orange rods, 28 orange rods and 35 orange rods.

3.16 INDIRECT COMPARISONS USING NUMBERS

The children can start using numbers to compare lengths when they are able to arrange numbers in order of magnitude. At first, make comparisons with numbers up to 10; then from 10 to 20; and finally from 20 upwards.

Obtain two pieces of string, both less than 1 metre in length, each being a whole number of yellow rods long. Ask a child, or group, which string is the longer and by how much? Measure each string using the paper strip marked yellow rods. Suppose one string measures 9 yellow rods and the other measures 16 yellow rods, then the latter is longer because 16 is greater than 9. The longer string is 7 yellow rods longer because 16 − 9 = 7, or 9 + 7 = 16, whichever way we look at the problem. Now put the strings side by side and measure their difference in length (Fig. 3.5). We should find it is 7 yellow rods, which checks our solution.

Fig. 3.5

Now use two strings, one between $5\frac{1}{2}$ and 6 yellow rods long, and the other between 6 and $6\frac{1}{2}$ yellow rods long. These strings must be carefully prepared beforehand. Measure the strings using the measuring strip marked yellow rods, to the nearest unit. We find that each string measures 6 yellow rods—and we say they are the same length, or they are equal in length.

When we place the strings side by side we see that one is slightly longer, but in most cases we cannot place items side by side to compare them and have to accept the lengths we are given. If we are not shown the strings but we are told only that each measures 6 yellow rods, to the nearest unit, we would say the two strings are the same length.

When children are ready they could be set individual work from work cards which include the following activities. Write answers in notebooks, or write labels to place near items.

Numbers Less Than Ten (2, 3 L1; 1, 8 L2)

1. Build two towers such that one is 2 orange rods taller or 2 yellow rods taller or 5 green rods taller.
2. Draw two straight lines, side by side, such that one is 5 orange rods longer or 6 green rods longer or 3 yellow rods longer.
3. Cut two strips of paper such that one is 5 green rods longer than the other or 2 orange rods longer or 5 yellow rods longer.
4. A paper strip is 6 orange rods long. Another strip is 4 orange rods longer. Cut out the longer strip. Ask similar questions.
5. The teacher prepares two strings, sticks or paper strips, each less than 1 m in length, and a whole number of orange rods long. The child measures the pair using the strip marked orange rods and says which is longer and by how much. Then he puts the pair side by side and measures their difference in length in order to check the calculation.
6. Working in pairs, the children measure the width of their hands in green rods. Who has the wider hand? How much wider? They also measure the lengths of their spans in green rods, and compare them. Include in *'Ourselves'*.

Numbers between Ten and Twenty (1, 2, 8 L2; 3 L3)

1. Cut two lengths of string so that one piece is 14 green rods longer than the other.
2. Prepare two paper strips, sticks or strings, less than 2 m in length, each measuring a whole number of orange rods. The child measures the strips in orange rods. Which is longer, and by how much?
3. Prepare two sticks, strings or paper strips, less than 1 m in length, each measuring a whole number of yellow rods. The child measures the sticks in yellow rods, and compares their lengths.
4. The teacher draws three or four straight lines, less than 1 m long, side by side on paper, each being a whole number of yellow rods long. The child measures the lines in yellow rods. How much longer is the longest line than each of the other lines?
5. Measure the width of the corridor and the width of the door using your feet. Which is the longer distance? How much longer?
6. Draw two curved lines (worms or snakes), less than 20 cm in length, on a card. Place Cuisenaire units on each worm to measure its length. Which worm is longer? How much longer?

Numbers above Twenty (1, 2, 8 L2; 3 L3; 3 L4)

1. Prepare pairs of strings, up to 4 m in length, each being a whole number of orange rods long. Measure the strings in orange rods and find their difference in length.

2. Prepare pairs of strings, up to 2 m in length, each being a whole number of yellow rods long. Measure the strings in yellow rods and find their difference in length.
3. Prepare two sticks or two strings, up to 1 m in length, each being a whole number of green rods long. Measure the sticks or strings in green rods. Which is the longer, and by how much?
4. Measure the length and breadth of the room using your feet. How many feet longer is the room than it is wide?
5. Measure the length and breadth of a small table in yellow rods. How much longer is the table than it is wide?
6. Place three different coloured skittles in the playground and measure their distances apart in feet or paces. Is it farther from the red skittle to the green skittle or the blue skittle? How many feet, or paces, farther?

3.17 THE USE OF A WHEEL TO MEASURE LENGTHS AND DISTANCES (1, 2 L2; 8 L3)

The use of a rolling wheel to measure lengths and distances is important, particularly for curved boundaries and roads on maps. A *trundle*, or *click wheel*, whose circumference is 1 metre could be used to measure and mark out distances, the results being expressed in turns. A *toothed cogwheel*, about 3 cm in diameter, from a Meccano or other construction set, could be fixed to a short axle and then rolled along boundaries of shapes to find their perimeters, or rolled along curved lines to find their lengths, in turns. For greater accuracy, lengths could be found in 'turns' and 'teeth'. The children could do these activities:

1. Use a trundle wheel to place two skittles 15 turns apart.
2. Use a trundle wheel to measure the distance between two skittles placed in the playground, e.g. 17 turns.
3. Measure reasonable distances in, and near to, the school using a trundle wheel, e.g. width of playground, the distance from the classroom door to the cloakroom, or the distance from the classroom door to the door of another classroom, etc.
4. Draw some curved lines on a work card. Measure the lengths of the lines in turns or teeth, or both, using a cogwheel. Which line is longest?
5. Draw three closed shapes on a work card. Roll a toothed wheel once around their boundaries to find their perimeters, in turns, or turns and teeth. Which shape has the longest perimeter?

3.18 THE NEED FOR STANDARD UNITS (1, 2, 8 L2)

The teacher could direct the following activities with a small group of children. Three or four sessions might be needed.

1. Each child measures out and cuts a length of wool 5 pencils long. Compare the lengths of wool. Are they the same? Why not?
2. Each child measures the length of the room using his feet. Compare the answers obtained. Why are they not the same?

The teacher could now mention other units, associated with the body, which were used to measure lengths and distances, e.g. cubits, feet, paces, yards, hands, spans and inches (thumb widths). Measure, and compare results, for the length of the desk in spans, the length of a stick in inches or the length of the room in cubits.

3. Each child measures out and cuts a length of wool 4 Cuisenaire orange rods long. Compare the lengths. Are they the same? Discuss.

The teacher then discusses with the children why we must all measure things using the same sized units in order to communicate lengths to one another. Telling someone that a stick is 5 pencils long is not good enough because that person will not know what a 'pencil' is. Feet and pencils are no good for measuring units because they differ in size. Cuisenaire orange rods would be suitable because they are all the same size. We need standard units to measure lengths and distances, for making things, and buying and selling goods.

The buying and selling of cloth in market places in earlier times could be talked about, and how yards and feet varied from stall to stall, and in different parts of the country, causing discontent. Some traders often employed small people for selling cloth. Why? Gradually, units of length were standardized, and their lengths displayed in markets, so that fair trading could take place, e.g. the foot was standardized in the fifteenth century. We often see in museums some of the standard measures which were once used.

Are weights and measures checked nowadays? This could be discussed.

Show the children a bamboo stick one metre long, and say this length, the metre, is a standard unit. Discuss its suitability for measuring rooms, corridors and playgrounds but not pencils, tables and chairs. Link with athletics if opportune, e.g. 100 m and 200 m races.

Next show a wooden dowel one decimetre long. This length, a decimetre, is another standard unit. Would this be suitable for measuring a table or chair? Why? What about the corridor or the width of your finger? Why not?

Let the children cut strings, and paper strips, 1 m long, by taking a copy of the metre stick.

Also let each child compare the decimetre stick and a Cuisenaire orange rod. What do you find? The orange rod and the decimetre are the same length. Therefore, we will still measure lengths using orange rods, but from now on we will call them decimetres.

Put a mat on the floor. Ask the children to roll a 1 metre trundle wheel along the mat once and compare the distance moved with the length of a metre stick. What do you find? How far is it around the edge of the wheel? Use the wheel to mark out 3 metres on the classroom floor.

3.19 MEASURING IN METRES ONLY (1, 2, 8 L2)

Set the children individual work based on the following activities. Compile work cards.

1. Place two skittles 5 m apart in the corridor using a metre string or stick.
2. Use a metre trundle wheel, and place two skittles 15 m apart in the playground or corridor.

3. Place two skittles anywhere in the playground and measure the distance between them, to the nearest metre, using a trundle wheel.
4. Measure the length and breadth of the playground, and of the school hall, to the nearest metre, using a trundle wheel.
5. Use a metre stick to measure out a piece of string 10 m long. Use this string and the metre stick to mark out distances of 17 m, 24 m, 35 m, etc.
6. Mark out a 40 m distance on the playing field. Work in pairs. Time your partner to run, walk, skip and hop this distance using a stopwatch or seconds timer. Who took the longer time in each event? Include in *'Ourselves'*.
7. Mark out 100 m on the playing field. Children work in pairs timing each other to run this distance, in seconds, using a stopwatch. Compare with the world record for this event. Graph these times for six or eight children. (*'Ourselves'*)

3.20 MEASURING IN METRES AND DECIMETRES (2 L2; 1 L3; 8 L4)

Ask the children to measure with a metre stick, lengths and distances in the classroom where a metre stick is clearly too long. Discuss the need for smaller units and introduce and use decimetre rods to measure them.

Follow this by talking about measuring lengths longer than a metre using decimetre rods only, and then with the metre stick *and* decimetre rods. For example, the length of the table is 13 decimetres or 1 metre and 3 decimetres. Bring out the point that we use two units to measure with rather than one because it is easier, more accurate and the numbers used are smaller.

Set individual work, involving metres, decimetres, and both, through the following activities. (Compile work cards.)

1. Place skittles in the corridor the following distances apart: 2 m 4 dm, 3 m 5 dm, 2 m 6 dm, using one metre stick and one decimetre rod only. Also put skittles 17 dm, 25 dm, and 19 dm apart, using only one decimetre rod.
2. Place skittles in the corridor more than 5 paces apart. Measure their distance apart in metres and decimetres using only one metre stick and one decimetre rod. Measure to the nearest decimetre. Give the answers in metres and decimetres.
3. Obtain a metre stick and place decimetre rods along it. How many decimetres in 1 m? How many in 2 m? 3 m? etc.
4. How many decimetres in 1 m 2 dm? 1 m 7 dm? 2 m 3 dm? 2 m 6 dm? etc.
5. Change 35 dm, 17 dm, 42 dm, 33 dm, etc., to metres and decimetres. Put two skittles 18 dm, 24 dm or 35 dm apart, using only one metre rod and one decimetre rod.
6. Give the child a paper strip 3 cm wide and 1 m long. How long is the strip? Place decimetre rods against the strip, and mark it off in decimetres. Label the intervals from 1 to 10, and write **decimetres** on the strip. Use this decimetre measuring strip to place cubes 7 dm, 5 dm or 9 dm apart, etc. Also use it to cut pieces of wool 5 dm, 4 dm, 8 dm, 12 dm and 14 dm in length.
7. Give the child a wooden strip 3 cm by $\frac{1}{2}$ cm in section and 1 m long. Ask the child to graduate it in decimetres, and number and label it as described in **6** above.

8. Measure the length and breadth of a table, to the nearest decimetre. Give the answers in decimetres, and in metres and decimetres.
9. Find the length and breadth of the room in metres and decimetres, to the nearest decimetre.
10. Find the width and height of a cupboard or door, in decimetres, to the nearest decimetre. Give the answers in metres and decimetres also.
11. Make a mark on the rim of a hoop. Roll the hoop once on the floor, and copy its circumference. Measure the circumference of the hoop in metres and decimetres and also give the answer in decimetres.

3.21 MEASURING IN DECIMETRES AND CENTIMETRES
(2 L2; 1, 2, 3, 8 L3; 2, 3, 8 L4)

Use centimetre squared paper and prepare strips 3 cm wide and 30 cm long. The teacher gives a child, or group of children, one strip each. Use pencils, notebooks, bottles and boxes to illustrate to the children that decimetre units are too long to measure small things. Short lengths are measured using the units along the longer edge of the strip you have been given. These units are called **centimetres** (Fig. 3.6). Demonstrate and ask the children to do the following. Go over the faint blue lines along one edge of the strip with a pencil, to a distance of about $\frac{1}{2}$ cm from the edge. Number the divisions from left to right from 1 to 30, midway along each interval. Print **centimetres** on the strip.

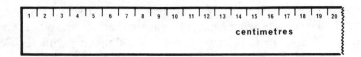

Fig. 3.6

Set individual work based on the following activities. (Compile work cards.)

1. Place a decimetre rod against the centimetre measuring strip. How many centimetres in a decimetre? How many in 2 dm? 3 dm? etc.
2. Place a Cuisenaire unit on the centimetre measuring strip, or centimetre squared paper. What is the height, width and length of the cube?
3. Use Cuisenaire units to make rows of length 15 cm, 12 cm, 22 cm, etc.
4. Measure the lengths of the various colours of Cuisenaire rods, in centimetres, using unit cubes.
5. Draw curved lines, snakes or worms on a piece of cardboard. Measure the lengths of the worms, in centimetres, by placing Cuisenaire units on them.
6. Draw closed shapes on a piece of cardboard. Measure their perimeters, in centimetres, by putting Cuisenaire units around their boundaries.
7. Use Cuisenaire decimetre and centimetre units to make rows of length 3 dm 2 cm, 2 dm 5 cm, 1 dm 7 cm, etc.
8. Use Cuisenaire decimetre and centimetre units to make rows of length 34 cm, 52 cm, 48 cm, 63 cm, etc.

9. Use centimetre cubes to make rows of length 1 dm 5 cm, 2 dm 3 cm, 1 dm 7 cm, etc.
10. Use Cuisenaire unit cubes to make rectangles:

    8 cm long and 5 cm wide,
    6 cm long and 4 cm wide,
    9 cm long and 7 cm wide,
    6 cm long and 6 cm wide, etc.

    How many cubes are there in each rectangle?
11. Use Cuisenaire rods (not cubes) to make rectangles the following sizes:

    8 cm long and 5 cm wide,
    9 cm long and 6 cm wide,
    7 cm long and 5 cm wide,
    10 cm long and 8 cm wide, etc.

12. Make rectangular boxes using Cuisenaire rods (not cubes) the following sizes:

    5 cm long, 4 cm thick and 6 cm tall,
    6 cm long, 4 cm thick and 4 cm tall,
    8 cm long, 5 cm thick and 4 cm tall, etc.

13. Draw straight lines, side by side, 12 cm, 18 cm, 22 cm and 28 cm long, using a straight edge and the centimetre measuring strip.
14. Give out rectangles with sides whole centimetres, e.g. 15 cm by 8 cm. Measure these rectangles, in centimetres, using the centimetre measure. Also give the answers in decimetres and centimetres.
15. On centimetre squared paper draw rectangles 12 cm by 14 cm, 15 cm by 6 cm, 4 cm by 14 cm, etc. Draw their diagonals and measure them, to the nearest centimetre. Which rectangle has the longest perimeter? the shortest perimeter? Which rectangle has the largest area? the smallest area? Make copies of these rectangles with sides half as long, or twice as long, etc.
16. Mark out six squares 5 cm by 5 cm on centimetre squared paper, and cut them out. Mount them on thin card and cut the card to the same size as the squares. Can you join the squares to make a box? What shape is the box? Find the area of one of the faces using a centimetre squared grid.
17. Use centimetre squared paper and mark out two rectangles 4 cm by 5 cm, two rectangles 5 cm by 6 cm and two rectangles 4 cm by 6 cm. Mount these rectangles on thin card and cut the card to the same size as the rectangles. Can you join the rectangles together with Sellotape to make a box. What shape is this box? Find the area of the faces of the box using a centimetre grid. Which face has the largest area? Which face has the smallest area?
18. Draw a decimetre square on centimetre squared paper. How many square centimetres in a square decimetre?
19. Draw a straight line near and parallel to the left-hand side of a piece of centimetre squared paper, and another line near and parallel to the bottom side (Fig. 3.7). Label the lines A and B. Mark small crosses on the paper 4 cm from A and 3 cm from B, 5 cm from A and 3 cm from B, 6 cm from A and 7 cm from B, etc. Instead of saying 5 cm from A and 7 cm from B we will just say five, seven. Now put crosses at three, six and at five, four and at two, eight and at four, four; etc.

When we write five, seven it looks like (5,7). Now put crosses at (2,3), (4,3), (8,2), (6,2), etc. Where is (4,0)? etc.

Plot crosses at the points (4,3), (8,3), (4,9) and (8,9) and join them. What shape do we get? Where is the centre of this shape?

Plot the points (1,5), (6,5), (1,4), (3,4), (3,1), (4,1), (4,4) and (6,4). Join up the points. What letter do I obtain?

I start at (2,3), then go to (4,6), then to (3,8), then to (4,5) and then to (7,8) walking in straight lines between stops. On centimetre squared paper draw a plan of my journey.

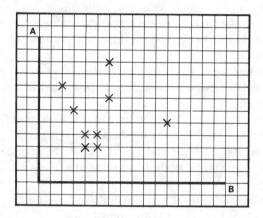

Fig. 3.7

20. Measure the lengths of various colours of Catherine Stern rods, to the nearest centimetre.
21. The teacher makes cardboard shapes, with straight sides, from art and craft scrap. Measure the sides of each shape, to the nearest centimetre, and find the approximate perimeters. Which shape has the longest perimeter?
22. Measure the lengths, breadths and heights of rectangular boxes, to the nearest centimetre.
23. Measure, to the nearest centimetre, the heights and diameters of cylindrical tins. Use a centimetre ruled paper strip, or tape measure, to find the circumferences of these tins, and then arrange them in order of girth.
24. Measure the height of one step in a flight of stairs, to the nearest centimetre. How far would you rise if you climbed 2 steps? 3 steps?
25. Measure your stride in decimetres and centimetres. How far would you walk in 2 strides? 3 strides? 5 strides? What is the length of a stride to the nearest decimetre? Use this length, and a calculator, to work out roughly how many strides you would need to walk 10 m and 30 m. Include in *'Ourselves'*.
26. A child measures, to the nearest centimetre, the lengths of the left feet of eight children. Who has the longest foot? Who has the shortest foot? Arrange the foot lengths in order of size. (*'Ourselves'*)
27. A child measures, in centimetres, the waists of six children, using a tape measure marked in centimetres. Find the largest, and the smallest, waist. Arrange waist measurements in order of size. (*'Ourselves'*)

28. Mark on a centimetre-ruled measuring strip the numbers from 0 to 150. Go up in 10's to 100, then in 1's to 150. Attach this to the wall from the floor vertically upwards. A small group of children use it to measure their heights to the nearest centimetre. Arrange these heights in order, tallest to shortest. Who is tallest? Who is shortest? How much taller is Bill than Jane? (*'Ourselves'*)

29. Use a centimetre measuring strip to find, in centimetres, your partner's reach. (Reach means from fingertip to fingertip with arms stretched out sideways to form a T-shape.) Who has the longer reach? and by how many centimetres? (*'Ourselves'*)

30. Use large wooden rectangular blocks of equal size.
    (a) Build different rectangular walls, one brick thick, containing 18 bricks. Measure the height and length of each wall, to the nearest decimetre, and to the nearest centimetre. If we painted the front of each wall, would we need the same amount of paint?
    (b) Build a rectangular wall 3 bricks tall and 5 bricks long. How many bricks are needed? Measure its height and length, to the nearest decimetre, and to the nearest centimetre.

31. Use some wooden rods 8 cm and 9 cm long from a Cuisenaire set. Show how some of these rods could be used to mark off distances of 16 cm, 17 cm, 18 cm and 24 cm. What about 1 cm? 10 cm? 7 cm? and 2 cm? Display the necessary rods on the table, end to end, side by side, or both, to illustrate the answers. (Use a calculator, if necessary.)

32. Use wooden sticks of length 1 dm, 3 dm and 9 dm. By putting all or some of these rods end to end, side by side, or both, show how they can be used to measure out distances of 1 dm, 2 dm, 3 dm, 4 dm . . ., up to 13 dm. (This activity could be done using instead Cuisenaire rods 1 cm, 3 cm and 9 cm long, with distances from 1 cm to 13 cm measured out. The rods could be displayed to show how each distance is obtained.)

33. Use Cuisenaire units, decimetre rods and a metre stick, if required, to find the number of centimetres in 1 metre. How many in 2 metres? 3 metres? etc.

34. Write 2 m 12 cm, 3 m 34 cm, 1 m 46 cm, etc., in centimetres.

35. Write 152 cm, 140 cm, 324 cm, 187 cm, 206 cm, etc., in metres and centimetres.

3.22 INTRODUCTION TO THE DECIMAL POINT (3 L3; 2, 8 L4)

An introduction to decimal notation is necessary to work towards Attainment Target 2, Level 4. It can be introduced by measuring lengths with two different units and then recording them. For example, 5 metres and 4 decimetres could be written in short as 5.4 metres, 6 decimetres and 3 centimetres as 6.3 decimetres and 2 metres and 34 centimetres as 2.34 metres, in the same way that £3 and 45 pence is written £3.45. The use of the decimal point in these cases is to act as a separator between two units, such as metres and decimetres or pounds and pence.

Questions, such as those now given, would give practice in the new notation.

1. Write in decimetres and centimetres: 5.6 dm, 8.7 dm, 4.6 dm, etc.
2. Write in decimetres, using a decimal point: 5 dm 6 cm, 4 dm 2 cm, 9 dm 7 cm, etc.
3. Write in metres and decimetres: 6.7 m, 7.6 m, 8.4 m, etc.

4. Write in metres, using a decimal point: 8 m 2 dm, 4 m 6 dm, 9 m 3 dm, etc.
5. Write in metres and centimetres: 1.62 m, 1.47 m, 3.25 m, 2.84 m, etc.
6. Write in metres, using a decimal point: 2 m 36 cm, 5 m 76 cm, 8 m 39 cm, and so on.

The next stage is to develop a deeper meaning of decimal notation and this needs to be discussed with work on tenths initially, and later with tenths and hundredths. The idea that 3.4 dm indicates 3 decimetres and 4 tenths of a decimetre could be developed side by side with tenths and linked with $3\frac{4}{10}$. Tenths and hundredths are needed to describe 2.36 m, which is a short way of writing 2 metres and 3 tenths of a metre and 6 hundredths of a metre. This needs connecting with 2 metres, 3 decimetres and 6 centimetres as well as 2 metres and 36 centimetres.

When a child has knowledge of decimal notation, involving only tenths, a start could be made to use it in calculation. Addition could be introduced by measuring the sides of a cardboard shape in decimetres and centimetres, expressing them in decimetres, then calculating the perimeter. For example, the sides of a triangle being 3 dm 2 cm, 2 dm 6 cm and 1 dm 4 cm could generate discussion on how to do 3.2 dm + 2.6 dm + 1.4 dm. Similarly, should the sides of a square measure 4 dm 3 cm, the perimeter would be 4.3 dm × 4. Suppose the lengths of two lines were 5 dm 2 cm and 3 dm 4 cm, the question 'How much longer?' could introduce 5.2 − 3.4 or 3.4 + ? = 5.2. Should the perimeter of a regular hexagon be given as 19.2 dm the length of a side promotes 19.2 ÷ 6.

After the children are able to do arithmetic involving tenths the teacher needs to provide opportunities for working in tenths and hundredths. The work with decimal fractions needs to be carefully integrated with length and other measuring activities in order to promote the need for, and justify the teaching of, the four rules with decimals.

Chapter 4

Time and the Calendar

Activities involving time in the infant school should not be confined only to the reading of the clock. We believe, in fact, that reading clocks should be delayed until children are able to understand the numbers involved and can appreciate the sophisticated ideas behind such instruments.

We could begin by comparing the duration of events by sight, after which intervals of time can be measured and compared using a count of some sort which will eventually lead to the use of an automatic counter. That time is measured in relation to the passing of events should be part of the children's experience, and in relation to this some idea of the origin and basis of the calendar should also be included. There should be some attempt at showing the primary periods of time to be the year and the lunar month, and that other periods are subdivisions of these.

Reading the clock can be preceded by activities which record the passing of events by means of a count. There is a pre-number stage in which the measure can be made by the collecting of items which are not counted. Comparisons of the duration of events can be made by comparing the collections. Such activities help the understanding of the fundamental concepts of number, *greater than*, *fewer than*, and *the same number as*. Later, the durations of events can be compared by comparing the numbers of collected items, or by comparing numbers counted aloud, so dispensing with collections. The need for a count can eventually be linked with the function of a clock as a mechanical counter. The gradual linking of the count with the clock is not helped by having at first a clock with two hands and a complicated number scale. It can be very confusing to have a numbered dial with two different kinds of readings on it. For this reason, and others, we suggest that it would be advantageous to have timers with one pointer initially. We find it not too inconvenient to use a modified seconds timer, or stopwatch, to time in minutes, and a clock with the hour hand removed to time in hours. Thus, hours and minutes would be recorded on separate instruments initially, but ultimately the advantages of a two-handed timer showing hours and minutes would be pointed out, and such timers used, when necessary.

Reading the time from digital clocks is also necessary. In these instruments electric pulses, regularly produced, mark the passage of time and control the number display. The time of day is visible but needs interpretation. When children can tell the time, involving minutes, from a 2-handed clock, and are learning to record it, connections should be made with digital clocks. For example, twenty past seven is written 7.20 and a quarter to eleven is written 10.45.

Some difficulty arises out of the use of language to describe periods of time. The meanings in colloquial English and the precise meanings are sometimes at variance. For

122

example, we use the word day when we mean the period of daylight whereas a day is a 24-hour cycle. We talk of the longest day and the shortest day so giving the impression that days alter in their duration. We also use the word morning to describe the period from midnight to midday whereas it commonly refers to the interval between sunrise and midday.

4.1 GENERAL SCHEME

General Scheme for the Timing of Events

1. Compare the duration of activities, which start together, by observation. Meanings of *longer time than*, *shorter time than* and *the same time as* will be introduced.
2. Time the duration of events, which do not start together, by collecting sand, water, marbles or cubes. Then compare rows of collected units, or amounts of water or sand, without using numbers, to find the longer time.
3. Compare the duration of events, which do not start together, using units of measure of some kind. Use numbers to describe the collected units and compare times by comparing these numbers. At first, only do activities which need small numbers. Number scales, which act as unit counters, would also be introduced when children understand number symbols.
4. Compare the duration of events using a pointer which moves on a numbered dial.
5. Compare the duration of events by counting aloud with the assistance of a mechanical counter.
6. Introduce rates of working, i.e. *faster*, *slower* and *quicker*.
7. Use mechanical timers more and gradually introduce standard units.
   Use a timer which has a pointer which takes 1 minute to revolve on a dial divided into 12 equal parts. Introduce minutes.
   Use a timer which has a pointer which takes 1 minute to revolve on a dial divided into 60 equal parts, and numbered 5, 10, 15, etc., up to 60. Introduce seconds, and measuring in minutes and seconds.
   Link counting aloud with timing in seconds.
   Use a 'minute' timer which has a pointer which takes 1 hour to revolve on a dial divided into 60 equal parts, numbered 5, 10, 15, 20, etc., up to 60. Introduce hours, and measure in hours and minutes.
   Use an 'hours' timer which has a pointer which takes 12 hours to revolve on a dial divided into 12 equal parts, numbered 1, 2, 3, 4, etc., up to 12. Time events in hours.
   Use a 'one-hour timer' or 'pinger' to time events in minutes.
   Use an 'hours' timer and a 'minutes' timer to measure intervals during the day, and then show the advantages of a 2-handed clock which records both hours and minutes.
   Read, and record, the time of day from a 2-handed clock.
   Relate activities to hours of the day, such as, breakfast is at 8 o'clock.
8. Tell the time of day from a digital clock.
9. Use a.m./p.m. and 24 hour clock notation to describe times of the day.

General Scheme for the Calendar and the Seasons

The topics mentioned so far have concerned only the measurement and comparison of intervals of time, but we must dovetail into this scheme, at appropriate stages, those items connected with the calendar and parts of the day.

1. Observation of the sun and moon to gain ideas about day and night; and morning, noon, afternoon and evening, leading to the concept of a day.
2. Dividing the day into various periods using daily events, and ordering these events, e.g. breakfast, dinner, tea and supper.
3. Observing the weather and plants, animals and birds, and acquiring the concept of seasonal events, their recurrence and the order of the seasons.
4. Naming days of the week, and ordering events during the week.
5. Observing the moon's phases and so developing the idea of a month. Noting the names of the months, and the number of days in each month.
6. Making a more detailed study of the environment leading to recognition of further differences in seasonal events, and the duration of the seasons in terms of months.

Timing events

4.2 NON-NUMERICAL WORK: COMPARING BY SIGHT THE DURATION OF EVENTS WHICH START TOGETHER (1, 8 L1)

Activities can be presented which, with discussion, lead to the use of the language of time. Some of the preliminary terms we need here are *finish first*, *finish last*, *finish together*, *takes a longer time than*, *takes a shorter time than* and *takes the same time as*. To do this the teacher could select activities to demonstrate and discuss in which two or more children start at the same instant to do something, e.g. put on a coat but leave the buttons undone. John finished first so he took less time, or a shorter time, than Bill. Or, Mary and Susan finished together, so they took the same time. We could also get two children to put on their coats if one starts when the other has nearly finished. Finishing first does not necessarily mean 'takes a shorter time than'. In this case we cannot say who takes longer because they started at different moments. To say who takes longer, or longest, we must get people to start together.

Do not, at this stage, use the descriptions *quicker than*, *faster than* and *slower than* because these are concepts based on time. Rates of doing things cannot be compared until after the children can compare intervals of time. Rates, therefore, will be studied after this background has been developed.

Some activities occurring naturally during the school day could be used to advantage in this context, e.g. dressing after PE, clearing up the room after craft work, and putting on of coats before going home. In the matter of dressing themselves some children need help, but they would all the time be encouraged to do what they can for themselves. Other activities, like those in **4** and **5** below, could be carried out with the class observing the participants and afterwards discussing what they saw. The remainder of the activities listed could be put on a card and instructions given orally. Children could work in twos or threes, one group at a time. (This would require two or three identical sets of items for each activity.) In all these activities the children start together. The teacher would need to be at hand to check given tasks and talk with the children about what happened.

1. Put a given number of bricks on top of one another to make a tower.
2. Put on a shoe (leave the lace untied).
3. Put on a coat (leave the buttons undone).
4. Run, hop, jump or skip a prescribed distance along the corridor, or playground, or playing field.
5. Have an egg and spoon race over a given distance.
6. Make identical jigsaw puzzles.
7. Build a shape on a pegboard being given a certain number of pegs, e.g. the teacher gives each child 12 pegs from which to make a rectangle.
8. Arrange six tins, or bottles, in order of height, tallest on the left.
9. Arrange six sticks, or strings, in order of length.
10. Use 12 pieces of card of different shapes. (Oblongs, triangles, circles and squares, all congruent.) Sort them into like shapes.
11. Use a card with symbols on it from **1** to **9**. Match number symbol cards with these numbers.
12. Use pieces of cardboard, 5 red, 3 blue, 2 yellow, 3 black, 6 white. Sort the pieces into various colours.
13. Use a large card with various shapes drawn on it, each shape being coloured. On each of these shapes the child fits an identical cardboard shape.
14. Put various plywood or plastic shapes into matching troughs or holes that are cut in a plastic or wooden base (an inset board).

4.3 NON-NUMERICAL WORK: COMPARING THE DURATION OF EVENTS WHICH DO NOT START TOGETHER (1, 8 L1; 1, 8 L2)

The next step is to compare the duration of activities which do not start together. The problem for the teacher at this stage is to present situations which under discussion show that we cannot always tell by looking alone whether one person took longer than another. If children do not start together then we have to apply some kind of test in order to aid our judgement.

The teacher arranges the class to observe while two children fill identical tins with sand, one starting when the other has nearly finished. Who finished first? Who started first? Who took the shorter time? Explain that finishing first does not necessarily mean 'takes a shorter time than' because they started at different moments. So who took the longer time? We cannot really tell in this case because they did not start together.

How can we solve this problem? Arrange for a third child to put beads, one at a time, into a box as the activity is undertaken by one of the children. This is repeated as the activity is done by the other child. Which box has more beads? Put the beads into two rows between thin wooden strips, or thread the beads on strings. Which row is longer? Which has more beads? For which child doing the activity were more beads put in the box? Who took longer? Thus, times can be compared without using numbers, and without the activities starting at the same instant.

The teacher could introduce the following test procedures, and encourage discussion about them, to groups of children who are ready to proceed further. Groups of two or three children, one group at a time, could use some of the tests demonstrated in order to compare the times taken for prescribed tasks. The tasks could be put on work cards and oral instructions given.

1. Compare times for two children to put on their coats, one starting after the other has finished, using a dripping, or very slowly running, tap. Adjust the tap to start with, push a glass or plastic container under it when the child starts, and quickly remove the container when the child has finished. Repeat this whilst the other child puts on his coat, collecting the water in an identical glass or plastic vessel. (Do not adjust the tap throughout the experiment because the flow will be affected.) Stand the containers of water, side by side, and compare the amounts (Fig. 4.1). Which contains more water? Who took the longer time?

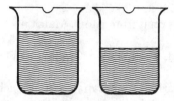

Fig. 4.1

Instead of having separate vessels to collect water we could use one, with a paper strip on it, and mark water levels each time (Fig. 4.2). Use this method to compare times for two or more children to put on their shoes, leaving the laces untied, and establish the terms 'takes the longest time', 'takes the shortest time' and 'takes the same time as'.

Fig. 4.2

If the tap is allowed to run very slowly the water could be collected in identical plastic beakers whilst each event takes place. Thus, rows of beakers of water could be displayed on a squared background to compare times (Fig. 4.3). The end beaker in each row would probably only be part full.

Suppose each child takes four full beakers, and part of another, to tie his shoes, then the water in the partly filled beakers has also to be compared to decide who takes the longer (Fig. 4.4).

Fig. 4.3

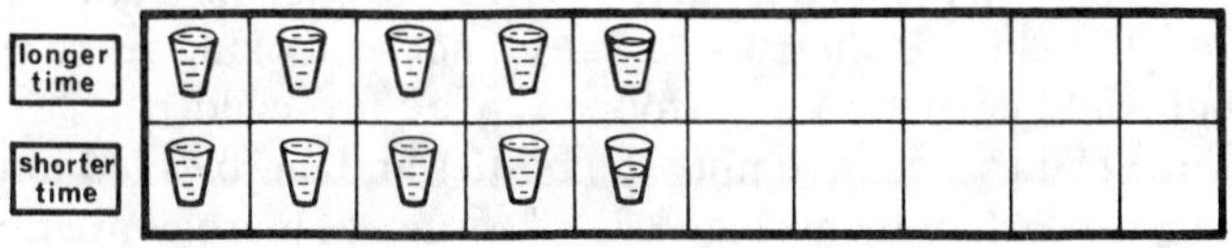

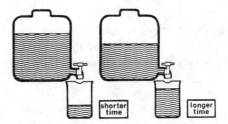

Fig. 4.4

2. Compare times for two or more children to fill given tins with sand or make a jigsaw puzzle or build a tower with bricks. Use a large transparent plastic bottle, fitted with a tap (an aspirator, see Appendix on Equipment) and run water from it as the event takes place. At first use two identical bottles, but later one bottle with a paper strip on it could be used.

When we use two bottles we can fill them both with water at the start and compare the amounts of water left. The jar with most water indicates the shorter time. Or, we can collect the water which runs from each bottle in identical containers and compare amounts (Fig. 4.5). The smaller amount represents the shorter time.

Fig. 4.5

When we use one bottle we can collect the water which runs out during each event in identical vessels, and compare amounts. Or we can collect the water which runs out in a plastic jug which has a paper strip on it. Mark the level of the collected water for each event. The smaller amount of water, shown by the lower level marked, represents the shorter time.

Another method is to fill the bottle at the start and mark the level of the water at the end of the event on the paper strip (Fig. 4.6). Repeat for the other timing and

Fig. 4.6

compare levels to decide when more water runs out. The higher marked level indicates the shorter time because a smaller amount of water runs out.

3. Have some plastic bottles filled with water or boxes filled with sand. These are to be emptied into a large bucket. Whilst a child empties the bottles another child maintains a steady feeding of marbles into a channel, closed at one end. (The child putting the marbles into the channel should be well away from the child doing the emptying because we do not wish the feeding of the marbles to become a tally of the emptying of the bottles. The child feeding marbles need not be looking at the child doing the emptying but could be started and stopped by a third child.)

    Two or three children could empty the bottles and marbles fed into channels by the same child for each of them (Fig. 4.7). The rows of marbles are then compared. Who took the longest time to empty the bottles? Who took the same time? Note that in this case we are using, and developing, concepts of the greater number and the lesser number in order to compare times. Also, when we compare groups of identical items then the greater number form the longer row.

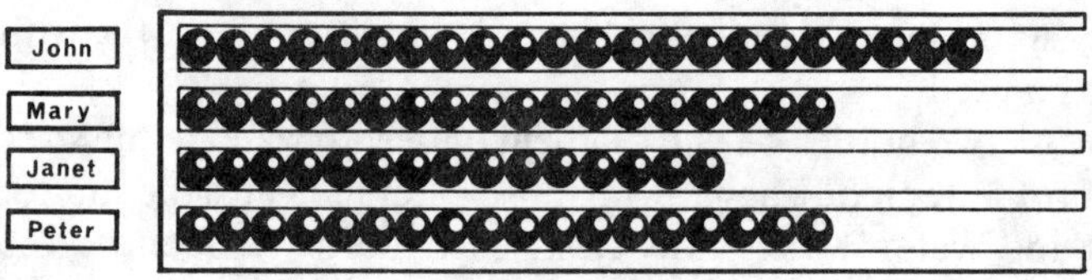

Fig. 4.7

    Cubes, or beads, dropped into a tin or box in a regular manner, could be used instead of marbles. The cubes could then be displayed in rows, or towers, side by side; the longest row, or tallest tower, represents the longest time. Beads could be threaded on strings, and placed side by side on the table in rows, or hung side by side on the wall, in columns.

4. Use two candles. Light one and let it burn throughout the morning activities, then light another to burn during the afternoon activities. Put the pieces of candle left, side by side, and compare them. Which is the longer? Did more candle burn in the morning or afternoon? Which takes the longer, morning school or afternoon school?

    Use birthday cake candles, which burn for 10–15 minutes, and compare the times between the end of morning assembly and the start of playtime, and the end of playtime and the start of dinnertime. Also, compare times spent on number activities, reading, daily news, painting, music and movement, etc. Every time a candle is used collect a card with a picture of a candle on it. (Draw the candles the same height as a new candle.) Any piece of candle left over at the end of this activity is placed against a new candle and a piece of the new candle equal to the length burnt away is chopped off. The latter piece is put with the 'candle cards'. Thus, the time for each activity can be represented by candle cards, and a part candle. Display the cards and pieces of candle in rows, side by side (Fig. 4.8). Which row shows the more candle burned? Which activity took the longer?

5. Compare times for various activities, which take less than 5 minutes, using a 5-minute sand glass. For example, ask two children to make a jigsaw puzzle. Stick a paper strip on the upper container of the sand glass and mark the sand levels at the

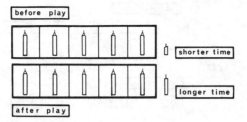

Fig. 4.8

end of each event (Fig. 4.9). The higher level indicates the shorter time because a smaller amount of sand has run out. Do *not* select activities which are longer and which would involve turning the timer over and making a count. The situation is too complex to record satisfactorily at this stage.

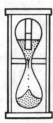

Fig. 4.9

6. Let two or more children build a number stair using Cuisenaire or Stern rods. While a child does this another child touches, in a regular fashion, coloured divisions on a paper or wooden strip, starting at one end and moving one division at a time towards the other end. The paper scale could be made from strips of 1 cm or 2 cm squared paper, joined together, with lengths coloured using felt pens (Fig. 4.10). When the

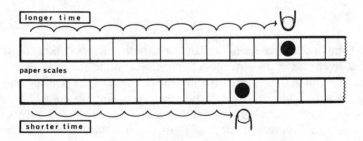

Fig. 4.10

child finishes the number stair the child who was touching the strip puts a counter on the scale to show how far he has travelled along it. Let the other children build the stair whilst the same child moves his finger along a similar paper strip. Compare distances travelled along the strips in order to compare times. The shorter distance represents the shorter time. Should the event take longer than a 'scales length', go back quickly to the other end of the strip, collect a cube, and start touching divisions

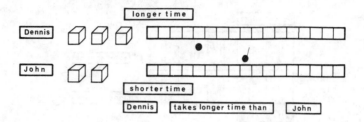

Fig. 4.11

again. Thus, each event can be recorded with cubes and a length on the strip (Fig. 4.11).

7. Use a timer, or stopwatch, with only one pointer which revolves once each minute, and which has a plain, ungraduated dial. A stopclock, or seconds timer, could be used. Place a narrow ring of gummed paper on the glass front of the timer in order to hide the numbers and divisions on the dial. This will leave visible part of the moving pointer revolving within a smaller plain face.

    At first compare activities which take less than 1 minute, e.g. let two or three children hop, in turn, across the room, or arrange six sticks in order of length, or arrange six tins in order of height. Zero the pointer of the timer initially, and as each child finishes mark the position of the pointer on the gummed ring of paper (Fig. 4.12). When did the pointer turn through the shorter distance? Who took the shorter time?

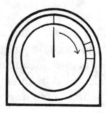

Fig. 4.12

Later, compare activities longer than one minute, such as making a jigsaw puzzle, copying a given shape on a pegboard, etc. Every time the pointer revolves once collect a cube and at the finish also mark the position of the pointer. Put the cubes, touching, in rows, side by side, on the table and compare them. Should one row contain fewer cubes it would represent the shorter time because it shows fewer turns of the pointer. In this case, fractions of a turn made at the end of each event need not be compared closely (Fig. 4.13).

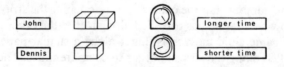

Fig. 4.13

If one row, however, contains the same number of cubes as the other, then part turns of the pointer recorded by the marks on the clock faces have to be compared closely to determine the shorter time (Fig. 4.14). Discuss this with the children.

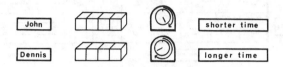

Fig. 4.14

4.4 NUMERICAL WORK: MEASURING AND COMPARING THE DURATION OF EVENTS

General Remarks

Numbers can be used to compare times indirectly when children have some grasp of them. At first the durations of events are measured using a count of some sort. The units of measure are then compared by placing them in rows, side by side, where possible, and the greater number found. The longer time can then be deduced and how much longer found if the calculation is not difficult. Children, initially, cannot deal with numbers abstractly but they are able to compare numbers and times when helped by some form of concrete representation. The activities suggested use various displays to aid thinking and enable numbers and times to be compared. Those activities involving larger numbers need to be delayed until children are ready for them.

Timing Events and Making Numerical Comparisons Involving Numbers Less Than Twenty (2 L1; 1, 2, 3, 8 L2)

The teacher could arrange the following activities into assignments for small groups of children. Some things will need discussion as they arise, e.g. the numbering of paper strips, and the reading of numerical results.

1. Compare times for two or more children, not starting together, to build a tower or to arrange eight bottles in order of height or to put on and button up a coat. Time each child by collecting water from a slow-running tap in a large jug. Empty this water into identical plastic beakers, up to marks drawn 1 cm below their top edges, so that no water will overflow. How many 'full' beakers were collected? Add to this number the partly filled beaker, if any, and then describe the size of the group as more than X but less than Y. Thus, we find that John takes between six and seven beakers to build the tower. Repeat this for the other children, then arrange the beakers in rows, side by side, with the partly filled beaker on the right of each row (Fig. 4.15). Put a number label against each row, and relationship labels against the rows representing the longest and shortest time.
   Should each child take five 'full' beakers and a part beaker, the water in the partly

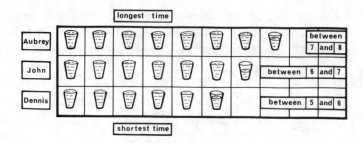

Fig. 4.15

filled beakers has to be compared carefully to decide which row contains more water, and so represents the longer time (Fig. 4.16). It is possible for rows to contain the same amount of water, in which case a **same time as** label would be used.

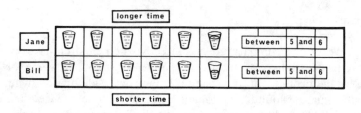

Fig. 4.16

2. Use 15–20 cardboard shapes. Find, and put into sets, the squares, triangles and circles. Use a slowly running tap to time each child. Collect the water in a plastic jug, which has on its outside a gummed paper strip marked in equal divisions (Fig. 4.17). Mark the water levels obtained and describe the heights of the water collected for each child by counting divisions. Describe fractions, for example, as just over five, about six and a half or nearly four. Thus, if John takes nearly eight divisions, and Mary takes just over seven divisions, Mary takes the shorter time. (If the marks on the paper strip are studied the children will see that nearly eight is greater than just over seven.)

Fig. 4.17

When children can order numbers up to about 20, and deal with number symbols from 1 to 9, we can ask them if there would be any advantage in numbering the divisions on the jug. (It enables one to read the number of divisions without having to count every time.) Number the divisions using symbols from 1 to 9, and 1 ten, 1 ten and 1, 1 ten and 2, etc., for numbers above 9 (Fig. 4.18). For future comparisons of time, therefore, use a graduated jug.

Fig. 4.18

3. Compare times for two or three children to match number symbol cards with pictures of groups of items or to arrange number symbol cards in order. Use a large transparent plastic bottle fitted with a tap (see Appendix on Equipment). On the outside stick a gummed paper strip marked in equal divisions, the strip extending to where the bottle starts to become narrower. Fill the bottle to the top of the strip, initially, and let water run out to time events. Find the number of divisions the water level has fallen for each event, such as just over four, about five and a half or nearly six, and then compare these numbers to compare times. At a later stage the advantages of numbering the divisions can then be discussed, and a bottle used with a numbered strip (Fig. 4.19).

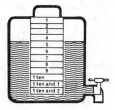

Fig. 4.19

4. An egg-timer (a 3–4 minute sand glass, see Appendix on Equipment), could be used to compare times to do things, e.g. complete a jigsaw puzzle or copy a figure drawn on squared paper. On each chamber of the timer stick a gummed paper strip, marked in 6 or 8 equal divisions (Fig. 4.20). If the level falls through 4 divisions for Dennis and just more than 3 divisions for John, the latter will take the shorter time.

Fig. 4.20

We could compare events which take longer than three or four minutes, e.g. the time for a dripping tap to fill various tins or bottles. Every time we turn over the sand glass, collect a cube. If the tin takes 3 cubes, and 4 divisions, to fill while the bottle takes 5 cubes, and 1 division, then the bottle takes longer to fill. The children could display the cubes in rows, side by side (Fig. 4.21). Which has the larger capacity, the tin or the bottle? How do we know? Discuss this.

Fig. 4.21

5. Let two or three children, in turn, arrange 8 sticks in order of length. Whilst each child completes the task Philip takes cubes from a box, one at a time, and puts them into a tin. (Keep the box and the tin in the same places throughout the activity so that the count is fairly regular.) The cubes put into the tin during this activity are sorted into tens and their number found, e.g. Heather takes fourteen cubes. This number could be compared with the efforts of the other children by putting the cubes in rows, side by side, if necessary (Fig. 4.22). Heather takes the longest time. Jack takes the shortest time. Heather takes 2 more cubes than George, and 5 more than Jack.

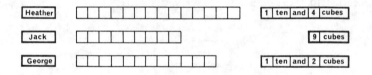

Fig. 4.22

We could use a cube 'counter' to find the number of cubes collected on each occasion. Why would one be useful? A paper strip, with divisions on it equal in length to the side of the cubes to be counted, and numbered from 1 to 50, would count up to 50 cubes, if they were placed against it (Fig. 4.23).

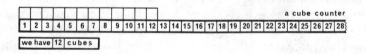

Fig. 4.23

6. For activities of longer duration a candle could be used. A paper strip, the same length as a new candle, and divided into equal intervals by paper folding, could be placed against the candle at the end of the activity to measure the amount burned down (Fig. 4.24). (Initially, make a mark on the candle one division from its lower end to show the lowest level to which it is to be burned. An elastic band can then be put on the candle at this mark to show clearly this level.) The number of divisions burned would be obtained by counting. Results could be, for example, that the

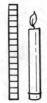

Fig. 4.24

candle burned down just over 3 divisions, or just less than 2 divisions, or about four and a half divisions. Compare the times between the end of morning assembly and the beginning of playtime, and the end of playtime and the beginning of dinnertime.

Would a numbered scale be better than a plain one? Discuss this. Make a numbered scale the same length as a new candle and divide it into 16 equal parts by paper folding (Fig. 4.25). Compare the duration of morning school and afternoon school. Should we use more than one candle collect a cube for each. Thus, 2 cubes and a partly burned candle which reads 3 divisions on the scale, means that 2 candles and 3 divisions of another were burned during the event.

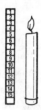

Fig. 4.25

Simple questions on differences could be asked. If a new candle has 15 divisions, and 5 divisions were burned, how many divisions remain? A harder problem would be to find how much longer, should one activity take 1 candle and 12 divisions, and another take 2 candles and 3 divisions. This could be solved by complementary addition: 1 candle, 12 divisions and 3 divisions more make 2 candles; and another 3 divisions gives 2 candles, 3 divisions. So, one activity is 6 divisions longer than the other in time.

Birthday cake candles could be used for activities of shorter duration. (A candle takes 10–15 minutes to burn.) The lengths of playtime, story time, news time, etc., could be compared.

7. Use a seconds timer, or a stopclock which has a gummed paper annulus stuck on its face to hide any previous graduations. (This timer has a large hand which revolves once in a minute.) Divide the gummed paper ring into 12 equal parts so that the approximate position of the pointer on the face can be described (Fig. 4.26). Zero the pointer initially, stop the timer at the end of the activity, and count the divisions turned through by the pointer, e.g. time children separately to hop or run across the yard and back or to arrange number symbol cards in order of magnitude or put six strings in order of length. The time taken for each event could be recorded on timer cards (Fig. 4.27). (Timer cards can be made easily using a rubber stamp clock face

a timer

Fig. 4.26

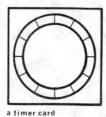

a timer card

Fig. 4.27

(see Appendix on Equipment). This stamp prints a circular dial divided into 12 equal parts, the divisions being numbered from 1 to 12. At this stage we do not want a numbered dial so the teacher could remove the numbers from a rubber stamp clock face with a sharp craft tool, or razor blade, in order to print such a dial. The child draws in the position of the pointer on the dial.)

The children, with help from the teacher, could display the timer cards, side by side, count the divisions, and make labels to describe the results (Fig. 4.28).

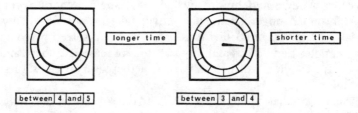

longer time

shorter time

between 4 and 5

between 3 and 4

Fig. 4.28

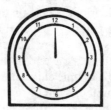

Fig. 4.29

The teacher can talk about how to describe the position of the pointer more accurately. Instead of saying between 4 and 5 divisions, use the descriptions just over four, just less than five or about four and a half, whichever is most appropriate. Also discuss the advantages of a timer with numbered divisions on its face. Get a timer, and fit on its face over the existing numbers and divisions, a gummed paper ring divided into 12 parts, and numbered from 1 to 12 (Fig. 4.29). For future activities use a numbered timer, and record and display results using 'timer cards' with a numbered dial. (Make these cards with a rubber stamp clock face.)

Timing Events and Making Numerical Comparisons Involving Larger Numbers (1, 2, 3, 8 L2)

The teacher could arrange the following activities into assignments for small groups of children.

1. Use a piece of strong thread about 100 cm long. The teacher ties a small piece of metal to one end, and the other end to a hook in the ceiling, allowing the metal mass to swing from side to side as a pendulum. Initially hold the mass out sideways, then release it, and each time it swings to and fro once put a cube into a box (Fig. 4.30). At

Fig. 4.30

the finish, if the mass has swung one way and is returning then count this as one oscillation. If the mass, however, has not yet swung completely one way then ignore this fraction. Use the pendulum to compare times for various children, in turn, to sort pieces of card into various colours or to arrange number symbol cards in order or to make a rectangle on a pegboard with 24 pegs. In each case find the number of cubes collected by putting them in tens, or by placing them against a 'cube counter'.

   If the pendulum swings 24 times for John, and 18 times for Tom, then Tom takes the shorter time, by 6 swings. Put the cubes in rows, side by side, if necessary, to obtain these results.

2. Activities can be compared by arranging for a child to touch, in a regular manner, the divisions on a numbered paper strip fixed to the wall (Fig. 4.31). The strip, 200 cm

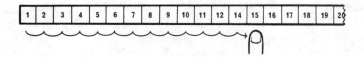

Fig. 4.31

long, could be marked in 2 cm divisions, and numbered from 1 to 100. The numbers could be spoken aloud as the child touches the divisions because this would help keep the count regular, and aid the learning of the counting sequence. Should the count be more than 100 the child collects a cube, goes quickly back to the beginning of the strip, and starts touching the divisions and counting again. Thus, 2 cubes and 23 on the strip would indicate that 2 hundred and 23 divisions were touched altogether.

Use this method to compare the times taken for two or three children, one after the other, to complete a jigsaw puzzle or put on and button up a coat or to take 24 pegs from a box of pegs and make a rectangle with them on a pegboard.

To compare the times for two or three people to perform an activity do *not* change the person who keeps the count by touching the strip.

4.5 COMPARING RATES OF WORKING BY SIGHT (1 L1; 2, 8, L2)

When the children can compare times, and understand the meanings of 'longer time than', 'shorter time than' and 'the same time as', we can introduce words which describe rates of doing things. The following activities need discussing with a child, or group of children, when they are in progress.

1. Let two children start together and tie their shoes, or hop across the room and back, or make a square with 25 pegs on a pegboard, or make a jigsaw puzzle, or arrange number symbol cards in order. Who finished first? Who finished last? Who took the longer time? Who took the shorter time? Who was the faster or the quicker? Who was the slower? Explain that when people start together to do the same thing the one who takes the shorter time is said to be the faster. He is quicker than the other. The one who finishes last is the slower. (*'Ourselves'*)
2. Run model cars down a sloping piece of wood after starting them together. Which car was fastest? Which car travelled slowest?
3. Let three or more children start together and put on their coats, or put 24 marbles in a tin, or run across the playground and back. Who finished first? Who finished last? Who was the fastest? Who was slowest? (*'Ourselves'*)
4. Use two plastic bottles, with taps, both filled with water to the same level. Turn on the taps at the same time, and collect the water in identical plastic jugs or buckets. Notice, and compare, the falling water levels in the bottles, and the rising water levels in the plastic buckets or jugs. Which bottle is emptying the faster? Discuss this.

4.6 TIMING EVENTS AND MAKING NUMERICAL COMPARISONS BY COUNTING (1, 2, 8 L2)

When children have learned the counting sequence up to, or beyond, a hundred, activities could be compared which last up to a minute and a half. The following activities could be arranged for small groups of children:

1. The teacher adjusts a tap so that it drips once in one or two seconds. (A plastic bottle

fitted with a tap will do just as well.) The children time, and compare, activities by counting the drips during each activity, e.g. build a tower, fill tins with sand, put 26 marbles in a box, hop along the corridor and back. Mary builds the tower in 14 drips, Jill builds one in 17 drips, so Jill takes longer by 3 drips.

2. Children could count aloud, using a metronome to keep time, while children run, hop, skip or jump prescribed distances on the playground. If Tom and John run around the playground separately, and the count reaches 23 and 26 respectively, then Tom takes the shorter time by 3 units. Which boy ran the faster? (*'Ourselves'*)

   When children become accustomed to the spacing of the count the metronome need not be used.

3. Make a pendulum about 100 cm long, set it swinging and count oscillations, or sideways movements, during each event. (An oscillation is equivalent to two sideways movements, to and fro.) Counting oscillations makes the numbers used much smaller than counting sideways movements, e.g. 42 sideways movements would be counted as 21 oscillations.

   When children become accustomed to the spacing of the counting sequence the pendulum need not be used, and children can count aloud, unaided, during events. A pendulum about 100 cm long has a sideways movement of 1 second approximately, and if the children imitate this count they are saying the numbers at intervals of 1 second approximately. Thus, we are giving children the concept of a second, and helping them estimate the duration of short events. If a child builds a tower whilst the class counts to 12 then he has taken 12 seconds approximately.

4.7 TIMING IN MINUTES AND SECONDS (1, 2, 8 L2; 3, 8 L3)

Arrange this section as a set of activities for small groups of children. With them we can introduce the standard units of time, minutes and seconds, to time events. We suggest that minutes are introduced first because the events timed involve reasonably small numbers. Later, to be more accurate, and when the children can cope with numbers up to 60, seconds can be introduced.

The timers suggested are made by altering existing clocks and timers in order to obtain simplified instruments with plain faces and one pointer. At a later stage graduations representing seconds are put on the face, and the divisions numbered 5, 10, 15, etc., up to 60. We can also encourage children to time in seconds by counting aloud.

1. Use a seconds timer, or a stopclock, with a gummed paper ring divided into 12 equal parts stuck to its face, and numbered from 1 to 12. (The pointer takes one minute to revolve once.) Time, and compare activities which take longer than a minute, e.g. making a jigsaw puzzle, or filling various containers from a slowly running tap. Each time the pointer revolves once collect a cube, and record the part turn made at the end on a timer card. Display the cubes, and timer cards, in rows, side by side, and also provide labels (Fig. 4.32). Thus, 6 cubes and a timer card showing 4 divisions would indicate that it took 6 turns and 4 divisions of another turn for the red tin to fill with water. The green tin filled with water in 8 turns and 6 divisions. It will be seen that the green tin took longer to fill. How much longer? In this case the answer, 2

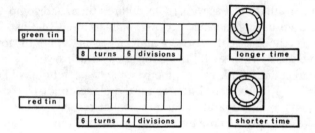

Fig. 4.32

turns and 2 divisions, is not difficult to obtain. Which tin has the larger capacity? How do we know?

Times could also be expressed as fractions of a turn, because 3 divisions are equivalent to a quarter turn; 6 divisions to a half turn, and 9 divisions to three-quarters of a turn (Fig. 4.33). If the pointer lies between 2 and 4 we would say about a quarter turn; between 5 and 7, about a half turn; between 8 and 10, about three-quarters of a turn; between 10 and 12, nearly one turn. Opportunities for developing simple vulgar fractions should be encouraged, particularly halves and quarters because they are often used in 'telling the time'. If Dennis took 6 turns and 5 divisions to make a jigsaw puzzle we could describe this time as about six and a half turns.

Fig. 4.33

2. The timers used so far have had pointers which revolve once in a minute. These same timers can be used to introduce standard units, and measurement in minutes is an easy step to take. Two and a half turns become two and a half minutes; three-quarters of a turn becomes three-quarters of a minute; and so on. Each child finds the approximate times, in minutes, using halves and quarters, for his partner to put on and button up a coat or to put on both shoes and tie them up or to walk around the playground once. A child finds the approximate times taken to fill a tin with water from a slowly running tap, or to burn a birthday cake candle, or to empty an egg-timer once, or to empty a 'five-minute' sand glass once, etc.

3. Before timing in seconds is introduced, the teacher could talk to the group of children who are ready to proceed to this, along the lines now suggested. The teacher shows a stopclock or seconds timer which has a pointer that revolves once in a minute over a dial marked in 60 divisions. Start the timer, let the pointer revolve once, and remind them that this interval is called a minute. To measure smaller intervals of time we divide the dial into 60 equal parts, and the pointer takes 1 second to move

through one of these divisions. In order to save counting when we use the timer the divisions are numbered, but not all, because there would be too many numbers on the face. Instead we only mark some of them, i.e. 5, 10, 15, 20, etc., up to 60. Count the divisions on the timer, starting at the zero position, and see whether the dial has been correctly numbered.

Start the timer, and stop it before the pointer has made a complete turn, and ask the children for how long, in seconds, it was turning. Children need plenty of practice reading a timer, under the guidance of the teacher, before they are asked to time events on their own.

Give activities based on the reading of this timer, or a similar one, to small groups of children. At first, time and compare the duration of activities done by two or three children which take less than 1 minute, e.g. hopping across the room and back, or running across the playground, putting on and buttoning up a coat or arranging 8 sticks in order of length, and arranging number symbol cards in order of magnitude. For example, Dennis takes 16 seconds, John takes 12 seconds, so John takes the shorter time by 4 seconds. John was the faster. (*'Ourselves'*)

Later, time events which take longer than a minute. Collect a cube at each turn of the pointer because we can easily forget, or become confused, about the number of turns should we try to count and remember them. 3 cubes and 12 divisions on the timer would tell us an event took 3 minutes and 12 seconds.

By talking with the group establish fractional relationships, that is, 15, 30 and 45 seconds respectively are equivalent to a quarter, a half and three-quarters of a minute.

Arrange for individual children. or pairs of children, to find the times, in minutes and seconds, for a party candle to burn, an egg-timer to 'empty', a five-minute timer to 'empty', a jar or tin to fill with water and a jigsaw puzzle to be completed.

With a group that is timing in seconds, the teacher could start a seconds timer and let the children count aloud so that the count keeps in step with the pointer. In doing this the children will become accustomed to the spacing of the sounds and this will help them, at a later stage, to estimate times, in seconds, by counting only. Also let the children count to sixty and see if a seconds timer, or stopwatch, not on display, registers sixty seconds while the count is in progress. If the counting pace is reasonably correct it helps children gain some appreciation of a minute.

The children should also use digital timers. Use those which will count up, or count down, in seconds, for up to 24 hours, display the time taken from the start and are push-button controlled. A child could start one and look at the seconds display changing 1, 2, 3, 4, ..., and count with it. After 59, instead of 60, it shows 1:00, which indicates that 60 seconds ≡ 1 minute. What happens next? What does 1:23 mean? Counting with the display, up to 60, regulates and fixes the counting pace which can later be used for estimating in seconds. Allow children to time those activities mentioned earlier, and others, using a digital timer, in seconds, and in minutes and seconds. Also to time events, such as sort a number of mixed shapes into squares, oblongs, triangles, etc., using both a digital timer and a seconds timer with a pointer, and compare results. Which is easier to use? Were the timings the same? Why not? Discuss this.

4.8 COMPARING RATES USING NUMBERS (1, 2 L2; 8 L3)

We can now encourage the children to use the words 'faster' and 'slower' after comparing the times taken in seconds or minutes for various people to do the same activity when they do not start together. This could be arranged as assignments for individuals or small groups of children.

1. Let two or three children run across the playground and back, or hop along the corridor and back, fill a bottle with water using a spoon or small vessel, or make a jigsaw puzzle, whilst another child times them with a seconds timer. (The children do these events separately.)

   Suppose John, Dennis and Peter took 15, 16 and 15 seconds respectively to run across the playground. Who took longest? Dennis, because 16 is greater than 15. Who was fastest? John and Peter took the same time. They ran equally fast, or at the same speed.
2. Use a plastic bottle fitted with a tap and filled with water. Find the time it takes to empty using a digital timer. Fill another identical bottle and find how long it takes to empty. Which bottle emptied the quicker?
3. Use clockwork cars, or other toys, brought to school by the children. Time them, separately, in seconds, over a prescribed length of corridor, or across the room, using a digital timer. Which toy travels fastest? Which was slowest? Now let the cars start together to check the result.

   Start the slowest car and a few moments later start the fastest car. What happens? The faster car catches up the other, and perhaps passes it. If one thing passes another, or catches it up, then it is travelling faster. Discuss this.

4.9 HOURS AND MINUTES: HOURS OF THE DAY

We can now proceed to timing longer intervals in hours and minutes using various timers. Initially, time the events in minutes, then hours and minutes, using a pointer which takes 1 hour to revolve over a dial divided into 60 equal parts. Later, count hours using a pointer which takes 12 hours to revolve on a dial divided into 12 equal parts. When both these timers have been introduced, use them together to time parts of the school day in hours and minutes. After this, use a digital timer.

An explanation of the day, and its division into two 12-hour intervals, can then be made. Using midday as the starting point we can find the hours when various events take place, such as the start of afternoon school, going-home time, teatime, bedtime, etc., using an 'hours' timer. Morning, noon and afternoon can also be thought of in terms of hours of the day.

Timing Events in Minutes and in Hours and Minutes (1, 2 L2; 3, 8 L3)

1. This activity is for pairs of children. Use a clock which has the hour hand removed. (A visit to the watch repairer may be necessary.) Stick over the dial a gummed paper annulus in order to hide previous divisions and numbers. Make a mark at the top of

the circle to indicate the starting position of the pointer. Put the pointer on the starting line, start the clock, and at the same instant start a stopwatch, or seconds timer, whose hand revolves once in a minute. Every time a minute passes make a mark on the paper dial at the tip of the pointer to record its position. After 5 minutes or so, quickly hand over to another pair who will keep marking the position of the pointer every minute. Repeat this until the pointer has returned to its starting position.

The teacher can then assemble the pairs of children. She would talk about the divisions, which represent minutes, on the timer, and number them in fives, starting at the initial mark (Fig. 4.34). Thus, the dial would be numbered 5, 10, 15, 20, etc., up to 60. Print **minutes** on the face of the timer. The teacher could talk about the time for one revolution of the pointer, or 60 minutes, being called one hour. How many minutes in a quarter hour? a half hour? and in three-quarters of an hour?

Fig. 4.34

Arrange for individual children to use this timer to find the duration of morning playtime, afternoon playtime, a school broadcast, etc.

Later, pairs of children could time events which take longer than one hour, e.g. the interval between the start of school and the beginning of dinnertime, or the start of afternoon school and the beginning of playtime, the end of playtime and going-home time, or the start of afternoon school and going-home time. (For each turn of the pointer, an hour, collect a cube. The number of turns is not likely to be forgotten or confused.)

2. Discuss with a group of children how to read, and use, a one-hour timer or 'pinger'. Such an instrument is sometimes found in the kitchen and is used to time things when cooking. This timer has numbers on it up to 60. Turn the pointer of the pinger to the 10 mark, and start a minute timer, at the same instant. What happens to the pointer of the pinger? The pointer goes from 10 down to zero, then the pinger stops. How many minutes were recorded by the minute timer whilst the pinger did this? It recorded 10 minutes, therefore, divisions on the pinger represent minutes. Use a pinger to time events. Suppose, at the start we put the pointer at 20, and at the end the pointer is on the 6th division. How long did the activity take? This involves finding the difference between 20 and 6, which could be done by complementary addition. (6 and 4 is 10, and another 10 is 20. 6 and 14 is 20, so the activity took 14 minutes. This answer can easily be checked by counting the divisions on the pinger from 20 down to 6, or from 6 up to 20.)

Let pairs of children use the one-hour timer to find the duration of morning playtime, afternoon playtime, a school broadcast, etc. (Compile a work card.)

3. The teacher could talk to the group of children who are to be given the next activity,

as early in the school day as possible, so that the clocks used could be referred to over a long period during the day. For one of the clocks use an ordinary cheap alarm clock with the minute hand removed. (This is quite easily removed using a small pair of pliers and a small screwdriver.) Stick over the dial a gummed paper annulus, divided into 12 equal intervals, in order to hide the previous markings and numbers. Use also the 'minutes' timer mentioned earlier which has a pointer which takes 1 hour to revolve. Start this timer, and the clock, at the same moment, and after 1 hour notice that the hand of the clock is opposite the first division on its face. In another hour it is opposite the second division, and in another hour it is opposite the third division. The divisions on the clock face, therefore, represent hours. Number the divisions 1, 2, 3, 4, etc. (Fig. 4.35). How long will it take for the hand to revolve once? Twelve hours—because there are 12 divisions in the circle. Print **hours** on the face of the timer.

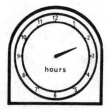

Fig. 4.35

    Children could use this timer individually, or in groups, to find the approximate length, in hours, of morning school and afternoon school, and the total time spent at school each day. (Use halves and quarters to approximate fractions of an hour.)
4. Time events in hours and minutes, using both an 'hours' timer and a 'minutes' timer. Start both timers together and read both instruments when the event has ended. If the pointer on the 'hours' timer is between 1 and 2 it indicates that more than 1 hour has passed. How much more can be found by reading the 'minutes' timer. If the pointer is on the 38 mark, the total time for the event is 1 hour and 38 minutes. Use these timers to find the length of the dinner break, morning school, and afternoon school, the time between the end of morning break and the start of afternoon break, and between the end of assembly and the start of afternoon school.
5. Time those intervals mentioned above using a digital timer which counts hours and minutes. If seconds are also recorded express times to the nearest minute.

The Day Divided into Hours: Finding Hours of the Day for Various Events (1, 2, 8 L3)

When talking to the children engaged in the next activity the teacher could talk about the hand of the 'hours' timer revolving twice a day. That is, daytime and night pass by while the hand makes two revolutions and this takes 24 hours.
    We partition a day into hours so that we can describe when things are going to happen, or did happen, and we number the hours in the period from midnight until noon, or midday, from 1 to 12. The hours after noon and until midnight are also numbered from 1 to 12.

We will use the middle of the day, *midday*, when the sun is highest in the sky as a starting point to count the hours. (Examine the lengths and directions of shadows cast by a stick during the day. The middle of the day is when the shadow is shortest.)

Using an 'hours' timer the children, in turn, could investigate as follows. Start an 'hours' timer at the end of morning school, which is about the middle of the day, or midday (Fig. 4.36). When do we start school again? The timer records about $1\frac{1}{4}$ hours. When is afternoon playtime? When does school end?

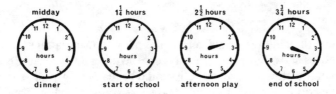

Fig. 4.36

Let the child take the 'hours' timer home and take note of the position of the pointer at teatime and at bedtime. On each occasion he or she would record the position of the pointer on a numbered timer card (Fig. 4.37). The child should also record the reading of the pointer when he or she wakes up.

Fig. 4.37

When waking in the morning the hand could be on the 8 (Fig. 4.38). During the night the hand has completed one turn, and moved 8 divisions on the next turn. One turn, or 12 hours after midday, takes us to *midnight* (Fig. 4.37). We then start to number the hours up to 12 again for the next revolution. The child brings the 'hours' timer to school that morning (carefully so that it will not stop), and records the hours for the start of school, morning playtime and dinnertime (Fig. 4.38). The pointer, therefore, revolves twice during the period from noon one day to noon the following day, and this takes 24 hours.

Fig. 4.38

A wall chart could be built up and displayed to show the hour of the day when various events occur (Fig. 4.39).

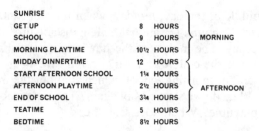

SUNRISE		
GET UP	8 HOURS	
SCHOOL	9 HOURS	MORNING
MORNING PLAYTIME	10½ HOURS	
MIDDAY DINNERTIME	12 HOURS	
START AFTERNOON SCHOOL	1¼ HOURS	
AFTERNOON PLAYTIME	2½ HOURS	AFTERNOON
END OF SCHOOL	3¾ HOURS	
TEATIME	5 HOURS	
BEDTIME	8½ HOURS	

Fig. 4.39

Following this the children could repeat the activity using a digital timer, instead, which counts hours and minutes. At midday zero the timer and start it. Record the times taken for each of the previous events. A list could be made (Fig. 4.39) to show the times of day when they occur. These times could now be expressed in hours and minutes. For example, get up could be 7.55; start of school 9.02; morning playtime 10.35, etc.

A group of children could find, using the 'hours' and 'minutes' timers or a digital timer, how much daylight there is in a December day by timing the period from sunrise to sunset. Sunrise and sunset times for a particular day of each month could be obtained from diaries or newspapers, and the number of hours of daylight also found by turning the hands of a clock from sunrise to sunset times and counting revolutions. The variation in the amount of daylight over the year could be shown by displaying the number of hours of daylight, for example, on the 15th day of each month, on a block graph. The amount varies from about 8 hours per day in December to as much as about 16 hours per day in June. In winter months the sun rises late and sets early, whilst in summer months the sun rises early and sets late. We talk about the 'days' getting longer and shorter when we wish to say that the hours of daylight are getting more or less, for a day is always 24 hours long. Encourage the children to observe sunrise and sunset times whenever the opportunity presents itself, so that the times for these events as predicted in diaries, etc., can be checked, roughly.

4.10 TIMING EVENTS WITH A CLOCK: READING THE TIME OF DAY

General Remarks

We can next introduce a clock, with two pointers, and show that the longer pointer records minutes, and the shorter pointer records hours, using an 'hours' timer and a 'minutes' timer. Further events can then be timed using a clock because both hours and minutes are recorded on the same instrument.

Following this a clock can be used to record the time of day, and the children taught to 'read a clock' and notice when events take place. Daily events can then be thought of, and ordered, in terms of hours of the clock.

Timing Events Using a Clock (2 L2; 8 L3)

Use a 'minutes' timer, 'hours' timer and an ordinary clock. Put their pointers on the starting marks, initially, that is, on the 60 for the minutes timer, and on the 12 for the hours timer and the clock (Fig. 4.40). When school commences, or immediately after assembly, start the timers and the clock, at the same instant, and then observe the pointers. The teacher could refer to the clock, roughly at hourly intervals, and talk with the children about the movements of the pointers.

Fig. 4.40

On the following day further discussion could take place. We have 2 pointers on the clock. What did the longer hand do? It kept in step with the pointer on the 'minutes' timer. The hand of this timer takes 1 hour to turn once so the longer hand of the clock takes 1 hour to turn once.

What happened to the shorter hand of the clock when the longer hand made its first turn? It moved to the 1. What happened to the shorter hand when the longer hand revolved once more? It moved to the 2. What was its position after another turn, and so on? What does the smaller hand of the clock do? It counts the number of times the longer hand has turned. How long does the longer hand take to revolve once? (60 minutes or 1 hour.) So the shorter hand of the clock records hours, and it takes 1 hour to pass from one number to the next number.

If we see the shorter hand of a clock is between the 4 and the 5, how many times has the longer hand revolved? It has made 4 complete turns, and part of another, which represents a time of more than 4 hours but less than 5 hours. If the longer hand has revolved between 5 and 6 times, where would the shorter hand be pointing? Discuss questions like these.

Also, talk about the movement of the smaller hand of the clock and the pointer on the 'hours' timer. We noticed that they also kept in step, which further substantiates that the shorter hand on the clock records hours.

The smaller divisions around the edges of the clock face represent minutes. How many minutes have passed if the longer hand moves from the 12 to the 1? from the 1 to the 2? from the 2 to the 3? etc. How many minutes if the hand moves from the 12 to the 2? from the 12 to the 3? from the 12 to the 4? etc.

Start the timers and the clock, together, on other occasions, after first putting their pointers on the starting positions. At various intervals read the times recorded by the instruments, and compare their results (Fig. 4.41). For example, the 'hours' timer reads 1 hour and a bit, and the 'minutes' timer reads 23 minutes. These timers indicate that 1 hour and 23 minutes have passed since they were started. Now look at the clock. Where is the shorter hand, or the hour hand? (Between the 1 and the 2.) Where is the longer hand, or the minute hand? (23 divisions from the start. This answer is obtained by counting the divisions carefully.) So the clock records 1 hour and 23 minutes.

Fig. 4.41

A clock, therefore, could be used to time events instead of an 'hours' timer and a 'minutes' timer together. We must remember, however, which hand of the clock records minutes and which one records hours.

Individuals, or pairs of children, could now use a clock, and both the timers, to find the durations of the following periods. Does the time read from the clock agree with the time recorded by the separate instruments?

1. start of school to the beginning of play
2. end of play to the beginning of dinnertime
3. beginning of dinnertime to the end of dinnertime
4. start of afternoon school to the beginning of playtime
5. beginning of afternoon play to going-home time
6. start of morning school to going-home time
7. start of afternoon school to going-home time

Reading the Time of Day from a Clock (2 L2; 3, 8 L3; 3, 8 L4)

We are now ready to use a clock to tell the time of day. A clock is a very complicated instrument which does the work of two instruments, and hours and minutes should be recorded separately, initially, so that they can each be understood.

For young children the natural divisions of a day into getting up time, dinnertime, bedtime, etc. are readily understood. Ideas of morning, noon, afternoon, evening and night can be gained by observing the sun's position in the sky, but they are probably more readily appreciated through the activities which take place during these periods, together with the language used to describe these happenings and when they take place. Partitioning the day into hours is an adult concept which enables happenings to be fixed within a frame of reference.

Telling the time uses the idea that the passage of time can be recorded by counting, and this might be better appreciated with a one-handed timer. Hours and minutes are also used at a stage when children have little, or no, appreciation of them. Also, on a clock, when the shorter hand points to the 1 we read it as one, but when the longer hand points to the 1 we read it as five, and this is very confusing, A knowledge of number symbols and notation up to 12, and numbers up to sixty is also essential. Some explanation of the numbering of the hours of the day is also necessary.

Children can be taught to tell the time in a mechanical fashion but an appreciation of the instrument and what the process really means takes some years to develop. We suggest that infant children should be given those experiences which will prepare the ground for the clock, and that we delay 'telling the time' until we have done this.

In teaching children to read a clock we could proceed as follows:

1. Read *hours* only.

    When talking with a group of children the teacher could use, if available, a clock with geared hands. (See Appendix on Equipment.) Put both hands on the initial mark (the 12) and then turn the minute hand around twice. Where are the hands now? The large hand is in the upright position and the small hand on the 2. This records 2 hours after midday or midnight because on a proper clock the large hand takes 1 hour to revolve, and the starting point is midday or midnight. We read this as two o'clock, and write it briefly as 2 o'clock.

    Turn the large hand around 3, 4, 7 and 8 times to illustrate three o'clock, four o'clock, seven o'clock, and eight o'clock, drawing particular attention to the positions of the hands.

    Use a rubber-stamp clock face, and on printed dials the children draw in the hands to show 1 o'clock, 5 o'clock, 9 o'clock, 12 o'clock, etc. Show the children printed dials with hands drawn in various 'o'clock' positions, and ask the children to read and record these times. Let the children use the geared model clock to show 5 o'clock, 10 o'clock, etc.

2. Talk to those children ready to proceed further about the *half hour*.

    Use a model clock, with geared hands. Put the hands in the midday or midnight position, turn the larger hand slowly around $3\frac{1}{2}$ times, and watch the smaller hand record the hours. It moves halfway between the 3 and 4. Explain that $3\frac{1}{2}$ turns, or $3\frac{1}{2}$ hours after midday or midnight, is called half past three.

    Now turn the large hand around $4\frac{1}{2}$, $6\frac{1}{2}$ and $10\frac{1}{2}$ times, and explain that the clock reads half past four, half past six and half past ten. In each case the minute hand registers half a turn whilst the hour hand lies between two numbers, the smaller of which shows the number of turns already made by the minute hand.

    Now give the following activities to individual children. Use printed clock faces with various 'half past' times shown and ask the child to read and record these times, e.g. half past five. Use cards on which half past times are written and ask the child to put the hands of a model clock at these times, or draw the hands to show these times on printed clock faces.

    Introduce the idea that half past two is called two-thirty, and half past four is called four-thirty, etc. Talk about this with the children doing these activities.

3. Talk with those children ready to proceed further, about *quarter past* using the model clock with geared hands. Turn the minute hand around one and a quarter, two and a quarter, three and a quarter times, etc., drawing attention to the positions of the hands each time. Explain that we read the time as quarter past one, quarter past two, etc.

    Set individual work. Draw 'quarter past' times on printed clock faces and ask the child to write down the times shown, e.g. quarter past four. Write various 'quarter past' times on cards and ask the child to draw in the hands showing these times on printed clock faces, or put the hands of a model clock at these times.

    When talking with the children doing the *quarter past* activities, introduce the idea that a quarter past two could also be referred to as two-fifteen, etc. Discuss this.

4. Talk to those children who are ready to proceed further about *three-quarter* turns.

Again use the model clock and turn the minute hand around one and three-quarter times, three and three-quarter times, etc., noting the positions of the hands each time. Talk about the fact that one and three-quarter turns is only a quarter turn less than two turns, and instead of saying three-quarters past one, we say a quarter before two, or a quarter to two.

Set individual work involving '*quarter to*' the hour. Show times drawn on clock faces and ask children to write these times down, e.g. quarter to four. Write times on cards and ask children to show these times on a model clock, or draw hands showing these times on printed clock faces. With these children introduce the idea that these times could be spoken of, and written as, the hour and forty-five minutes, e.g. two forty-five, or 2.45, means two and three-quarter hours after midday or midnight, and is the same as a quarter to three.

5. Use printed clock faces and ask each child or group of children to draw the hands on clock faces to show the times when they have breakfast, start for school, have dinner, start afternoon school, finish afternoon school, have tea and go to bed. Talk about the results of this exercise with the child or group.

6. Talk with those children ready to proceed further about the reading of times from the model clock with geared hands, when the minute hand travels through twelfths of a revolution. There are 12 large intervals on a clock face so the minute hand takes 5 minutes to sweep through each division because 1 turn takes 60 minutes. Explain the sequence five past, ten past, fifteen past, twenty past, twenty-five past, thirty past, thirty-five past, forty past, forty-five past, fifty past and fifty-five past, and initially use these descriptions. If the minute hand makes 3 turns, and 4 parts of a turn, after midday or midnight the clock reads twenty past three. Instead of fifteen minutes past two we say quarter past two, and instead of thirty minutes past three we say half past three. Instead of saying thirty-five minutes past we say twenty-five minutes to, and instead of forty minutes past we say twenty to, etc. Talk about these changes.

Now set individual work. (Compile work cards.) Draw the hands on a printed clock face to show five past six, five to eight, ten past seven, ten to eight, etc. Also show times drawn on clock faces and ask the children to write down these times. Draw hands on clock faces showing these times: 7.10, 4.20, 3.35, etc.

7. The teacher could next deal with reading a clock to the nearest minute. Practice exercises can be provided similar to those described earlier.

8. Introduce a digital clock which shows the time of day (not one with a 24-hour display). Ask the children to describe times from the display in words, e.g. 11.22 is 22 minutes past 11 o'clock, and 9.42 is 42 minutes past 9 o'clock. Being able to describe 8.38 as 22 minutes to 9 o'clock involves calculation such as $38 + ? = 60$ or $60 - ? = 38$ so for many children 38 minutes past 8 o'clock is quite acceptable. When using a two-handed (analogue) clock the calculation needed to convert a time such as 2.36 into 24 minutes to 3 o'clock is easier because the clock face is often used to assist the thinking involved. Analogue clock users may probably offer 20 minutes to 10 o'clock more readily for 9.40 than digital clock users.

9. After this the children can proceed to simple questions involving addition and subtraction, using a model clock with geared hands, and turning the hands forwards or backwards from an initial position. It is twenty past six. What time will it be five minutes later? ten minutes later? etc. What time was it five minutes earlier? ten

minutes earlier? etc. At first, set questions in which the hour does not change. Later we can set more difficult questions, e.g. it is ten to eleven. What time will it be in five minutes' time? ten minutes' time? fifteen minutes' time? twenty minutes' time? It is now a quarter to three. What time will it be in half an hour? It is now quarter past two. What time was it half an hour ago?

10. We can also work out lengths of time using a model clock by turning the hands from an initial position to a final position, and counting the minutes between. At what time do we go out to play? When does play end? How long was playtime?

At what time did we start mathematics and when did we finish? How long did we spend doing mathematics?

Initially, only involve differences in time up to half an hour, then up to an hour and then more than one hour, e.g. at what time do we start school and when do we stop for playtime? How long is this interval?

We could also use the *Radio Times* or *TV Times* and work out how long some of the programmes last, e.g. 'Blue Peter' starts at 5.05 and finishes at 5.35. When is 5.05? When is 5.35? How long is the programme?

4.11 RECORDING TIMES OF THE DAY: A.M./P.M. AND 24-HOUR-CLOCK NOTATION (2 L2; 3, 8 L3; 3, 8 L4)

In everyday conversation we need to use words such as morning, afternoon and evening to describe when something took place or will take place. We say 'I will meet you tomorrow evening at half past eight', 'Did you see the programme on TV yesterday evening at eight o'clock?' 'The train leaves at ten-thirty tonight'.

When we record times of the day we also need to make it clear whether the event happened during the first 12 hours, between midnight and midday, or during the second 12 hours between midday and midnight. This is necessary when timetables for buses and trains or times of radio and TV programmes are being printed. At present both the a.m./p.m. notation and 24-hour-clock systems are in use and children need to know about them, but the a.m./p.m. notation is gradually being used less and being replaced by the 24-hour-clock system.

Talk with the children about the following:

1. To record that an event took place between midnight and midday, during early morning, morning or before dinner, we write **a.m.** after its time of occurrence. We write **p.m.** after it if it took place between midday and midnight, during the afternoon, evening or late at night. **A.m.** and **p.m.** are abbreviations for the Latin *ante meridiem* and *post meridiem*, which mean before noon and after noon.

What happens at 10.30 a.m.? We go out to play. What happens at 3.45 p.m.? We go home from school. How do I write eleven o'clock in the morning? two o'clock in the afternoon? half past six in the evening? twenty past ten at night? etc. Ask similar questions and then set these exercises.

Write down quickly, eleven o'clock in the morning, five o'clock in the afternoon, quarter past eight in the morning, twenty past six in the afternoon, half past seven in the evening, etc.

Write times on the blackboard, or on a work card, and ask children to describe them in words, e.g. 6.00 p.m., 7.30 p.m., 8.20 a.m., 1.40 a.m., etc.

Ask about journeys, e.g. a train leaves X at 8.00 a.m. and arrives at Y at 10.30 a.m. How long did the journey take? Proceed to questions such as—a train leaves X at 11.00 a.m. and arrives at Y at 3.00 p.m. How long did the journey take? (The hands of a clock could be turned from one time to the other to help with the working.)

2. A more modern way of describing times is to number hourly intervals of the day from 1 to 24 using midnight as the starting point. All times are written using four digits—the first two digits record hours and the last two record minutes. Thus 12.30 hrs means 12 hours and 30 minutes after midnight. This would bring us to 30 minutes after midday, or 12.30 p.m. Similarly 16.45 hrs means 16 hours and 45 minutes after midnight, or 4 hours and 45 minutes after midday, which is 4.45 p.m.. Midday is written as 12.00 hrs, while 1.00 p.m., 2.00 p.m., 3.00 p.m. and 4.00 p.m. are written as 13.00 hrs, 14.00 hrs, 15.00 hrs and 16.00 hrs, and so on. Three minutes past two in the afternoon is written as 2.03 p.m. or 14.03 hrs. Notice that minutes are written using two digits and if necessary a 0 is put before the minutes number to fill a space. In a similar way 1.00 a.m., 2.00 a.m., 3.00 a.m. and 4.00 a.m. are written as 01.00 hrs, 02.00 hrs, 03.00 hrs and 04.00 hrs. In this case a 0 is put before the hour number to fill a space.

Children need plenty of oral and written work on the changing of a.m./p.m. times to 24-hour-clock times because railway, bus and air timetables, and digital watches, use this notation. A clock face with numbers from 0 to 24 written around it, from 0 to 12 for the first turn and from 12 to 24 for the second, could be used to help children convert times. Thus, 1 o'clock could be seen as both 1 hr and 13 hrs after midnight.

Simple questions, of the types shown, could be set:

1. Write 3.00 p.m., 5.00 p.m., 12.00 p.m., 6.00 p.m., 4.00 a.m., 8.00 a.m. in 24-hour-clock notation.
2. Write 4.32 p.m., 6.15 p.m., 9.36 p.m., 9.45 a.m., 10.15 a.m., 7.05 p.m. and 7.50 a.m. in 24-hour-clock notation.
3. Write these times another way: 08.30 hrs, 10.15 hrs, 13.45 hrs, 16.00 hrs, 15.30 hrs, 18.04 hrs and 09.05 hrs.
4. A train leaves X at 12.40 hrs and arrives at Y at 13.50 hrs. How long does the journey take?
5. A train leaves X at 09.30 hrs and arrives at Y at 11.05 hrs. How long does the journey take?

The calendar and the seasons

4.12 PARTS OF THE DAY AND THE ORDERING OF DAILY EVENTS (8 L1; 8 L2)

We must not only compare the duration of events which happen in a short period of time, but prepare the ground for an appreciation of recurring events which could act as markers to describe the duration of activities which take longer times. Our lives are run on a daily basis, and this interval being rather long is divided into smaller periods. The concept of a day, and its subdivisions, need particular attention and these can be associated with what we do in a day. The teacher could talk to the children about things they do, see and feel regularly, and the order in which they occur, because these experiences are used to mark the passage of time, and describe when future events will take place.

1. When it is dark we go to bed to sleep and we get up when it is light in order to do work, or go to school. When dark it is nighttime and when light it is daytime. We experience light, dark, light, dark, etc., and we go to school, sleep, go to school, sleep, etc., when it is daytime, nighttime, daytime, nighttime, etc.
2. The passage of time is also marked by periods for eating. After we get up we have breakfast. In the middle of daytime we have dinner. Some time later we have tea, and just before we go to bed we have supper. Daytime can be thought of as the period during which we have breakfast, dinner, tea and supper, in this order. (*Note*: If the children are not accustomed to this sequence of meals, the teacher should use the one familiar to them whenever meal times are mentioned.)
3. The sun provides light. We can see the sun when the clouds are not hiding it. Its light is bright and we feel its warmth. When cloudy we cannot see the sun but light and warmth, although not very strong, still manage to pass through the clouds. (A torch and pieces of paper of different thicknesses will help this discussion.)

   The sun, after it rises, gets higher in the sky, then descends and finally sets. (Encourage the children to observe sunrise and sunset, and the movement of the sun across the sky, at convenient times. Sunrise occurs about schooltime, and sunset about teatime, during winter months.) The period of sunlight, or daylight, is called daytime; and we divide it into morning, noon and afternoon. During the morning the sun gets higher in the sky. At midday, or noon, it is at its highest point, and during the afternoon the sun gets lower. The period just before sunset we call evening. Thus, daytime is the sequence morning, noon, afternoon and evening, and within these periods we have breakfast, dinner and tea respectively.

   A day is a period of light followed by a period of darkness, and is the sequence morning, noon, afternoon, evening and night. A wall chart, with events arranged in order around a circle, could be used to display this information (Fig. 4.42). Coloured pictures which help the illustration could be cut from magazines and stuck on the chart, e.g. pictures of sunrise, sunset, children at school, a family at breakfast, a boy or girl asleep in bed, etc.

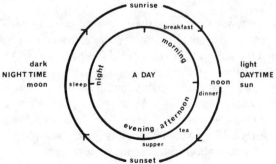

Fig. 4.42

4. Children could be helped to put in order various daily happenings and to say in which part of the day an event occurs or is going to occur. A set of picture cards showing various daily events could be made and the exercise, to put these in order, given to individual children. The order chosen could be discussed after the arrangement is made.

   A list of daily activities could also be displayed on a chart and illustrated with coloured pictures cut from magazines. Daily happenings, and when they occur, could be the subject of discussion in 'talking time', or included by the children in their 'news'. Daily events would often be included in the stories read or told in 'story time'; and further ideas gained from books in the 'book corner' through reading or looking at pictures, and from reading and dramatizing poems. (*'Ourselves'*)

   (a) What we do in the morning:
       Get up—eat breakfast—come to school—do our writing, diary, number work and reading.
   (b) What we do at midday or noon:
       Have dinner. This is dinnertime.
   (c) What we do in the afternoon:
       Start school again—do painting, modelling. Have our story—go home—eat tea.
   (d) What we do in the evening:
       Go out to play. Watch children's television programmes. Have supper—go to bed.
   (e) What we do at night:
       Go to bed. Sleep.

5. After the sun sets it becomes dark and if it is not cloudy we see the moon. It can look like a large white-yellow disc, or crescent shape. The moon 'shines' at night so that nighttime is not completely dark, particularly at full moons. Just before a new moon nighttime is very dark. Light from the moon is called moonlight. (Light from the sun is called sunlight, and when we receive it we say it is daylight.) During winter months we sometimes see the moon when we are on the way to school and again about teatime. Encourage the children to look at the moon and draw its shape. These important observations will be used later when talking about a month. We also see the stars when it is night.

4.13 SEASONAL EVENTS (8 Levels 1–4)

Encourage the children to take notice of their surroundings, in particular the weather, and plants, animals and birds. Observations of the environment is started with lower infants and continued throughout the infant and junior schools. At first, observations are sketchy, but these initial experiences are added to in successive years, so giving an appreciation of seasonal activities. Probably, children living in the country will be able to notice many more seasonal changes than town children. Flowers, berries and nuts can be collected, and birds, animals and trees observed. As a result of these observations, talk about the sort of things which happen in spring, summer, autumn and winter.

   The ideas children acquire about the seasons depend very much on where they live and what their interests are. Work concerning the seasons could take place through the following activities:

1. Collect nuts, berries, fruits, leaves and flowers, and display them on the nature table. Record the seasons when the items are generally seen.
2. In 'talking time', discuss the weather for each season, and the plants, flowers, etc., that are seen. Talk also about what the children do after school, the games that are played, etc.
3. Talk about seasonal festivals such as Christmas and Easter; also the harvest festival, and when the school holidays occur.
4. Look at, and talk about, various pictures which show the countryside at different times of the year.
5. Collect coloured pictures from magazines, or old calendars, which show seasonal activities and country scenes at various times of the year.
6. Make collages to show spring, summer, autumn and winter.
7. Read poems about the seasons, months of the year, birds, flowers, etc.
8. Many stories read to the children in 'story time' include information about the seasons, so would some of the books found in the 'book corner'. Impressions could be similar to those listed below:

   (a) In winter:
   Christmas holidays—Christmas presents—cold weather—rainy—snow—ice—frost—warm clothes—wear gloves and a scarf—cloudy skies—daylight is poor so we use electric lights a lot—dark in the mornings when we go to school—dark about teatime—cannot go out to play after tea—some trees have no leaves—no flowers in the hedgerows—few vegetables in the garden.

   (b) In spring:
   Easter holiday—Easter eggs—weather is a little warmer—not so cloudy—showery and windy—trees are in bud and leaves start to grow—hazel catkins, willow catkins, daffodils, snowdrops, crocuses, primroses—frog's spawn—birds make nests—plant seeds in the garden.

   (c) In summer:
   Haymaking time—summer holiday—go on holiday—go to the seaside—weather is hot and sunny—wear thinner clothes—short-sleeved shirts—some garden vegetables are ready to eat, such as radishes, lettuce, carrots and potatoes—we eat salads—long evenings—go out to play after tea—play cricket—lots of flowers in the hedgerows—pick bilberries and blackberries—strawberries and plums—harvest time.

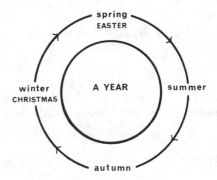

Fig. 4.43

(d) In autumn:
Weather gets colder—cloudy skies—rainy and windy—wear warmer clothes—trees lose their leaves—flowers die—collect hazel nuts, conkers, chestnuts and acorns—rose hips.

The pattern of events just mentioned is then repeated. We call this period a year. Thus, a year is the sequence spring, summer, autumn and winter (Fig. 4.43).

4.14 DAYS OF THE WEEK (8 L2; 8 L3)

When some notion of a day has been gained we can explain that days are given special names—Monday, Tuesday, Wednesday, Thursday, Friday, Saturday and Sunday. These days make a week, and when they have passed we use these names again to describe the days of the next week, and so on. Display these names on a wall chart, putting them in order around a circle (Fig. 4.44). How many days make a week?

Fig. 4.44

The teacher could talk to the children about what they do on the various days of the week, and the activities for a typical week listed on a chart and displayed. The children could also be encouraged to write the day name at the beginning of each work assignment.

4.15 THE CALENDAR AND THE SEASONS

General Remarks

Phases of the moon could be studied to build the idea of a month as about 30 days. Months can be named and related to the seasons in order to give some idea of a year.

Idea of a Month (2 L2; 8 L3)

The teacher would encourage the children to observe the moon all through the year, but the period from October to February is particularly suitable for observation, when the sky is clear, because the moon can be seen when coming to school, soon after school or early in the school day. Try to arrange for the class to see the moon each day from school, but when this is not possible ask the children to look at the moon when coming to or going from school, or when at home. (Ask for some assistance from home.)

Fig. 4.45

Ask each child to look at the moon, draw its shape every two or three days, and stick the shapes, in order, on a paper strip. (Draw the moon shapes obtained on circles of the same size, and cut off the pieces not required, before mounting the shapes on the strip (Fig. 4.45)). After a week or so ask the children what they notice about the shape of the moon? After about five weeks look at the moon shapes mounted on the strip and talk about, and identify, a new moon, a full moon and an old moon. Following this, ask the class to find the number of days between new moons. The teacher could select a suitable new moon as the starting point by consulting a diary. Ask the children, starting on the day of the new moon, to observe and record the passing of the days until the next new moon. Record the days by making a tally with beads on a string or ticks in a row of squares (Fig. 4.46). How many days between new moons? Repeat this until the next new moon, and so on, and let the children find that the moon is new at regular intervals of 29 or 30 days. This period is called a month.

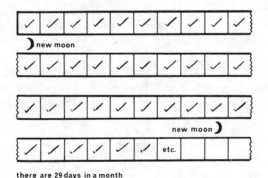

Fig. 4.46

The Calendar and the Seasons (2,8 L3; 8 L4)

Verify, by observation, that after 12 or 13 moons certain natural events happen again, e.g. trees come into leaf, crocuses bloom, conkers are ready, frogs spawn, etc. This period is called a year. Special names, the names of seasons, are given to various parts of the year to describe main features, e.g. spring—the season of growth.

The seasons are determined by the sun. Our calendar is based on the sun, and the year is divided into twelve calendar months. These are slightly different from moons because calendar months last generally 30 or 31 days.

The sun's behaviour can be judged by finding, and comparing the amounts of daylight each day. A solar year is roughly the number of days between successive 'longest' days, or 'shortest' days, and this period is longer than twelve moons but shorter than thirteen moons.

Further Notes

A solar year is the interval of time between two successive spring equinoxes, which is about 365 days 5 hours and 49 minutes, or $365\frac{1}{4}$ days. (This is generally found by measuring the interval between equinoxes over a long period and calculating the average time between successive ones.) A yearly calendar could not include a fraction of a day but we get over this difficulty by having a calendar based on a four-year period of 365, 365, 365 and 366 days. The interval has the same number of days as four solar years. A year containing 366 days is called a leap year.

The names of the months, and the Julian calendar, could be included in discussions about the Romans, because our present calendar is a modification of the Julian calendar. Traces of the early Roman ten-month year are seen in the names September, October, November and December.

The names of the days could also be talked about. Later Romans named them after heavenly bodies, i.e. Saturn, Sun, Moon, Mars, Mercury, Jupiter and Venus. Why? Some of these days were renamed in Britain after the Anglo-Saxon and Norse invasions to cater for their gods, i.e. Tiw's day, Woden's day, Thor's day and Friia's day.

Our calendar is difficult to understand, and much discussion of it is needed, particularly with upper junior and secondary children. Calendar reform could also be considered.

The months are named January, February, March, April, May, June, July, August, September, October, November and December. The teacher could display these names on a wall chart by putting them in order around a circle (Fig. 4.47). Stick

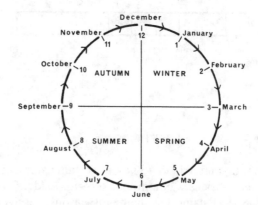

Fig. 4.47

coloured pictures on the chart to illustrate monthly scenes, and also indicate roughly the periods of the seasons.

Also deal with the number of days in the months. September, April, June and November have 30 days, and the remainder, except February, have 31 days. February has 28 days generally and 29 days in a leap year.

A chart could be fixed to the wall to record children's birthdays, commencing dates for the seasons and important days such as Good Friday, Easter Sunday and Christmas Day (Fig. 4.48). (Spring begins on March 21, Summer on June 21, Autumn on September 23 and Winter on December 22.) Label the beginning of the strip January 1, and the end December 31, and write the cumulative total of the days in each region, as well as the date. We then find that 365 or 366 days make a year.

1	2	3	4	5	6		362	363	364	365
NEW YEARS DAY		Mary Smith				↔		George Jones		
1	2	3	4	5	6		28	29	30	31
		JANUARY						DECEMBER		

Fig. 4.48

A year can be thought of as 365 days, or the time from one birthday to the next, or from one Christmas Day to the next, etc. If the wall chart is examined the duration of the seasons will be seen.

Spring includes the end of March, all April and May, and the beginning of June.
Summer includes the end of June, all July and August, and the beginning of September.
Autumn includes the end of September, all October and November, and the beginning of December.
Winter includes the end of December, all January and February, and the beginning of March.

Arrange the following investigation activities for individuals, or small groups of children:

1. The children could study in greater detail the plants, animals, trees and birds in their surroundings, and record the dates when various things were seen.
2. Details of the weather could also be kept so that seasonal changes could be detected.
   Midday temperatures could be recorded daily for each month, and the results shown by block and line graphs. These graphs, or some of them, if drawn to the same scale, could be displayed side by side and temperatures compared. Was it generally warmer in June or February? or warmer in September than October? What happened to the temperature during March? What was the highest temperature recorded in March? and the lowest?
   Each day in a particular month could be described as either **dry**, **showery** or **heavy rain**, and a block graph drawn of these categories. What kind of day is most common? Were there more dry days than wet ones? The number of dry days and wet

days could be compared for different months, e.g. February and May. We could then ask whether May was drier than February.

Each day in a particular month could be classified as **very sunny**, **sunny** or **very little or no sun**, and a block graph drawn. Was March a sunny month? Did March have more very sunny days than May?

We could also classify each day as being **windy**, or **not very windy**, and investigate whether some months are generally windy, or not.

4.16 FUTURE WORK

So far we have introduced units of time, measured the duration of events with timers, and compared the duration of events and rate of doing things. We have also developed the meanings of day, month and year, and the formation of the calendar. Finally, we introduced the clock and telling the time.

Later, work in school could proceed in two directions. On the one hand, deal with speed and involve distance/time graphs. This would concern the reading of timetables, the finding of distances on maps, fares and fuel consumption. On the other hand, give further considerations to the calendar, and various methods and instruments for measuring time. Geometrical work on position, which establishes the need for grids, could lead to discussion of lines of latitude and longitude, and of time in other parts of the world.

Chapter 5

Capacity and Volume

Capacity means the amount of space inside a container. Volume refers to the amount of space taken up by an object. Capacities of vessels are expressed in liquid measure, the main unit of which is the litre (approx $1\frac{3}{4}$ pints). Volumes are described in terms of cubic capacity, units being cubic metres, cubic decimetres and cubic centimetres.

Children will be introduced to both systems because the litre and its subdivisions are used in everyday life for buying liquids, and cubic measure is used extensively in scientific and mathematical fields. The two systems can easily be connected, for the volume of a cubic decimetre is equivalent to a litre, that is, a millilitre is equivalent to a volume of 1 cubic centimetre. Also, the mass of a litre of water is 1 kilogram, that is, the mass of 1 cubic centimetre of water is 1 gram. Hence, if we buy 110 ml of liquid, of specific gravity 0.9, its volume is 110 cubic centimetres, and its mass 99 g. The example just mentioned shows the ultimate connection between measures of liquid, cubic capacity and mass, illustrating the ease of calculation required. This linkage will not be shown in the work done with infant and lower junior children but the foundation is being laid for its emergence in the future.

5.1 GENERAL SCHEME

The following stages are necessary, in the order given below:

1. Volume and capacity are more difficult to appreciate than length because they have more dimensions. These concepts are built on length so that fundamental ideas cannot be developed until certain aspects of length have been dealt with, e.g. the water rises farther up this jar so this vessel holds more, or this row of cubes is longer than that row so they take up more room, etc.

   Comparisons of lengths must come before some of the tests used to compare capacities.
2. Next should come the comparing of capacities and volumes using different tests, together with the learning of basic vocabulary, such as *larger capacity than, same volume as, holds less than*, etc. It should be remembered that vocabulary helps thinking and concept formation. Capacities are considered first because the filling of containers is familiar to most children on entering school, and elementary ideas are present already. The concept of volume is much more difficult and preparatory work should be introduced later than capacity because many tests concerning volume rely on capacity. To form ideas about volume children need plenty of experience in

immersing solids in water, noting the water level and the liquid displaced. The building of solids with bricks, and modelling with plasticine, is also essential.

   Children should realize that tests are necessary to compare capacities and volumes correctly, because visual estimates are often incorrect.

3. We measure capacities and volumes in terms of measuring units. We find how many of these units are contained in the item, and the number describes its size. We can also compare capacities using numbers.

4. In order to communicate ideas it becomes necessary to introduce standard units. Introduce liquid measure initially and measure capacities in litres, half litres, decilitres and centilitres, but not at the same time. Introduce them, one at a time, when finer measurements are required to be more accurate, or to describe the capacities of smaller containers. The millilitre is too small to be included at this stage; indeed, the centilitre is quite small enough.

   Measurement of volume in cubic measure cannot be advanced very far with infant and lower juniors because units depend on standard measures of length; also cubic decimetres are a little too large, whilst cubic centimetres are too small. A start can be made building solids with cubes, and the cubic centimetre introduced as a building unit, enabling volumes of small solids to be described. Until children can deal with numbers up to 500 or so the work cannot be further developed because most reasonably sized items have volumes of this magnitude, or beyond, in cubic centimetres.

5.2 EQUIPMENT

Requirements

A collection of tins, bottles, jars, boxes, jugs and other containers of various shapes and sizes. In particular, large and small fruit tins, large and small jam jars, cream cartons, beakers, cups, egg-cups, table spoons, Oxo cube boxes (dozen size), cornflour packets, coffee tins, Vim containers, Bisto boxes, cereal packets, salt boxes, yoghurt containers, stones, pebbles, builders' bricks, rectangular pieces of metal, pair of large metal bolts, detergent containers, etc. Often 6 or more of the same container will be needed. 2 dozen yoghurt containers, small cream tins, or plastic beakers, of the same make are useful for representing capacities of vessels.

   Fill containers with dried peas, rice, sand, wooden cubes (Stern), shells, marbles, beads and water.

   Plastic buckets and bowls, and large jars, which will hold capacities up to 5 or 6 litres.

   Plastic jugs, ungraduated, of capacity half litre and 1 litre approximately. Sets of standard liquid measures including litre, half litre, decilitre and centilitre containers.

   2 or 3 displacement cans, at least 1.5 dm in diameter by 3 dm tall. 2 or 3 boxes of Cuisenaire rods with extra cubic centimetres, if required. A good supply of Centicubes. Stern unit cubes, two or three hundred. Also other cubes, 2 cm and 3 cm, for building towers, etc.

   2 sets of mathematical shapes—one of wood—the other set being made of plastic and the containers hollow so that they can be filled, e.g. children could discover that the

capacity of a pyramid is one-third of the capacity of a prism of the same base and height. Plasticine for modelling.

Preparation

Apparatus needed must be readily at hand before the tasks are set. Mark the tins, jars, bottles, boxes, in such a way that they can easily be referred to, using colours, letters, numbers or stickers with emblems or pictures. Specific reference can be made to items, and it helps with recording, and the giving of instructions, e.g. compare the capacities of the green and red tins; the green tin holds more than the red one.

5.3 RECORDING

It is useful to have item cards with **tin**, **bottle**, **box**, **jar** on them; also cards with colours **red**, **green**, **blue**, etc.; also relationship labels **holds more than**, **holds the same as**, **holds less than**, **larger capacity than**, **same capacity as**, **smaller capacity than**, **same volume as**, **larger volume than**, **smaller volume than**, **taller**, **narrower**, **shorter**, **wider**, etc. At first answers could be accepted orally by the teacher. Later, the recording could consist of putting two containers on the table with a relationship label between. After this item cards and a relationship label could be used; and finally, recording could be the copying of sentences into a book, or the writing of labels.

Initially, use the labels **holds more than**, **holds less than** and **holds the same as**, and orally use the descriptions 'same capacity as', 'larger capacity than', and 'smaller capacity than'. Later, a **holds** label and a **capacity** label could both be put near an item. Finally, a **capacity** label only would be used. Obviously the teacher must give the child a lot of assistance in selecting various labels and writing labels, and making written statements in notebooks. Recording is greatly helped by the preparation and use of answer sentences, into which the children write their answers, e.g. . . . **larger capacity than** . . . **smaller capacity than** . . .

5.4 INTRODUCTORY ACTIVITIES (1, 8, 10 L1)

The teacher collects boxes, tins, bottles, jars, wooden blocks, pebbles, stones and containers of different shapes and sizes. The children handle the shapes, roll them along the floor, build with them, fit them inside each other, fill them with sand and water and pour from one container to another, tear some along the seams and examine the pieces, etc. Through play children become familiar with some of the attributes of these items. The teacher has to hold regular chats with the whole class, or group, about the shapes, pointing out similarities and differences, and focusing attention on particular aspects and developing correct vocabulary. During these talks, each lasting a few minutes, children could be asked to select particular shapes, to pick up and feel items, and talk about them. Include questions and details as suggested in the next paragraph, and afterwards the children could be directed, two or three at a time, to do individual work based on some of these ideas.

From what are the items made? Find those made of glass, wood, tin, stone, plastic or cardboard. Feel and look at the surfaces of the objects. Some have flat faces, others have curved faces. In what way do they feel and look different? Discuss. Find shapes with flat faces only, or curved faces only, or flat and curved faces. We also see straight and curved edges. Feel the edges, look at them and talk about the differences. Now, examine objects and point out straight and curved edges. Look at the shapes of faces. Find oblongs, triangles, circles and squares. Find more of these shapes on other things in the classroom. Sort out containers which look alike. We have cylinders and rectangular boxes mainly. Why is this box called rectangular? Compare two boxes, bottles, tins, etc. Which is taller? wider? shorter? narrower?

The above activities, together with talking and questioning, lead to a natural introduction to capacity.

5.5 COMPARING CAPACITIES: NON-NUMERICAL (1, 8 L1; 1, 8 L2)

The following activities, asking 'Which holds more?', are presented to the class, or group, as a problem to be solved. Can the children offer solutions which use the material introduced by the teacher? By talking with them, various procedures are suggested and carried out which provide the answer to this question.

1. The teacher puts two tins the same shape and size, side by side. Which is taller? Which is wider? Look at them from different directions. Are they the same size? Will they hold the same amount of water? How can we tell? Fill one tin with water and pour it into the other. What happens? Now pour the water back into the first tin. Repeat this, pouring from one to the other carefully. What happens to the water? Does it overflow? or just fit? We say that the tins hold the same amount, or have the same capacity. We expect this really because the tins are the same height and width. Record the result by putting the tins on the table with **same height**, **same width**, **holds the same as** labels alongside.

   Repeat this experiment with two boxes, filling them with dry sand.

   During the next few days let the children, two or three at a time, experiment with other identical pairs of tins, boxes and bottles, filling them with water or sand and pouring from one to the other.

2. A few days later the teacher would again talk with the class, or group. She requires two tins, not necessarily the same shape, such that one can be put inside the other. Ask which is the taller? the wider? and which holds more?

   Fill one tin with water and pour it into the other, or as much as you can. What happens? Having found which holds more, pour water from the smaller into it and look into the larger tin. What do you notice? Now fill the larger and pour water into the smaller. What happens? Introduce the descriptions and labels **holds more than** and **holds less than**.

   Now put one tin inside the other. The outside tin is longer, wider and thicker so it holds more than the tin inside it. Conversely, if one tin fits inside another it must hold less because it is smaller in all directions.

   During the next few days the children, two or three at a time, and working individually, could be given pairs of boxes and tins, one of each pair being able to fit inside the other. At the beginning ask which holds more. Then pour water from one to the other, and also fit one inside the other, to check the estimate. The answer is given orally to the teacher. The child also puts the containers on the table with **holds more than** and **holds less than** labels against appropriate containers. (The teacher would help the child to select these labels.)

3. Use a glass vessel, or transparent container, and fix a gummed paper strip on the outside from top to bottom, and show two bottles, or tins, to the children. (Put a distinguishing mark on one bottle.) Which has the larger capacity? The teacher fills one of the bottles with water, pours it into the glass vessel, marks the water level on the paper strip, and then pours the water back into the bottle again. She fills the other bottle and pours its contents into the glass vessel. What happens? Where is the water level? Is it higher or lower than the level made by the first bottle? Which bottle holds more or has the larger capacity? How can we tell? Discuss. Was your estimate correct? Rub out the marks on the strip, and repeat the experiment but this time pour water from the bottles into the jar in the opposite order. Discuss again. Then, verify the result by pouring water directly from one bottle to the other (use a funnel).

   The teacher would then set individual work based on this demonstration to two or three children at a time, if sufficient apparatus is available. Use pairs of tins, boxes and plastic bottles, and pour into a transparent polythene container which is not very wide. The child estimates which has the larger capacity at the beginning and then performs the test. (Also include pairs of items having the same capacity.) The child checks his answer by pouring directly from one container to the other, or putting one inside the other should this be possible. Deal with answers as described in the previous section.

4. Use two tins, and a plastic bottle larger in capacity than both. Stick a paper strip down the side of the plastic bottle. Completely fill the bottle, pour water into one tin, and mark the level of the water left in the bottle. Now fill the bottle again and pour water from it into the other tin. Compare the level of the water in the bottle with the level in the previous case. When was more water poured out, and into which tin? So, which tin holds more? Which has the larger capacity? Verify the result using another method.

   Now set individual work to two or three children at a time, if sufficient apparatus is available. Use pairs of tins of the same capacity as well as different capacities. Up to now the children have used **holds more than** and **holds less than** labels to record results, and the teacher has used larger capacity than and smaller capacity than in conversation. A child could start to use **larger capacity than** and **smaller capacity than** labels when the teacher decides he is ready for this. Children could use both kinds of label to record results for a while and later only use 'capacity' labels. Children would also give oral answers.

5. Use two tins, or boxes, of different capacities. Ask a child which has the larger capacity. Let two children fill each to the brim with wooden cubes. (Stern cubes.) Shake the tins as you fill them so that the cubes settle into the larger spaces. The teacher then empties each tin, and arranges the cubes, touching and end to end, in two rows side by side. Which row is the longer? Which row has more cubes? Which tin holds more cubes? Which tin has the larger capacity? Check the result using another method. The teacher repeats this with another pair of containers, and uses labels to record the results.

The teacher now sets individual work to three or four children at a time based on this demonstration. Compare the capacities of two boxes, two tins, or a box and a tin, using Stern or other similar sized cubes. Check the answer by pouring sand from one to the other. Do *not* compare tins of the same capacity using this test. The cubes inside each tin could pack themselves differently so that the rows obtained are not the same length, but differ by one or two cubes. This would indicate that the capacities are different, and this result would be contradicted by the other test. These remarks also apply to the next section.

6. Talk with the class, or group, about comparing the capacities of two tins by filling them with marbles or beads. Place the marbles in rows confined between three wooden strips (Fig. 5.1). Which is the longer row of marbles? Which tin holds more marbles? Which tin has the larger capacity? Check using another method.

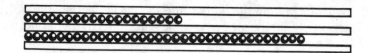

Fig. 5.1

The teacher now sets this activity to one or two children at a time, but working individually. Use pairs of tins, boxes or jars.

7. Use tins of the same size such as cream, bean or instant coffee tins, or the plastic or cardboard beakers used in coffee vending machines. Compare the capacities of two larger containers by filling them with water or sand using the smaller identical tins or beakers. Fill one of the containers and stand the empty tins (or beakers) used in filling, in a row on a squared background. (One tin per square.) If part of a tinful is needed at the end then treat it as a full tin—or ignore it—depending on the amount poured from it. Discuss this point.

   Then make a row with the tins used to fill the second container alongside the first row. Which row of tins (beakers) is the longer? Which row of tins contains more water? Which container needs more water to fill it? Which container holds more? Stand the containers on the table with **holds more than**, **holds less than** or 'capacity' labels near appropriate containers.

   The teacher could repeat this, if necessary, using another pair of containers. Then set individual work to one or two children based on this demonstration. Use sand to fill pairs of boxes, and water to fill tins and other vessels.

8. (a) Use two identical glass jars, or transparent plastic containers, and place them side by side. Are the jars the same width? Are they the same height? Pour a cupful of water into each jar and examine the columns of water. They are the same height. Repeat, using first a tin of water, and then a tin of sand. Discuss.

      Now let the children take it in turns to try this experiment throughout the day. Establish the following day with the class or group that if we pour the same amount of sand or water into containers of the same size then the columns are the same height.

   (b) The teacher talks to the class or group again. She uses two tins of different capacity and asks one of the children to find which holds more by pouring water from one to the other.

The teacher then fills each tin with water and pours it into the two jars mentioned in **a**. What happens to the water levels? Which jar has the higher water level? Which tin was emptied into this jar? This one—the one that holds more. Repeat, with another pair of containers, if necessary.

Let the children take it in turns during the day to do this activity. That is, find the tin with the larger capacity by pouring water from one to the other, then pouring the contents of both tins into identical vessels and noticing the water levels.

Establish when the group meets again that different amounts of water rise to different levels when they are poured into vessels of the same size, and the larger amount rises to a higher level. Also that equal amounts of water rise to the same level when they are poured into identical vessels.

(c) Put the two identical jars side by side on a table. Obtain two tins, or bottles. Which holds more? Say which. Now fill them with water, and pour their contents into the glass jars. Which jar contains more water? How can we tell? Which tin was poured into this jar? So, this tin has the larger capacity. Did you estimate correctly? Check, pouring water directly from one to the other.

Now put the two tins, side by side, on the table. Which holds more? Which is the taller? Which is wider? Put labels alongside the tins, **taller**, **shorter**, **narrower**, **wider**, **holds more than**, **holds less than**.

Let the children work individually throughout the next few days to find the tin or box of larger capacity using this method, given pairs of tins or boxes. (Use dry sand for boxes.) Always estimate the larger capacity before doing the test. Record the results using 'holds' or 'capacity' labels as just described.

Establish that it is not always the taller vessel that has the larger capacity. We must compare widths as well as heights in order to consider which holds more. In many cases guessing is not good enough, and we rely on one of the tests previously mentioned to provide an answer.

9. Use a set of four plastic containers of different shapes and sizes, but with the same capacity. (These can be made by pouring a tin of water into different plastic vessels, and cutting off their tops at the water level.) Ask which is the tallest. Which is widest? Which has the smallest capacity, also the largest? Check by pouring water from one to another; and water from each container into four identical transparent plastic vessels. Clarify that the same capacity does not necessarily mean the same width and height. Label the tallest, and narrowest. Also, put a **same capacity as** label near them.

Let the children, working individually, do this experiment within the next few days.

10. Talk with the class or group. Put glass and polythene jars of different shapes and sizes, side by side, on the table. Pour a tin of water into each. Look at the levels. Do the jars contain the same amount of water? The levels are not the same, but the jars all contain a tinful. Why are the levels different? Ask a child to arrange the jars in order of width, and look at the levels of the water. What do you notice? The water rises most in the narrowest jar, and least in the widest. As the jars get narrower the water rises higher. Discuss. Repeat, if necessary, putting a bottle of water in each, or two tinfuls.

Let the children work individually and do this experiment within the next few days.

11. Obtain pairs of tins, or boxes, which do not fit inside one another completely. Place a pair side by side. Ask which is taller. Which is wider? Which has the larger capacity? How can we tell? Pour water or sand from one to another, also into identical transparent containers, to answer this question.

Put the tins on the table with labels against them. Use **taller**, **shorter**, **wider**, **narrower**, **larger capacity than** and **smaller capacity than** labels.

Establish that width and height must be taken into account when comparing capacities and that our senses are still not often good enough to make accurate estimates. We must rely on a test of some kind to obtain correct answers.

Let the children, two or three at a time, and working individually, compare the capacities of tins and boxes in the manner just described. Estimate first and then do the test. Use labels to record results.

12. Individual work for three or four children at a time. Use 3 tins, 3 plastic containers or 3 boxes. Estimate which has the largest capacity and which has the smallest capacity. Ask the child to check his answers using one of the methods listed below. Each work card could include a different method for checking the estimate. (Five different work cards needed here.)

(a) Pouring water or sand from one to another.
(b) Filling each container using a transparent vessel which has a gummed strip on its outside.
(c) Pouring the contents of each into a jar which has a gummed paper strip on its outside.
(d) Pouring the contents into identical polythene vessels standing side by side.
(e) Filling each container with marbles or beads, and matching rows.

5.6 COMPARING VOLUMES: NON-NUMERICAL (1, 8 L2)

The teacher could next introduce elementary ideas about volume to the class, or group, by doing and discussing the following activities:

1. Show two towers, as described below, one built with red cubes and the other with yellow cubes. Ask each time which is taller, wider, thicker? Which tower has more wood in it? Which takes up more room? That is, which has the larger volume? How can we tell? Pull the towers apart and place the cubes, touching and end to end, in two rows, side by side. Are the rows the same length? Which row has more wooden cubes in it? Which row takes up more room? Which tower had the larger volume? Introduce orally the descriptions **same volume as**, **larger volume than** and **smaller volume than**.

Make two rectangular towers:

(a) Same width, height and thickness. Same volume.
(b) Same width and thickness, but different heights. Taller has larger volume.
(c) One taller, wider and thicker. Larger in all directions has larger volume.

(d) Same width, but one taller and narrower than the other, with different volumes.

(e) Same width, with one taller and narrower than the other, but the same volume.

These sessions with rectangular towers could cover a period of a week or so. Each day, for two or three minutes, the teacher would show two towers which differ according to one of the requirements listed. The teacher would ask the children to compare heights, widths and thicknesses, to decide which tower takes up more room, and so find the larger volume. Following this the test would be performed.

Being shown towers of various heights, widths and thicknesses should help the children realize that volumes cannot always be compared correctly at first sight. Sometimes, when one tower is clearly longer than the other in all directions, it is possible to 'see' the larger volume. In most cases, however, a comparison test which uses change of shape is needed to give a correct visual result.

The children could work in pairs, one or two pairs at a time. Each child would build a tower and compare it with the tower made by his partner according to height, width, thickness, more wood, more room, and then volume. They would then perform the test to check the comparison of volume.

2. Show two cylinders of plasticine as described below. Which piece has the larger volume? Which piece is longer? Which is thicker? Which piece has more plasticine? In each case, roll the thicker piece into a cylinder the same thickness as the other, and compare lengths, to decide this. Which piece takes up more room? Which has the larger volume? Throughout the activity use, and explain, the word volume, and the descriptions larger volume than, smaller volume than and the same volume as. (A thing has a larger volume if it takes up more room, and things have the same volume if they take up the same room.)

   Make two plasticine cylinders:

   (a) same thickness and length
   (b) same thickness but different lengths
   (c) same length but different thicknesses
   (d) one piece thicker and longer than the other
   (e) one longer and narrower than the other.

   This activity could be spread over a week or so, and each day the teacher would spend two or three minutes comparing the volumes of pairs of cylinders. A child from the group could change the thickness of the cylinder whilst the teacher controls the activity and channels the discussion along profitable lines.

   As a result of these experiences the children should realize that comparisons of volume cannot always be made correctly at first sight. A test procedure which involves a change of shape is often needed.

3. Individual work for two or three children. Compare the volumes of two or three different coloured lumps of plasticine. Check your estimate by rolling the lumps into cylinders of the same thickness, and comparing their lengths. Put cylinders on the table, larger volume on the left. Give oral answers and also place **larger volume than** and **smaller volume than** labels near appropriate pieces.

4. (a) Obtain two large metal bolts, or other objects, both the same size. Which is longer? Which is thicker? Which bolt has more metal? Which takes up more

room? Do the bolts have the same volume? The bolts are the same size, they contain the same amount of metal, they take up the same amount of room, so they have the same volume. Talk about this.

Use a transparent plastic jug, or bucket. Stick a paper strip on the outside from top to bottom, partly fill it with water, and mark the level. Tie a thin string to each bolt, lower one into the water, and mark the water level again. What happens to the level as the bolt enters the water? Watch the level as the bolt is removed? What happens if the bolt is moved about under the water? Discuss. Why does the water rise? The bolt takes up space under the water so it forces the water up the jug. Remove the first bolt, and notice that the level goes down to the lower mark again. Then, put the second bolt into the water. Where is the level now? Opposite the higher mark again. The level rises the same distance for both bolts. The teacher could repeat this demonstration using two identical house bricks and a polythene bucket.

Explain that if we put things having the same volume under water in a container, separately, the water rises the same distance.

Let the children do individual work, one or two at a time, based on this demonstration. Use two balls of plasticine of the same diameter and lower them into a polythene jug. Lower two identical bolts into a polythene jug or use two identical tins (with lids) filled with sand and lower them into a polythene container. Ask, in each case, which item takes up more room before they are put in the water. Should the items have the same volume display them on the table with a **same volume as** label alongside.

(b) Use two metal bolts, one being longer and thicker than the other. Which is longer? Which is thicker? Which has more metal? Which takes up more room? Which has the larger volume?

Repeat the experiment of **a** using these bolts. Which bolt makes the water go farther up the jug? Which takes up more room under the water? The teacher could also compare the volumes of two balls of plasticine of different diameters, and then put them in the water.

Establish that should we put things having a different volume under water in a container, separately, the water rises different distances, and the object with the larger volume makes the water go up farther.

Let the children do individual work, two or three at a time. Using two metal cylinders, one being longer and larger in diameter than the other, then two cylindrical tins, filled with sand, one being taller and larger in diameter than the other (instant coffee and powdered milk tins), two balls of plasticine of different diameters, and lastly two plastic bags of different sizes filled with sand. Find the item of each pair which takes up more room, by inspection, then put them under the water, separately, and remember which one makes the water level go up farther.

Display each pair on the table with **larger volume than** and **smaller volume than** labels alongside. Tell the teacher which one makes the water rise more.

The items **must** have strings tied around them beforehand by the teacher. Also explain that the objects must be lowered into the water. Push your hand into the water and see what happens to the level. This is why we must keep our hands out.

(c) Individual work for two or three children. Obtain two pebbles or stones of different sizes, a lump of plasticine and a stone, a bag of sand and a piece of metal, and a bolt and a lump of plasticine. The teacher must tie strings securely to these items beforehand. Ask which item of each pair takes up more room, or has the larger volume. Lower each item into a transparent vessel containing water to check the estimate. Display pairs of items with 'volume' labels alongside.

5. (a) Obtain a large tin, two identical transparent vessels and a tray. Stand the tin on the tray and fill the tin with water so that it is on the point of overflowing. Use two metal bolts of the same shape and size with thin strings tied to them. Ask the children which bolt takes up more room. Which has the larger volume? Discuss this and lower the bolts, separately, into water contained in another transparent vessel, if necessary.

   Now lower one bolt into the tin. What happens? The water overflows. Why does it overflow? The bolt takes up room and pushes some water out. Pour the water that has collected in the tray into one of the transparent vessels. This vessel now contains the water that was pushed out.

   Prepare the tin and tray as they were initially, and lower the other bolt into the water. What happens? Why? Do you think this bolt pushed out more water than the other? Discuss. Now pour the water from the tray into the second identical transparent vessel.

   Stand the vessels alongside one another. What do we notice? The water levels are the same. Which vessel contains more water? The vessels contain the same amount of water. The bolts pushed out the same amount. Why do you think this was so? Because they took up the same room under the water. We said at the beginning that the bolts had the same volume so we would expect them to push out equal amounts of water, and this is what happened.

   (Use a displacement can to do this experiment should one be available which is a suitable size. Many cans are too small for school use with young children because they only take objects up to 3 or 4 cm wide. A can which will hold reasonably large objects would be about 1.5 dm in diameter and 3 dm tall. Let the children pour water into this can, and lower things into it, so that they will be familiar with it before the demonstration.)

   (b) On another occasion the teacher could repeat the procedure of **a**, but using two metal bolts, one of which is longer and thicker than the other. Which is longer? Which is thicker? Which takes up more room? Which has the larger volume? If we lower the bolts, separately, into the tin and collect the water which overflows, which bolt will push out more water, or will they push out the same amount? Discuss this and then do the experiment. Establish that the bolt with the larger volume pushes out more water because it takes up more room.

   Now set individual work to one or two children at a time. Use two lumps of plasticine, two pebbles, two metal bolts, two tins filled with sand, a tin filled with sand and a lump of plasticine, a pebble and a metal bolt. (These items must have strings attached to them by the teacher beforehand.) The child has to estimate which of each pair has the larger volume and then check the answer by displacement. Display items in pairs with **larger volume than** and **smaller volume than** labels alongside.

6. Compile work cards, giving individual work for one or two children at a time. Use three stones, pieces of metal, lumps of plasticine or plastic bags of sand, which have strings tied to them. Estimate which has the largest volume and which has the smallest volume. Check the answer by putting items in water contained in a transparent plastic vessel and comparing the rises in water level. On another card the child could be asked to check the result by comparing amounts of water displaced, this being displayed in three identical transparent plastic vessels. Display items with **volume** labels; also give oral answers.

7. Children work in pairs, one or two pairs at a time. A child makes three or four rectangular towers with wooden cubes. Use a different colour of cube for each tower. His partner estimates which has the largest volume and which has the smallest. Check the answers by making and comparing rows of cubes from each tower. Put the rows alongside one another on a squared background.

5.7 MEASURING CAPACITIES AND VOLUMES (2 L1; 1, 2, 8 L2)

When children can deal with numbers, capacities and volumes can be described using them. Use numbers less than ten initially; then to twenty; then beyond twenty. Containers, with their lids removed, can be used as measuring units. Capacities can be recorded using **holds** labels at first, but **capacity** labels can be used sometime later when children appreciate their meaning. Volumes can be recorded using **volume** labels. The activities are meant to be done individually by three or four children at a time. Compile work cards for these activities. (See Sections 1.11, 1.14 and 1.15 of Chapter 1 for other numerical work on capacity and volume.)

   The following activities are designed to be carried out under supervision by individual children:

1. Build three towers containing 8 cubes, 14 cubes and 17 cubes, and arrange them on the table with the largest volume on the left. (Use Stern cubes, or larger cubes.)
2. Make three rectangular towers using 8 cubes, 12 cubes and 20 cubes. Which has the largest volume?
3. Make different rectangular towers, each containing 24 cubes. Are the towers the same height? Have they the same volume?
4. Pour water into various transparent polythene containers, two cups in each. Do the vessels contain the same amount of water? What do you notice about the levels of the water? Why are they different?
5. Pour water into identical transparent polythene vessels, three beakers in each. Do the vessels contain the same amount? What do you notice about the levels of the water? Why are they the same height?
6. This activity involves numbers less than ten. The child measures out the following amounts of water or sand: 3 beakers, 5 jam jars, 4 fruit tins, 6 bottles, 9 egg-cups, 7 cups, 5 Oxo cube boxes and 8 Vim cartons. Use dishes, boxes, jugs or bowls to display the amounts, on the table, one at a time, with a number label and the measuring unit alongside, e.g. near a box which contains 7 cups of sand is placed a **7** label and a **cup**.
7. This activity involves numbers larger than ten. The child measures out these quantities of sand or water: 15 cups, 16 Oxo boxes, 22 egg-cups, 12 beakers, 13

cream cartons, etc. Display each amount, separately, in a box, dish, jug or bowl, together with a number symbol label and the measuring unit used.

8. Which is the heavier, 2 cups of marbles or 1 jar of sand? 6 cream cartons of shells or 4 cups of sand? 2 beakers of wooden cubes or 10 egg-cups of dried peas? 3 Oxo boxes of sand or 2 cups of wooden cubes? etc.

9. Find the capacities of tins and boxes using a smaller container filled with sand or water, and describe the number required. (Match each unit emptied into the tin or box with a cube or bead. Thus, 8 cubes at the end would indicate that 8 units were used. Tallying, and then totalling, is superior to counting and remembering what the previous count was.) Often the answer will have to be recorded as **larger capacity than** ....., **smaller capacity than** ....., because the measuring unit will not fit a whole number of times in the larger vessel, e.g. the bottle has capacity larger than 2 jam jars and less than 3 jam jars.

   Measure the capacity of a salt box with an Oxo box, a Bisto box with an Oxo box, a large fruit tin with a jam jar, a beaker with an egg-cup, an egg-cup with a tablespoon, a jam jar with an egg-cup, a bottle with a jam jar, a bottle with a beaker, a cornflakes packet with a salt box, a cup with an egg-cup, a large fruit tin with a beaker, a small fruit tin with an egg-cup, a large fruit tin with a cream carton, a cereal packet with a cup and a bucket with a large fruit tin.

10. Measure the amount of water displaced when a stone, a lump of plasticine, a tin of sand, or a metal bolt, is put into a tin filled to the brim with water. The child uses a small container, such as an egg-cup, a dessert or tablespoon, or cream carton to measure with, e.g. the water pushed out was more than 6 egg-cups and less than 7 egg-cups.

5.8 MEASURING CAPACITY TO THE NEAREST UNIT (2 L1; 1, 2, 8 L2)

Up to now we have expressed capacities between limits, such as more than 7 egg-cups, less than 8 egg-cups. We are now going to measure to the nearest unit. That is, if the measuring unit is less than half full we ignore it, if half full or more we count it as one unit.

The teacher fills a cup with sand using an egg-cup, and a salt box with sand using an Oxo box, to illustrate this. (Keep a tally with cubes as each unit is emptied into the larger container.) Suppose we use 6 full egg-cups and more than half of another, we would record this with a **7 egg-cups** label.

Now set individual work, for two or three children at a time. (Compile work cards.) Ask the children to find, using sand or water, the capacities, to the nearest unit, of a bucket using a bottle, a jam jar using an egg-cup, a fruit tin using a jam jar, a bottle using a cream carton, a coffee tin using an Oxo box, etc. The teacher would help the child with the labelling, if required.

Also measure to the nearest egg-cup, or other container, the amount of water pushed out when a stone, a lump of plasticine, a metal object, and a tin of sand, is lowered into a tin filled to the brim with water. (Compile a work card.)

5.9 DIFFERENCES IN CAPACITY AND VOLUME: NUMERICAL (1, 2, 3, 8 L2)

Ask a child from the group to find, using beakers, to the nearest beaker, the capacities of a plastic bottle and a tin. Then ask which has the larger capacity and how much larger it is than the other. Treat the subject as now described.

Suppose the bottle is 4 beakers, and the tin 14 beakers, in capacity. Then, the tin is larger in capacity than the bottle, because $14 > 4$. Also, their difference in capacity is 10 beakers, because $14 - 4 = 10$, or $4 + 10 = 14$, whichever way we look at it.

Many children will not be ready for this abstract approach and we could put two rows of beakers, side by side, on a squared background, to represent the capacities, and find their difference in a more concrete fashion. If we do not have enough beakers to do this we can represent the beakers pictorially, and then will have two rows of pictures side by side. Or, we can just represent the beakers by rows of ticks made, one in each square, on squared paper, and finally compare the number in each row. We could represent the beakers with wooden cubes, and compare two rows of these, if necessary.

Specially prepared cards for recording purposes are also useful (Fig. 5.2). Similar cards could also be made for recording volumes, by substituting the word 'volume' for 'capacity' in Fig. 5.2.

```
                              I find
        capacity of                              capacity of
     . . . . . . . . . . . . . . . .          . . . . . . . . . . . . . . . .
            is                                      is
     . . . . . . . . . . . . . . . .          . . . . . . . . . . . . . . . .
            . . . . . . . . . has larger capacity than
                 by . . . . . . . . . . . . . . . . . . . . . . .
            . . . . . . . . . has the same capacity as        . . . . . . . . . . . . . . . .
```

Fig. 5.2

Now set individual work for two or three children at a time. Prepare work cards on the following topics:

1. A child builds two towers, side by side, such that one has a volume of 6 cubes more than the other, or 12 cubes more, or the same volume as, etc. Place a number label near each tower to describe its volume.
2. Work in pairs. Each child builds a tower with less than 20 cubes. Which tower has the larger volume? Find their volumes, and the difference in volume.
3. Use pairs of pebbles, lumps of plasticine, pieces of metal and tins of sand. Put each item under water and measure the water displaced in egg-cups, cream cartons or other suitable units. Which item in each pair has the larger volume? How much more water does the larger item push out?
4. Find the capacities of the following pairs of items, in the units stated, to the nearest unit, and their difference in capacity:

    large fruit tin and small fruit tin in beakers, a fruit tin and a jam jar in egg-cups, a beaker and a cup in egg-cups, a bottle and a jam jar in beakers, large and small fruit tins in egg-cups, cereal packet and washing powder box in salt boxes, a blancmange box and a Bisto box in Oxo boxes, a Bisto box and a salt box in Oxo boxes, a bottle and a jam jar in egg-cups, a cereal packet and a washing powder packet in beakers, etc.

5. A child uses three boxes, three bottles or three tins. He arranges them in order of capacity, by estimation, with the largest on the left. He then measures the capacity of each using a cream carton, or Oxo box, and again arranges them in order of capacity. Were you correct in your estimate? How much larger is the largest than the smallest?
6. A child uses three or four lumps of plasticine, pebbles or pieces of metal, and arranges them in order of volume, by inspection, with the largest on the left. Find out how much water each item displaces in egg-cups, or other suitable units, and arrange the items in order of volume again. Find how much more water the largest pushes out than the smallest.

5.10 INTRODUCTION TO STANDARD UNITS OF LIQUID MEASURE: THE LITRE (1, 2, 3, 8 L2; 8 L3)

1. At a teaching session ask children from the group to find the capacity of a tin by filling it with sand using an Oxo box, an egg-cup and a cream carton. Compare the answers obtained and discuss the need for standard measures. The teacher shows a litre measure and uses it to fill two or three large containers with water. The answers are to be recorded as more than ..... litres and less than ..... litres. (Up to now standard measures have not been put in the capacity and volume corner. They are kept by the teacher until children can appreciate the need for them.) Then set individual work for two or three children at a time. Compile work cards.
   (a) Put 1 litre, 4 litres and 3 litres of water into different containers.
   (b) Use a common balance, and kilogram and half-kilogram masses, to find the mass of 1 litre of water, together with the container. Establish that it is between 1 and $1\frac{1}{2}$ kg.
   (c) Find the capacities of various containers using a litre measure, e.g. large plastic bucket, plastic bowl, large tin, etc. Record answers as more than ..... litres and less than ..... litres.
2. The children, with the teacher's help, find the capacities of two or three containers, to the nearest litre, by filling them with water using a litre measure. Following this, ask one or two children at a time to find the capacity of a plastic bucket, a plastic bowl and a large tin, to the nearest litre.
3. Measuring to the nearest litre is not often accurate enough and the litre is much too large a unit to measure some containers with. Discuss these points with the children. Show a half litre measure but do not name it yet. Ask a child to use it and fill a litre measure with water, and establish that a litre measure holds two of these measures, so the new container is a half litre.
   Ask a child to measure the capacity of a container in half litres, to the nearest half litre, and then to express the amount in litres. Check the result by filling the same container using a litre measure and a half-litre measure, if required.
   Suppose a bucket holds 19 half litres. This is 9 litres and 1 half litre. Check by filling the bucket in this manner. (To help this calculation the child could use the 19 tallying cubes, arrange them in pairs, and obtain 9 pairs with 1 left over.)
   Explain that half a litre is written as $\frac{1}{2}$ litre, and that 2 litres and 1 half litre is written in short as $2\frac{1}{2}$ litres. Connect with $\frac{1}{2}$ kg when recording mass, etc.
   Now set individual work to one or two children at a time. (Compile work cards.)

(a) Find the capacities of bowls, buckets and large tins in half litres, to the nearest half litre. Express the answer in litres. Record orally, and also write down:
..... half litres $\equiv$ ..... litres and ..... half litre

(b) Pour nine half litres, six half litres, five and a half litres, and then three and a half litres of water into a bucket. Give oral instructions.

(c) Pour 3 litres and a half litre, 2 litres and a half litre, $4\frac{1}{2}$ litres and then $2\frac{1}{2}$ litres of water into a bucket. Write amounts on cards.

(d) Find the capacity of the teachers' kettle in litres and half litres. Take home a $\frac{1}{2}$ litre measure and find the capacity of your kettle. (This would involve parents in the child's mathematical work.) Which kettle holds more? How much more? Sort out kettle sizes for the class. Illustrate graphically. Relate to the project '*Ourselves*'.

(e) How much do you drink each day? This activity requires parental help. Should the results be expressed in cups full or beakers full, ask the children to convert them to litres. This can be done by pouring the required number of cups or beakers into a half litre measure. (Bring the measuring unit to school.) How much does your mother drink each day? your father? Include in '*Ourselves*'.

(f) How much water is used at home for washing up dishes? Record the amount used each washing up and then find the total amount. (Assistance would be needed from parents. The child also needs to be able to deal with hundreds. Calculators could be used.) This activity entails choosing a measuring unit such as a jug, a milk bottle, a saucepan or a jug graduated in pints or litres. The results can be discussed at school. How many times a day is the washing up done? How much water is used each time? When was most water used? In order to decide who used most water each day the children would probably need to change their results into a common unit, such as litres. Discuss this. To change results the measuring unit could be emptied the required number of times into litre and $\frac{1}{2}$ litre measures. Measuring units, therefore, need to be brought to school. Some of the information could be illustrated graphically. Do the activity at a weekend. ('*Ourselves*')

5.11 INTRODUCTION TO THE DECILITRE (1, 2, 3, 8 L3)

1. The teacher illustrates and discusses with a group that the half litre is still too large for measuring the capacities of some containers, or measuring out small quantities, e.g. a jam jar is smaller than a half litre, and to say that its capacity is half a litre is perhaps not good enough.

   Show a decilitre. Ask a child to fill a litre measure with it by pouring water and establish that ten of these containers fill a litre. This container is called a decilitre, so 10 decilitres $\equiv$ 1 litre. Explain that decilitre is written as **dl**.

   Compile work cards and set individual work to one or two children at a time.

   (a) How many decilitres in half a litre? Establish that it is 5, by pouring water.

   (b) Pour 8 decilitres of water into a tin, 5 decilitres of sand in a jar, 7 decilitres of water into a bottle, etc. Put a number label near each amount.

   (c) Use a common balance, and centicubes, to find the mass of 1 dl of wooden beads, Cuisenaire unit cubes and dried peas. If necessary give the answers as larger than .... and smaller than ....

(d) Measure the capacities of the following containers in decilitres, to the nearest decilitre: medium fruit tin, squash bottle, jam jar, large fruit tin, beaker, cup, Oxo cube box, salt box, cornflour box, cereal packet and jug. Use water or sand. Record as: **capacity of** .... **is** .... **dl**.

(e) Use containers larger than a litre in capacity, such as buckets, saucepans, jugs and large tins. Measure their capacities in decilitres, and also in litres and decilitres, e.g. the jar has a capacity of 21 dl or 2 litres and 1 dl.

(f) Pour into large containers these quantities of water: 13 dl, 16 dl, 1 litre 2 decilitres, 1 litre 4 decilitres, etc. Put a label near each amount.

2. Individual work for one or two children at a time. Use a transparent plastic jug of about 1 litre in capacity. The teacher tells the child to do the following things:

> Stick a gummed paper strip outside it from top to bottom.
> Carefully fill the jug with water, one decilitre at a time, marking the levels on the paper strip, and numbering them 1 dl, 2 dl, 3 dl, 5 dl, etc.
> Continue until the jug is graduated nearly to the top, which will be about 8 or 9 dl.

Compile a work card. Ask the child to find the capacities of tins, bottles and jugs by filling them with water from this measuring jug, and also by pouring water from various containers into it. Answers will be given to the nearest decilitre.

This exercise is relatively easy if the measuring jug is larger than the capacity of the vessel to be measured. When the measuring jug is smaller in capacity the activity involves a little arithmetic, e.g. suppose our jug measures up to 8 dl, and we have a tin of larger capacity to measure. We could pour 8 dl into the tin, fill the jug again to the 8 dl mark, and pour water into the tin until it is full. We note that the level of the water remaining in the jug is near the 2 dl mark, so we poured another 6 dl into the tin. Therefore, the total capacity of the jar is 8 dl + 6 dl, or 14 dl. This could be expressed as 1 litre 4 dl.

Further practice can be gained if necessary. Compile a work card. Ask the children to measure out these quantities of water, using the measuring jug only: 16 dl, 15 dl, 18 dl, 26 dl, 3 litres 4 dl, etc.

3. Individual work for one child at a time. Instructions are given orally.

The child puts a stone, or large pebble, into a tin filled to the brim with water and measures the amount of water pushed out to the nearest decilitre. The child now measures the water pushed up by the pebble when it is placed in water contained in the graduated jug mentioned in 2, the previous section. He puts water into the jug, initially up to one of the decilitre divisions, then hangs the pebble in the water and reads the level again to the nearest decilitre. The difference in levels tells us the amount of water pushed up, e.g. should the level move from the 4 dl mark to the 8 dl mark we would say that 4 dl of water has been pushed up. Did the pebble push out the same amount of water from the tin as it pushed up when placed in the jug?

Repeat this exercise using a lump of plasticine, a piece of metal and a small tin of sand. Select these items so they are as large as possible. That is, each one goes into the graduated jug with little room to spare. The water pushed out would then be more than 3 decilitres.

4. Obtain a decilitre and a half litre measure. Pour water from the decilitre into the $\frac{1}{2}$ litre. How many decilitres does it hold? (5) Use both these containers to measure out 4 dl of water. How is it done?

5. Make a 3-dl and a 5-dl container using two plastic bottles. (Put the required amount of water into a bottle, mark the water level, then cut off the top of the bottle at this level.) The child is asked to go to the sink and use both these containers to measure out 2 dl of water. How is it done? Then the child is asked to measure out 1 dl of water.
6. The teacher uses plastic bottles to make a 5-dl and an 8-dl container. The child, at the sink, uses both these containers to measure out 3 dl of water. How is it done? Then the child is asked to measure out 2 dl of water.

5.12 INTRODUCTION TO THE CENTILITRE (1, 2, 3, 8 L3)

The decilitre is too large to measure some containers. Illustrate this by asking children to select, from a collection, those containers which could suitably be measured using decilitres, and those which could not, giving reasons for their choice. Show a centilitre measure. Ask a child to fill a decilitre measure with water from the centilitre measure and establish that $10\,cl \equiv 1\,dl$. Explain that the centilitre is written as **cl**. Also ask a child to measure the capacity of a small tin or bottle, to the nearest centilitre, using the measure.

   Then set the following exercises to be done individually by two or three children at a time. (Compile work cards.)

1. Pour into various plastic containers and tins these amounts of water using a centilitre measure: 7 cl, 6 cl, 14 cl, and 18 cl. Place a number label near each container.
2. How many centilitres in a decilitre? Find out by pouring water. Change these amounts into decilitres and centilitres: 16 cl, 14 cl, 24 cl, 27 cl, etc.
       Record as ..... cl $\equiv$ ..... dl and ..... cl.
3. Pour into various plastic containers and tins these amounts of water using a decilitre and a centilitre measure: 15 cl, 22 cl, 32 cl and 26 cl.
4. Find the capacities in centilitres, and in decilitres and centilitres, of the following containers: Oxo box, egg-cup, cup, jam jar, beaker, small fruit tin, small cream tin, plastic cream carton and instant coffee tin. Near each container place a capacity label, e.g. 18 cl, or 1 dl 8 cl.
5. Find by pouring water or sand how many centilitres in a decilitre, and how many decilitres in a half litre. Without pouring water can you find how many centilitres in a half litre?
6. Find by pouring water how many centilitres in a decilitre and how many decilitres in a litre. Without pouring water can you find how many centilitres in a litre?
7. How much water does a hamster, gerbil, guinea pig or rabbit drink each week, in centilitres?
8. How much water does your dog drink daily? How much milk does the cat drink? This is a week-end activity which could involve parents and children working together. The child takes home the necessary measuring unit.
9. How much do you drink daily? Find this out in cups or beakers. At school, measure the capacity of your cup or beaker in centilitres. Calculate the amount you drink each day in centilitres. (Use a calculator.) Change to litres, if appropriate. (*'Ourselves'*)

10. In the project '*Ourselves*' find out how much water is wasted if we leave a tap dripping. (The teacher adjusts a tap so that it drips 20 or 30 times per minute.) The water collected could be measured after 1 hour, in centilitres, and possibly changed to litres, e.g. 114 cl ≡ 1 litre 14 cl. Using this result the amount of water lost each day could be estimated. Use a calculator.

5.13 INTRODUCTION TO STANDARD UNITS OF VOLUME: THE CUBIC CENTIMETRE (1, 2, 3 L3; 8 L4)

Give each child a Cuisenaire unit, or Centicube, to measure. It is 1 cm wide, 1 cm thick and 1 cm tall. It is a **centimetre cube**. The room taken up by this cube is called one cubic centimetre. The amount of room inside boxes, and the amount of space which things take up, can be measured with these units. Children, when recording, could write cubic centimetres at first, and **cub. cm** later. The abbreviation cm^3 is not suitable for young children.

Compile work cards for the following activities, individual work for two or three children at a time.

1. Ask a child to make three rectangular buildings with Cuisenaire unit cubes, or Centicubes, having volumes of: 8 cubic centimetres, 12 cubic centimetres and 16 cubic centimetres.
2. Ask a child to find the volumes of the other Cuisenaire rods by making equivalent rods with unit cubes, e.g. the brown rod has a volume of 8 cubic centimetres.
3. Make six different shapes, with Centicubes, each having a volume of 16 cubic centimetres.
4. Find the amount of room in the carrying compartments of model lorries by filling them with wooden centimetre cubes. Write down—the volume of the lorry is . . . . . cub. cm.
5. Find the volumes of small boxes by filling them with Centicubes. The cubes could be joined together to make blocks of ten blocks of ten, and if necessary could be put together to form a hundred. How many cubes are there? This activity provides an opportunity to develop number notation and place value.
6. Using only Cuisenaire orange rods and unit cubes, put out the following amounts of wood: 35 cubic centimetres, 62 cubic centimetres, 58 cubic centimetres and 29 cubic centimetres. Also, if appropriate, ask questions involving hundreds, e.g. 146 cubic centimetres.
7. Find the volumes of small boxes, filling them with Cuisenaire rods and calculating the number of cubic centimetres involved. For example, an Oxo box contains 16 dark green rods. Each dark green rod has a volume of 6 cubic centimetres, so the Oxo box has a volume of 6 × 16 (or 96) cubic centimetres. The numbers involved with larger boxes would make calculation more difficult and a calculator could be used.

5.14 DECIMAL NOTATION (3, 8 L4)

Talk with the group. When we are measuring capacities in litres and decilitres we can write the answers more quickly, e.g. 2 litres and 4 decilitres ≡ 2.4 litres. When we find capacities in decilitres and centilitres we can also do this, e.g. 2 dl and 2 cl ≡ 2.2 dl. Explain that the dot, or decimal point, is being used as a device to separate units of different denomination. This notation provides a much quicker way of writing things down.

Compile work cards as follows:

1. Find the capacity of a plastic bucket, a plastic bowl and a large instant coffee tin, in litres and decilitres. Write the answers a quicker way.
2. Find the capacity, in decilitres and centilitres, of a small instant coffee jar, a plastic detergent bottle, a plastic squash bottle, a large fruit tin and a Vim container. Write the answers a quicker way.

   Later, when children realize that 2 dl and 4 cl ≡ $2\frac{4}{10}$ dl, the notation 2.4 dl has another interpretation. Here, .4 is another way of writing $\frac{4}{10}$. When the decimal point is used in this sense a more difficult mathematical meaning of decimal notation, and place value, is being developed.

5.15 FINAL COMMENT

So far we have introduced liquid measure, except for the millilitre, and made a start in measuring volume in cubic centimetres. Future work would be to connect the cubic decimetre with the cubic centimetre and the litre, and the millilitre with the cubic centimetre. Volumes could be measured in cubic centimetres and capacities in millilitres, and decimal notation developed further, e.g. 3 dl and 4 cl ≡ 3.4 dl ≡ .34 litre, or 1240 cubic centimetres ≡ 1.24 litres.

The notation **cm³** could also be introduced. We also need to proceed further with displacement and show that the amount of water displaced represents the volume of the object because this principle is used to find volume. The kilogram could also be explained as the mass of a litre of water, and activities set involving mass and volume leading to the idea of density. Measuring jars graduated in cubic centimetres and millilitres can be made by the children. The advantages of finding capacities by using the jars, rather than by filling and counting, can then be clearly demonstrated.

Chapter 6

Heaviness and Mass

A common balance can be used to compare, and measure, weights or masses. Masses or quantities of material are measured in grams and kilograms and should we use these units to balance an object then we are finding its **mass**. This point is not generally made clear in schools and it causes confusion at a later stage when children are being told about mass and weight. We suggest that if an object be balanced with grams we should encourage the children to say that its mass is 20 g and not that its weight is 20 g, the latter being the usual practice. In class we should ask children to find masses of objects rather than to weigh them.

6.1 CONCERNING THE MEASUREMENT OF MASS

The kilogram is rather too heavy to use as an introductory unit of mass because it is a source of danger to the feet of children if dropped from a table. This problem can be eliminated if kilogram bags of sand are used rather than metal masses and if common balances are placed near to the floor. Measuring with kilograms, however, has the advantage that numbers would be small should strong balances be used which measure up to 5 kg.

The gram should be introduced after the kilogram because it is very small. Objects must be chosen with care for measuring activities because the grams could easily be greater than the size of the numbers the child could handle. Interlocking plastic centimetre cubes, Centicubes, each of mass 1 gram, are extremely useful. They may be used singly in some circumstances, or be joined together to form 10-g blocks, or be put into 100-g bundles. The use of these cubes in measurement activities gives valuable ideas about place value and various arithmetical processes.

Children should, at first, use common balances to measure mass, and only later use compression balances. (A compression balance has a pan resting on top of a spring.) Spring balances, with hooks and scale pans, are awkward to handle, but could be used by juniors.

Problems often arise as a result of school apparatus. Beam balances with hanging pans often fall over when masses are put on them, or the pans are not large enough to hold the object concerned. Strong solid common balances are needed for young children to use. These balances should be checked regularly to see that they balance when the pans are empty and, if necessary, adjustments made.

Objects placed on common balances do not often balance the measuring units, unless specially prepared by the teacher, and inequality needs to be described far more than it is. If the article is larger than 12 g and smaller than 13 g then this should be recorded. It is sometimes possible to describe a mass as just under x, or just larger than y, but this requires an enlightened judgement of the balance.

A compression balance enables the mass of an object to be read to the nearest unit and in this respect it is superior to the common balance. It is also quicker to use but it involves the reading of a scale. A better understanding of the scale is obtained if the instrument is graduated by the children themselves under the guidance of a teacher.

6.2 GENERAL SCHEME

1. Personal sensory experiences of heaviness leading to the development of vocabulary. Compare amounts of like substances for heaviness using sight and feel.
2. Study the effects of the larger amount, and the heavier amount, on a common balance, a compression balance and a spring.
3. Compare amounts of like substances for heaviness using a common balance, a compression balance and a spring. Establish that the larger is the heavier.
4. Compare amounts of different substances for heaviness. Establish that heaviness cannot be compared by looking. The larger is not necessarily the heavier.
5. Establish that instruments are needed to compare objects for heaviness. Our senses are not reliable, particularly when objects feel just as heavy, or nearly so.
6. Describe and compare, the heaviness of objects in terms of smaller units of measure, but without the use of numbers.
7. Describe and compare the heaviness of objects in terms of equivalent units of measure and then use numbers.
8. Introduce standard units of mass, the kilogram and half kilogram. Find and compare masses of objects using a common balance and kilogram and half-kilogram masses.
9. Graduate and use a compression balance to find masses to the nearest half kilogram.
10. Introduce the gram. Find masses in grams, using a common balance.
11. Link arithmetical procedures, particularly addition and subtraction, with the measurement of mass in grams, using Centicubes arranged in 100-g bundles and 10-g blocks.
12. Graduate compression balances in grams and use them to measure to the nearest 100 g, 50 g and 10 g. Develop arithmetic further.

6.3 EQUIPMENT

Tins, stones, plastic bottles, wooden blocks, metal objects, lumps of plasticine, marbles, beads, shells, cubes of wood, cubes of metal, dried peas, large nails, nuts and bolts, metal washers, bags of shells, bags of sand, bags of marbles, bags of cubes, strong elastic bands, metal helical springs.

Metric standard masses—use kilogram and half-kilogram metal masses: 100 g and 50 g stacking masses; 100 g, 50 g and 10 g metal masses. Kilogram and half-kilogram bags of sand. A good supply of Centicubes.

Strong spring balance 0–5 kg range. More sensitive balances 0–3 kg, 0–1 kg ranges. Various compression balances with 0–750 g, 0–1 kg, 0–5 kg ranges. *Cover* graduations and numbers on the dials with plain gummed white paper, before doing own graduations.

Strong common balance with 0–5 kg range; others with 0–2 kg and 0–3 kg ranges.

The tins and bottles could be painted different colours, numbered or lettered, or marked with symbols, pictures or coloured stickers. This enables containers to be referred to easily, e.g. the red tin is heavier than 12 marbles.

Tins, boxes and bags of various substances, many of which should be an exact number of kilograms, half kilograms, or grams. Nuts and bolts, metal washers, etc. These items could be arranged in pairs for purposes of comparison.

6.4 DEMONSTRATIONS INVOLVING THE COMPARISON OF LIKE SUBSTANCES: 'HEAVY', 'LIGHT', 'HEAVIER', 'LIGHTER'. (1, 8 L1)

Initially, various experiences of heaviness could be given. These would be direct (holding objects to feel the difference) or indirect (using a balance for example). These should lead from children's natural oral descriptions of what they experience to the appropriate and acceptable vocabulary. The indirect experiences where the effects of heaviness are seen when various objects are put on a balance, or hung on a spring, must be interpreted in the light of the former direct experiences.

We suggest that at first, with the class or group of children, the teacher shows materials prepared beforehand, performs the tests, conducts the questioning and promotes discussion along the following lines, and as a result introduces new words and ideas concerning heaviness.

1. Use a bucket and invite the children to pick it up when it is empty or contains a little sand. Then put in a large quantity of sand and invite them to try to lift the bucket again. Discuss the fact that it is harder to pick up in the second case. Introduce the words **heavy** and **light**.
2. Use two cylinders of plasticine of the same diameter but different lengths and of different colours, one of which is markedly heavier than the other (masses about 500 g and 200 g). Hold the cylinders side by side, and ask which piece has more plasticine (Fig. 6.1). Establish that the lumps are the same width, and that one is longer, and that this one has more plasticine. The children could look at this another way if the teacher rolls the cylinders into balls, and holds the balls side by side. Does the lump with more plasticine make the larger ball?

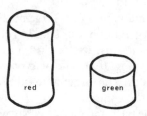

Fig. 6.1

Give the children in the group the balls to hold, one after the other, on the palm of one hand, or at the same time with one on each palm. Ask them to close their eyes when doing this. Do the lumps feel the same or different? (The lumps do not feel the same.) Try to obtain the reply, or suggest, that one presses down more on the hand. Which lump does this? Tell the children that the lump which feels as though it presses down more on the hand is said to be heavier. The other lump is not so heavy, or lighter. Ask them to pick up the lumps again and find the heavier and the lighter.

The teacher could now put the lumps in the opposite pans of a common balance. What happens? The heavier lump makes the balance go down. Verify this again by letting the children hold the lumps in their hands. This lump is heavier because it contains more plasticine. Now put the lumps on the balance with the heavier lump on the other pan. What happens now? The heavier lump makes the other pan go down. Let the children hold the lumps in their hands again and identify the heavier. Can you see the larger piece? Is the larger piece the heavier lump? Put it on the balance to find out.

Next, the teacher puts the plasticine lumps, one at a time, in the pan of a compression balance which has a pointer and marks the final positions of the pointer. (Cover the dial of the balance beforehand with gummed white paper in order to hide the previous graduations and numbers.) What happens to the pointer in each case? Establish that the larger piece makes the pointer turn farther. Is this the heavier lump? Check by holding. Where does the pointer go for the lighter lump?

Following this the teacher ties strings around the lumps of plasticine and hangs them, one at a time, on the end of a metal spring or strong elastic band which is fixed to a long nail in the wall. (A sheet of paper is placed behind the spring so that the end can be marked before and after the lumps are attached. Ensure that the lumps do not scrape against the wall, or touch it, otherwise the spring will not be properly stretched.) Establish that the larger piece stretches the spring more. Let the children pick up the lumps and find the heavier, and establish it is this one which stretches the spring more.

3. With a group of children the teacher could use two identical transparent plastic bottles containing water, one being nearly full and the other about half full. Stand them side by side. Which bottle has more water? Which has the larger amount of water? Ask the children to close their eyes, pick up the bottles one by one, and find the heavier. Put the bottles on opposite pans of a common balance. What happens? (The balance goes down on the side with the heavier amount of water, that is, the side with the larger amount of water.) Put the bottles on a compression balance and also hang them from a spring and talk about what happens. Establish that the larger amount of water, or the heavier amount, causes more turning or more stretching and that the larger amount is also the heavier.

4. Use two transparent bags containing about 500 g and 250 g of dried peas. Hold up the bags. Which contains the larger amount of peas? Probably the larger amount could not be identified with certainty just by looking. Pour the peas into two identical glasses, or plastic jars or jugs (Fig. 6.2). The peas occupy the jars to different levels, and the jars are the same width. The larger amount is the jar with peas to the higher level. Talk about this with the children.

Pour the peas back into the bags and mark the bag with the larger amount. Let the children hold the bags, one after the other, on the palms of the hands, and find the

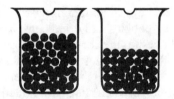

Fig. 6.2

heavier lot of peas. Is it the bag with the larger amount? Put the bags on a common balance and a compression balance, and hang them on a spring. Talk about the effects produced by the larger amount, and the heavier amount, in each case. Establish that the heavier is also the larger amount.

   The teacher could also compare bags of sand, bags of shells, bags of pebbles or bags of marbles.

5. Use two transparent plastic bags containing about 100 and 50 wooden cubes respectively. Put the bags side by side and ask the children to select the bag with more wood in it. Verify the result by emptying out the cubes and placing them in two rows, side by side. The longer row has more cubes and the larger amount of wood. Put the cubes back into the bags. Ask the children to pick up the bags and find the heavier lot of cubes. Put the cubes on common and compression balances, and hang them on a spring, and observe what the heavier amount does, and what the larger amount of wood does.

6. The teacher could use two transparent bags containing about 100 and 50 marbles. Ask the children to pick up the bags and find the heavier lot of marbles. Which is the larger amount of marbles? Verify the latter by putting the marbles in two rows, side by side, between three long wooden strips. The longer row of marbles has the larger amount. Then put the marbles on a common balance, and a compression balance, and hang them on a spring, and discuss the effects produced.

6.5 PRACTICE ACTIVITIES CONCERNING 'HEAVIER AND LIGHTER', 'HEAVIEST AND LIGHTEST' (1, 8 L1)

Up to now the teacher has organized various materials in order to introduce vocabulary and ideas connected with heaviness. The children should now be able to find the larger amount, or the heavier object, on their own. Arrange the following exercises for individual children.

1. The child compares two quantities of like substances, one of which is noticeably larger and heavier than the other (Fig. 6.3). The teacher prepares beforehand,

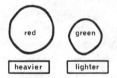

Fig. 6.3

lumps of plasticine, plastic bottles containing water, and bags of wooden cubes, marbles, sand, shells, small pebbles and dried peas. The child finds the heavier by picking up the objects. The results are checked by the child using a common balance, a compression balance and a spring. Results are displayed by placing pairs of items on the table with **heavier** and **lighter** labels near them.

2. A child is given a transparent polythene bag partly filled with sand. Ask him to put a larger amount of sand into an identical bag, just by looking, and then to check the result using a compression balance.

3. Give the child a bag of cubes. Ask him to put into an identical bag a heavier amount of cubes. He then checks the result using a common balance.

4. The teacher puts out two noticeably different amounts of like substance, and asks the child to select, by looking only, the heavier amount. A balance or spring is used to check the result.

5. Give a child three amounts of like substance that are noticeably different in weight. He finds the lightest and heaviest and checks the answers using a compression balance or spring.

6. A child watches another child hang two transparent plastic bags containing different amounts of the same substance in turn on a spring and mark the position of the end of the spring, or put the bags on a common balance, or put the bags on a compression balance and mark the position of the pointer each time. The child observing has to identify the heavier bag and the lighter bag.

7. A child watches another child hang three plastic bags of differing amounts of the same substance on a spring, separately, and mark the position of the end of the spring, or put the three bags on a compression balance and mark the final position of the pointer each time. The child observing has to identify the heaviest bag and the lightest bag.

8. The teacher puts different amounts of a like substance in pairs of identical tins and replaces the lids. Shells, peas or sand could be used. The child has to find the tin containing the larger amount of the substance. Encourage the child to detect the heavier by picking up the tins, but if they feel much the same to put them on a balance or hang them on a spring to identify the heavier. The child may look inside the tin in order to check the answers. (This activity could be done by two children. One puts the substance in the tins and the other finds the larger amount.)

6.6 DEMONSTRATIONS INVOLVING THE COMPARISON OF LIKE SUBSTANCES: 'JUST AS HEAVY' (1, 8 L1; 8 L2)

It might be possible to compare two amounts of the same substance by sight if one were appreciably larger than the other. Similarly, the heavier can be detected when the amounts feel distinctly different. When the weights are nearly the same it is not easy to feel the heavier, and accurate statements cannot be made about which is heavier and which is lighter. That is, personal judgements are no longer reliable.

In such cases balances and springs have to be relied upon and decisions based on the effects seen. That is, we rely on the interpretation of indirect experiences. If the amounts of the material produce the same stretch on a spring, the same amount of turning of a pointer, or they balance, then they are **just as heavy as** one another.

Establish these points by means of the following activities which could be demonstrated by the teacher and discussed with a group of children.

1. Use identical plastic bottles filled with water. Which contains the larger amount of water? The water from one bottle could be poured into the other and would just fit, so the amount of water is the same in each bottle. Which do you think is heavier?

   Ask the children, in turn, to pick up the bottles of water. Do they feel the same or different? Are they just as heavy? Is one heavier? Establish that they feel much the same but this is not certain. The teacher puts the bottles, one after the other, on a compression balance and records the position of the pointer each time. What is noticed? The pointer turns the same amount. This means the bottles are just as heavy as one another. Hang the bottles, one after the other, on a spring and mark the positions of the end of the spring before and after each bottle is attached. What is seen? The spring stretches the same amount. Put the bottles on the opposite arms of a common balance. What happens? The arms remain level, that is, the bottles are just as heavy because the amounts balance. Try balancing the bottles *beforehand*. Some balances stick at the pivot and objects declared to be just as heavy by a spring or compression balance may appear to be different when placed on a common balance.

   Explain that the bottles of water, or other objects, are described as being **just as heavy as** one another when instruments show balance, or the same amount of stretching or turning. That is, one is not heavier or lighter than the other.

2. Give a child a bag containing about fifty 3-cm cubes. Ask him or her to put the cubes, touching, in two rows, side by side, so that the rows are the same length, but without counting the cubes. (The rows of cubes could be put on a squared paper background.) Ask the children of the group which row has more cubes? Which row has more wood? Have the rows the same amount of wood? The teacher now puts each row of cubes into identical plastic bags. Which bag of cubes do you think is heavier?

   Let the children pick up the bags. Do they feel the same or different? Is one bag heavier? Are the bags just as heavy? Establish that they feel much the same but it cannot be said with certainty that they are just as heavy.

   The teacher could then put the cubes on a compression balance and also hang them on a spring. Are the bags just as heavy? How do you know?

   Talk about the same amount of wood being just as heavy. Would different amounts of wood be just as heavy? The teacher could, with a group of children, compare unequal rows of cubes, if necessary, to deal with this question.

3. Use two transparent bags containing 80 and 90 marbles and mark the bags with different coloured stickers. Hold the bags, side by side, and ask which has the larger amount of marbles. Talk about the bags looking much the same and that it is not easy to tell. Ask the children in turn to pick up the bags and hold them on the palms of their hands. Which bag of marbles is the heavier? Discuss this with the children. The bags feel much the same so a decision cannot be made with certainty. However, ask the children to choose a bag.

   The teacher now puts the bags on a compression balance. Which is the heavier? Did you choose the right one? Do you think the heavier bag has the larger amount of marbles? Put the marbles from the bags in two rows, side by side, between three long sticks. Which row has more marbles? Which bag contained the larger amount? Did you select the right one? Did the heavier bag contain the larger amount of marbles?

Activities **1**, **2** and **3** of this section would show the children that amounts cannot always be compared at first sight nor heaviness compared by picking things up, particularly when objects look and feel much the same. In these cases a balance or spring must be used and a decision made which is based on what happens to these instruments.

6.7 PRACTICE ACTIVITIES CONCERNING 'JUST AS HEAVY' (1, 8 L1; 8 L2)

The children should now be able to do the following activities individually with guidance from the teacher. The children could be given instructions orally and could reply orally. Objects could be displayed on the table with **just as heavy** labels alongside.

1. Give a child a bag of wooden cubes. Using one-to-one correspondence he puts the same amount of cubes into another bag and checks the result by putting the bags on a common balance.
2. One child partly fills a plastic bottle with water. Another child, by only looking, puts the same amount of water into an identical bottle. The children check the result with a compression balance.
3. Give the child a tin partly filled with sand. Using a common balance he puts the same amount of sand into an identical tin. Are the tins of sand just as heavy?
4. The teacher puts about 500 g and 400 g of sand into two transparent polythene bags and sticks different coloured stickers on them. Ask a child to look at the bags. Which has the larger amount or are they the same? The child now picks up the bags. Which is the heavier, or are they just as heavy? He checks the answers by putting the bags on a compression balance.
5. Ask a child to roll a lump of plasticine into a ball, then with more plasticine to prepare another ball having the same amount of plasticine. He checks the result with a common balance. Should the amounts not be the same he adds small pieces of plasticine to the smaller until the lumps balance. Is there the same amount in each lump now?
6. Give a child two transparent bags each containing 60 marbles. Ask the child to put the bags on a compression balance. Do they contain the same amount of marbles? The child checks the result by emptying the bags and putting the marbles in two rows side by side, between three long sticks.
7. Give a child three transparent plastic bags each partly filled with sand. Arrange it that two of the bags contain the same amount. The child uses the compression balance to find the bags containing the same amount of sand.
8. Give a child a bag containing ten 100-g metal stacking masses. Ask a child, without counting, to put the same amount of metal into another bag. (To do this he could build a tower with the given pieces and make another tower alongside which is just as tall. Or he could make a row with the given metal pieces on a squared background and make a row, just as long, alongside.) The child checks the result using a compression balance.
9. The teachers puts four, four and eight 100-g stacking masses into three identical tins,

fitted with lids, and marks the tins with different coloured stickers. Tell the child that metal pieces have been put inside the tins. Which tin has the largest amount of metal inside it? Have any of the tins the same amount of metal inside? Ask the child to pick up the tins in order to answer these questions. The child now puts the tins on a compression balance and answers the same questions. Were your answers correct? Verify these answers by opening the tins and building towers with the metal pieces.

6.8 DEMONSTRATIONS LEADING TO THE COMPARISON OF DIFFERENT SUBSTANCES (1 L1; 8 L2)

So far the children have compared amounts of like substances by sight and heaviness and have found that decisions are often difficult to make and not always reliable. They have been using instruments to compare amounts and weights in cases of doubt. The teacher has also tried to establish that the larger amount is always the heavier, and the heavier is always the larger amount. This leads to the idea that a balance or spring could be used to find the larger amount or the heavier.

The teacher could develop the idea that amounts and heaviness cannot be compared by sight and that greater reliance has to be placed upon instruments. This particularly applies when quantities of different substances are compared. The following demonstrations and discussions could illustrate these points.

1. Obtain two identical tins, with lids, and label them with different coloured stickers. Put six metal 100-g stacking masses inside each tin.

   Show the tins to a group of children. Tell them that the tins have pieces of metal inside. Have they the same amount of metal inside or not? Can we tell by looking? No, we cannot see inside the tins. Can we tell by picking them up? Let the children pick up the tins and find out. The tins feel much the same but we cannot be sure.

   The teacher now puts the tins on a compression balance. The pointer turns the same amount for each tin. What does this mean? The tins contain the same amount of metal. Verify this by taking off the lids, making towers with the pieces, and comparing these towers.

2. Use two identical powdered milk tins, with lids, one nearly full of sand and the other one about a quarter full. (Label them with different coloured stickers.) Tell the children that the tins contain sand. Do they contain the same or different amounts of sand? We cannot tell by looking. Let the children pick up the tins. They feel different. Which is the heavier? Which tin has the larger amount of sand? The teacher puts the tins on a compression balance to check the answer. Let the children look inside the tins to compare the amounts of sand.

3. Fill a bottle with sand and an identical bottle with water. Ask the children whether they think one is heavier than the other or whether they are just as heavy. Pick them up to find out and then put the bottles on a compression balance to check. Are we right? Can we tell by looking? Explain that the heavier is not the larger because the substances are not the same.

4. Obtain a metal ball about 4 cm in diameter and with plasticine make a ball of the same size. (Or, sellotape together eight 100-g stacking masses to make a cylinder,

and make a plasticine cylinder of the same height and diameter.) Show the children these objects. Which is heavier? Let the children find the heavier ball by picking them up, and then use a balance to check the answer. Establish that they look the same size but they are not just as heavy as one another because they are different substances. The heavier is not larger.

5. Obtain a tennis ball and a ball of plasticine which is smaller, but heavier, than the tennis ball. (Or use an orange and a large hollow rubber ball.) Show the children these objects. Which ball is heavier? Let the children pick them up to find the heavier and then check the result with a compression balance. Display the balls on the table with **heavier** and **lighter** labels alongside. Establish that the heavier ball is smaller in size than the lighter one, and that the heavier cannot be found by sight when different substances are being compared.

6.9 PRACTICE ACTIVITIES FOR LIKE AND UNLIKE SUBSTANCES: 'HEAVIER', 'LIGHTER' AND 'JUST AS HEAVY' (1 L1; 8 L2)

Arrange the following activities for individual children. Compile work cards and, if necessary, read them to the children or give oral instructions. Accept oral answers and encourage the children to use **heavier**, **lighter** and **just as heavy as** labels.

1. Into pairs of identical tins, or boxes, the teacher puts different amounts of dried peas or sand. A child picks up a pair of items which look the same, finds the heavier, and then checks the answer using a compression balance. He displays the pairs of items with **heavier** and **lighter** labels alongside. (Use tobacco tins, powdered milk tins, dried fruit packets, etc.)
2. The teacher prepares pairs of parcels, some of which are just as heavy as one another. A child uses a spring to find the heavier and the lighter of each pair, and pairs just as heavy.
3. The teacher puts various objects into a box, e.g. bags of shells, sand, marbles and cubes, wooden blocks, lumps of plasticine, fairly large pebbles, metal objects, etc.
    A child takes out a pair of items and finds the heavier. He checks the answer using a common balance and displays the pair with **heavier** and **lighter** labels alongside. He repeats this with other pairs of items.
4. Give the child a bag, or tin, containing sand, dried peas or cubes of wood. Ask the child to use a common balance to prepare a bag of sand just as heavy.
5. The teacher puts various objects into a box. Give the child an item from the box. The child uses a spring to find items from the box that are lighter and heavier than the given item.
6. Give a child a bag of sand. He then uses a compression balance to prepare a bag of wooden cubes heavier than the bag of sand, and a bag of shells lighter than the bag of sand.
7. The child uses identical plastic beakers and a compression balance. Which is the heavier, a beaker of sand or water? a beaker of sand or shells? a beaker of marbles or sand?
8. A child partly fills a plastic bottle with water. He uses a compression balance to prepare a bag of sand just as heavy as the bottle of water.

9. Obtain a wooden cube of about 5 cm side. Let the children make a plasticine cube of approximately the same size. Are the cubes just as heavy as one another? Which is the heavier? Use a common balance to check the answer.
10. Obtain a bottle of milk and an identical bottle of sand. Pick them up. Are they just as heavy? Check the answer using a compression balance. Which is the heavier?
11. The teacher provides identical transparent plastic containers, e.g. milk bottles, beakers or jugs. A small bag of sand is given to the child. Amounts of flour, earth, polystyrene chips and cornflakes are measured out on a common balance to be just as heavy as the sand. Put each substance into a plastic container, and display the containers side by side. Are amounts that are just as heavy also the same size?
12. Obtain a collection of spherical, or nearly spherical, objects, e.g. a large metal ball bearing, an orange, a golf ball, a table-tennis ball, a tennis ball, a plasticine ball, etc. Ask a child to find a ball which is smaller than another but heavier. The child uses a common balance to check the results. Display the balls in pairs with **heavier** and **lighter** labels alongside.
13. Give the child three or four objects. He uses a compression balance to find the heaviest and lightest.
14. The teacher partly fills three identical tins or boxes with sand. The child uses a common balance to arrange them in order of heaviness, from heaviest to lightest.
15. Give a child four objects. He picks them up and arranges them in order of heaviness, from heaviest to lightest, and then checks the order using a common balance.

6.10 DESCRIBING AND COMPARING OBJECTS FOR HEAVINESS USING MEASURING UNITS NON-NUMERICALLY (1, 8 L2)

1. The teacher, beforehand, partly fills tins of sand so that they balance a number of identical units, e.g. 15 marbles, 10 wooden cubes, 7 nuts and bolts, etc. She could stick different coloured labels on the tins and pictures of the measuring units to be used.

    Ask a child to balance the green tin with marbles, the red tin with nuts and bolts, etc. Talk with the child about the results. Display the objects on the table with a **just as heavy** label alongside (Fig. 6.4).

Fig. 6.4

2. The teacher could partly fill two tins with sand so that they balance 6 and 10 identical nuts and bolts. Ask a child, or group of children, to find the heavier tin by picking up the tins. Check the result with a common balance.

    The child is then asked to balance each tin with nuts and bolts on the common balance. Ask him to arrange the nuts and bolts in two rows, side by side, on a squared background, and put each tin near the row it balances. (Fig. 6.5). (Squared paper enables the bolts to be spaced out evenly so that the two sets can be compared without counting.) Talk with the children about the display. Which row has more nuts and bolts? Which row has more metal? Which row is the heavier? Which tin balanced this row? Which tin is the heavier? Put **heavier** and **lighter** labels near the tins.

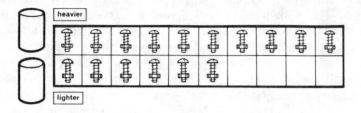

Fig. 6.5

Children from the group could now use this method to compare pairs of items, but the items have to be prepared beforehand by the teacher. She could partly fill tins or bags with sand, shells, dried peas, small pebbles or marbles, so that they just balance a number of wooden cubes, metal bolts, metal washers, large nails, large metal nuts and lumps of metal. (Lumps of metal could be hectogram and half-hectogram stacking masses.) Prepare the tins and bags so that they balance no more than twenty units.

Collections of nails, cubes, washers, bolts, nuts and lumps of metal could then be placed in rows, side by side, on a squared paper strip, to be compared. Cubes could also be compared by building towers with them or putting them touching in rows, side by side. Metal washers and stacking masses could also be built into towers and compared.

Ask individual children to compare the heaviness of bags of sand which have been specially prepared to balance 7 and 10 bolts, 10 and 18 wooden cubes, 5 and 8 hectogram stacking masses, 8 and 15 large nails, 12 and 18 metal washers, 7 and 13 pieces of metal (50-g stacking masses), etc.

6.11 USING NUMBERS TO DESCRIBE HEAVINESS (2 L1; 1, 2, 8 L2)

A careful control of the activities which follow is necessary in order to direct the number work into those regions which the children can understand and handle. Initially, select activities involving numbers to ten; then up to twenty; and finally beyond twenty. The activities listed below illustrate what could be done but precise details are left to the teacher.

1. The teacher prepares bags or tins of sand, shells and dried peas so that they balance wooden cubes, metal nuts, metal washers, nuts and bolts, old sparking plugs, hectogram and half-hectogram stacking masses. Keep the bags or tins and their appropriate measuring units in the same box. Individual children could then be asked to balance these bags and tins with appropriate units, and describe the results.

   Initially, the children could display the answers by arranging items on the table with **just as heavy** and number labels alongside, or by drawing a picture of the items if the numbers are reasonable (Fig. 6.6). Older children could make written records such as **The bag is just as heavy as 6 nails**. Recording is aided by giving the children sentences to copy in which the missing words have to be inserted, e.g. The . . . . . . is just as heavy as . . . . .

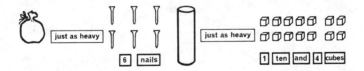

Fig. 6.6

2. Ask a child to use a common balance and to prepare bags of sand just as heavy as eight cubes, six nails, fifteen marbles and twenty washers, etc.
3. A child could use a compression balance to prepare bags of sand or dried peas just as heavy as nine lumps of metal, sixteen metal washers, seven nuts and bolts, etc.
4. Ask a child to use a common balance to find which is the heavier, six cubes or twelve marbles, three bolts or eight washers, seven nails or fifteen cubes, three pieces of metal or nine cubes, twenty marbles or ten metal washers, thirty shells or twenty-four acorns, etc. Display the objects with appropriate labels (Fig. 6.7).

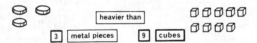

Fig. 6.7

5. The teacher prepares bags of sand, dried peas and shells so that they are lighter than twenty prescribed measuring units, but not necessarily an exact number.

   Individual children could then balance the bags with marbles, wooden cubes, metal nuts, metal washers, metal bolts, nuts and bolts or stacking pieces. Suppose a child is asked to find the number of nails as heavy as a bag of dried peas. He might find, using the common balance, that the bag is lighter than 14 nails but heavier than 13 nails. He could record this with the help of the teacher as shown in Fig. 6.8.

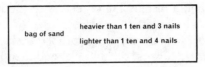

Fig. 6.8

When a child has a fuller knowledge of notation this could be written as shown in Fig. 6.9.

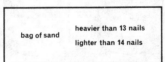

Fig. 6.9

Recording is greatly assisted if the teacher gives the child basic sentences to copy from cards, or prepared sentences on slips of paper, into which missing details are written (Fig. 6.10).

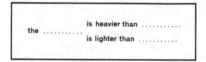

Fig. 6.10

6.12 USING NUMBERS TO COMPARE OBJECTS FOR HEAVINESS (2 L1; 1, 2, 3, 8 L2)

The teacher could prepare pairs of tins, or bags of sand, to just balance a number of cubes, nuts and bolts, large nails, pieces of metal, etc. Ask individual children to find the lighter of each pair.

Initially, ask the child to pick up a pair of tins and find the lighter. He then balances each tin with specified units, finds the number of units in each case, and displays these units in rows, side by side, on a squared paper strip (Fig. 6.11).

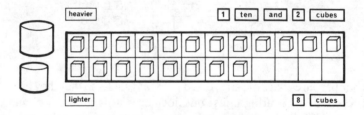

Fig. 6.11

Suppose the tins balance 8 cubes and 1 ten and 2 cubes, then the former is the lighter because 8 is fewer than 1 ten and 2. Talk about this with the child. Arranging the cubes in rows helps the child to draw this conclusion should he not be able to deal with these numbers mentally. He should display the objects with the appropriate number and **heavier** and **lighter** labels alongside.

If a child balances bags of sand with pieces of metal (stacking masses), the metal pieces could be built into two towers, side by side, and their numbers compared (Fig. 6.12).

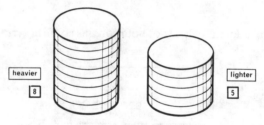

Fig. 6.12

6.13 INTRODUCTION TO STANDARD UNITS: THE KILOGRAM AND HALF KILOGRAM (1, 2, 8 L2)

1. The teacher could show the children a kilogram mass and ask them to hold it whilst taking care to see that it is handled near the floor for safety's sake. Say that this piece of metal has a mass of 1 kilogram and that we call it a kilogram mass. It is not correct to say it weighs 1 kilogram: what is felt when it is picked up is its weight, but its mass is the amount of metal essential to this weight.

   She could then produce some 1-kilogram bags of sand and show, on a balance, that each one balances the 1-kilogram mass. These bags of sand can be used in future activities to measure amounts because they are safer to handle. The children should use a strong common balance, designed to measure up to 5 kg, and placed near to the floor. Should the kilogram bags of sand prove too large to fit on the balance the metal kilograms could be used instead.

2. The teacher prepares boxes of earth, sand and pebbles, and parcels of old books, up to 5 kg in mass, where each is an integral number of kilograms. The children find the masses of these boxes and parcels using a common balance. They could record the masses by filling in the missing details in a sentence copied from a card, or written on a recording slip (Fig. 6.13).

---

the mass of the .... is .... kilograms

Fig. 6.13

3. A child puts sand in a bag so that it feels just as heavy as a kilogram mass. He then uses a balance to check his estimate, and adds or removes sand until the mass equals 1 kilogram. Repeat this activity using earth, pebbles, pieces of plasticine, and dried peas.

4. The teacher prepares a bag of peas, a tin of sand, a bag of earth, a large pebble, a plastic bag of potatoes, a large swede, etc., all less than 5 kg in mass, and not an integral number of kilograms. Use a common balance to compare these items with a kilogram mass, e.g. the tin of sand has a smaller mass than 1 kilogram, or the bag of potatoes has a larger mass than 1 kilogram.

   Also balance each object with kilograms and find their approximate masses. Record the answers by copying and completing sentences written on a card (Fig. 6.14).

---

the .... has a larger mass than .... kilograms
has a smaller mass than .... kilograms

Fig. 6.14

5. The teacher could introduce half-kilogram metal masses and bags of sand. The

children could use a balance to find how many of these bags and metal pieces are needed to balance a kilogram bag. The idea of a half in this and other situations already encountered could be discussed and compared.

Let individual children compare items with a half-kilogram mass, such as 2 cups of sand, a Dienes block, 3 cups of wooden cubes and a cup of dried peas. He could find, for example, that 2 cups of sand have a larger mass than a half kilogram, a cup of dried peas has a smaller mass than a half kilogram, and so on.

Ask individual children to use a common balance to measure out 4 half kilograms of sand, 5 half kilograms of pebbles, 3 half kilograms of sand, etc.

6. The teacher prepares tins and bags of materials so that they just balance a number of half-kilogram masses (no more than 10). Use peas, sand, earth, pebbles, conkers, nails, metal washers, marbles and wooden cubes. Ask individual children to find the masses of these items using a common balance. Record answers by completing sentences written on slips of paper, or by copying and completing sentences (Fig. 6.15).

the . . . . has a mass of . . . . half kilograms

Fig. 6.15

7. Kilogram masses could be balanced with half kilograms and the relationship of halves to wholes could be recorded for 1, 2, 3, 4 and 5 kilograms (Fig. 6.16). Some of the children could be asked to continue the pattern further without using a balance. How many half kilograms would balance 8 kilograms? 7 kilograms? 10 kilograms?

. . . . half kilograms balance 1 kilograms
. . . . half kilograms balance 2 kilograms
. . . . half kilograms balance 3 kilograms
. . . . half kilograms balance 4 kilograms
. . . . half kilograms balance 5 kilograms

Fig. 6.16

8. The teacher could, with a child or group, balance 7 half kilograms with kilograms and a half kilogram. That is, 7 half kilograms balance 3 kilograms and 1 half kilogram. This could be recorded by completing a sentence (Fig. 6.17).

. . . . half kilograms balance . . . . kilograms and a half kilogram

Fig. 6.17

Individual children could now balance 3 half kilograms, 5 half kilograms, and 9 half kilograms with kilograms and a half kilogram.

9. The teacher could with a child or group introduce the notation ½ for one half. This might have been encountered before in other activities. Also introduce kg as the abbreviation for kilogram. Show number cards involving half kilograms, or write them on the blackboard, to help practise interpreting this notation: 3½ kg means 3 kilograms and 1 half kilogram, 5½ kg means 5 kilograms and 1 half kilogram, etc. Also explain that four kilograms and one half kilogram is written down quickly as 4½ kg. Find the cards which have written on them three and a half kilograms, five and a half kilograms, seven and a half kilograms, etc. Encourage the children to use this notation when recording.

10. Individual children could use the objects listed in paragraph **4** of this section, together with such items as a shoe, a blackboard rubber, a Dienes block, parcels of books, a bottle of water, and wooden off-cuts. Find their approximate masses using kilogram and half-kilogram masses. Record results by completing sentences (Fig. 6.18).

```
                   has a larger mass than   .......1½..... kg
the  ....sand.....
                   has a smaller mass than  .......2...... kg
```

Fig. 6.18

6.14 GRADUATING AND USING A COMPRESSION BALANCE: KILOGRAMS AND HALF KILOGRAMS (1, 2, 8 L2)

So far the children have used a common balance to measure masses in kilograms and half kilograms. If, however, a bag of sand has a larger mass than 2 kg and a smaller mass than 2½ kg we cannot say whether the sand is nearer 2 kg or 2½ kg in mass. We cannot measure to the nearest unit, generally, using a common balance.

A compression balance graduated in kilograms would enable us to measure to the nearest kilogram, and one graduated in half kilograms would enable us to measure to the nearest half kilogram. We could then say that a box has a mass of 2 kg if the pointer is nearer 2 than 3, or 2½ kg if the pointer is nearer 2½ than 3.

This is one of the reasons why children should be encouraged to use compression balances. Children could, initially, use common balances because handling kilograms and half kilograms provides the 'feel' of these units. Standard masses have then to be totalled and this provides useful experience involving cardinal number, number language and addition. To use a compression balance and merely read numbers from a dial does not give an understanding of cardinal number of notation, or provide an appreciation of the measuring units.

When children are able to use a common balance and deal easily with kilograms and half kilograms they are ready to use a compression balance.

1. The teacher should prepare, before the teaching session, to make an existing compression balance suitable for the occasion. She needs a compression balance,

that is, an instrument with a scale pan and a pointer. The usual type of instrument has a pointer which rotates over a circular dial. Use an instrument which measures up to 5 kg. Cover the existing numbers, and graduations, with gummed white paper. That is, stick a paper annulus on the glass covering the circular dial so that the pointer is still visible within the ring.

Having completed this preparation the teacher, with the children, graduates the instrument to read half kilograms. Mark the initial position of the pointer. Put on the pan, one at a time, half kilogram masses, and mark the positions of the pointer. Exchange two ½ kg masses, on the pan, for a kilogram mass whenever possible. Count the number of kilograms on the pan, each time, and write the number of kilograms against the mark at the end of the pointer. In this way we build up a scale ½, 1, 1½, 2, 2½, 3, 3½, 4, 4½, and 5.

2. The teacher arranges for individual children, at first, to put objects whose masses are an integral number of half kilograms on the instrument, and read their masses. Also to measure out quantities such as 2 kg of sand, 1½ kg of pebbles and 2½ kg of sand.

3. After this the teacher would put items, less than 3 kg, on the balance and ask children from the group to read these masses. This would be followed by individual children finding masses for themselves, to the nearest ½ kg.

4. Give a child a pair of objects, each less than 3 kg in mass. Ask the child to measure the masses of these objects, to the nearest ½ kilogram, and find their total mass, and how much larger one mass is than the other. The mass of each object could be displayed using ½ kg bags of sand or metal pieces to help the child answer these questions.

Record the answers by copying and completing sentences (Fig. 6.19)

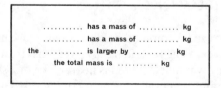

Fig. 6.19

6.15 INTRODUCTION TO GRAMS (1, 2 L2; 2, 8 L3)

Up to now masses have been measured using kilograms and half kilograms. Explain that these units are too large to measure the masses of smaller items. This leads to the introduction of grams.

Activities involving grams could occur when the children are becoming familiar with the use of numbers up to 100 and so would provide excellent opportunities to develop number words, notation and place value, and do some simple calculations.

Centicubes could be used to balance items. These plastic cubes, of side 1 cm, each have a mass of 1 gram. At first balance small items with these gram masses put on singly. Later they can be joined together to make multiple masses, and put on in bars or blocks, to make measuring quicker.

The teacher also needs to select the items used before presenting them to the children in order to control the numbers. Keep below a hundred grams at first and then proceed to slightly larger masses.

1. The teacher could with a group of children find masses of small items using a common balance and 1-gram cubes. The following objects, whose approximate masses are given, could be used: plastic ballpoint pen (7 g), yoghurt carton (10 g), plastic egg carton (12 g), a small cardboard box (15 g), plastic squash bottle (28 g), large plastic detergent bottle (36 g) and a spark-plug (50 g).

   After each item has been balanced, the grams, when possible, are sorted into groups of ten. Each group of ten cubes is made into a 10-g block. The 10-g blocks are placed on the left of the 1-g cubes left over. If the squash bottle is balanced, for example, the 1-gram cubes can be structured into two 10-g blocks and eight separate 1-g cubes. How many cubes is this? (Two tens and eight ones) What is this number? (Twenty-eight) How do we write twenty-eight? (28) What is the mass of these cubes? (Twenty-eight grams). The plastic bottle, the gram masses, and a **28 gram** label could be displayed on the table.

2. Individual children could use the common balance to find the masses of the following articles: ballpoint pen, pencil, matchbox, two drawing pins, a penny, a very small pebble, one or two pieces of screwed-up paper, etc. If balance cannot be obtained describe the mass of the item as between x and y grams.

3. A child could find the masses of these larger items using grams: small cardboard box, yoghurt carton, plastic egg-box, a four-inch nail, a Stern ten block, etc. Form the cubes into 10-g blocks when finding the mass of each item. Display the 10-g blocks and 1-g cubes, and recording labels, near each item, e.g. 2 tens 5 ones, or 25, depending on the stage the child has reached.

4. A child makes four different shapes with Centicubes, each having a mass of 24 grams.

5. A child uses Centicubes to make shapes with these masses: 15 grams, 24 grams, 35 grams, and so on.

6. Talk about the inconvenience of having to sort 1-g cubes into tens to find the masses of objects. The children then make 10-g blocks and use them and 1-g cubes to find the masses of these items using a common balance: a small plastic Fairy Liquid bottle, a large plastic Fairy Liquid bottle, a small cream tin, a small plastic squash bottle, 4 Cuisenaire orange rods, a Stern 6-block, 10 Cuisenaire yellow rods, 6 Stern unit cubes, a cardboard egg box, a spark-plug and a 6-inch nail.

   If balance cannot be obtained describe the mass as between x and y grams. Display each item with a mass label alongside, e.g. 3 tens 5 grams, or 35 grams, whichever is appropriate.

7. Display, using 1-g cubes and 10-g blocks, these masses: 26 grams, 17 grams, 32 grams, 40 grams, 29 grams, etc. Put the 10-g blocks to the left of the 1-g cubes.

8. Use 10-g blocks and 1-g cubes to measure out these amounts of sand: 18 grams, 27 grams, 39 grams, and so on.

9. The children who can handle numbers involving tens and ones, and masses to a hundred grams, could be introduced to numbers beyond a hundred, and measure masses in the 100–200 gram range. The teacher needs to prepare and assemble suitable objects. The following articles, amongst others, could be used: large empty

fruit tin, 3 Dienes flats, 3 Stern 10 blocks, 3 six-inch nails, 30 Stern unit cubes, a packet of tea (125 g), a tablet of soap, etc.

Ask a child to balance a large carrot with 10-g blocks and 1-g cubes. Then sort the 10-g blocks into sets of ten, and put an elastic band around each set. Explain that ten tens are called a hundred, so these masses are 100 grams. Arrange the 100-g bundles on the left of the 10-g blocks, and the 10-g blocks on the left of the 1-g cubes. Suppose there is 1 hundred-gram bundle, 2 ten-gram blocks and 4 gram cubes on the table after the exchanging. How many cubes are there? (One hundred, two tens and four.) What number is this? (One hundred and twenty four.) How do we write this number? (1 hundred 2 tens 4 ones, at first.) Place the carrot, the 100-g, 10-g and 1-g masses together with number labels on the table.

The teacher could supervise a child, or group, and assist them with recording whilst the masses of the other objects listed previously are being found.

10. When the children are ready the recording could be simplified by writing 124 g, 165 g, and so on. The abbreviation g for gram is introduced; and hundreds, tens and ones labels are gradually phased out.

The masses of objects measured could then be increased to about 500 g. These could be balanced with 100-g metal stacking masses, 10-g blocks and 1-g cubes, because the 100-g metal pieces would occupy less room on the balance. (Balance the metal pieces with 10-g blocks before using them to establish that they are 100-g masses.)

The children could then measure out sand, earth, lentils, or make plasticine balls, of these masses: 120 grams, 174 gram, 135 grams, 146 grams, etc.

They could also measure the masses of these items: a Mars bar, a large blackboard rubber, a cup of peas, a cup of sand, a medium-sized potato, an orange, a large onion and a Dienes block.

11. The children put folded paper and cardboard pieces into different sized envelopes to make pretend 'letters', find the mass of each letter, in grams, and the cost of posting it. Postal rates for letters could be looked up from a Royal Mail letter rate leaflet.

12. Float tin lids, small open boxes or other containers on water and put 1-g, 5-g, 10-g and 50-g masses on them. Find the largest mass each one will carry before sinking.

6.16 DIFFERENCES IN MASS: NUMERICAL WORK (1, 2, L2; 3, 8 L3; 3 L4)

1. The teacher specially prepares lumps of plasticine each with a mass an integral number of grams below 20 g. Other objects could also be used if they meet these requirements.

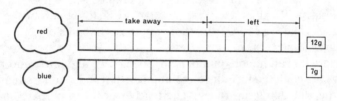

Fig. 6.20

The teacher with a group of children uses two pieces of plasticine and balances them with 1-g cubes. The masses of the pieces of plasticine are to be compared by displaying the cubes, fixed together in two blocks, side by side, on the table (Fig. 6.20).

Talk about how many cubes balance each lump of plasticine and what their masses are (12 g and 7 g). Which piece has the larger mass? How much larger in mass is it? Talk could proceed on methods of finding this out. We could take from the longer block as many cubes as are in the shorter block and leave some behind (12 take 7 leaves 5): so one piece is 5 g larger than the other.

At another time she could, in dealing with this situation, talk about the difference between the number of cubes, looking to see up to what point the blocks are the same length in the display and observing the 'extra' cubes in the longer block. She could show how to find the number of 'extra' cubes, the difference between the masses, by counting on ($7 + ? = 12$), or by removing the 'extra' cubes in the longer row or by counting back ($12 - ? = 7$).

2. Set practice exercises based on these ideas. For example, a child could use a matchbox and a small cardboard box, each less than 20 g in mass. He finds their masses using gram cubes and a common balance, and forms each lot of cubes into a block. He compares the blocks of cubes and finds the larger mass, and how much larger it is.

A child, or pair of children, could use a plastic ballpoint pen, a yoghurt carton, a plastic egg-box and a small empty cardboard box. He finds the mass of each using a balance and 1-g cubes, and forms them into blocks. The blocks of cubes are then displayed, side by side, and labelled with the masses of the cubes in each block. Which block is longest? Which article has the largest mass? Which block is shortest? Which thing has the smallest mass? Arrange the blocks in order from the largest mass to the smallest mass. Suppose the order is cardboard box (15 g), egg-box (12 g), yoghurt carton (10 g) and pen (7 g). Is the box larger in mass than the yoghurt carton? How much larger? How much smaller in mass is the pen than the box? Is the mass of the pen and the yoghurt carton together larger than the mass of the box? Write down how much larger or smaller in mass the yoghurt carton is than each of the other items.

3. The teacher should also talk with the children about comparing larger masses. Two prepared tins of sand, pieces of plasticine, and other selected objects could be used. Suppose we use a small tin (43 g) and a small plastic bottle (28 g). The 1-g cubes which balance each item are formed into 10-g blocks and displayed near each object together with number labels (Fig. 6.21).

The children should be questioned about the larger mass. How can we tell? More 1-g cubes balanced the tin. The teacher should make the point about looking first at the 10-g blocks and not at the 1-g cubes.

The children, individually or in pairs, could be given pairs of items, in the 10 g–100 g range. They find the mass of each object and the larger and smaller mass. The results are displayed as shown in Fig. 6.21.

4. Using a prepared pair of objects a child, or pair of children, find the mass of each using 1-g cubes and a balance. (3 Cuisenaire orange rods in a small cardboard box and a cardboard egg-box could be used.) Structure the cubes into 10-g blocks. Then record the masses of each item, and use Centicubes to find how much larger in mass

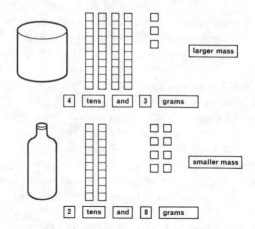

Fig. 6.21

one object is than the other. This could be done by adding cubes to the smaller mass to make it up to the larger mass, or taking cubes from the larger mass to make it the same mass as the smaller. Recording could be assisted by copying and completing sentences written on a card (Fig. 6.22).

The mass of .... is .... tens .... ones grams
The mass of .... is .... tens .... ones grams
        The .... has the larger mass
    It is .... tens .... ones grams larger

Fig. 6.22

5. Similar activities could now be done by a child, or pair of children, to find the larger and smaller mass, and how much larger, using other selected pairs of objects. The objects should balance gram masses. (If they do not the teacher should help the child find the mass to the nearest gram by considering the behaviour of the balance.)

    Suitable pairs of objects which could be used are: a small plastic bottle (28 g) and a small cream tin (44 g), 4 Cuisenaire orange rods inside a small cardboard box (42 g) and a small plastic detergent bottle (31 g), a spark-plug (50 g) and a medium fruit tin (60 g), a small blackboard rubber (82 g) and 5 plastic ballpoint pens inside an elastic band (36 g), or a large fruit tin (102 g) and a large plastic detergent bottle (36 g).

6. At an appropriate time for the child, after he or she has done sufficient comparison exercises, the teacher could arrange a teaching group to demonstrate and discuss the finding of the differences in mass by a formal method. One-gram cubes and 10-g blocks would be used as a concrete base for the thinking to be involved in the process. The 10-g blocks can easily be split into ten 1-g cubes, demonstrating the process of decomposition (Fig. 6.23). To find the difference in mass between 43 g and 28 g we could take away the smaller mass from the larger mass, that is, 43 g take away 28 g (Fig. 6.23). We see there are not enough 1-g cubes in the mass of the tin to be able to take away 8 cubes. We restructure the mass of the tin from 4 tens and 3 ones into 3 tens and 13 ones. The teacher should be sure this step is appreciated; that is, there are the same number of cubes as before but they are arranged in a different

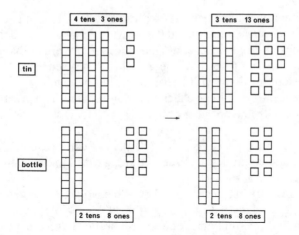

Fig. 6.23

way. We can now take away 8 cubes, followed by 2 ten-blocks, leaving one 10-g block and five 1-g cubes. The difference in their mass in 15g.

When sufficient illustrations of the process have been given the teacher could show the formal way of recording which follows the steps taken in the concrete situation.

$$4 \text{ tens} \quad 3 \text{ ones} \quad \text{take away} \quad 2 \text{ tens} \quad 8 \text{ ones}$$
$$3 \text{ tens} \quad 13 \text{ ones} \quad \text{take away} \quad 2 \text{ tens} \quad 8 \text{ ones}$$
$$1 \text{ ten and } 5 \text{ ones left}$$

This may later be expressed in a different form

$$4 \text{ tens} \quad 3 \text{ ones} \qquad\qquad 3 \text{ tens} \quad 13 \text{ ones}$$
$$2 \text{ tens} \quad 8 \text{ ones} \quad \text{·take away} \quad 2 \text{ tens} \quad 8 \text{ ones}$$
$$\overline{\qquad\qquad\qquad\qquad\qquad 1 \text{ ten} \quad 5 \text{ ones} \quad \text{left}}$$

and eventually put in the usual column format

$$
\begin{array}{cc}
3 & 10 \\
\cancel{4} & 3- \\
2 & 8 \\
\hline
1 & 5 \\
\hline
\end{array}
$$

Similar pairs of items, as mentioned in **5** of this section, could now be used by the children as individual exercises. Having found their masses they would use the decomposition method to calculate the difference in mass. This would lead to practice exercises without the use of apparatus for those children who are successful, and understand the previous stages of this section.

6.17 ADDITION: NUMERICAL WORK (1, 2 L2; 3, 8 L3; 3 L4)

Addition could be introduced and developed by finding the total mass of two or three objects. At first involve tens and ones, and later hundreds. Masses of objects would be found on a common balance and represented by 10-g blocks and 1-g cubes.

Initially, at each stage, only record the individual masses and their total mass. Later a more formal layout should be encouraged, and as grams are exchanged for 10 g carrying numbers could be written down. Cubes should still be used. Finally work cards containing practice exercises done with apparatus could be given.

None of the results should be checked with a balance. The practical result would not generally agree with the answers obtained.

1. Find the total mass of an egg carton (12 g) and a cardboard box (15 g). Combine the two masses and count first the number of 1-g cubes followed by the number of 10-g blocks (12 g + 15 g = 27 g).

    Find the mass of an egg carton (12 g). What would be the mass of four of these egg cartons? (12 g + 12 g + 12 g + 12 g = 48 g)
2. Proceed to find the total mass of a squash bottle (28 g) and a cardboard box (15 g). Combine the masses, then sort the 1-g cubes into 10-g blocks. Count the 1-g cubes and then the 10-g blocks (28 g + 15 g = 43 g).

    Find the mass of a large plastic detergent bottle (36 g). Use cubes to find the mass of two of these bottles (36 g + 36 g = 72 g).
3. Hundreds could be introduced. Find the total mass of a squash bottle (28 g), detergent bottle (36 g) and a medium-sized fruit tin (60 g). In this case the 10-g blocks could be grouped into tens to form 100-g bundles (28 g + 36 g + 60 g = 124 g).

    Find the mass of a small plastic detergent bottle (28 g). Use cubes to find the mass of four of these bottles (28 g + 28 g + 28 g + 28 g = 112 g).

6.18 GRADUATING AND USING A COMPRESSION BALANCE: GRAMS (1 L2; 2, 3, 8, L3; 3 L4)

1. The teacher obtains a compression balance which measures up to 1 kg. Cover the original scale on the circular face of the balance with a gummed paper ring. Supervise a child, or group, whilst 100-g metal stacking masses are placed on the balance, one at a time. (Before doing this establish that a metal stacking mass balances, on a common balance, ten 10-g Centicube blocks, so its mass is 100 g). Mark the initial position of the pointer and the positions as the 100-g masses are put on. Talk about the total mass on the pan at each stage and write the appropriate number near the mark at the end of the pointer. The circular dial would be marked 0, 100, 200, ... , 800, 900. Stop at 900 otherwise thousands would need to be introduced.

    Children could now place objects on the balance and the positions of the pointer read to give their masses. Descriptions such as just larger than 300 g, or just smaller than 600 g, could be discussed and used. The middle positions between the 'hundred' marks could be considered, and a mass described as about 350 g, if appropriate. Masses could also be measured to the nearest 100 g.

    Individual children should be given plenty of opportunity to find masses, up to 900 g, using this instrument. They could also use it to measure out quantities such as 200 g of sand.

2. The teacher could, when the children are ready, proceed a step farther and graduate a balance to read up to 950 g in 50 g intervals. Initially, balance some of the 100-g and 50-g metal masses which are to be used with 10-g blocks on a common balance to establish that they are 100-g and 50-g masses. Use an instrument which measures up to 1 kg and cover the dial with a paper ring. Put the masses on 50 g at a time and whenever possible exchange two 50-g masses for one 100-g mass. Talk about the total mass on the pan at each stage, how that number is written and write it near a mark at the end of the pointer. The scale would read 0, 50, 100, 150, ... , 900, 950.

   The teacher could then put items on the balance and children could read their masses, to the nearest 50 g. Then ask individual children to find masses of various items, and measure out quantities, e.g. 450 g of sand.

3. The next stage would be for the teacher and children to graduate a balance in 10-g intervals. Use an instrument which measures up to 750 g or 1 kg. Put 100-g masses on at first and put in the 'hundred' marks. Then start again with an empty pan and put on 10-g masses one at a time whilst marking and numbering the pointer positions. When appropriate exchange ten 10-g masses for one 100-g mass.

   The teacher would then ask the children to read the masses of various objects placed on this instrument to the nearest 10 g.

4. Arrange for individual children to find the masses of various items to the nearest 10 g using the compression balance graduated in 10-g intervals.

5. Find the mass of a half litre of water, sand, marbles, wooden cubes and shells, using a compression balance graduated in 10-g intervals. Include the container in each case.

6. Give a child a pair of objects. Use a compression balance graduated in 10-g intervals to find their masses to the nearest 10 g. Which is the larger mass? How much larger is it? (The child could count along the scale from one mass to the other, or he might be capable of calculating the difference.)

7. A child needs three or four objects each less than 800 g, a compression balance and some 100-g masses. He picks up each object and estimates its mass to the nearest 100 g. (To do this he picks up 100-g masses until they feel just as heavy as each object.) He records the estimates then puts each item on the balance and reads its mass to the nearest 100 g. How much larger or smaller were the estimates than the actual masses?

8. Ask a child to pick up three or four bags of sand or other items and to find the largest and smallest masses. Then put the items one at a time on a compression balance and find their masses to the nearest 10 g. Were the correct items selected? Arrange the objects in order of mass from the largest to smallest. How much larger in mass is the largest than the smallest?

9. Do the exercise described in **8** using instead small identical tins containing quantities of sand, water or dried peas.

10. A child uses a compression balance graduated in 10-g intervals to find the masses to the nearest 10 g of the following pairs: a cup of dried peas and a cup of sand, a cup of marbles and a cup of wooden beads, and a cup of wooden cubes and a cup of sand. In each case find how many grams larger one item of the pair is than the other.

11. Find, using a compression balance, the mass of an empty half-litre metal measure to the nearest 10 g. Then find the masses of a half litre of water, a half litre of sand and

a half litre of wooden cubes. What mass of cubes, sand and water does the measure hold?

6.19 FURTHER ACTIVITIES (2, 3, 8 L3; 3 L4)

The teacher could also include the following activities for those children who are ready for them:

1. Ask questions about shopping. Ensure the arithmetic is reasonably straightforward.
   If sugar costs 35p for 500 g, how much will 100 g, 200 g, 400 g and 900 g cost? How much sugar could be bought with 21p, 49p and 70p?
   If 100 g of tea costs 44p what will 400 g, 500 g, 50 g, 25 g and 250 g cost? How much tea could be bought with 22p, 66p, 110p, 33p and £1.32?
2. Set questions which concern the buying of small or larger amounts. For example, a 50-g tube of toothpaste costs 65p whilst a 125-g tube of the same kind costs £1.09. A 125-g tablet of soap costs 33p whilst a pack of two 75-g tablets of the same brand costs 45p. Which is the better buy?
3. Pick up four items and arrange them in order of mass, largest to smallest, then put them on a common balance to check the answer. Do not use any standard masses but only balance items one with another.
4. Use a common balance to find to the nearest gram the mass of 30 marbles. Use this result to estimate the masses of 60, 90, 120, 150 and 75 marbles.
5. Use a compression balance to compare the masses of twenty 2p coins and forty 1p coins. Have they the same mass? The teacher could introduce the following argument:

   20 twopences balance 40 pennies
   so 10 twopences balance 20 pennies
   and 1 twopence balances 2 pennies.

   Talk with the child about this argument very carefully. Who do you think this coin, a twopence, is worth twice as much as this coin, a penny? (It has twice the mass and twice as much metal.)
6. Use a compression balance to compare the masses of twenty old 5p coins and ten 10p coins. What do you find? They have the same mass. Help the child to form the argument that:

   20 fivepences balance 10 tenpences
   so 10 fivepences balance 5 tenpences
   and 2 fivepences balance 1 tenpence.

   Why do you think this coin, a tenpence, is worth two of these fivepences? (One is twice the mass of the other and has twice as much metal so is worth twice as much.)
7. Using a bathroom scale, graduated in kilograms, the pupil keeps a monthly graphical record of his or her mass during the year. Stones and pounds could be talked about, possibly, should the scale be graduated in Imperial and metric units. ('*Ourselves*')

8. A group of children each find their mass using a bathroom scale. They arrange their masses in order, largest to smallest, and illustrate them with a block graph. (*'Ourselves'*)

9. You have a common balance and one 1-g, one 2-g, one 4-g and one 8-g mass. What masses could be measured out if all or some of these masses are put in one pan of the balance only? Record each result briefly; e.g. $12\,g = 8\,g + 4\,g$; $7\,g = 4\,g + 2\,g + 1\,g$. (Answer: 1 g, 2 g, 3 g, 4 g, ... , 14 g, 15 g.)

10. You have 4 masses of 1 g, 2 g, 5 g and 10 g and a common balance. What masses could be measured out using some, or all, of these masses if they are put on the same pan of the balance? Are there any masses less than 18 g which cannot be measured out? (4 g, 9 g and 14 g) Could 4 g, 9 g and 14 g be obtained if both scale pans were used? Give details.

11. You have a common balance and one 1-g, one 3-g and one 9-g mass. What masses could be measured out if all or some of these masses are put in both pans, or only in one pan, of the balance? Give brief details, e.g. $5\,g = 9\,g$ on one pan and $3\,g + 1\,g$ on the other pan. (Answer: 1 g, 2 g, 3 g, 4 g, ..., 12 g, 13 g).

12. With a group of children the teacher could carry out the following activity and discussion. Hang a metal helical spring from a nail. Behind it fix a long strip of white paper. Use a spring which will easily support up to 600 g and extend about 2 or 3 cm for each 100 g. Tie a small box or tin to the end of the spring to act as a mass holder. Mark the position of the end of the spring on the paper.

    Put 100 g in the mass holder and mark the position of the bottom of the spring again. Repeat this for masses of 200 g, 300 g, etc., up to 600 g. Write alongside each mark the number of grams needed to stretch the spring that far.

    Ask the children where they think the end of the spring would be if a mass of 350 g was put in the box. Put 350 g in the box and mark the end of the spring. Then put 50 g, 150 g, 250 g, 450 g and 550 g, in turn, in the box and mark the positions with the appropriate numbers.

    The teacher could then put various items, whose masses are 600 g or less, in the box and ask the children to read the mass of each item from the scale to the nearest 50 g.

    Ask individual children to use the graduated spring to find the masses of a pair of objects to the nearest 50 g and then calculate their difference in mass.

    Ask a child to pick up four or five objects and find the largest and smallest masses. He then uses the graduated spring to measure these masses and consequently to arrange them in order, starting with the largest mass.

Chapter 7

Surface and Area

The surface of an object is the part we see and can touch. It is the boundary of a solid. With young children the surface can be imagined to be a very thin skin which encloses the material inside it. With a blown-up balloon a thin sheet of rubber encloses air and this rubber is the surface of the balloon. The surface of a plastic bag filled with sand is the plastic bag. With a cardboard box the surface is the thin layer of cardboard from which it is made. These analogies, though unsuitable from a mathematical point of view, at least put the children some part of the way towards knowing what a surface is.

7.1 GENERAL SCHEME

The following points should be considered when dealing with surface and area.

1. Comparison of lengths should precede some of the tests used to compare surfaces because they are based on the former.
2. The building of vocabulary is very important, particularly in the early stages when comparison tests are introduced and fundamental ideas are being developed.
3. Measuring surfaces should then be tackled and the word **area** introduced. Children must be helped to realize that surfaces are measured by placing items on them and counting the number needed. Initially, use specially selected shapes so that an integral number of units fit on them. Then use shapes where units do not fit and the answers have to be expressed between limits. Finally, encourage children to describe an area approximately using one number, such as 'about 12 squares'.
4. The need for standard units is then considered. The **square metre**, **square decimetre** and **square centimetre** are introduced, and areas of surfaces found. These units are not introduced at the same time. The square decimetre is the first unit to deal with because it is a reasonable size for covering things. The square metre can be introduced as a unit for larger surfaces, but it is rather large and there are not many suitable surfaces to measure. Finding the area of the classroom floor is difficult because units cannot be fitted over it; finding the area of the playground or school hall would involve numbers which are too large and also demand too many covering units.

   The square centimetre is rather small, and certainly surfaces would not be covered with cardboard centimetre squares because the task is too difficult and time consuming. A centimetre grid, however, does save the situation. Areas of small faces of boxes, and lids from tins, can be found but most containers have faces whose areas are larger than 100 square centimetres.

Apart from an introduction to these units we cannot proceed very far in finding areas. We have to wait until children can deal with larger numbers.

7.2 EQUIPMENT

A collection of tins, bottles, jars, boxes and other containers of various shapes and sizes. Solid objects, such as pieces of metal, stones, pebbles and wooden blocks. Various prisms, pyramids and spheres. In particular, tin lids, box lids, Vim containers, Bisto boxes, salt boxes, biscuit tins, Oxo boxes, cereal packets, table jelly boxes, tea packets, macaroni boxes, porridge boxes, cornflour boxes and suet boxes.

Cover surfaces with Cuisenaire and Stern unit cubes, bottle tops, buttons, beads, marbles, plastic circles, plastic rectangles, plastic hexagons, 2.5 cm plastic squares (abacus tablets), 5 cm plastic squares, 10 cm plastic squares, cardboard decimetre squares and newspaper metre squares.

Shapes needed for tessellations: plastic squares, rectangles, right-angled triangles, equilateral triangles, isosceles triangles, rhombuses, parallelograms, circles, semi-circles, quadrilaterals, hexagons, pentagons and octagons.

Various cardboard shapes, such as rectangles, triangles, circles, etc., as described in the text.

Centimetre squared paper, 2 cm squared paper, 5 cm squared paper and triangular grid paper.

Transparent plastic grid ruled in centimetre squares.

7.3 SURFACE: INTRODUCTORY ACTIVITIES (1, 8, 9, 10 L1)

Use a collection of boxes, bottles, jars, tins and other containers. Also solid objects, such as pieces of metal, wooden blocks, stones and pebbles. Sets of mathematical shapes are also necessary because they include pyramids and prisms of various kinds. Let the children play with them, and sort them, as described in Chapter 5, 'Capacity and Volume', under Section 5.4, *Introductory Activities*.

The teacher needs to hold up various shapes, such as cylinders, rectangular boxes, and various prisms and pyramids, and talk to the children about them. These talks would be to the whole class and last three or four minutes. The talks would introduce ideas about faces, edges, corners, curved and flat faces, straight and curved edges, and names of shapes, such as rectangle, circle, triangle, rectangular box, cylinder, ball and pyramid. Children would also be allowed to handle the shapes. The next paragraph indicates some of the points to be included. Further details can be obtained from Chapter 8, 'Shape and Space', Section 8.3.

The surface of an object is the part we see and touch. Often surfaces are split into regions called faces by boundaries called edges. Faces may be flat or curved, enclosed by straight or curved edges. On looking at solids we see faces of various shapes, rectangles, squares, triangles and circles, mainly. Some solids, such as a ball, an orange, a lump of plasticine, have one surface only and no edges and corners. Consolidate these ideas by talking about solids from the class collection. Ask children to sort solids into sets according to shapes of faces, or the nature of their faces or edges. When we ask children to compare sizes of two faces we enter the province of area, e.g. does this face cover more than that one?

7.4 DIRECT COMPARISONS: NON-NUMERICAL (1, 8, 9, 10 L1)

1. The teacher obtains two boxes with rectangular flat faces. Pick out a face on each box such that one face will surround the other when they are placed together. Cover these faces with coloured gummed paper for identification purposes. Ask the class which face covers more surface, the red or the green. How can we tell? Get a picture or jigsaw puzzle and put each surface on it in turn. Which leaves more picture showing? Which surface covers more of the picture? Which surface is larger? Then put the boxes together with the red and green faces touching. The face which lies inside the other has the smaller surface, e.g. the red surface covers more than the green surface (Fig. 7.1).

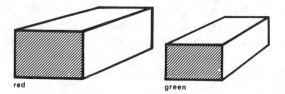

red   green

Fig. 7.1

The teacher then cuts these faces from the boxes so that the children can see more clearly what is being done. We have a red rectangle and a green one. Which is the longer? Which is the wider? Which rectangle has the larger surface, that means, covers more? Put one rectangle on the other. If it goes inside the other it has a smaller surface; if it more than covers the other rectangle it has a larger surface.

The children could then do the following activities, individually, during the next few days:

(a) Give the children cardboard shapes, such that one can be put inside the other, as follows: a rectangle and a circle, a circle and a triangle, two circles, two rectangles, a square and a rectangle, two triangles, two irregular shapes, etc. Ask which is the larger surface of each pair. Also use sets containing three cardboard shapes and ask which is the largest surface and the smallest. (Put sets of shapes on the table with the larger or largest on the left in order to give answers.)

(b) Use boxes with various faces painted different colours, or marked with a picture or symbol. The teacher selects faces from different boxes such that one fits inside the other. Ask the child which is the larger surface, the red or the green? the face marked with a cat or the one marked with an apple?

No more than two or three children would do the activities at a time because only a few sets of shapes would be available. When most children have done these activities the teacher proceeds as described in paragraph **2**. Children who have done the activities in **1** could then start the activities in **2**, whilst other children complete the activities of **1**.

2. The teacher next uses two boxes of the same shape and size, e.g. cereal packets. Ask

the children if any of the faces are the same on both boxes. Put faces together to test this. Explain that when faces fit exactly they are the same length and width, and also cover the same amount. That is, they have the same amount of surface.

The teacher takes one of the boxes, removes the top face, and cuts the remaining piece carefully down the seams. What shapes are the faces? How many faces have we? Are any of these faces exactly the same? Ask a child to fit them together and find identical shapes. We have two pairs of equal rectangles and an odd rectangle. Did this rectangle have a partner? If so, where did it fit? In order to find out fit this rectangle against the faces of the box which was not taken apart.

The teacher would then set different activities to be done individually. No more than three or four children would do them at a time.

Give the child six rectangles, two of which are the same. Find the rectangles which cover the same amount. Also use sets of triangles, quadrilaterals, circles and assorted shapes. Put shapes on the table with those that cover the same amount on the left.

When most of the children have completed the activities of **2** the teacher again talks to, and shows things to, the whole class or a group as described in **3**.

3. Get a cereal box and cut it open along the seams. Retain two different side faces and the bottom face.

   The teacher uses the two side faces. Which is the longer? Which is wider? Establish by fitting them together that they are the same length but different widths. Which rectangle has the larger surface? The narrower rectangle will just fit the wider one in one direction but there is spare room in the other direction. So the wider rectangle has the larger surface.

   Now compare the rectangle from the bottom with the smaller of the side faces. Which is longer? Which is wider? Here, one rectangle is longer but their widths are the same. Which surface is the larger? The teacher fits the shorter rectangle on the longer one. It just fits one way but there is room to spare in the other direction. So the shorter rectangle has the smaller surface.

   Now provide individual work for four children. Supply two sets of four rectangles, cut from thin card, of the same width but with different lengths. For each set find the largest and smallest surfaces. Also supply two sets containing four cardboard rectangles of the same length but different widths. For each set find the largest and smallest surfaces.

4. When most of the children have done the activities mentioned previously the teacher would again talk to the group or class explaining that surfaces cannot always be compared by putting them together, so we cut one surface up and see if the pieces can be put inside the boundary of the other.

   Use a rectangle 20 cm by 10 cm cut from thin red card, and another 15 cm by 12 cm cut from white card. Demonstrate, fitting one rectangle on the other, that one is longer but narrower. Which rectangle has the larger surface, the red or the white? Show that one rectangle is not surrounded by the other when we put them together, so we cannot tell by looking which is the larger. Cut off the projecting piece made by the red rectangle and after cutting it again place the red pieces on the projecting piece made by the white rectangle. We see that the red pieces more than cover the white rectangle, so the red surface is larger than the white one. Discuss this.

   The teacher can repeat this with other pairs of shapes cut from different coloured cards, initially asking the children which shape has the larger surface, and then carrying out the test to check the estimate.

Although this test seems easy to perform most children find it difficult cutting one of the faces into suitably shaped pieces with which to cover the other surface. Demonstration by the teacher, however, will provide valuable experience and food for thought.

7.5 INDIRECT COMPARISONS: NON-NUMERICAL (1, 8, 9, 10 L2)

The teacher talks to the class, or group, explaining that in many cases surfaces cannot be compared as described in the previous section because they cannot be picked up and put together, neither can they be cut into pieces.

1. The teacher uses two rectangular pieces of paper, one 10 cm by 10 cm, the other 20 cm by 10 cm, and puts them on the tables well apart. She also uses plastic squares of 5 cm side (see Appendix on Equipment). Ask the children how we can compare these surfaces without moving them from the tables, but using the plastic squares. (The rectangles need not necessarily be this size, nor the plastic squares. Use measuring squares, however, at least 2.5 cm in side, preferably larger, and make rectangles so that an integral number of squares fit on them. Children find larger squares easier to handle.)

   The teacher could ask a child to fit squares on each surface, and place the squares from each surface, touching, side by side, in rows (Fig. 7.2). Which row of squares is longer? Which row of squares covers more? Which rectangle was covered with these squares? Which rectangle has the larger surface? Check this, putting the two rectangles together directly.

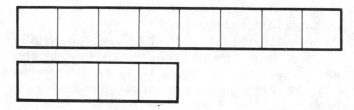

Fig. 7.2

   Afterwards two or three children at a time could do individual work. That is, each child is given specially prepared rectangles to compare using plastic squares. Thus, two or three pairs of rectangles and sufficient squares would be needed. Record answers by putting **covers more than** *and* **covers less than** labels against appropriate rectangles. Also accept oral answers using the descriptions 'larger surface than' and 'smaller surface than'.

2. Work in pairs. Each child makes a shape on the desk using equal plastic squares, or rectangles. Which has the larger surface? Then, without mixing up the squares from each shape, place them in two rows, touching, and side by side. Which row of squares has the larger surface? Who made the shape formed by this row of squares?

3. The teacher demonstrates the following activity using two rectangles with sides an

integral number of Stern unit cubes. Use reasonably small rectangles, e.g. 5 by 8, and 6 by 4. Which covers more? Put Stern cubes on each, then arrange the cubes in two rows, side by side. (Put cubes along a straight edge to arrange them because it makes the task easier and quicker.) Which row covers more? Which rectangle was covered by this row? Which rectangle has the larger surface? Check the result by putting the rectangles together, if this is possible.

Now set individual work. Two pairs of rectangles and sufficient cubes would enable two children at a time to do this activity. (Be sure the cubes fit on the rectangles 'exactly'.)

4. The teacher demonstrates to the class, or group, using a cardboard triangle and a circle, one clearly larger in surface than the other. Which surface is the larger? Fit equal plastic circles on each, in some cases going over the edges slightly, but in other cases not quite going to the edge. Then arrange the circles in rows and compare the sizes of the rows. Which row of circles covers more? Which shape did these cover? Which shape has the larger surface? Test the answer, if you can, by placing one surface on the other.

Three or four children could now do individual work based on this demonstration. Compare pairs of surfaces using plastic circles, bottle tops, buttons, coins, marbles, beads and Stern or Cuisenaire cubes. Vary the shapes of the surfaces to be compared as much as possible using some with curved boundaries as well as those with straight sides. Put circles, cubes, buttons and coins against the edge of a wooden strip so that they just touch, and then take the strip away, to arrange them in straight rows. Arrange beads and marbles in rows between three wooden strips (Fig. 7.3).

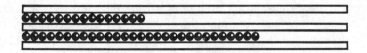

Fig. 7.3

5. Two or three children could work individually using plastic geometrical shapes. Put shapes of the same size together on the table and see if they tessellate, that is, fit together to cover a flat surface. Try rectangles, squares, right-angled triangles, scalene triangles, isosceles triangles, parallelograms, rhombuses, circles, semi-circles, quadrilaterals, pentagons, hexagons and octagons.

If the teacher has not enough of a particular shape others can be copied by drawing around one on cardboard, and cutting out the pieces. All these shapes can be purchased, except for scalene triangles and quadrilaterals, but if you make one of each, copies can be made as described earlier.

Patterns can also be made on plain paper by drawing around these shapes, and colouring in the regions. Octagons placed together form an interesting pattern because of the square regions between them. Quadrilaterals also make a pleasant pattern if four colours are used where corners meet. Squared paper and triangular paper can also be used for pattern building and colouring.

6. The teacher asks the class to collect tin lids with rims, box lids with shallow sides, plastic plates and saucers, of various shapes. She puts them in pairs so that one item has a larger surface than the other? Which is the larger? Place beads or marbles on

each item and check your estimate by matching rows. This activity is for one or two children working individually.

7. Carefully cut a rectangular box along its seams, select two or three different faces and give them to the child. Which is the largest face, and the smallest face? Check your estimate by fitting buttons, bottle tops, cubes, plastic squares or triangles on each face, and then compare the surfaces by comparing the rows of units. Two or three children could work individually on this activity.

7.6 MEASURING SURFACES INVOLVING ONLY WHOLE UNITS (1, 2, 8, 10 L2)

Surfaces can be described using numbers when children can deal with them. Initially, select activities which involve small numbers.

The teacher talks to the class, or group, and explains that surfaces are measured by placing units on them, and counting these units. When we measure a surface like this we say that we find its area. If we say the rectangle has a larger area than the triangle we mean the rectangle has a larger surface, or covers more, than the triangle. If two faces of a box have the same area we mean that they cover the same amount. We will now use this word when describing surfaces.

Get a piece of cardboard, cover it with plastic squares, and ask the children to count them. (Select a piece of card on which squares will just fit.) Explain that the result will be recorded as **cardboard covers the same as 9 squares** using item cards, number cards and relationship cards. When recording, place labels, such as **covers less than**, **smaller area than**, **covers more than**, **larger area than**, **covers the same as**, **the same area as**, alongside the item concerned. Initially, the children can use a 'covers' label and an 'area' label to describe the same result. Later, when its meaning becomes clearer, only 'area' labels would be used.

The following activities include numbers up to ten, and are intended to be done individually. No more than two or three children would be doing them at the same time. Put the instructions for these activities on cards and on the back of each card make brief notes of any special paper or measuring units needed. Number the cards and put them in polythene envelopes. Sometimes a card and any specially prepared shapes needed for the activity could be put in a larger numbered envelope, or a numbered box. Many children will probably not be able to read the cards so the teacher must read the card to the child, or read the card and tell the child what to do. The children could give oral answers but encourage children to record the areas by putting number symbol cards alongside. Children able to write numbers would make their own labels. The largest area could always be put on the table on the left and the smallest to the right. This would help the teacher check the answers speedily.

1. Use 5-cm plastic squares to cover rectangles 10 cm by 10 cm, 10 cm by 20 cm and 15 cm by 10 cm. The child measures these areas in squares and finds the largest area and the smallest.
2. The child makes three different shapes on the table containing 5 squares. Do these shapes have the same area? Repeat, making shapes with 7 triangles, 9 rectangles and 6 squares.

3. Ask the child to make rectangles with 6 squares, 8 squares and 9 squares. Which rectangle has the largest area?
4. The child draws shapes on 2-cm squared paper containing 6 squares, 5 squares, 8 squares and 7 squares. Which shape has the smallest area?
5. The teacher prepares a work card with shapes drawn on it like those shown in Fig. 7.4. Ask the child to describe the area of each shape.

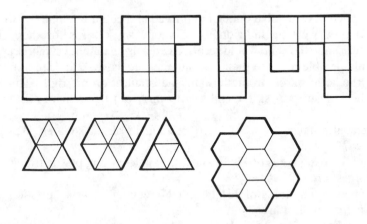

Fig. 7.4

6. The teacher draws shapes on a work card, or prepares cardboard shapes, as shown in Fig. 7.5. The child has to find the areas of the shapes, and the largest area.

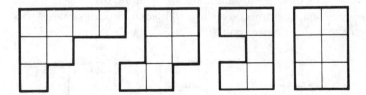

Fig. 7.5

7. Which shapes have the same area? Prepare a work card (Fig. 7.6).

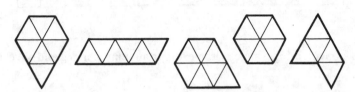

Fig. 7.6

8. On 2-cm squared paper a child draws three different L-shapes each with an area of 8 squares, and four different T-shapes each with an area of 9 squares. Which letter T is the best shape? Which letter L?
9. On 2-cm squared paper draw six different shapes each having an area of 8 squares.
10. Use 2-cm squared paper. Draw and colour in different shapes each with an area of 3

squares. Use the lines on the paper to make the sides of these shapes (two shapes). Next, colour in different shapes each having an area of 4 squares (five shapes are possible). (If a shape is rotated or turned over it will produce the same shape. Also squares cannot be joined at a corner.) Multilink cubes could be used instead of drawing shapes. Three or four could be joined together, placed flat on the table, and looked at from above. Different shapes can then be displayed.

The following activities involve numbers up to 20 and could be done by two or three children at a time working individually. Compile work cards for these activities. Alongside each shape the child would record its area using number symbol cards. Some children would be able to write their own number labels. Ask the children to display shapes with the largest area on the left and the smallest on the right. This helps the teacher to check answers. Ask the children to carry out the activities listed below.

1. Make rectangles having areas of 15, 16, 12 and 18 plastic squares. Which has the largest area?
2. Make shapes having areas of 11, 15 and 18 triangles, using plastic triangles. Which has the largest area?
3. Make shapes having areas of 13, 14 and 17 rectangles, using plastic rectangles. Which has the smallest area?
4. Make shapes having areas of 12, 15 and 16 plastic hexagons. Which covers the most?
5. Using centimetre ruled squared paper (do not call them centimetre squares, yet), make five different shapes having areas of 15 squares.
6. Using triangular ruled paper, make five different shapes having areas of 14 triangles.
7. Make five shapes having the same area on a geoboard.
8. Show the child shapes drawn on a squared blackboard, or squared paper (Fig. 7.7). Find their areas. (No more than 20 squares in area.)

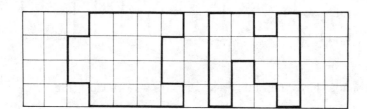

Fig. 7.7

9. Repeat **8** above, using shapes drawn on triangular paper, and give answers in triangles.

These activities involve numbers larger than 20. Individual work for two or three children. Alongside each shape the child records its area using a number label.

1. Ask the child to draw on centimetre-ruled squared paper shapes having areas of 25 squares, 36 squares, 28 squares, 45 squares, etc. Compile a work card.
2. The teacher cuts out rectangles with sides an integral number of centimetres, e.g. 8 cm by 5 cm, 7 cm by 5 cm, 6 cm by 9 cm, 6 cm by 7 cm, 9 cm by 9 cm and 7 cm by

10 cm. The child covers the rectangles with a centimetre-squared grid and finds their areas. Arrange them on the table in order of area, with the largest on the left. Compile a work card.

7.7 MEASURING SURFACES APPROXIMATELY (1, 2, 8, 9 L2)

The teacher cuts out a cardboard rectangle 7 cm by 12 cm and uses 2.5-cm squares to find its area. Demonstrate to the child, or children, and explain that 3 rows of 5 squares more than cover the rectangle, so its area is less than 15 squares. But 2 rows of 4 squares, or 8 squares, do not quite cover the rectangle. The area is less than 15 squares and more than 8 squares, and would be recorded thus. We could also say the area is between 8 and 15 squares.

If 18 squares only just more than cover a shape an answer just less than 18 squares would be acceptable. Also, just more than 13 squares would be suitable if the surface just exceeded this amount. The form of the answer depends on how well squares fit inside the boundary of a surface.

Later, when the children can judge pieces around the edge of a shape to be more or less than half a square or fit the pieces together in the mind's eye to make the equivalent of whole squares, an area can be expressed *approximately* using one number, e.g. about 8 squares. This is the ultimate aim to be sought after and children should be encouraged to express areas in this way as soon as they are capable of doing so.

In the activities mentioned below record the results as less than x and more than y, between x and y, just less than x, just more than y, whichever is most appropriate. Compile work cards so that two or three children could work individually on the various activities.

Numbers up to 20

The child uses 2.5-cm squares to find the areas of the bottom face and a side face of a tea packet, the bottom face of a washing powder packet, the smaller side face of a washing powder packet, the bottom face and the smaller side face of a salt packet, the bottom face and the smaller side face of a porridge box, the largest face of a Bisto box and the largest face of a rice box.

Numbers Sometimes More Than 20

1. The child uses 2.5-cm plastic squares to find the areas of the faces of a macaroni box, the largest face of a porridge box, the largest face of a cornflour box, the cover of an exercise book and the faces of a cereal packet.
2. Use a transparent plastic grid marked in centimetre squares. (Do not call them centimetre squares yet.) Place the grid over the following things and find their areas approximately by counting squares: the faces of an Oxo box, a tea packet and a jelly packet.
3. Obtain cardboard squares 10 cm by 10 cm and let the child use them to find the

approximate areas of a page from the *Radio Times*, and a sheet of newspaper. (To make cardboard squares draw around a plastic 10-cm square on to a piece of cardboard and cut out the pieces.)

7.8 INTRODUCTION TO STANDARD UNITS: THE SQUARE DECIMETRE AND THE SQUARE METRE (1, 2, 8, 10 L2)

The teacher talks to a child, or group of children, developing the topic along these lines. Up to now we have been measuring areas in squares, triangles, circles, etc. This seems reasonable, but if we have to describe the size of a surface to someone it is not sufficient to say it is 10 squares or 14 triangles. Why not? Bring out that it all depends on the sizes of the squares or triangles. We cannot compare things fairly if the squares I use to cover things with are larger than yours. We must all use measuring units of the same size, but they must also be a convenient shape.

What plastic shapes will cover a flat surface, such as a table-top, without leaving gaps? Give the children geometrical shapes to find those which tessellate. Children could work individually, or in pairs, if the investigation is spread over a few days, and they take turns to use different shapes. Probably the children will know some shapes which tessellate through previous work but this is an opportunity to investigate further. We find congruent squares, rectangles, isosceles triangles, scalene triangles, equilateral triangles, rhombuses, parallelograms, quadrilaterals and hexagons will fit together— but circles, pentagons and octagons will not.

The teacher continues to develop the theme. We now know possible shapes from which to choose a measuring unit for area. Of these, the square is the best. Why? Remember that rectangular surfaces are probably more common than any other in our everyday lives, and we need to find their areas for trading purposes. Think of rectangles about you—walls, doors, windows, pieces of wood, builders' bricks, exercise books, football pitch, etc. One reason why squares are chosen is because they are easier to fit on rectangular surfaces than triangles, rectangles, parallelograms or other shapes.

The Square Decimetre

Show the children a square 10 cm by 10 cm. This is a standard unit for measuring surface. Measure the sides of this square using a Cuisenaire orange rod, which is 1 decimetre in length, or use a centimetre measuring strip, measure it in centimetres, and recall that 10 centimetres is called a decimetre. This square is a decimetre square and we describe the area it covers as 1 **square decimetre**. Talk about things in the classroom which could be measured with squares of this size, e.g. desk tops, windows, doors.

At first the abbreviation **sq. dm** could be used. Later, when children have some knowledge of indices, dm^2 could be written instead.

Set the following activities which are intended for three or four children at a time, working individually. Some of the activities may be put on work cards.

1. Cut out for the child cardboard shapes such as rectangles, L-shapes, T-shapes, H-shapes, etc., composed of an integral number of decimetre squares. The child

finds the areas of these shapes in square decimetres by covering them with decimetre squares.

2. A child makes different shapes, each having an area of 10 square decimetres, using decimetre squares. Make the shapes on pieces of newspaper and carefully draw around their boundaries and cut them out. Have the shapes the same area? Have they the same perimeter?

3. Using decimetre squares cut from thin card, the child finds the areas of the following items: a sheet of newspaper, a page from a magazine, a tea towel, a face towel, the desk top, a cupboard door, an exercise book, the largest face from a cereal packet, the whole surface of a cereal packet, a sheet of drawing paper and the largest face of a biscuit tin. Record answers as less than x and greater than y, between x and y, just more than x, just less than y or give an estimate using one number. Make sure the numbers involved are less than 100. (Some of the more able children may be able to find upper and lower approximations of area, or give a one-numbered estimate, using only one decimetre square to measure the surface. Do not force this issue but let the idea come from the children.)

The Square Metre

When the children have completed the activities of the previous section, concerning the square decimetre, the teacher talks with them again.

Show a metre square made from newspaper sheets joined together and cut to size. Ask a child to fit a metre rod against its sides to measure it. Establish that it is a metre square, and the area it covers is called a **square metre**. This is another standard unit. What kinds of things would we measure with units of this size?

Ask each child to make a newspaper metre square by drawing around the square made by the teacher. (Probably three or four children could do this at a time in the corridor outside the classroom.) When six or more squares have been made the teacher would organize the children into pairs. Ask each pair to find the approximate areas of the classroom door, a cupboard door, a window and a table cloth. Only one or two pairs at a time would do this activity.

7.9 INTRODUCTION TO STANDARD UNITS: THE SQUARE CENTIMETRE (1, 2 L2; 8 L3)

After the square metre the teacher could show a 1 cm by 1 cm square and establish, by measuring, that it is a **centimetre square**. Talk about it covering 1 square centimetre and that it is a standard unit for measuring small surfaces. Would it be awkward to fit squares of this size on surfaces to measure them? Why? Show a transparent plastic grid marked off in squares and check to see whether they are centimetre squares or not. Would this be better to use? How do we use it? To illustrate the latter point allow children, under your guidance, to find the areas of specially prepared rectangles 6 cm by 5 cm, 4 cm by 8 cm, etc. by square counting. (Introduce **sq. cm** as an abbreviation.)

The teacher then shows centimetre-squared paper and talks about the sizes of the small squares. He shows some shapes drawn on this paper, composed of whole squares, and asks a few children in the group to find these areas by square counting. (Again make sure the numbers are less than 100.)

   The children would then, three or four at a time, and working individually, do the various activities mentioned below, many of which could be put on work cards.

1. Use assorted shapes composed of centimetre squares only, e.g. rectangles, T-shapes, L-shapes, H-shapes, etc. The child finds their areas by placing them under a centimetre grid and square counting.
2. On centimetre squared paper the child draws shapes with areas of 35 sq. cm, 39 sq. cm, 62 sq. cm, 83 sq. cm and 58 sq. cm.
3. On centimetre-squared paper the child draws rectangles 8 cm by 4 cm, 7 cm by 5 cm, 6 cm by 6 cm and 8 cm by 5 cm. Find their areas, and the rectangles with the largest and smallest areas. Also find their perimeters. Does the rectangle with the largest area have the longest perimeter?
4. The child draws six different shapes on centimetre-squared paper having an area of 60 square centimetres. Find the perimeters also. Has the shape with the smallest area the smallest perimeter?
5. The teacher draws the letters T, H, L, F and E on centimetre-squared paper with areas less than 100 sq. cm. Ask the child to find their areas, the largest area and the smallest area.
6. How many sq. cm in a sq. dm? Get the child to fit a centimetre grid over a decimetre square to find out.
7. Draw a rectangle 3 cm by 2 cm on centimetre squared paper. What is its area? Copy the rectangle so that its sides are twice as long, and find the area of this larger rectangle. How many times larger in area is this rectangle than the smaller one?
8. Draw a square 4 cm by 4 cm on centimetre-squared paper. Keeping to the lines, divide the square into two parts of equal area. (Rotations and turn-overs of a previous answer are considered to be the same answer.) Can you find and draw six different ways?
9. Using centimetre-squared paper the teacher compiles work cards with shapes on them including half squares. Find the area of each shape. Include those with whole number answers before those with halves (Fig. 7.8).

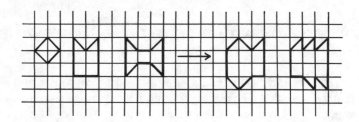

Fig. 7.8

10. Draw a 2-cm square on centimetre-squared paper. Within this square draw a shape with an area of 3 square centimetres. Diagonals of squares may be used as sides as well as the lines on the paper. No lines must cross. Rotations and turn-overs of a previous answer are considered to be the same. Try to find, and draw, seven different ways.

11. On centimetre-squared paper draw a 2-cm by 2-cm square. Within the square draw a shape with an area of 2 sq. cm. See **10** above, for the rules. Try to find, and draw, five different ways.

7.10 WORKING WITH TRIANGLES (3, 8 L3; 3 L4)

Ideas about finding the areas of triangles could be developed with those children who are ready for them. The activities suggested below would be done in the order given. Compile work cards where appropriate.

1. The child draws a rectangle 8 cm by 6 cm on centimetre-squared paper. What is its area? Cut out this rectangle. Draw a diagonal of the rectangle and cut it into two triangles. Compare the triangles. What is the area of one of the triangles?
2. The child draws a square of side 8 cm on centimetre-squared paper. What is its area? Cut out the square. Draw its diagonals, and cut out the four triangles. Compare the triangles. What is the area of one of the triangles? Two of the triangles?
3. The teacher shows square-cornered triangles drawn on centimetre-squared paper. The child uses the following method to find the areas of the triangles. (Answers should be less than 50 sq. cm.)

   On centimetre-squared paper draw two copies of one of the triangles. Cut out the triangles, fit them together to make a rectangle and find the area of the rectangle by square counting. What is the area of one of the triangles? Find out by calculating one half of the area of the rectangle.
4. The teacher again shows square-cornered triangles drawn on centimetre-squared paper. (Areas should be less than 50 sq. cm.) The child finds their areas in the following way.

   On centimetre-squared paper draw a copy of one of the triangles. Draw another triangle upside down on top of it, and touching, so that the two triangles form a rectangle. Square count the area of the rectangle and then calculate the area of the triangle, i.e. one half the area of the rectangle.
5. The teacher shows triangles, not square-cornered, drawn on centimetre-squared paper. (Areas less than 50 sq. cm.) Arrange the triangles in order of increasing difficulty. Do not involve halves in early calculations, e.g. one half of 23 sq. cm is 11½ sq. cm.

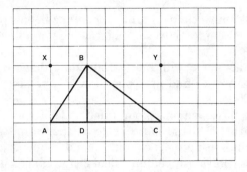

Fig. 7.9

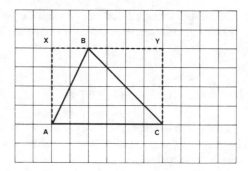

Fig. 7.10

The child finds their areas by dividing each one into two square-cornered triangles (Fig. 7.9). Triangle ABC could be split into two square-cornered triangles if BD was drawn or visualized in the mind's eye. The area of triangle ABD is one half the area of rectangle AXBD. That is, one half of 6 sq. cm, or 3 sq. cm. The area of triangle BDC is one half of the area of rectangle BDCY. That is, one half of 12 sq. cm, or 6 sq. cm. Therefore, the area of triangle ABC is 3 sq. cm + 6 sq. cm, or 9 sq. cm.

6. The teacher shows triangles, not square-cornered, drawn on centimetre-squared paper. The child finds their areas by putting each triangle just inside a rectangle. The area of the rectangle can be square counted and the area of the triangle calculated as one half the area of the rectangle.

   To find the area of triangle ABC, in Fig. 7.10, we could enclose the triangle ABC just inside the rectangle ACYX. This is the same length as the base of the triangle and the same width as the height of the triangle. The area of rectangle ACYX is counted to be 24 sq. cm. The area of the triangle ABC is one half of 24 sq. cm, or 12 sq. cm. This procedure is merely an extension of the method used in **5**. Talk about this with the children.

7. Draw, on centimetre-squared paper, a triangle, a rectangle, a pentagon, a hexagon, a 7-sided shape and an octagon, each having an area of 8 sq. cm.

7.11 FURTHER WORK FINDING AREAS APPROXIMATELY (3 L3; 4, 8 L4)

The teacher could talk with a child, or group, about the finding of areas of shapes, on which whole squares do not 'exactly' fit, by including the following activities:

1. Show a circle, or other shape, with a curved boundary, drawn on centimetre-squared paper, and discuss how to find upper and lower approximations of area. (Keep numbers below 100.)

   To find a **lower approximation**, colour in and find how many squares fit inside the boundary of the shape. Then use another colour of pencil and shade in those squares at the boundary which just project over it. Total the squares just coloured and add this number to those previously coloured, and this gives an upper approximation for the area. (An **upper approximation** is given by the number of squares which make a shape that just projects over the boundary of the original shape.) We might find that the area of our shape is between 56 and 68 sq. cm, and we would record this as such.

Now ask the children to find approximations of area for the following shapes by drawing around them on centimetre-squared paper and totalling squares: a 50p piece, a squash bottle top, a milk bottle top, the bottom of a detergent bottle and the bottom of a Vim container. Also the lids of an instant coffee jar, a powdered milk tin, a custard powder tin and a drinking chocolate tin. (Compile a work card or work cards.)

Also find in square centimetres, using a centimetre-squared grid, approximations of area for the faces of an Oxo box, a tea carton, a jelly packet and a salt box. Also the bottom face of a cereal packet and the bottom face and smaller side face of a Bisto box. (Compile a work card.)

2. When children have done the activities just mentioned, the teacher would explain how to express an area approximately using one number.

Show a shape with a curved boundary drawn on centimetre-squared paper. (Keep numbers below 100.) Colour in the squares which fit inside the boundary of the shape and find how many there are. Then go around the edge of the shape and examine carefully the part squares, not yet coloured, inside the boundary. Any part square which is larger than, or equal to, half a square in area count as 1 square. Any part square smaller than half a square do not count. This procedure measures each part square to the nearest square. Keep a tally and mark the part squares as they are dealt with. Add the 'squares' around the edge to the number of whole squares inside the shape. Should the number of whole squares inside the shape be 58 and the number of 'squares' around the edge be 12, then the approximate area would be 70 squares. As each square covers 1 sq. cm the area of the shape would be 70 sq. cm.

Now ask the children to find the approximate areas of the following by drawing around them on centimetre-squared paper, and square counting: the bottom of a detergent bottle, the bottom of a Vim tin, a milk bottle top, the lid of a coffee jar, the lid of a powdered milk tin and the lid of a drinking chocolate tin. (Compile a work card.)

3. The children could then find the areas of some of the shapes just mentioned using a different method.

Repeat the previous procedure up to the point where the areas of the part squares around the shape and inside the boundary are to be found. Go around the inside of the shape and put pieces together in the mind's eye, to make up equivalent whole squares, e.g. that piece and that piece together cover roughly a square, so does that piece, and that piece and that piece cover roughly a square, and so on. Keep a tally of the equivalent whole squares, as this procedure progresses, and shade in the part squares already taken into account. Add the total of the equivalent squares to the number of whole squares inside the shape.

If we compare the areas of shapes found using both these methods we find they agree reasonably closely. The latter method, however, is more accurate.

Also find, using a centimetre grid, approximate areas for the faces of an Oxo box, a tea carton, a jelly box and a salt box. (Compile a work card.)

7.12 FINAL COMMENT

We have compared surfaces, measured them with various shapes, and discussed the need for and used standard units. The work has been deliberately selected to keep numbers less than a hundred. Initially, measuring units just fitted the shapes considered, then areas were described between limits, and finally areas were expressed approximately using one number. Future work could be to find areas of shapes by square counting using larger numbers, to show the relationship between standard measures and work towards the formulation of rules for calculating the areas of rectangles and triangles. The dimensions of these could involve tens and units, and vulgar and decimal fractions, so generating the need for learning further arithmetical techniques. Prisms, pyramids and cylinders could be measured and their surface areas determined.

Chapter 8

Shape and Space

We live in a world of shapes and this aspect of our surroundings contains much to be examined and discussed. There is an accumulation of associated language used to describe the shapes we see, pick up or feel, and this for the child could come, amongst other places, from the home, from playing with other children and from the teacher. Much of the initial work dealt with in this chapter comes from an examination of shapes together with an introduction and/or extension of appropriate language connected with these shapes. Initially three-dimensional shapes are examined and ideas about surfaces, faces, edges and corners are developed. Such work could be dealt with non-numerically, and numbers only introduced at a later stage.

The aim is not only to introduce vocabulary but to examine more closely words such as **larger**, **bigger** and **smaller**. Young children use these words then comparing objects to mean different things. They might say larger when they mean fatter, taller, wider, thicker and heavier, and often ideas are confused. The taller thing is not necessarily heavier, the longer rectangle does not always cover more, the taller jar does not always hold more, etc. We have to show that larger and smaller are not sufficient terms to use when comparing things which involve many variables. If we say that line A is bigger than line B, then we could only mean that A is longer than B. To say that rectangle A is bigger than rectangle B leads to different interpretations—longer, wider or covers more. We must try to ensure that the language used is as precise as possible.

We must also concern ourselves with the descriptions '**the same as**' or 'the same' when applied to things. These could mean the same length, width, size, shape, and so on. Here again we can help children to specify the property they are talking about and use terms such as same width, same height, same capacity, etc. When objects are the same shape and size we call them **congruent**, and showing that things are congruent is an important mathematical tool, for what we know about the one then applies to the other. What do we mean by the same shape? To answer this we need to compare corners and sides of shapes, that is, deal with **similarity** as well as congruence.

We can also introduce the names of common mathematical two- and three-dimensional shapes. This includes the names of polygons, prisms and pyramids, and how they are identified. At this stage we are supplying vocabulary and ideas that are necessary for future work.

8.1 GENERAL SCHEME

The following topics could be included:

1. Experiences with three-dimensional objects. Curved and flat surfaces, straight and

curved lines, and corners. Recognition of oblongs, squares, circles and triangles. Sorting solids.
2. Sorting in terms of taller, wider, thicker, thinner, narrower, shorter and longer.
3. Larger and smaller in terms of capacity.
4. Larger and smaller in terms of 'covers more'.
5. Sorting solids according to the number of faces, edges and corners. Names of polygons.
6. A more detailed study of rectangles and triangles.
7. Congruent shapes.
8. Prisms and pyramids, their names, and how they are recognized.
9. Square corners. Squares, rectangles and square-cornered triangles. Sorting involving square corners.
10. Parallel lines, parallelograms and rectangles.
11. Covering surfaces with congruent shapes. Measurement of surface.
12. Comparing corners of plane figures.
13. Making prisms, pyramids and cones.
14. Elementary ideas about circles.
15. Angles thought of in terms of rotation.
16. Line symmetry of plane figures, and plane symmetry of solids.
17. Similar shapes, congruent shapes and caricatures.
18. Number patterns derived from geometrical patterns.

8.2 GENERAL REMARKS

From the beginning in each classroom there could be a 'making' box containing assorted three-dimensional shapes, and also various shapes displayed on a 'shapes' table. Some shapes could be hung from the ceiling. Many of the shapes would be empty containers of foodstuffs, or other household goods, such as cardboard boxes, plastic bottles and containers, and tins. Most of the collected shapes would be rectangular prisms or cylinders, so the collection needs supplementing with other prisms made from wood, cardboard or plastic. Sets of hollow mathematical shapes consisting of various prisms and pyramids can be bought, and when filled with sand or water their volumes can be compared. Prisms can be made by joining plastic or cardboard congruent rectangles, and pyramids by joining congruent isosceles triangles.

A set of two-dimensional plastic and cardboard shapes is also needed. Some can be obtained by carefully cutting faces from boxes. Many, however, would have to be bought because they are not generally found on containers, e.g. some of the regular polygons, parallelograms, trapezia, different types of triangle, etc.

On the 'shapes' table we could display interesting items, such as an Oxo cube, a wooden building brick, a cheese sector, a ball, a cylindrical pencil, a hexagonal pencil, a circular table mat, a wooden cone, a triangle made with Meccano-like strips, a pebble, a picture of a starfish, etc. In fact, anything which is interesting from the point of view of shape. Mathematical shapes made by the children could also be included, e.g. a cube or pyramid. Items involving basic shapes that are included in craft work could also be displayed such as models made from cardboard cylinders.

Shapes to be brought from home for building and sorting are as follows:

Rectangular prisms—cereal, dried peas, suet, custard, lentil, biscuit packets, etc.
Square-based prisms—tea cartons, Oxo boxes, biscuit packets, etc.
Circular prisms or cylinders—fruit tins, drinking chocolate tins, Smartie tubes, fruit pastille tubes, etc.
Triangular-based prisms—Toblerone box, Biarritz chocolate box
Square-based pyramid—a Terry's Pyramint box
Truncated pyramids—Quality Street box, Cadbury's Roses box, yoghurt cartons, cream containers, plastic beakers, etc.
Hexagonal prism—Terry's chocolate box
Octagonal prism—orange and lemon fruit slices container
Miscellaneous items—plastic containers of all kinds, interesting shaped boxes and other items, e.g. Easter egg boxes

Special equipment which could be used is as follows:
Plastic and wooden cubes of various sizes
Wooden building blocks—prisms, pyramids, arches, etc.
Cuisenaire rods
Hollow plastic prisms and pyramids (volume relation models)
Stern cubes and Stern rods
Logic blocks—shapes for sorting—squares, oblongs, triangles, circles and regular hexagons
Attribute blocks—shapes for sorting (similar to Logic blocks)
Decimal set
Dienes 10 mm Multibase blocks
Polydron—construction set for building certain 3-D shapes
Clixi—construction set for building 3-D shapes
Geometrical strips—for making polygons
Various plastic shapes—triangles, rectangles, circles, regular pentagons, regular hexagons, regular octagons, rhombuses, trapezia, parallelograms, etc.
Wooden and plastic squares of different sizes, e.g. 2.5 cm, 5 cm, 7.5 cm
Plastic or wooden mathematical shapes—various prisms, pyramids, Platonic solids, truncated prisms and pyramids, spheres, etc.

For further details see the Appendix on Equipment.

8.3 SORTING SOLIDS: NON-NUMERICAL ACTIVITIES (1, 8, 9, 10 L1)

Activities could be given to the children which consist of sorting the shapes according to properties or attributes that the children can see in them. For example, it could be that various three-dimensional shapes are being used to build houses or fortresses. In this activity sorting takes place, the most appropriate pieces being selected for various parts of the building. Some shaped blocks are best for walls, others make towers, whilst others can be put on the tops of towers. Much of the sorting is incidental and need not be made into formal exercises.

Many ideas about shapes are gained incidentally by 'playing' with solids from the 'making' box, from which children can select those shapes particularly needed for the objects they are making. Cuisenaire and Stern rods, Dienes Multibase blocks, and

Poleidoblocs, could be used in addition to empty food containers. Lego bricks are also useful. Houses and fields could be made for farm and zoo animals, garages for model cars or enclosures for objects which are being sorted and so on. Boxes and tins could be fitted together to make model boats, trains, buses, etc.

More formal exercises could be arranged by asking the children to sort a collection of shapes according to a property of their own choosing, or an attribute suggested by the teacher, e.g. some will roll, some will slide, some will both roll and slide. When the shapes are sorted into sets they can be placed in groups on the floor or table, together with a naming card made with the help of the teacher (Figs. 8.1, 8.2, 8.3 and 8.4).

The teacher could perhaps spend a little time each week holding up solids and talking about them to the class and allowing the children to pick them up and feel their faces.

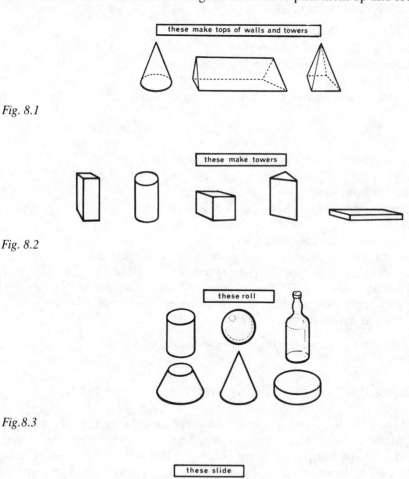

these make tops of walls and towers

Fig. 8.1

these make towers

Fig. 8.2

these roll

Fig.8.3

these slide

Fig. 8.4

Faces could be tested for flatness by resting a Cuisenaire orange rod on them. If the rod fits the face anywhere, and in any direction, that face is flat. Edges could be tested for straightness by holding a stretched string alongside them. The edge is straight if the string fits the edge everywhere. New words and ideas can be introduced, such as **flat face**, **curved face**, **straight edge**, **curved edge**, **corner**, **cylinder**, **cube**, and so on. Thin plastic or cardboard shapes could also be shown and words like **triangle**, **square**, **oblong** and **circle** introduced. (At this stage shapes are distinguished by sight and not by any definite mathematical properties.)

As an activity for individual children, or pairs of children, a sorting box could be provided which contains squares and circles. Each shape could be of a variety of sizes, including some of the same size. Circles the same size as a given circle could be searched for. Squares of the same size as a given square could be searched for. Instructions to find sets of larger circles than the given circle, or larger squares than the given square, could be given. The children could be asked to find smaller circles or smaller squares.

Through talking about and handling shapes, both two- and three-dimensional, a vocabulary is built up which could help children distinguish objects in more mathematical ways.

The teacher might now arrange for the objects in the 'making' box to be sorted by individuals or pairs of children. Some of the things which the children could look for, at the suggestion of the teacher, are listed below:

1. those with only flat faces
2. those with only curved faces
3. those with flat and curved faces
4. those with no edges
5. those with only straight edges
6. those with only curved edges
7. those with a corner or corners
8. those with no corners
9. those with a square face
10. those with a circular face
11. those which are the same size.

For individual children, or pairs of children, activities could be devised which involve sorting by using a posting box. Shapes could be 'posted' and those found which 'just fit', or are 'the same size as', the posting holes (Fig. 8.5). The words larger and smaller could be used when we try to post various circles in the circular hole, or various squares in the square hole.

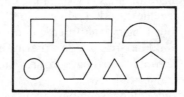

Fig. 8.5

For individual children, or pairs of children, sorting exercises could be given using thin plastic or cardboard shapes:

1. Squares of three or four different sizes could be put on top of one another and sorted into sets of squares of the same size.
2. Triangles of three or four different sizes could be sorted into sets of like triangles.
3. Circles of three or four different sizes could be put into sets of like circles.
4. Various shapes could be sorted into circles, triangles, squares and oblongs.
5. Given miscellaneous shapes, two or three of which are exactly the same, to find these shapes.

Specialized apparatus could also be used:

1. Cuisenaire or Colour Factor rods can be put into sets of the same colour, or sets of the same size.
2. Various Dienes Multibase blocks could be sorted into pieces of the same size.
3. Poleidoblocs could be sorted into sets of shapes exactly alike.
4. Cubes of three or four different sizes could be put into piles of cubes of the same size. Which cubes are smallest? Which are largest?
5. Spherical beads of three or four different sizes could be sorted into sets of the same size.
6. Beads of different shapes (spherical, cubical and ellipsoidal), could be sorted into sets of like beads.
7. A collection of farm animals or zoo animals could be sorted into sets of those that are the same shape and size.

The results of this sorting could be checked by the teacher and then the original set of shapes could be examined further for things 'bigger' or 'smaller' than an item first selected. Discussion could lead to ideas of bigger in the sense of longer, taller, wider and thicker, and from this we develop a study of length as described in Chapter 3. The following activities, however, could be particularly valuable and could be arranged as activities for individual children or pairs of children:

1. Five or six Meccano-like strips, of different lengths, could be arranged in order of length. Which is shortest?
2. Three or four pieces of string, of the same thickness, could be compared for length. Which is longest?
3. Wooden dowels, or bamboo canes, could be arranged in order of length. Which is the longest?
4. Use Cuisenaire, Colour Factor or Stern rods. Find a rod the same length as this one (black rod). Find a rod longer than this one (blue rod). Find a rod shorter than this one (yellow rod). Arrange these rods (yellow, blue, brown, pink) in order of length. Are two yellow rods longer than three green rods?
5. Bottles, jars and boxes could be arranged in order of height, tallest on the left.
6. Tins and plastic containers could be arranged in a row in order of width, widest on the left. Is the tallest container the widest?
7. Three or four cords or strings could be compared for thickness by feeling them and looking at them. Which is the thickest?

8. Three or four wooden dowels of different thicknesses could be compared. Which is the thinnest rod?
9. Cardboard rectangles of the same width could be arranged in order of length. Are they the same width? Which is the shortest?
10. Cardboard rectangles of the same length could be arranged in order of width. Are they the same length? Which is the widest? Which is the narrowest?
11. Use Invicta Attribute blocks. Sort them into thick and thin, large and small circles, large and small squares, large and small triangles, large and small oblongs and large and small hexagons.
12. Given three or four cardboard rectangles of different colours, lengths and widths, to find a rectangle longer and wider than the blue rectangle; or longer and narrower than the white rectangle.
13. Given three or four wooden dowels of different colours, lengths and thicknesses, to pick a rod longer and thicker than the red rod; or shorter and thicker than the blue rod; etc.
14. Given three or four tins of different colours, heights and widths, find a tin taller than the red one, or wider than the green tin, or taller and narrower than the red tin.

Many of the collected shapes, if hollow, could be filled, by a child, with sand or water, and the contents of the containers poured from one to another. This would lead to the idea of bigger in the sense of 'holds more', and introduce a study of capacity as described in Chapter 5.

If the teacher shows a child or group of children two solids of the same material such as balls of plasticine, she could talk about the larger piece being the heavier. This is experienced directly by the child if he holds the pieces of plasticine, one in each hand, or seen indirectly if he places them on opposite pans of a balance or hangs them, in turn, from the end of a spring or elastic band. From these activities the teacher is able to develop further ideas about mass and heaviness as described in Chapter 6.

If the teacher immerses two stones, of different sizes, in identical plastic buckets, initially containing water to the same level, the children can see that both levels rise but not to the same extent (Fig. 8.6). One stone pushes the water level up higher because it

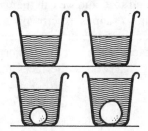

Fig. 8.6

must take up more room in the bucket. Bigger in this sense refers to the stone which takes up more room. The stone which pushes the water up more is said to have the larger volume.

The teacher could also fill the buckets to the brim with water when they are standing on plastic trays, tie strings around the stones, lower them into the buckets, and pour the water pushed out into each tray into identical plastic beakers. Rows of beakers could then be compared in order to see which stone pushes out more water, or has the larger volume (Fig. 8.7). Further work on volume could be developed as described in Chapter 5.

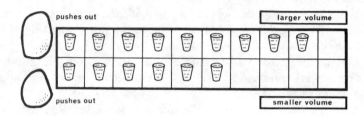

Fig. 8.7

Whilst handling solids, and looking at them, the children gain ideas about flat and curved surfaces and learn to distinguish the shapes of various faces. Besides this, the teacher could ask whether the green face on this box is bigger than the red face on that box. (Use rectangular boxes.) This would involve the comparison of lengths and widths of rectangles, and the amounts of surface they cover. Such an activity leads to various tests for comparing surfaces, and measuring surfaces, as described in Chapter 7.

Provide a child, or group of children, with large rectangular boxes, such as cornflake packets. Each box could be cut down its side edges and the cardboard opened out. This enables the faces to be seen more easily. The box could then be reconstructed again for folding, and joining the side faces with Sellotape.

On another occasion, as an exercise for individual children or pairs of children, rectangular boxes with no lids could be cut along their side edges, opened out flat, and faces compared by looking. What shape is each face? Do any faces look the same? Cut out the faces and put them on top of one another to find those that are the same. When examining these results the teacher could discuss what we mean by the same. If two shapes just fit on top of one another, their sides are the same, and their corners are the same. They have the same shape and size, and we call them congruent. We will use this word from now on when referring to shapes exactly alike.

Each child, or pair of children, could then colour congruent faces of the box the same colour using crayons, and put the faces of the box together again on the desk to form the shape of an opened out box (Fig. 8.8). Stick the faces together with Sellotape and rebuild the box.

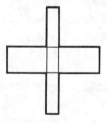

Fig. 8.8

At another time a few children working individually could cut out the faces of a rectangular box, and colour congruent faces the same colour. Which faces are the longest? Which faces are widest? Can you find a face, or faces, longer, and wider than the others? (The answers can be arrived at, and checked, by putting the rectangles together with their sides touching.) Which face covers most? Find out by putting the faces on top of one another, and seeing if the boundary of one of the faces surrounds the boundaries of each of the other faces. Such a rectangle will cover more than the others. See Chapter 7 'Surface and Area'.

Again, a child, or pair of children, could take apart a cylindrical box, such as a Smartie tube. Take off the lid, and push out the bottom. What shape is the bottom? Cut down the side face, and spread it out flat (Fig. 8.9). What shape is the flattened out face?

Fig. 8.9

To display the parts of the tube stick them on to a piece of thin cardboard using strong glue (Fig. 8.10).

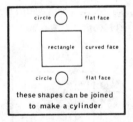

Fig. 8.10

Give these children rectangular pieces of paper of different lengths and widths. Bend each piece of paper around so that two opposite sides meet, and join these sides with Sellotape. What shapes have been made? Display the cylinders, together with other cylindrical containers found in the 'making' box, or brought from home.

8.4 SORTING 2-D AND 3-D SHAPES: NUMERICAL ACTIVITIES (2 L1; 10 L2)

8.4.1 Sorting Solids: Numerical Activities (2 L1; 10 L2)

We cannot study shapes in much detail unless we use numbers. When children can deal with numbers up to ten, or even before this, we can associate certain shapes with particular numbers. Up to now we have only asked that shapes be recognized by their geometrical form. Many of the activities listed below use numbers as a basis for describing and sorting shapes.

1. A child, or pair of children, could sort out the collection of three-dimensional shapes in the 'making' box, or from the 'shapes' table, and find those with one face, two faces, three faces, four faces, five faces, six faces, one curved face and two flat faces. Display the shapes on the table with an appropriate label (Figs. 8.11 and 8.12).

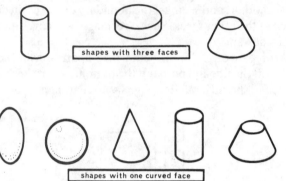

shapes with three faces

Fig. 8.11

shapes with one curved face

Fig. 8.12

2. Ask a child, or pair of children, to describe a given solid in terms of faces, edges and corners. Only use a cylinder, cone, sphere, triangular-based pyramid, square-based pyramid and a hemisphere, in order to keep numbers below ten. (The hemisphere could be made with plasticine.) The answers could be given by filling in numbers in a box, opposite appropriate words, on a prepared sheet (Figs. 8.13 and 8.14), or they could be given orally.

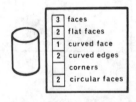

3	faces
2	flat faces
1	curved face
2	curved edges
	corners
2	circular faces

Fig. 8.13

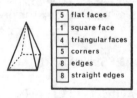

5	flat faces
1	square face
4	triangular faces
5	corners
8	edges
8	straight edges

Fig. 8.14

3. We could, at this stage, introduce the names of some solids. It is better to introduce the new names one at a time. At a 'talking time', hold up each solid, name it and talk about its features. Introduce the **rectangular box**, **cylinder**, **sphere** and **pyramid**.

8.4.2 Sorting Flat Shapes: Numerical Activities (2 L1; 10 L2)

1. Prepare various plastic and cardboard two-dimensional shapes, consisting of various triangles, four-sided figures and polygons. Ask children individually to find those shapes with three sides, four sides, five sides, six sides and eight sides. Display the shapes on the table with a label (Fig. 8.15).

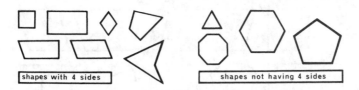

Fig. 8.15

2. At a 'talking time' session, hold up the shapes mentioned in the previous paragraph and ask the children to tell you the number of sides and the number of corners for each. Establish that a three-sided shape has three corners, a four-sided shape has four corners, a five-sided shape has five corners and a six-sided shape has six corners. Suppose a shape has eight corners. How many sides would it have? Show an eight-sided figure to check the answer.

   Talk about the fact that we generally describe a shape according to the number of sides it has, and some shapes with straight sides have special names. Show three-, four-, five-, six- and eight-sided plane figures with straight sides and introduce their names. (When four-sided shapes are displayed we could name rectangles but describe the remainder as four-sided. Point out that both squares and oblongs are rectangles. Do not, however, discuss side and angle properties of squares and oblongs at this stage but merely rely on recognition of geometrical form.) Put these shapes with name labels on various tables (Figs. 8.16 and 8.17). Also display names and shapes on a wall chart.

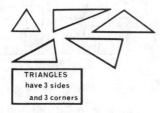

Fig. 8.16

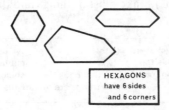

Fig. 8.17

3. Give a child, or pair of children, a set of polygons, regular and irregular, together with the name labels **triangles**, **pentagons**, **hexagons**, **octagons**, and **four-sided shapes**. Sort the shapes according to their number of sides.

4. Give a child, or pair of children, various plastic and cardboard four-sided shapes with both straight and curved sides (Fig. 8.18). Ask them to find squares, oblongs, rectangles, shapes with four straight sides and shapes with four curved sides.

Fig. 8.18

5. Give a child, or pair of children, various cardboard shapes with boundaries consisting of straight and curved sides, some shapes being regular (Fig. 8.19). Find those shapes with four sides, three sides, two sides, six sides, one side, five sides, eight sides, only three curved sides, and only one curved side. Also find triangles, rectangles and hexagons.

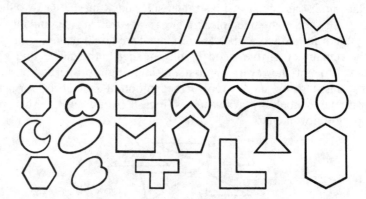

Fig. 8.19

6. At 'talking time' ask the children to point out square, oblong, rectangular and circular faces, which can be seen in the classroom. (Note that square and oblong faces are both rectangular.) Make a list of things and display their names on a wall chart (Fig. 8.20).

blackboard	window pane
table top	cupboard door
front cover of writing book	sheet of paper
these things are rectangular	

Fig. 8.20

7. For the next activity the teacher collects a ball, rectangular box, cube, cylinder, triangular prism and pyramid, square prism and pyramid, hexagonal prism and pyramid, and a plasticine hemisphere. Ask a child, or a pair of children, to select those solids with a circular face, a triangular face, a square face, an oblong face, a hexagonal face, all its faces flat, both flat and curved faces, and to put the solids on the table with teacher-prepared labels (Figs. 8.21 and 8.22).

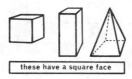

Fig. 8.21

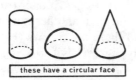

Fig. 8.22

8.4.3 Triangles (2 L1; 10 L2)

Use Meccano-like strips. The teacher could arrange that a child makes triangles with sides the same length, with two sides the same length, and with sides of different lengths. The teacher could, on discussing what was made, introduce the term **equilateral** to describe a triangle with three equal sides, but should not yet introduce names for other types of triangle because they are not so easily distinguished as the equilateral triangle.

Give the child a box which contains various cardboard and plastic triangles. Ask him to find triangles with all sides equal. Then ask him to find triangles with three corners the same shape. What does he notice about the corners of a triangle with equal sides? (They all look the same.)

The teacher needs three plastic triangles, isosceles, equilateral and scalene, and a fairly large cardboard box. On the face of the box draw around the triangles and then cut triangular holes with a sharp craft tool. Cover one face of each triangle with red gummed paper and mark the corners with various symbols for identification purposes (Fig. 8.23). Also stick a Cuisenaire unit cube on the red face of each triangle to hold on to when the triangle is picked up. The following activity could be set for individual children who are ready. Ask the child to post each triangle through the appropriate hole of the 'posting box' in as many ways as possible with the red face uppermost. Two triangles can only be posted in one way. The other triangle can be posted in three different ways because the differently marked corners of the triangle all fit a particular corner of the posting hole. Talk with the child about the meaning of this result, that is, the corners of this triangle are the same, and its sides are the same. This verifies what we see when we look at an equilateral triangle.

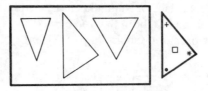

Fig. 8.23

8.4.4 Rectangles: Squares and Oblongs (2 L1; 10 L2)

Compile a work card for this activity, or give oral instructions. Ask the child to make a row with 8 pegs on a pegboard—then put another row of 8 pegs directly beneath—then another row—and so on—until there are 5 rows (Fig. 8.24). What shape have you made? (A rectangle.) How many pegs long is it? (8) How many pegs wide? (5) Are these numbers the same? (No) Make more shapes with 3 rows of 6 pegs, 4 rows of 7 pegs, 5 rows of 8 pegs, etc. Ask each time what shape is made, how many pegs long it is and how many wide, and whether these numbers are the same. Establish that these rectangles, called oblongs, are longer one way than the other using, if necessary, a stretched string to compare side lengths.

Fig. 8.24

Next arrange for the child to make a row with 5 pegs—then put another row of 5 pegs directly beneath—then another row—and so on—until there are 5 rows (Fig. 8.25). (Compile a work card or give oral instructions.) What shape is made? (A special rectangle called a square.) How many pegs long is it? (5) How many wide? (5) Are these numbers the same? (Yes) Compare the length and width of the square using a stretched string. Is the length the same as the width? (Yes) Make more shapes with 4 rows of 4 pegs, 6 rows of 6 pegs, 7 rows of 7 pegs and establish that these are squares, and that a square is a special rectangle which has the same length and width.

Fig. 8.25

Give oral instructions, or make a work card which instructs the child to colour on 2-cm squared paper a row of 6 squares—then a row of 6 squares directly beneath—then another row—and so on—until he or she has coloured in 4 rows (Fig. 8.26). What shape is this? (A rectangle called an oblong.) Now colour in some more rows in order to change this shape into a square. How many units wide, and long, is the square? Make more shapes consisting of 4 rows of 8 squares, 3 rows of 7 squares, 6 rows of 9 squares, etc. Change each of these oblongs into squares by colouring in extra rows. How many units long, and wide, is each square?

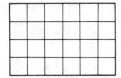

Fig. 8.26

Compile a work card. On 2-cm squared paper the child draws rectangles 6 units long and 4 units wide, 5 units long and 3 units wide, 7 units by 5 units, 8 units by 6 units, 4 units by 4 units and 6 units by 6 units. Which of these rectangles are squares? Colour them red.

The teacher prepares a work card which uses 1-cm squared paper. On it she draws rectangles 7 cm long and 4 cm wide, 8 cm long and 7 cm wide, 9 cm long and 9 cm wide, 6 cm long and 5 cm wide, 7 cm long and 7 cm wide, and 9 cm long and 8 cm wide. Ask the child to find those rectangles which are square.

Prepare a set of cardboard rectangles, some square and some nearly square. The child finds the squares using a stretched string.

8.4.5 Congruence (2 L1; 2, 10 L2)

We could extend ideas about congruence by setting a child individual work, in the context of these activities. Compile work cards where necessary.

1. The teacher could stick pictures of objects on pieces of cardboard, and ask a child to trace these pictures. To do this he has to travel over the lines of the picture with a pencil. (Use paper clips to fix the tracing paper firmly to the card.) The tracing and the picture are congruent. Why? (Because the copy of the picture is the same shape and size as the picture.)
2. The teacher makes a shape with pegs on a pegboard and the child is asked to make a copy alongside. (Or the children could work in pairs—one makes the shape and the other copies it.) Initially use rectangles (Fig. 8.27), but later make L-, H-, E-, F- and T- shapes.

Fig. 8.27

3. Work in pairs. One child makes a shape with plastic squares, triangles, etc., and the other child copies it (Fig. 8.28).

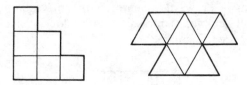

Fig. 8.28

4. The teacher could draw, on 2-cm squared paper, various shapes mostly with square corners. Start with oblongs, squares, T-shapes, etc., and proceed to more compli-cated shapes (Fig. 8.29). A few shapes could be included where the squares have been crossed diagonally. (The shapes could be mounted on rectangular pieces of cardboard, and covered with PVC film, before being given to the children.) Ask the child to draw copies of the shapes on the same kind of squared paper.

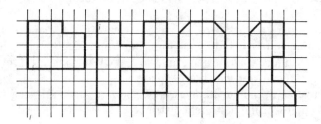

Fig. 8.29

5. Work in pairs. One child builds a tower, or makes a rectangular box with cubes, Dienes blocks or Poleidoblocs, and the other child makes a copy. Initially the tower can be built alongside the original one, but later ask for the copy to be built on the floor, or chair, at the other end of the room.
6. A child could be asked to sort out solids in the 'making' box or from the 'shapes' collection, and find pairs of shapes that are congruent.
7. At 'talking time' look at things in the classroom and ask children to point out items which are exactly alike. If possible, bring the items side by side, and compare them, to check the replies. (This activity needs to be teacher-directed with necessary discussion about the objects chosen.)

8.4.6 Prisms (2 L1; 10 L2)

When children know the names of certain polygons we can introduce prisms made from them.

Use congruent plastic oblongs and squares, and arrange for a child, or small group of children, to sort them out, and pile the pieces on top of one another and build towers. At 'talking time' the teacher could examine these towers with the group of children. The pieces could be piled on top of one another with their edges overlapping, and corners projecting, in a disorderly manner (Fig. 8.30). If the pieces are turned around slightly, some in one direction, some in another, we notice that corners and edges sometimes coincide and we obtain a regular arrangement (Fig. 8.31).

Fig. 8.30

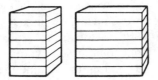

Fig. 8.31

Explain that these shapes are called **prisms**. Demonstrate that another square could be fitted on the tower in a number of ways. Show that we could turn this square so that it fits in four different positions, which indicates that its corners are the same, and its sides the same. When we put another oblong on the pile of oblongs it can be turned only in two ways to fit, otherwise it would project over the edges. This experience gives rise to the idea that the adjacent sides of an oblong are different, but its corners are the same.

Children, working individually or in pairs, could then be asked to build towers using congruent plastic shapes, e.g. squares, oblongs, various kinds of triangle and regular polygons. When these are built the teacher could ask questions about the shapes used to build the particular tower. Which sides are equal? Which sides are longer than which others? Are the corners the same?

Next, ask the group of children to make towers with congruent squares and oblongs (Fig. 8.31), and to look at these towers from across the room. Talk with the children about these prisms having a rectangular outline when seen from the side. Also that prisms can be built with thin slices of the same size and shape. Both these prisms are rectangular prisms because they are built with rectangles but the one made with squares could also be called a square prism. As an activity ask individual children, or pairs of children from the group, to look in the 'making' box and see if any rectangular prisms can be found.

Arrange for individual children, or pairs of children, to build towers using sets of congruent equilateral, isosceles and right-angled triangles. Afterwards ask the children to look at the towers from the side, and talk with the children about the construction of each tower. Is the tower a prism, or not? If it is a prism, what is its name?

Towers could also be built by individual children, or pairs of children, using congruent plastic circles, pentagons, hexagons and octagons. Discuss with the children whether the towers are prisms, or not. Also talk about the names of the prisms, and introduce the special name **cylinder** to describe the circular prism.

Ask a child, or group of children, to find the following from the class collection of three-dimensional shapes: **rectangular prism**, **square prism**, **hexagonal prism**, **pentagonal prism** and **octagonal prism**. Display the prisms with name labels. (Note that the square prism also needs a rectangular prism label.)

8.4.7 Pyramids (2 L1; 10 L2)

At a 'talking time' session, the teacher could stand triangular-, square-, pentagonal-, hexagonal-, octagonal- and circular-based **pyramids** on the table. Ask the children if they know what these shapes are called. (Pyramids.) What do they notice about them? (They taper to a point and they have triangular faces.)

These pyramids all rest on one face which we call the base. A pyramid is named after the shape of this base. Pick up a pyramid and examine the face on which it was resting. How many sides has it? What is this 5-sided shape called? (A pentagon.) So this is a pyramid on a pentagon, or a pentagonal-based pyramid.

Pick up each pyramid, ask the children to examine the base and identify it, and so name the pyramid. Explain that a circular pyramid is called a **cone**. Display various pyramids and label them.

8.4.8 Further Numerical Work with Solids (2 L1; 2,10 L2)

When a child can deal with numbers up to twenty, or beyond, we can ask him to describe solids in terms of faces, edges and corners. The teacher could prepare cyclostyled sheets to help the child record this information (Fig. 8.32).

shape	
flat faces	straight edges . . . .
curved faces	curved edges. . . . .
total faces	total edges . . . .
corners	

Fig. 8.32

Ask individual children to examine faces, edges and corners of these solids: sphere, hemisphere, cube, rectangular box, cone, cylinder, triangular prism and pyramid, square-based prism and pyramid, pentagonal-based prism and pyramid, hexagonal-based prism and pyramid.

8.5 FURTHER ACTIVITIES WITH 2-D AND 3-D SHAPES: MAINLY NUMERICAL (2 L1; 10 L2; 10 L3)

8.5.1 Sides and Corners of Squares and Oblongs (2 L1; 10 L2)

At a 'talking time' session with a group of children, the teacher could use a large cardboard square with its corners coloured red, green, blue and yellow, in order to distinguish them. Place the square on a piece of paper and draw along the sides adjacent to the red corner, and so copy the square corner (Fig. 8.33). Will the green, blue and yellow corners of the square also fit this corner? We find they just fit; therefore, all the corners of the square are the same.

Fig. 8.33

If any shape has corners the same as those of a square we say that these corners are square. Get an oblong, and fit its corners into the square corner drawn on paper (Fig. 8.34). Are the corners of the oblong square? We find that an oblong has four square corners.

Fig. 8.34

Now hold the square and the oblong on top of each other and put one corner of each shape together (Fig. 8.35). We find they always just fit, which further demonstrates that oblongs and squares have the same shaped corners.

Fig. 8.35

The teacher needs a plastic square and oblong, and a fairly large cardboard box. On one face of the box draw around the oblong and square and then cut out square and oblong holes (Fig. 8.36). Also mark one corner of the square, and oblong, with a red

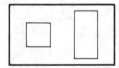

Fig. 8.36

pen. Arrange for each child from the group to post these shapes into the box and then talk with the children about what was done and seen, and what the results show. (The red corner of the square fits four different corners of the posting hole, and each time the square goes into the box. This means that a square has sides the same length as well as corners the same shape. The red corner of the oblong fits all the corners of the rectangular hole but the oblong cannot always be posted. This means that its sides are not all the same length, but its corners are the same shape.)

The teacher could make a collection of rectangular boxes and tins, with lids, some of which are square, e.g. shoes boxes, biscuit tins and sweet boxes. (Some food boxes could be fitted with lids in order to obtain boxes with square lids.) Remove the lids from the boxes and ask individual children, or pairs of children from the group, to find those that are square. Some lids could be clearly seen not to be square but those which are square, or nearly square, are hard to distinguish. Now ask the children to put the lids on the boxes and find the square ones, and non-square ones, by considering the number of ways each lid fits its box. Talk with the children about the lids along the following lines. This lid fits its box four different ways, so its sides are the same length and its corners the same shape, therefore, it is a square. This lid, however, fits its box in only two ways so it is oblong but not square. Colour the edges of this oblong lid red, green, blue and orange (Fig. 8.37). The lid fits the box in two ways as shown. This means that the red and orange edges of the lid are the same length, and the blue and green edges of the lid are the same length. Therefore, opposite sides of an oblong are the same length.

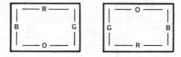

Fig. 8.37

Talk with the children about rectangles being shapes with four square corners. Squares and oblongs are both rectangles and their opposite sides are the same length. So we can say that the opposite sides of a rectangle are equal in length.

8.5.2 Finding Square Corners (2 L1; 10 L2)

At a 'talking time' session with a group of children, the teacher could use a plastic square and right-angled triangle, and put a corner of the triangle on top of a corner of the square, points together, and one side coincident (Fig. 8.38). Which is bigger, the

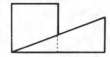

Fig. 8.38

corner of the square or triangle? Discuss this. (The corner of the triangle is smaller than a square corner.) Compare another corner of the triangle with a square corner (Fig.

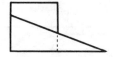

Fig. 8.39

8.39). These corners are the same, so this corner of the triangle is square. Finally, compare the other corner of the triangle with a square corner. We find that this particular triangle has a square corner, and two corners smaller than square corners. Also compare the corners of a square and a pentagon (Fig. 8.40). We find that a pentagon has corners larger than a square corner.

Fig. 8.40

Show the children how to make a square corner by folding a piece of paper (Fig. 8.41). Do not tell them it is a square corner, but having made one, compare it with a corner of a square. We can use this paper square corner as a basis for describing other corners by fitting it against them. Let the children in the group make their own square corners and then find other square corners in the classroom, e.g. corners of an exercise book, a door, a window pane, a sheet of paper, etc. List the results, or give oral answers.

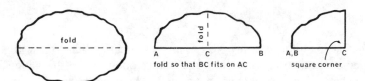

Fig. 8.41

The teacher prepares a set, or sets, of cardboard acute-angled, right-angled and obtuse-angled triangles. As an activity, individual children from the group could be asked to find, by only looking, those triangles with a square corner, a corner larger than a square corner, a corner smaller than a square corner or all its corners smaller than a square corner. Ask them to check the results by testing the corners with a paper square corner, and to display the triangles on the desk. Label each display (Figs. 8.42 and 8.43).

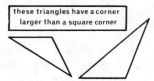

Fig. 8.42

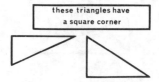

Fig. 8.43

Prepare a set or sets of cardboard four-sided shapes (Fig. 8.44). Individual children from the group could also be asked to find, just by looking, those shapes with one square corner, two square corners, no square corners, only one corner larger than a square corner, two corners larger than a square corner, only one corner smaller than a square corner or two corners only smaller than a square corner. Ask them to check the results by testing the corners with a paper square corner.

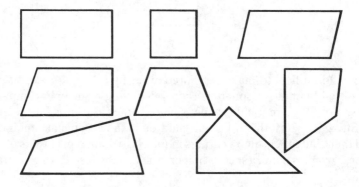

Fig. 8.44

Ask the group of children, a few at a time if necessary, each to join together four congruent geometrical strips, and place the shapes obtained on the table (Fig. 8.45). Discuss each shape. Is it a square? If not, why? (The corners are not square.) If yes, check the corners with a square corner. Then ask each child to put a paper square corner on his shape between two adjacent strips, and adjust the corner and make it square. Notice that when you alter one corner the other corners also change, and that when one corner is square the others are also square. Check this.

Fig. 8.45

Now arrange that the same children each use two pairs of geometrical strips of different lengths, and join them in the order long, long, short, short, to make four-sided shapes (Fig. 8.46). Put the shapes on the table. Talk with each child about the shape he or she has made. Is it a rectangle? Could you change its corners and make it into a

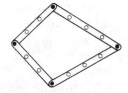

Fig. 8.46

rectangle? (No) The shape you have made is like a kite. If you pick up the shape it will close. How could you stop it from closing? Discuss this, and ask the children to make the shapes rigid.

Next, ask each of these children to use two pairs of geometrical strips of different lengths and join them in the order long, short, long short (Fig. 8.47). Each child puts his shape on the table, and the teacher talks with the children about what has been made. Is it a rectangle? If yes, check its corners with a square corner. If not, could the shape be changed into a rectangle? Ask each child to fit a square corner on the framework he has made and adjust its shape so that it makes a rectangle. Are opposite sides of a rectangle the same length? Discuss this.

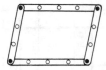

Fig. 8.47

8.5.3 Parallelograms and Parallel Lines (2 L1; 2,10 L2)

1. In 'talking time', with a group of children, the teacher selects two pairs of geometrical strips of different lengths, puts them together, and establishes that the longer strips are the same length, and the shorter strips are the same length. He, or she, then joins the strips to make a parallelogram (Fig. 8.47). Talk with the children about this shape. (The corners are not square and opposite sides are the same length.) This shape is a **parallelogram**. A parallelogram has opposite sides parallel, that is, they are the same distance apart. Railway lines are parallel, as are the opposite edges of a table, the opposite sides of a sheet of paper, etc.

   Ask the children to point out parallel lines in the classroom. Could we find twelve different pairs? Discuss the results. Could we also find lines which are not parallel? Point them out.

2. Ask the children, a few at a time if necessary, each to draw on plain paper, with a straight edge, two straight lines which cross. Talk with these children about the lines. Are they parallel? (No) Why not? Because they get closer together, then meet, and then get farther apart. Now ask the children to draw two straight lines which do not get closer together. This is difficult. Discuss some of their efforts and decide whether the lines will eventually meet, hence, are not parallel.

Give each child some squared paper and ask them to draw two parallel lines on it. Talk about this task. Is it easy to do? How are the lines kept the same distance apart? Establish that we draw one line, go up *x* units from its ends, make marks and then join these marks. To join these marks we only need to draw over one of the ruled lines. Suppose we draw a line, go up five units at one end and eight units at the other, make marks and then join them with a straight edge. Would the lines be parallel? Try it and see.

3. Individual work for the group of children. Ask each child to draw two straight lines across a piece of squared paper and on top of the ruled lines (Fig. 8.48). Are the lines parallel? Now draw two straight lines down the paper on the printed lines. Are these lines parallel? Each child shades in the shape enclosed by the parallel lines. Talk with the children about each shape. What is it called? (A rectangle.) Is it also a parallelogram? (Yes.) Tell them that a parallelogram with square corners is given the special name of rectangle.

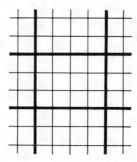

Fig. 8.48

Now give each child triangular ruled paper. Ask him to draw two pairs of straight lines, crossing, on top of the ruled lines, and colour in the shape enclosed by these lines. The shape could be like the one shown in Fig. 8.49. Talk with the children about each shape. Are any sides parallel? Which ones? Is the shape a parallelogram? (Yes.) Is it a rectangle? Why not?

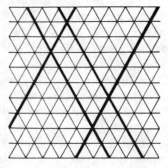

Fig. 8.49

4. Demonstrate what follows to a small group of children. Use cardboard cylinders (Smartie tubes). Cut one down the side squarely with the top edge, and the other

obliquely (Fig 8.50). Spread out the faces and talk with the children about the shapes obtained. Establish that both shapes are parallelograms, and that one is also a rectangle because its corners are square.

Fig. 8.50

5. Individual work for pairs of children. Each pair marks out a rectangle on squared paper and cuts it out. Then they fold the rectangle round, and join two of its opposite sides with Sellotape, to make a shape. Name the shape. (A cylinder.)
   Now use triangular paper. On it, each pair marks out a parallelogram, and cuts it out. Fold it round and join two of its opposite sides with Sellotape to make a shape. Name the shape. (A cylinder.)
6. Compile a work card, or give oral instructions. Ask a child, or children, each to make a row with 10 pegs on a pegboard. Put another row of 10 pegs beneath but slightly to one side, and another row, and so on, until we have 6 rows (Fig. 8.51). What shape has been made? Suppose the rows of pegs were put directly beneath each other. What shape would be made?

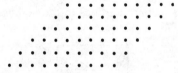

Fig. 8.51

7. Compile a work card, or give oral instructions. Ask a child, or children, each to make a parallelogram with geometrical strips. How can the shape be stopped from closing up? Insert an extra strip to make it rigid (Fig. 8.52). We have split the parallelogram into two shapes. What are these shapes? What do you notice about these triangles? (They are the same, or congruent.)

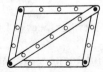

Fig. 8.52

8. Compile a work card, or give oral instructions. Ask a child to select congruent equilateral triangles from a box of assorted plastic shapes, and then fit them together to cover a sheet of paper without leaving gaps. The triangles are allowed to project

over the edges of the paper (Fig. 8.53). Ask the child to point out any parallel lines that can be seen. Study the pattern and then make parallelograms using 2 triangles, 8 triangles and 12 triangles. Could you make one with 5 triangles? (No.)

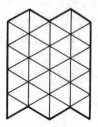

Fig. 8.53

9. Compile a work card, or give oral instructions. Give a child a right-angled triangle, not isosceles. Ask him to select a congruent triangle from a box of shapes, and put the triangles together to form a rectangle; then a parallelogram (Fig. 8.54). Establish

Fig. 8.54

that a rectangle or parallelogram could be made from two triangles. Ask the child to find more triangles and see if they will fit together to cover a sheet of paper (Fig. 8.55). Find different sets of parallel lines in the arrangement of triangles.

Fig. 8.55

8.5.4 Fitting Shapes Together to Cover Surfaces (2 L1; 2, 3, 10 L2)

Compile work cards, or give oral instructions, for the following activities:

1. A child, or pair of children, could use about 20 congruent rectangles and see whether they could be fitted together to cover part of the desk top. What patterns have you made? Find sets of parallel lines within the arrangements.

   Ask each child to make patterns, like those shown in Figs. 8.56 and 8.57, on pieces of plain paper, by drawing around a rectangle. Colour in the patterns using three or

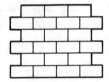

Fig. 8.56

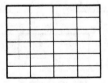

Fig. 8.57

four different colours. Look at a brick wall. Do you see a pattern like one you have just drawn? Make a 'brick-wall' pattern using Cuisenaire rods.

If necessary, show these children that rectangles can also be fitted in a 'herring-bone' pattern (Fig. 8.58). Ask them to make such a pattern using congruent rectangles or Cuisenaire red rods. Also draw a 'herring-bone' pattern on plain paper by drawing around a plastic rectangle, and colour it in using four different colours.

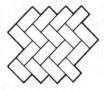

Fig. 8.58

2. Ask a child, or pair of children, to cover a part of the desk top by fitting together about 20 congruent plastic shapes. Use squares, circles, square-cornered triangles, equilateral triangles, regular hexagons, regular pentagons and regular octagons. Which of these shapes do not fit together? (Circles, regular pentagons and regular octagons.)
3. Arrange for a child, or children, each to make a pattern on a piece of plain paper by drawing around a plastic triangle and colouring in the regions. Also, to make patterns using only a circle, a regular hexagon, a regular octagon and an equilateral triangle. When octagons are fitted together notice that the regions between them are square (Fig. 8.59).

Fig. 8.59

4. Give a child, or pair of children, congruent plastic squares, equilateral triangles, right-angled triangles, and specially prepared cardboard shapes as shown in Fig. 8.60. (These shapes can be just covered with plastic pieces if the right ones are selected.)

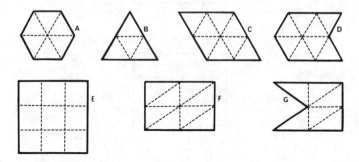

Fig. 8.60

Which is the best shape to cover the cardboard triangle B? From the various plastic shapes find those with corners the same as the corners of the cardboard triangle, and use them for covering. What shaped pieces did you use? (Equilateral triangles.) Would the same shaped pieces be best to cover the cardboard square E? Try fitting them, and see. In this case we find that plastic pieces with square corners fit best because they fit the corners of the square. When square-cornered triangles and squares are tried we find that the squares just fit, but that the triangles do not. Now try covering the rectangle F, and then the other shapes. Display each cardboard shape on the table together with the best shaped unit for covering it.

Which is the bigger shape, A or C? What could we mean by bigger in this case? We could mean longer, wider or covers more. What shaped units cover both A and C? (Small equilateral triangles.) How many triangles are needed to cover each shape? A needs 6 triangles and C requires 8 triangles, therefore, C covers more than A. (At the pre-number stage the triangles could be displayed in rows, side by side, to determine the greater number.) Does C cover more than D? and F cover more than G? and A cover more than B? Questions of this nature introduce the idea of area, and these topics are dealt with in greater detail in Chapter 7 'Surface and Area'.

8.5.5 Congruence and Area (2, 10 L2)

We will briefly mention a few activities for individual children involving congruence, which lead to important ideas connected with area. Work cards could be compiled which deal with these activities, or instructions given orally.

1. A child uses four congruent square-cornered triangles, not isosceles, and with two of them makes a rectangle, and with the others makes a parallelogram (Fig. 8.61). Talk with the child about the rectangle and parallelogram covering the same amount of surface because they are both formed with two congruent triangles. Conversely, one of the triangles covers half as much as the rectangle or parallelogram. (Later we

Fig. 8.61

could say that the areas of the rectangle and parallelogram are equal, and that the area of the triangle is half the area of the rectangle or parallelogram.)

2. Ask a child to draw a triangle on thin cardboard, cut it out, draw around it, and then cut out another triangle. Next, fit the triangles together. Are they congruent? Make a parallelogram with the triangles. Talk with the child about the parallelogram covering twice as much as one of the triangles, and that the triangle covers half as much as the parallelogram.
3. Ask a child to draw a parallelogram on triangular ruled paper, and cut it out carefully (Fig. 8.62). Draw a diagonal, cut along it, and divide the parallelogram into two triangles. Are the triangles congruent? Does the parallelogram cover twice as much as one of the triangles?

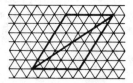

Fig. 8.62

4. A child uses four congruent square-cornered plastic triangles and fits them together to form a parallelogram (Fig. 8.63). Talk with the child about the parallelogram covering four times as much as one of the triangles.

Fig. 8.63

5. Ask the child to draw a square of side 12 units on centimetre-squared paper, and cut it out. Draw its diagonals, cut along them, and cut the square into four triangles. Fit the triangles together and see if they are congruent. Talk with the child about the diagonals dividing the square into four equal parts, about the square covering four times as much as one of the triangles, and about a triangle covering a quarter as much as the square.
6. Give a child four congruent isosceles square-cornered triangles. Fit the triangles together. Are they congruent? Make a square with the triangles. Establish that the shape is a square by testing its corners with a paper square corner, and comparing its sides by putting sides of triangles together. Talk with the child about the square covering four times as much as one of the triangles.

7. Give a child six plastic equilateral triangles. Fit the triangles together to make a hexagon. Establish that the hexagon covers six times as much as one of the triangles.
8. Ask a child to make eight different shapes on centimetre-squared paper so that each contains 20 squares, and to find the perimeter of each shape. Which shapes have the largest and smallest perimeters? Have these shapes the same area? An area of 20 squares produces many shapes with different perimeters. What do you notice about the shape with the largest perimeter? (It is long and narrow.) What do you notice about the shape with the smallest perimeter? (The squares are clustered together.)

8.5.6. Comparing Corners (11 L2)

We dealt with this topic in a specialized way when we talked about square corners (Section 8.5.2, *Finding Square Corners*, earlier in this chapter). We will now compare corners which are not necessarily square.

1. The teacher could talk with a child, or group of children, about the following test. To compare two corners we could put them on top of one another, points coinciding and one side coinciding (Fig. 8.64). We can then see which is the larger, or smaller corner, depending on where we focus our attention.

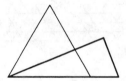

Fig. 8.64

   Compile work cards and set individual work. Each child needs practice in comparing the corners of cardboard triangles, quadrilaterals and other polygons, firstly by inspection, and then by fitting the corners together to check the results. Each shape could be numbered or lettered, and its corners painted different colours, so that questions could be asked about particular corners, e.g. which is the larger, the red corner in shape A, or the blue corner in shape B? Also, arrange for some of the corners that are compared to be the same.
2. Compile a work card or give oral instructions. Use numbered triangles with their corners marked in different colours. Ask a child, or children, each to select a triangle, look at its corners, and say which is the largest, and the smallest, e.g. the red corner is largest, the blue corner is smallest. Copy each of the corners of the triangle

common side

Fig. 8.65

by drawing along the sides forming them, and draw these copies on top of one another with their points coinciding and one side of each coinciding (Fig. 8.65). Place the corners of the triangle on top of the copied corners again so that the colours of the largest and smallest can be identified. Compare these results with the initial estimates. Repeat this process with other triangles.

Also put the corners of a cardboard quadrilateral in order of size, by inspection, and then check the estimate using the procedure just mentioned.

3. Compile a work card, or give oral instructions. Ask a child, or children, each to make triangles with three geometrical strips of the same length, with three strips of different lengths and then with three strips, two of which are the same length. Compare the corners in each triangle, taken separately, by drawing along the sides forming each corner, on top of one another (Fig. 8.65). Before doing this, however, the child finds the largest, smallest or equal corners in each triangle, by inspection.

Talk with the child about a triangle with equal sides, an equilateral triangle, having three equal corners, and a triangle with unequal sides having unequal corners. Where is the largest corner of a triangle? (Opposite the longest side.) Where is the smallest corner of a triangle? (Opposite the shortest side.) Also establish that a triangle with two equal sides has two equal corners. Where are these equal corners? (Opposite the equal sides.) Introduce the term **isosceles** for this kind of triangle.

8.5.7 Isosceles Triangles (2, 10 L2)

1. Arrange for individual children to use two congruent square-cornered triangles, and fit them together to make a larger triangle. Find equal sides and corners in the larger triangle. What is the special name for this kind of triangle? (Isosceles.)
2. On squared paper draw isosceles triangles. (Use the ruled lines as construction lines.) The teacher could direct this activity with a group of children. Draw a line down the paper x units long, and mark it AB (Fig 8.66). Through B draw a line across the paper, mark off y units each side of B, and obtain points P and Q. Join AP and AQ with straight lines. Carefully cut out the triangle APQ. Fold the triangle in order to find equal sides and corners. We find that two sides are the same length, and two corners are the same. What is the special name for this triangle? (Isosceles.)

Fig. 8.66

The children could now, without much assistance, draw other isosceles triangles to dimensions of their own choosing, or provided by the teacher. (The dimensions given would be AB, BP and BQ.)

3. Make a work card which asks a child to draw on centimetre-squared paper a square of side 10 units, then to cut out the square, draw its diagonals and cut along them, so

obtaining four triangles. Are the triangles congruent? Fit them on top of one another to find out. Has each triangle a square corner? Which angles, and sides, look the same? Fold the triangles and see whether the sides, and angles, which look the same, coincide. Are the triangles isosceles?

4. Make a work card which asks a child to draw on centimetre-squared paper a rectangle 16 units long and 10 units wide, then to cut it out, draw its diagonals and cut along them, so obtaining four triangles. Are any triangles congruent? Are any triangles isosceles? Fit the triangles together, and fold them, to answer these questions.

8.5.8 Making Three-Dimensional Shapes (2 L1; 10 L2; 10 L3)

1. Write instructions on a work card. Ask a child to examine the faces of a cube. What shape are they? Are the faces congruent? Make a cube by joining together cardboard squares with Sellotape. (The congruent squares could be obtained by drawing around a plastic square.)

2. Compile a work card, or give oral instructions. Ask a child to obtain a rectangular box, with a lid, such as a cereal packet. Cut the box, or tear it carefully, along its edges to obtain six rectangular faces. Compare the faces by fitting them on top of one another. Are any congruent? Which ones? Then rebuild the box by sticking the rectangles together with Sellotape.

3. Give a child six rectangular pieces of cardboard, or thin plastic rectangles, which can be joined to make a rectangular box. Compile a work card, or give oral instructions. Do you think you could make a rectangular box with these rectangles? Sort them and see. (Six rectangles are needed, three congruent pairs.) Now make a rectangular box by sticking the rectangles together with Sellotape.

4. Give a child four cardboard or plastic rectangles, and two squares, which can be joined to make a rectangular box. Compile a work card, or give oral instructions. Do you think you could make a box with these pieces? Put the pieces on the table, side by side, and show how you would join them. Then make the box by joining the pieces with Sellotape. Is it a prism? Stand it on the table on one of its square faces. Is it a square-based prism?

5. Compile a work card, or give oral instructions. Use congruent cardboard rectangles 10 cm by 8 cm. Ask a child, or pair of children, to draw around one or two such rectangles and make copies.

   Join the longer sides of three rectangles together to make a prism (Fig. 8.67). What kind of prism is it? Can its shape be altered? (No, it is rigid.) Make triangular end-pieces for the prism by standing it on thin cardboard and drawing around its ends. What kind of triangle is needed?

Fig. 8.67

Join four rectangles together by their longer sides to make a prism. Can the shape be altered? (Yes.) Stand the prism on a piece of card, alter its shape until its base is square, and draw around its end in order to make a square end-piece. Make a square face for the other end of the prism, in a similar way.

Make pentagonal, and hexagonal prisms, by joining together five, and six, rectangles. Draw around their ends on thin cardboard in order to make end-pieces.

6. Arrange for a group of children to each make a cylinder by folding a rectangular piece of thin cardboard round and joining opposite sides with Sellotape. Draw around the ends of the tube to mark out circular end-pieces.

7. Compile a work card, or give oral instructions. Use cardboard congruent isosceles triangles. (The teacher could give a child, or pair of children, one or two such triangles to draw around in order to obtain copies.) What kind of triangle is being used? (Isosceles.) Are the triangles congruent? (Yes.)

Join three triangles with Sellotape as shown in Fig. 8.68. Fold the shape so that AB and BC meet, and then join these sides together. Put the shape on the table so that it rests on its open end. What shape has been made? (Pyramid.) What shape is its base? (Triangle.) What kind of pyramid has been made? (A triangular-based pyramid.)

Join together four, five and six isosceles triangles in the manner described above, and make other pyramids, and name them. Fit a base to each pyramid, if required.

Fig. 8.68

8. Compile a work card, or give oral instructions. Give a child a cardboard obtuse-angled sector of a circle of about 15 cm radius, to draw around on thick paper (Fig. 8.69). Cut out the paper sector, bend it around until the straight edges meet and join them with Sellotape. What shape is obtained? (A pyramid.) What is the shape of the open end? (A circle.) Put the pyramid on the desk resting on its open end. What is the special name for this pyramid? (A cone.)

Fig. 8.69

8.5.9 Circles (2 L1; 10 L3)

Compile work cards and give oral instructions concerning the following activities:

1. Ask a child to fix the end of a piece of string to the classroom floor with a drawing pin. At the other end of the string make a loop. Into the loop push a stick of chalk, and keeping the string taut, move around and draw a chalk line on the floor (Fig. 8.70). Discuss with the child the shape traced out. (A **circle**.) The drawing pin is at the **centre** of the circle. The **radius** of the circle is the distance from the centre to the boundary. The boundary is called the circumference.

Fig. 8.70

2. A child, or a few children, could each mark out a circle on thick paper by drawing around a circular plastic plate. Cut out the circle, and then fold it in half a number of times (Fig. 8.71). What do you notice about the creases made on the circle? They are straight lines which cross at the centre of the circle. Mark the centre of the circle, draw two straight lines from the centre to the edge, and cut the circle along these lines into two sectors. With the sectors make cones. Which cone is like a lampshade? Which is like an ice-cream cornet?

Fig. 8.71

3. A child, or group of children, could each mark out a paper circle by drawing around a circular plastic plate. Cut out the circle, fold it in half, then in half again. Open out the circle and join the points where the creases meet the circumference by means of straight lines (Fig. 8.72). Look at the four-sided figure so formed. Are the sides equal in length, and the corners square? What shape do you think it is? (A square.) Cut out the four-sided shape, and fold it to see whether its sides are equal, and corners the same, to check that it is a square. Cut the square into triangles, after drawing the diagonals, and compare these triangles. Are they congruent? Fold each triangle to find equal sides and equal corners. Are the triangles isosceles?

Fig. 8.72

4. A child, or group of children, could each mark out a paper circle by drawing around a plastic plate. Cut out the circle, fold it in half, in half again, then in half again (Fig. 8.73). Open out the circle and join the points where the creases meet the circumference of the circle by means of straight lines. How many sides has this shape? Cut out the eight-sided shape, and by folding it compare sides and corners. Is it a regular octagon?

Fig. 8.73

   Mark the corners of the triangles which meet at the centre with a coloured pen. How many triangles are there? Cut out the triangles and fit them together. Are they congruent? (Yes.) Fold each triangle to find equal sides and corners. Are the triangles isosceles? Remake the octagon by putting the triangles together, side by side, on the table.

5. A child, or group of children, could each mark out a circle by drawing around a plastic plate. Cut out the circle and fold it in half twice. (Not in quarters.) Open out the circle and join the points where the creases meet the circumference with straight lines (Fig. 8.74). Cut out the four-sided shape so formed, compare its sides and angles, and identify it. (A rectangle.)

Fig. 8.74

6. The teacher could discuss this activity with a group of children. Get a hoop or large cardboard circle, place it on the floor, and look at it from different positions. Do you see a circle? We see a shape like a squashed circle called an ellipse. Stand as far as possible from the circle, look at it, and walk towards it. We see a narrow ellipse at first, and as we walk nearer the ellipse gets wider until it becomes a circle. A circular object when observed obliquely appears as an ellipse.

   Find other circles in the classroom and look at them from different positions so that they appear elliptical, e.g. bottom edge of a circular lampshade, top edge of a cylindrical tin, top edge of a cup, the rim of a plastic bucket, the edge of a circular plate, etc.

7. Arrange for a child, or group of children, each to make a cylinder with plasticine. Each child cuts a cylinder with a knife and looks at the shape of the face made by the cut (Fig. 8.75). He repeats this, varying the direction of the cuts. What shapes are the

cut faces? (Generally an ellipse.) How could we obtain a circular cut face? (Hold the knife parallel to one of the circular ends of the cylinder and cut.) Ask each child to look at an elliptical cut face from different places and notice that its shape also appears to change. Could an ellipse appear as a circle? Where would the viewing position be for this to happen?

   Each child could now make two plasticine cones, then cut one cone to obtain a circular-cut face, and the other to obtain an elliptical-cut face.

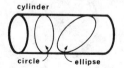

Fig. 8.75

8. Arrange for a pair of children to do as follows. On thin cardboard draw around a circular tin lid and cut out a circle. Hold the circle near a wall in a dark corner, or cupboard, and shine a torch at it. Shine the torch at the circle from directly in front, and obliquely, and observe the shadow produced. From where do you shine the torch to produce a circular shadow? From where do you shine the torch to obtain an elliptical shadow?

   Also, keep the torch still but slowly turn the cardboard circle. Can you obtain circular and elliptical shadows in this case?

8.6 ANGLES, SYMMETRY, SIMILARITY AND NUMBER PATTERNS (2, 3 L2; 5, 10, 11 L3; 5, 10, 11 L4)

8.6.1 Angles (2, 11 L2; 10, 11 L3)

Introductory work on angles has been confined to the comparison of corners, and the recognition of angles. We have not yet used the word angle but talked about corners being the same, or one corner being larger than another. The corners examined have been seen as fixed, unchangeable, parts of cardboard shapes.

   We could now introduce the term **angle** to describe an amount of turning, and then apply the idea of movement to the corners of plane figures. Thus, corners can then be seen from a static point of view and from a rotational point of view.

   The teacher could demonstrate with apparatus and discuss ideas about turning as described in the following activities.

1. Use two geometrical strips hinged at one end. Put the strips on top of one another initially and then turn one of the strips whilst the other strip is kept still (Fig. 8.76). The two strips make a corner, or an angle.

   Make an angle with another pair of strips in the manner described earlier and then compare the angles (Fig. 8.77). Which is the larger? Fit them on top of one another to check the estimate. Which strip was turned more? Which angle is the

Fig. 8.76

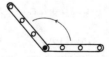

Fig. 8.77

larger? The larger angle, therefore, was made by turning the strip around more.

The teacher, or a child, could now make an angle (by moving one strip only), and another child asked to make a larger angle with the other pair of hinged strips. Repeat this activity but ask the second child to make a smaller angle.

Also deal with equal angles, and establish that they are made by turning the strips through equal amounts (Fig. 8.78).

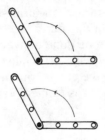

Fig. 8.78

2. Also use a piece of white cardboard to which a pointer has been attached with a bayonet paper clip. Mark the initial position of the pointer, turn the pointer a little and mark its final position (Fig. 8.79). Put the pointer on the initial mark again, turn the pointer, and again mark its final position. Did we turn the pointer more the first or second time? When did the pointer turn through the larger angle?

Also turn the pointer through an angle, and then turn the pointer through the 'same angle'.

Fig. 8.79

3. Ask children from the group to demonstrate. One child stands facing a mark on the wall, and turns once, twice or three times in a clockwise direction. Another child watches, and then turns through a larger angle, a smaller angle or the same angle as directed.

4. Ask children from the group to demonstrate. A child stands facing a mark on the wall and turns in a clockwise direction, but less than a complete turn. Another child watches, and is asked to turn through a larger angle, a smaller angle or the same angle as directed.

5. The children in the group could stand up and face a mark on the wall. Ask them to make one turn clockwise, two turns clockwise, three turns anticlockwise, one turn anticlockwise, etc. Explain that **clockwise** is turning about to the right, and **anti-clockwise** is turning about to the left.

   In a clockwise direction make two and a half turns, a quarter-turn, three-quarters of a turn, two and a quarter turns, one and three-quarter turns, etc.

   In an anticlockwise direction make two and a quarter turns, one and a half turns, three and a quarter turns, one and three-quarter turns, etc.

   Explain that *right-turn* means a quarter-turn to the right, *left-turn* means a quarter-turn to the left, *right-about-turn* means a half-turn to the right and *left-about-turn* means a half-turn to the left. Let the children face a wall and then give a series of commands, e.g. left-turn—left-turn—right-turn—left-about-turn. What single command would now bring you to face the wall again? (Left-turn.)

6. Arrange for these activities to be done individually by a group of children.

   Each child uses two Meccano-like strips hinged at one end, and does as follows. Keep one strip still and move the other strip through a quarter-turn anticlockwise (Fig. 8.80). What kind of corner is formed? (A square corner.)

Fig. 8.80

A quarter-turn makes a square corner. Tell the children that another name for a square corner is a **right angle**. So a quarter-turn, or a square corner, both make a right angle.

Put the strips together again, and turn one strip through a quarter-turn, then another quarter-turn, both anticlockwise (Fig. 8.81). What happens to the strips? (They make a straight line). Thus, two right angles make half a revolution. Two quarter-turns make a half-turn, so two square corners should fit together to make a straight line.

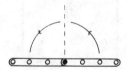

Fig. 8.81

Give each child two square-cornered triangles, and put the square corners, side by side, points coinciding (Fig. 8.82). Do the corners form a straight line? Put a straight edge against the line to check this; or stand the triangles, corners together, on the table top.

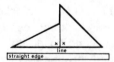

Fig. 8.82

The children put the strips together again, and turn one strip anticlockwise through a quarter-turn, a quarter-turn, a quarter-turn, and a quarter-turn, pausing at each stage (Fig. 8.83). Observe that four quarter-turns make a whole turn. Another way of saying this is that in turning through four right angles we turn one revolution.

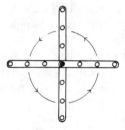

Fig. 8.83

Each child now gets four plastic shapes all of which have a square corner, and puts the square corners together (Fig. 8.84). These corners fit together, thus verifying that four square corners added together are equivalent to one revolution.

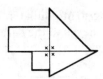

Fig. 8.84

To sum up, therefore, the children could find that one turn is equivalent to four right angles, a half-turn is equivalent to two right angles and that two right angles form a straight line (having been told that a quarter-turn is called a right angle).
7. Drawings of pairs of hinged geometrical strips could be put on cards. A child uses a pair of hinged geometrical strips and opens them so that they look like the drawings on the cards. The child has to say whether the angle turned through is less than a right angle, or greater than a right angle. Should an angle turned through be larger than a right angle, the child describes its approximate size, e.g. more than two right angles and less than three right angles, that is, between two and three right angles.

Also ask the child to describe each angle using fractions of a turn, e.g. more than a half-turn and less than three-quarters of a turn.

8. Compile a work card. Ask a child to do the following activities and describe the angles turned through in terms of right angles, and quarter-turns. Describe the angle turned through by a door when it is opened, a handle or knob when the door is unfastened, a key when a door is locked or unlocked, the front cover when a book is opened and the large hand of a clock between two and three o'clock.

9. Compile a work card. Ask a child to describe in terms of right angles, and quarter-turns, the angles turned through by the large hand of a clock in moving from the 12 to the 6, the 3 to the 9, the 9 to the 12, the 3 to the 6, the 1 to the 4, the 2 to the 8, the 10 to the 1 and the 7 to the 4. (Use a model clock face to obtain the answers, if necessary. All turning is considered clockwise.)

10. Write instructions on a work card and give the child large cardboard triangles, quadrilaterals and other polygons. Describe the angles of each shape as being equal to, greater than or less than a right angle. Use a corner of a square to test for right angles, if necessary.

11. Compile a work card. A child uses a set of cardboard triangles, quadrilaterals and other polygons. Find those shapes with a right angle, with an angle smaller than a right angle, with an angle larger than a right angle and with two angles smaller than a right angle, etc.

12. Ask a child to fit congruent regular hexagons together on the table. Notice that three corners fit together, and these corners are equal (Fig. 8.85). A corner of a hexagon can be thought of as one-third of a turn.

Fig. 8.85

13. Arrange for a child to fit congruent equilateral triangles together on the table. Notice that six corners fit together, and they are equal (Fig. 8.86). A corner of an equilateral triangle can be thought of as one-sixth of a turn.

Fig. 8.86

14. Arrange the instructions on a work card and give a child cardboard scalene triangles which are congruent and have their corners marked with symbols, or different colours. (Suppose the corners are marked **x**, **o**, and ∗.) The child compares these triangles. Are they congruent? Compare angles marked **x**. Are they equal? Compare corners marked **o**. Are they equal? Compare angles marked ∗. Are they equal? Fit two triangles together to make a parallelogram and then fit four paral-

lelograms together (Fig. 8.87). Which 6 corners fit together to make the equivalent of one turn of a pointer, or 4 right angles? (2 crosses, 2 stars and 2 circles) This means that 2 stars, 2 crosses and 2 circles add up to 4 right angles. What do 1 cross, 1 star and 1 circle add up to? (2 right angles.) Is your answer correct? Check your answer by looking at the edges of the pattern of triangles. Notice that 1 star, 1 cross and 1 circle form a straight line, which is 2 right angles.

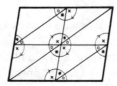

Fig. 8.87

Notice that the angles of a triangle are marked * (star), **o** (circle) and **x** (cross). What is the sum of these angles? (2 right angles, because star, cross and circle form a straight line.)

The child can check this. Compile a work card which asks the child to do as follows: Draw a triangle on gummed paper, cut it out, and mark its corners with arrows. Tear off the angles and carefully stick them side by side on white paper (Fig. 8.88). Do they form a straight line? Check with a straight edge.

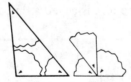

Fig. 8.88

15. Put on a work card for individual children. Draw a four-sided shape on gummed paper, cut it out, and mark its corners with arrows. Tear off the corners and stick them side by side on paper (Fig. 8.89). The corners make an angle equivalent to one

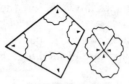

Fig. 8.89

turn of a pointer. How many right angles in one turn? What do the angles of a four-sided shape add to? (Four right angles.) Are we surprised at this result? A four-sided figure can be divided into two triangles, and the angles of these triangles form the angles of the quadrilateral (Fig. 8.90). If the angle sum of a triangle is two right angles, then the angle sum of two triangles is four right angles.

Fig. 8.90

8.6.2 Symmetry of Two-dimensional Shapes about a Line (10, 11 L3)

A two-dimensional shape is symmetrical about a line if its boundary is the same shape and size on both sides of the line, but facing opposite directions. Compile work cards and give oral instructions in order to arrange individual work concerning the following activities.

1. Fold a piece of paper and prick out a line of holes with a pin through both thicknesses of paper. Start at the fold, make the holes, and finish at the fold. Open out the paper and examine the lines of holes (Fig. 8.91). Notice that every hole on one side of the fold has a partner on the other side. Find partners and encircle them with coloured pencil lines. Talk with the child about partners being the same distance away from the fold because they originate from the same pinprick. The lines of holes are the same shape and size but facing opposite directions. The fold divides the shape into two congruent parts. The shape is divided in half by the fold, and the boundary is balanced about the fold. The fold is called a **line of symmetry**.

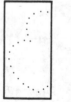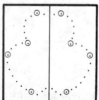

Fig. 8.91

   Make more symmetrical shapes this way, join the pinpricks, and carefully cut out the resulting shapes.
2. In a fold on a piece of paper a blob of ink or paint is dropped, and this is pressed out flat as the two faces of the paper are pushed together (Fig. 8.92). Examine the ink

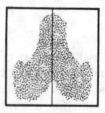

Fig. 8.92

blot and notice that it is the same shape on both sides of the fold, hence, it is symmetrical. Where is the line of symmetry? Make other ink blots using blobs of different coloured paints.

3. Cut a jagged edge on a folded piece of paper. Open out the paper and examine the shape obtained (Fig. 8.93). Is it symmetrical? Where is the line of symmetry?

Fig. 8.93

Now fold a piece of paper, as if to make a paper square corner, and cut a jagged edge on it. Open out the paper and examine the shape (Fig. 8.94). Is it symmetrical? This shape is balanced about two lines of symmetry.

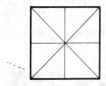

Fig. 8.94

4. Give a child a plastic or cardboard oblong, square, circle, isosceles triangle, scalene triangle, equilateral triangle, regular hexagon, regular octagon, regular pentagon and parallelogram. Draw around each shape on paper and carefully cut out the copied figures. Find the lines, or line, of symmetry of the shapes by paper folding, and draw in these lines (Fig. 8.95).

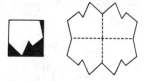

Fig. 8.95

A line of symmetry divides a shape into two equal parts. If we fold a shape so that the parts on both sides of the fold match exactly then the fold marks the line of symmetry. Some shapes can be folded in more than one way, e.g. a square has four lines of symmetry and a circle has an infinite number.

Find out how many lines of symmetry each of these shapes has: a square, a regular pentagon, a regular hexagon and a regular octagon (4, 5, 6 and 8). A study of lines of symmetry of regular figures develops gradually the idea that an n-sided figure has n lines of symmetry.

5. Prepare paper scalene, isosceles and equilateral triangles. A child folds each to find lines of symmetry.

We cannot find a line of symmetry by paper folding on the scalene triangle. This means that all its sides are of different lengths, and its angles unequal.

An isosceles triangle has one line of symmetry so that corresponding sides and angles (sides and angles which partner one another), on opposite sides of the line, are equal. Talk with the child about this, and ask him to draw in the line of symmetry, and mark equal sides and angles (Fig. 8.96).

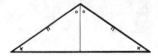

Fig. 8.96

An equilateral triangle has three lines of symmetry. On this triangle a child could mark equal angles and sides by considering symmetry about one line, and then mark equal angles and sides by considering symmetry about a different line (Fig. 8.97). All the angles and sides are now marked, thus showing that this triangle has equal angles and sides.

Fig. 8.97

6. Prepare thin cardboard shapes such as those shown in Fig. 8.98. Ask a child to hold a mirror vertically on the table, and place a shape flat on the table with a side touching the surface of the mirror, then observe the shape of the cardboard and its mirror image (Fig. 8.99). Repeat this with the other cardboard pieces. Talk with the child about what is noticed. (The mirror edge acts like a line of symmetry separating the actual cardboard shape and its image.) By drawing around each card, make complete drawings of each shape and its image.

Fig. 8.98

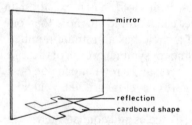

Fig. 8.99

7. The teacher could make a set of work cards using squared paper, each showing a shape in front of a 'mirror'. The child could copy each shape and the mirror line, and then draw the image and so make a symmetrical figure (Fig. 8.100).

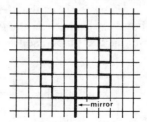

Fig. 8.100

8. Consider capital letters of the alphabet. On squared paper, a child draws those with one line of symmetry and then those with two lines of symmetry.
9. The teacher could draw symmetrical shapes on squared paper. Stick the squared paper on thin cardboard and make work cards. Cover the cards with thin transparent PVC film on both sides. Let the children draw lines of symmetry on each shape with a coloured felt-tipped pen. (The surfaces of the cards can be rubbed clean with a damp cloth, and the cards used again.)

8.6.3 Plane Symmetry of Three-dimensional Shapes (10, 11 L3; 11 L4)

A solid is symmetrical about a plane (a flat sheet) if its boundary (the surface) is the same shape and size on both sides of the plane, but facing opposite directions. Compile work cards and give oral instructions in order to arrange the following activities for individual children:

1. The child needs a plane mirror, and small wooden cubes, rectangular blocks, cylinders, cones, and other prisms and pyramids. (Poleidoblocs could be used, and other shapes made with plastic pieces from a geometrical set.) Ask a child to hold each solid with one of its faces resting on the mirror and observe the shapes of the solid, its image and the composite shape of image and solid. The teacher could talk about the results with the child. (A cylinder and its image form a cylinder twice as long. A cone and its image are cones joined by their bases, and make a solid with 1 edge, 2 faces and 2 corners. A square-based pyramid produces a solid with 8 faces, 6 corners and 12 edges.)

    Talk with the child about each solid and its image being the same shape and size, and that corresponding points on the surface are directly opposite one another with respect to the mirror's surface. Hence, the composite shape is symmetrical. We could also imagine that each composite shape is cut in half should the mirror's surface be considered a slicing position for a knife.
2. A child makes a cube, a rectangular prism, a cylinder, a cone, a ball, a square-based pyramid, etc., using plasticine. Each shape could be cut in half, and the halves rested on the surface of a mirror, on those faces made by the cuts. Observe that the

half-pieces, and their images, rebuild the original shapes. The mirror is the **plane of symmetry** in each 'completed' solid.

3. Ask a child to make a shape with wooden cubes on the desk. (The shape could be made with Multilink cubes instead.) Stand a piece of cardboard vertically on the desk and resting against one of the faces of the shape (Fig. 8.101). Pretend the cardboard is a mirror, and build the 'image' on the other side of it. Remember to match colours of cubes as well as the shape itself.

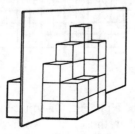

Fig. 8.101

4. Ask a child to find shapes in the classroom, and bring items from home, that are symmetrical. Indicate their plane, or planes, of symmetry, by showing with chalk lines where you would cut them in half, if this were possible, e.g. chair, table, wastepaper basket, milk bottle, lampshade, light bulb, door knob, beaker, cup, etc.

5. Ask a child to sort out the classroom collection of mathematical shapes and find those which are symmetrical. How many planes of symmetry has a rectangular box? a cube? a square-based prism? a hexagonal prism? a cylinder? and a triangular-based prism?

6. Solid objects look flat when they are seen from a long way off, and many present symmetrical outlines. Show a child outlines of common solid objects, drawn on cards. Ask him to identify them, and point out lines of symmetry (Fig. 8.102). The outlines shown are those of a ball, a beaker, an egg, a bottle and a table. Ask the child to draw symmetrical outlines of some other objects that are found at home, or school. He then asks another child to identify them.

Fig. 8.102

7. A pair of children could look at magazines and find pictures of various objects which are symmetrical, or very nearly symmetrical. (Advertisements provide a rich source for symmetrical layouts and patterns.) They could cut out these pictures, draw in their lines of symmetry, and display these pictures on a wall chart. The teacher could talk with these children about each picture and consider whether it is symmetrical, or very nearly symmetrical.

8. Ask a pair of children to consider the world of living things, e.g. plants, birds, fish,

animals, insects, trees, flowers, etc. Make a list of some symmetrical, or nearly symmetrical, things. Draw outlines or obtain pictures of these things, display them on a wall chart, and draw in their lines of symmetry. (Why do you think living things are symmetrical in shape? An interesting topic for discussion.)

8.6.4 Similar Shapes and Caricatures (2 L2; 3, 10 L3; 3 L4)

So far we have developed congruence as a topic, and applied it in other fields, whenever possible, e.g. symmetry. **Similarity** and **caricature** have not been previously mentioned, and with congruence could be introduced via the following activities.

1. Using a film strip, or coloured slide, and a projector, demonstrate to the group of children the enlargement of the picture by projection on to a screen. Discuss the idea of two identical slides being congruent. Discuss the picture on the slide and its enlargement on the screen—the idea of these two pictures being similar. There is enlargement, the shapes are maintained and there is no distortion.

    Again with this group of children, show a square of side 3 units drawn on centimetre-squared paper. Ask each child to copy the square exactly, and also make a copy with sides twice as long (Fig. 8.103). Talk about A and X being **congruent**. This means that the sides of X and the sides of A are the same lengths; and the angles of X and the angles of A are equal.

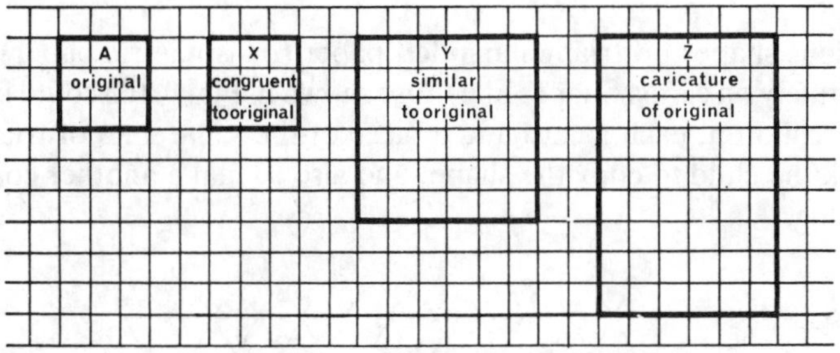

Fig. 8.103

The copy, Y, 6 units by 6 units, is said to be **similar** to the original, A, see Fig. 8.103. Similar means the same shape. This requires that the corners of the copy are the same as the corners of the original, and the sides of the copy are multiples of the sides of the original, e.g. twice as long, or half as long, etc. Look at the corners of A and Y and compare them. They are the same—all right angles. The original shape was square, and if we double the sides our copy, Y, is a larger square. Thus, shape is preserved.

Now ask each child to make a copy of the square so that its sides across the page are doubled, and those down the page are trebled (Fig. 8.103). This gives an oblong, Z, 6 units by 9 units, and this is not similar to A because its shape is different. The corners of A and Z are equal, but the sides of Z are not all the same multiple of the sides of A. Some sides have been doubled, some trebled, and because the sides have been treated differently the shape of Z is different from the shape of A. A copy, such as this, is called a caricature.

2. Draw various shapes on centimetre-squared paper and mount them either on separate cards, or all on the same card. Shapes like those shown in Fig. 8.104 could be used. Give a child, or group of children, each a card and a piece of centimetre-squared paper. Ask each child to make a copy of the shape (or one of them), to make another copy of the shape with sides twice as long, and then to make a copy of the shape with sides three times as long. Also make a caricature by doubling the side lengths in one direction and trebling them in the other.

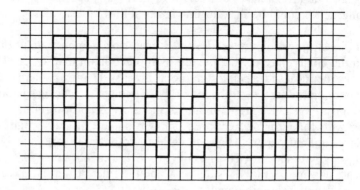

Fig. 8.104

3. Draw various shapes on triangular-ruled paper (or isometric paper), and mount them separately on cards. Shapes like those shown in Fig. 8.105 could be used. Give a child, or children, each a card and a piece of the same kind of triangular-ruled paper. Ask the child to copy the shape, and also to make another copy with sides twice as long.

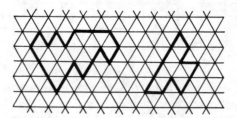

Fig. 8.105

4. A caricature is a distorted view of a shape. Ask a child to look at cartoons in newspapers and make a collection of caricatures of well-known people, and, if possible, their photographs. What features have been unfairly treated?

5. The teacher could demonstrate as follows, and talk with a group of children. Use a balloon. Blow it up a little and draw various shapes on it with a felt pen, such as a circle, or triangle. Blow up the balloon a little more and observe the shapes again. Talk about the ways in which the shapes have changed. Do you think they are

congruent to, similar to, or caricatures of, their original shapes? Repeat this a few times, until the balloon is blown up tightly.

Then clean the ink from the balloon, draw more shapes on it, and ask the children to observe changes in the shapes as the balloon is gradually let down. Again talk with the children about these changes.

6. The teacher could ask a child, or group of children, to do the following things, and talk about them.

Look at your face in a flat mirror. The image and your face are the same size and shape; they are congruent.

Now look into a convex mirror. The image of your face is much smaller than your face, but it still looks like you because they are the same shape. Your image and your face are similar. Also look at a postage stamp, or coin, through a concave lens.

Hold a concave mirror a short distance away from your face. The image of your face is much larger than your face, and only a part of your face can be seen at once. Your nose, mouth, eyes, etc., are the same shapes as their images, but much smaller, so these items are similar to their images. A coin, or postage stamp, could also be examined through a convex lens.

7. Arrange as an activity for an individual child. When you have your photograph taken, is the photograph congruent to, similar to, or a caricature of, yourself? Look at a photograph and various enlargements of it. Are they similar?

8. The teacher sticks squared paper on to thin cardboard and makes work cards showing three or four rectangles, two of which are similar (Fig. 8.106). Ask a child to find the similar rectangles.

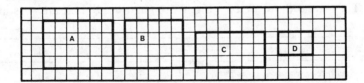

Fig.8.106

9. The teacher sticks squared paper on to thin cardboard and makes work cards showing three or four shapes, of which two are similar (Fig. 8.107). Ask a child to find the similar shapes. (Use E-, F-, H-, L- and T-shaped figures.)

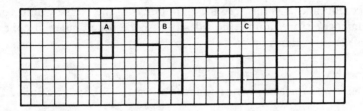

Fig. 8.107

10. The teacher, or child, could make a rectangular prism with cubes. (Use 3-cm cubes.) Another child could make a copy, and also another copy but with sides twice as long. (Twice as long means twice as tall, twice as wide *and* twice as thick).

The shapes copied can gradually be made more complicated. That is, to a basic rectangular prism add projecting pieces or remove some cubes.

11. A child could build three rectangular prisms with cubes, of which two prisms are similar. Another child has to identify the similar shapes.

12. On centimetre-squared paper the teacher could draw shapes which enclose 3, 4, 5, 6, 7 and 8 small squares. A child could make copies of these shapes with sides twice as long, and find the number of small squares in each shape. Then he could make a table (Fig. 8.108), and write his answers in it.

Number of small squares in original shapes	3	4	5	6	7	8
Number of small squares in copies with sides twice as long						

Fig. 8.108

Questions which could be asked about the completed table are as follows:
What do you notice about the numbers in the top row and their partners in the bottom row? (The numbers in the bottom row are four times larger than those in the top row.)

Could you complete this sentence? If we double the sides of a shape the number of small squares enclosed is increased . . . . . times.

13. A pair of children could build shapes on the desk containing 3, 4, 5, 6, 7 and 8 cubes and then make copies with sides twice as long, and find the number of cubes in each copy. They could draw a table (Fig. 8.109) and write their answers in it.

Number of cubes in original shapes	3	4	5	6	7	8
Number of cubes in copy with sides twice as long						

Fig. 8.109

Questions which could be asked about the completed table are as follows:
Look at each number in the bottom row and the number directly above it. How many times larger is the number in the bottom row than its partner in the top row? (Eight times.) Is this true for all numbers in the table? Could you complete this sentence? If we double the sides of a shape the number of cubes needed is increased . . . . . times.

8.6.5 Geometrical Work Involving Number Patterns (2, 3 L2; 3, 5 L3; 3, 5 L4)

The teacher could show to a group of children some shapes that are related to one another. The shapes could be built by the teacher on the desk, or drawn and displayed on squared or triangular paper. Children in the group could be asked to indicate what the next shape or shapes in the series would be. Questions asked, and their answers, could then establish the numbers of unit shapes in each shape of the series. On examining this series of numbers it is possible to find their connection, continue the series, and so predict the number of items in one of the shapes without having to build it, and the preceding shapes.

The following activities illustrate what is intended, and they could be given to individual children, or pairs of children. The teacher could compile work cards and give oral instructions to arrange the activities.

1. Use plastic or wooden squares to make the shapes shown in Fig. 8.110, and then build the next three shapes in the series. Write down the number of small squares in the first shape, second, third, etc., up to the seventh shape. (1, 2, 3, 4, 5, 6 and 7.) Now continue the series until you have twenty numbers. Use this number series in order to find the number of small squares in the 8th, 10th, 15th and 20th shapes.

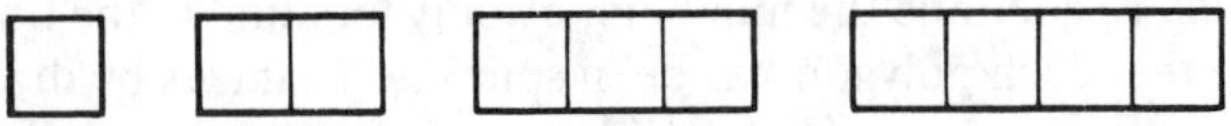

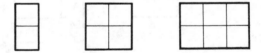

Fig. 8.110

2. Use plastic squares to make the shapes shown in Fig. 8.111, and then build the next three shapes in the series. Write down the number of small squares in the first shape, second, etc., up to the sixth shape. (2, 4, 6, 8, 10 and 12.) Continue this number series until you have twenty numbers. Use this series to find the number of small squares in the 8th, 10th, 13th, 15th, 17th and 20th shapes.

Fig. 8.111

3. Use matchsticks to make the shapes shown in Fig. 8.112, and then build the next three shapes. Write down the number of matchsticks in the first shape, second, etc., up to the sixth shape. (4, 7, 10, 13, 16 and 19.) Continue the series until you have twenty numbers. How many matchsticks are there in the 7th, 9th, 11th, 16th and 18th shapes of the series? Which shape of the series is made with 31 matchsticks?

Fig. 8.112

Write down the number of matchsticks in the perimeter of each shape. (4, 6, 8, 10, 12 and 14.) By continuing the series find the number of matchsticks in the perimeters of the 8th, 10th, 12th and 15th shapes. Is there a shape with 19 matchsticks in its perimeter? (No—all perimeters are even numbers, and 19 is an odd number.)

4. On a work card the teacher draws irregular polygons like those shown in Fig. 8.113 and a table like that shown in Fig. 8.114. Ask a child to draw a similar table, then to look at the polygons and record in the table the number of sides and triangles in each.

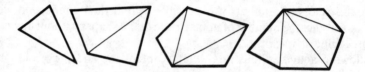

Fig. 8.113

Number of sides in polygon	3	4	5	6	7	8	9	10
Number of triangles in polygon	1	2						

Fig. 8.114

Ask the child to continue the numbers, by only looking, in the bottom row of the table. Notice that each polygon has been split into triangles by drawing lines from one corner to other corners. If we do this to an 8-sided shape, and a 9-sided shape, how many triangles would we obtain? Draw irregular 8- and 9-sided polygons, split them into triangles, and check some of your results. (The children may need assistance in drawing the 8- and 9-sided irregular shapes.)

5. Use plastic squares to build shapes like those shown in Fig. 8.115, then make the next three shapes.

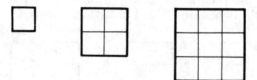

Fig. 8.115

Find the number of small squares in the shapes, and record the results in a table (Fig. 8.116).

	1st Shape	2nd Shape	3rd Shape	4th Shape	5th Shape	6th Shape	7th Shape	8th Shape
Number of small squares	1	4						

Fig. 8.116

Could you continue the series of numbers and find the number of squares in the 7th and 8th shapes? How many in the 10th shape? (The 3rd shape has 3 times 3 squares, the 4th shape has 4 times 4 squares, the 5th shape has 5 times 5 squares, etc. So the 10th shape has 10 times 10 squares, or 100 squares.)

We could use another method to answer these questions. Write down the numbers that we have so far, and beneath them their differences (Fig. 8.117). Could you continue the differences? How do the bottom numbers grow? Write in some more

Fig. 8.117

bottom numbers. Can you see how to put in the top numbers now? How many squares in the 9th shape? and 10th shape?

6. Suppose the squares of paragraph **5**, above, were made from matchsticks. Write down the number series giving the numbers of matchsticks in the perimeters of the first six shapes. (4, 8, 12, 16, 20 and 24.) Continue the series and find how many matchsticks are in the perimeters of the 10th, 15th and 20th shapes.

7. Use equilateral triangles, or triangular-ruled paper. Build shapes like those shown in Fig. 8.118, and then the next three in the series. Write down the number of small triangles in the first shape, second shape, third shape, etc., up to the sixth shape. (1, 4, 9, 16, 25 and 36.) Study this sequence of numbers and continue it. (Notice that 4 = 2 times 2, 9 = 3 times 3, 16 = 4 times 4, etc.) How many triangles in the 8th, 9th and 10th shapes?

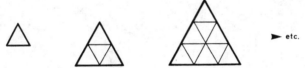

Fig. 8.118

We could continue the series by studying the growth of differences (Fig. 8.119). (Notice also that the number of small triangles in the shapes can be expressed as 1, 1 + 3, 1 + 3 + 5, 1 + 3 + 5 + 7, etc.) Find the number of triangles in the 8th, 9th and 10th shapes using this pattern.

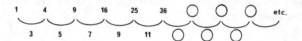

Fig. 8.119

Suppose we made the shapes with matchsticks instead of equilateral triangles. Write down the number series giving the number of matchsticks in the perimeters of the first six shapes. (3, 6, 9, 12, 15 and 18.) Continue the series and find the number of matchsticks in the perimeters of the 8th, 10th and 12th shapes.

Write down the number series giving the number of matchsticks in the first five shapes. (3, 9, 18, 30 and 45.) Could you continue the series and find the matchsticks in the 6th, 7th, 8th and 9th shapes? Write down the numbers you have so far, and put their differences beneath (Fig. 8.120). Could you continue the differences, and then fill in numbers on the top line?

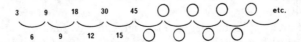

Fig. 8.120

8. Copy shapes like those shown in Fig. 8.121 on squared paper, and draw the next three shapes in the series. Write down the number of small squares in the 1st shape, 2nd shape, 3rd shape, etc., up to the 6th shape. (1, 3, 6, 10, 15 and 21.)

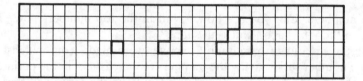

Fig. 8.121

Continue this series using differences and find the number of small squares in the 7th, 8th and 9th shapes (Fig. 8.122). (Notice that in the 2nd shape there are 1 + 2 squares. In the 3rd shape there are 1 + 2 + 3 squares. In the 4th shape there are 1 + 2 + 3 + 4 squares.) How many squares are there in the 7th shape?

Fig. 8.122

Suppose the shapes were made from matchsticks instead. Write down the series giving the number of matchsticks in the perimeters of the first six shapes. (4, 8, 12, 16, 20 and 24.) How many matchsticks in the perimeters of the 8th, 10th and 12th shapes?

Write down the number of matchsticks in the first four shapes. (4, 10, 18 and 28.) Use differences to continue the series, and find the number of matchsticks in the 6th, 8th and 10th shapes (Fig. 8.123).

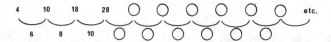

Fig. 8.123

8.7 FUTURE WORK

Future work could extend the ideas in this chapter, and treat many of the topics in a more numerical fashion, without making calculation difficult. Length, area and volume could be investigated, the units of measure gradually becoming smaller as the need for accuracy increases.

The finding of areas of rectangles and triangles, and volumes of rectangular boxes, gradually leads to the use of symbols and formulae. Surface areas of prisms and pyramids could be found because they are formed from rectangles and triangles.

Volumes of prisms and pyramids could be found using measuring vessels, and volumes of stones or pieces of metal by displacement.

Angular measurement in degrees could be introduced, and ideas formed about angle sums of triangles, quadrilaterals and other polygons. Various triangles, quadrilaterals and polygons could be drawn, and prisms and pyramids made from cardboard.

Different kinds of triangle and quadrilateral could be examined for side and angle properties.

Similarity could include the drawing of similar shapes on squared paper and the building of similar solids with cubes. The latter activities involve enlargement and reduction in size, and the idea of scale. Areas of similar shapes could be found and compared, as well as volumes of similar solids.

The need for reference lines and grid systems would be established in order to fix the position of points on planes, and the surfaces of cylinders and spheres. Particular attention could be given to Polar and Cartesian co-ordinates.

Chapter 9

Using and Applying Mathematics—Further Activities

9.1 INTRODUCTION

The *National Curriculum (Mathematics)*, by devoting two of its Attainment Targets to 'Using and Applying Mathematics', reminds us that it is not sufficient only to develop knowledge, skills and understanding but that a balance be maintained between these and the using of mathematics effectively. This demands that children, even from the early years of their mathematical education, should begin to work independently and to plan and carry out tasks for themselves.

When, in 1982, the Cockcroft Report highlighted the need for such a balance it suggested that the effective use of mathematics could take place in the solving of problems. Here, problems were held to mean those met with in everyday situations, those within mathematics itself and those which were in the extended form of investigations. Many applications of mathematics in everyday situations involve the use of that mathematics which is to be found in Chapters 1 to 8 of this book and examples of some kinds of that work have been included in those chapters. Further examples of the applications of mathematics are included in this separate chapter especially where they relate to cross-curricular projects and to projects which could arise from children's literature. Some of the activities included concern problem-solving and investigations. As far as problems within mathematics itself is concerned these often do not pertain to one branch of mathematics and in any case we are more concerned to use them so that children may meet and develop the processes of problem-solving itself. (Two books which deal with the processes of problem-solving are included in the bibliography.)

As a basis for this work on the application of mathematics children need to be well-motivated and prepared to undertake tasks which may be unfamiliar to them. The teacher should not only be concerned to plan her programme to meet Attainment Targets 2–8 and 10–14 but in meeting those in ATs 1 and 9 encourage her children to be more independent of her and to be prepared to try to use their knowledge, skills and understanding in the tackling of unfamiliar tasks in which their thinking needs to be flexible and in which they can display a measure of creativity. The amount of time taken in performing these applications may vary greatly. Some may be opened up so that the child has freedom to explore the question. For example, a closed task might be to find the sums of prescribed sets of numbers, such as $3 + 2 + 5$, $2 + 5 + 2$, etc., whereas the open task may be to find possible scores each time a set of three darts is thrown at a dartboard, similar to that shown in Fig. 9.1.

Fig. 9.1

Other tasks might be opened up so that a collection of appropriate information has to be made before any conclusions can be drawn. This may mean a group of children have to work co-operatively and value each other's contribution. For example, if, within the context of a project the teacher conjectured that, 'Most families prefer to use gas to heat their homes', the children to whom this statement was addressed would need to decide how they could answer this: namely, what information would be necessary, how it could be obtained and from whom.

Throughout this chapter solution hints are given with many of the problems for the convenience of the reader. It is not intended that these be seen as the only strategies for obtaining solutions. Different children will explore different ways of obtaining a solution, all of which should be valued. These different ways of approaching the same problem could be reviewed with the children, who may come to see that their own starting point might be equally valid.

The applications have been accorded Attainment Targets and level numbers where they are thought to be appropriate. Many of the tasks belong to several Attainment Targets and these are indicated in the section headings. These ATs and levels cater for all the activities included in the section and do not describe any one particular task.

Many of the activities included could be tackled at different levels with the knowledge, skills and understanding appropriate to those different levels. The use of concrete material, or a calculator, might reduce the level of a task considerably. The teacher, however, needs to select those tasks which could be tackled at the attainment level of her children. Indeed, many of the problems do not need high attainment levels of mathematics in order to effect their solution. What is more important very often is the process by which a solution may be obtained. Children must be willing to tackle the task, to work systematically, to try various ways out of possible impasses, to learn from the experience and to make valid judgements, perhaps about possible emerging patterns and to draw conclusions.

It is to be remembered that with children, as with everyone else, nothing succeeds like success. Children will enjoy doing what they feel they will be successful at. This does not mean always doing what they are familiar with. With the right attitude and encouragement children often surprise us with what they are able to tackle successfully.

The additional applications in this chapter are contained within the headings:

Number
Money
Shape and Space
Puzzles
Children's Literature
Integrated Projects

9.2 NUMBER

9.2.1 Sharing (2, 3 L1; 2, 3, 8 L2)

An activity which is fruitful, in engaging children in meaningful discussion towards a solution, concerns the sharing of a bag of dog biscuits among four dog bowls. This may be done with a group of eight middle or top infants with the teacher present. The children are shown a bag of whole dog biscuits of different colours and shapes. The teacher has ensured that the bag contains a multiple of four of each colour or shape. The children are given four bowls and asked to share the biscuits 'fairly' for the dogs to eat.

Some 6-year-olds, given this task, distributed the biscuits on a 'one for this one, one for that one' basis with scant regard to the shape and colour of the biscuits. Other children, of the same age, began by sorting the biscuits by colour and shape before a 'one for this one' distribution to the bowls. Some children, in performing the distribution, realizing they had plenty of each colour, began by distributing them in twos.

This activity may be varied to include some broken pieces of biscuit with the multiples of four whole biscuit varieties. Experience has shown that some children continue with a one-to-one correspondence sharing between biscuits and bowls for whole biscuits, and on being left with the pieces put these together in four piles which they estimate to be equal. On being questioned about whether these piles are equal there has ensued a lively discussion between those children who think the piles are equal and those who do not. At this point the teacher could intervene and steer the children's thoughts to what could be done to make the distribution really 'fair'. This has led some children to think of using a balance. The group then carried out the balancings and the adjustments which need to be made.

A further variation is to provide a bag of broken dog biscuits.

The activities now being suggested could be done with a group of eight children working together, some doing the sharing whilst others observe. The teacher and all the children would talk together and discuss what is being done, whether the sharing is fair, what could be done instead, what adjustments are needed, and so on, until each task is completed. The sharing procedure could then be repeated by other members of the group. Some of the situations involve equal sharing whilst others need the proposing and acceptance of an equivalence rule.

1. Eight apples are shared fairly between two children.
2. Twelve pennies are shared equally among three children.
3. A group of children share a segmented chocolate bar among themselves: e.g. an 8-piece bar among two or four children; an 18-piece bar among three or six children.
4. Share out a packet of Iced Gem biscuits. Initially use whole biscuits, e.g. 30 biscuits, 5 of each colour, each with icing, among five children.
   Next use some whole biscuits, some with their icing tops broken off but loose in the packet. Arrange it so that the wholes and parts can be equally shared, e.g. 15 whole biscuits, 5 icing tops and 5 biscuit bottoms, between four children.
5. Two bananas are shared equally among three children.
6. The children have to determine an acceptable rule for sharing marbles when some

of the marbles are larger than others, e.g. 2 large and 6 small marbles among four children, or 2 large and 7 small marbles among three children.
7. Some Smarties could be equally shared out, e.g. 20 Smarties between five children; 18 Smarties between three children; 13 Smarties between four children and 17 Smarties between five children.
8. A group of children are divided into two smaller groups, given the box of construction kit, and asked to share the contents fairly between the groups.
9. At an appropriate time after a group has done some cooking in school the cakes could be shared out, e.g. a patty tin of 12 fairy cakes among six or eight children, or a patty tin of 9 fairy cakes among three, six or four children.
10. Some pennies are shared between two children so that one child has two more pennies than the other, e.g. 12 pennies or 14 pennies.
11. Some sweets are shared among two children so that one child has three more sweets than the other, e.g. 11 sweets or 15 sweets.
12. A sum of money, given in multiple value coins, is shared amongst a group of children. Ensure there is exact sharing, e.g. one 5p and two 2p among three children, one 10p and one 2p among two children, one 10p and three 2p among four children, and one 20p and two 2p among three children.

9.2.2 Notation and Ordering (2 L2, 3)

1. Use digits chosen from 3, 4 and 6, to make numbers between 10 and 100. The digits in each number must be different. Arrange these numbers in order of size, least to greatest. (34, 36, 43, 46, 63 and 64)
2. What numbers between 10 and 100 can you make with different digits chosen from 2, 4, 6 and 8? Arrange them in order of size. (24, 26, 28, 42, 46, 48, 62, 64, 68, 82, 84 and 86)
3. Use the digits 2, 3 and 5 to make numbers greater than 100. The digits in each number are to be different. Arrange the numbers in order of size. (235, 253, 325, 352, 523 and 532)
4. Use the digits 2, 4, 5 and 6 to make numbers between 100 and 1000. The digits in each number are to be different. Arrange these numbers in order of size. Which is least? Which is greatest? (There are 24 different numbers. 245 is the least. 654 is greatest.)

9.2.3 Addition (2, 3 L2)

1. Use Cuisenaire rods, or Unifix, to find three different numbers which add to 10. Can you find four different sets? (1, 2, 7 and 1, 3, 6 and 1, 4, 5 and 2, 3, 5)
2. Use Cuisenaire rods, or Unifix, to find three numbers which add to 12, two of the numbers being the same, e.g. 1 + 1 + 10. Can you find three more sets? (2, 2, 8 and 3, 3, 6 and 5, 5, 2)
3. Use the numbers from 1 to 9 and add two or more of them to produce answers of 15, if no number is repeated. For example, 6 + 2 + 7, 8 + 7 are allowed but 3 + 3 + 9 is not. Find eight more different ways.

9.2.4 Putting Numbers into Sets (2 L2; 3 L3, 4)

1. Arrange the numbers 3, 4, 5, 6 and 8 into two sets, the numbers in each set having the same total. (8, 5 and 3, 4, 6)
2. Move a number from one set to the other so that the numbers in each set have the same total (Fig. 9.2).

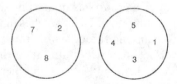

Fig. 9.2

3. Arrange the numbers 1, 2, 3, 4, 5, 6 and 7 into two sets such that the numbers in each set have the same total. Can you find four different ways of doing this?
4. Arrange the numbers 1, 2, 3, 4, 5, 6, 7 and 8 into three sets, each set having the same total. Can you find three different ways of doing this?

9.2.5 Dominoes (2, 3 L1; 3 L2)

1. Use a normal domino set. Place the dominoes on the table with their dots showing. The task is to pick two dominoes so that the total number of dots is four. Can you find six different ways? Draw them.
2. Pick three dominoes from a normal set so that the total number of dots is five. Can you find eight different ways? Draw them on squared paper.

9.2.6 Making Numbers (2 L2; 3 L3, 4)

1. Use three of the digits, 2, 4, 7 and 8, and one + sign to make other numbers. No digit can be repeated, e.g. 47 + 2 will make 49. How many different numbers can you make? Record how you made them. (There are 12.) Which is least? $(24 + 7 = 27 + 4 = 31.)$ Which is greatest? $(87 + 4 = 84 + 7 = 91.)$
2. Make up number statements which include one − sign to produce the numbers 2, 5, 7, 9, 12, 15 and 26, e.g. $9 − 7 = 2, 25 − 20 = 5, 34 − 22 = 12$.
3. Make up ten different number statements which include one + sign and one − sign to make the number 8, e.g. $6 + 7 − 5 = 8, 23 + 5 − 20 = 8$.

9.2.7 Finding Numbers (2 L2; 3 L 3, 4)

1. A number divides exactly by 3 and 4. It lies between 30 and 40. What is this number?
2. A number is between 30 and 40. It is odd and divides exactly by 3. Its units digit is greater than its tens digit. What is this number?

3. A number lies between 20 and 50. It divides exactly by 2, 3 and 7. What is this number?

4. Start at my head and move towards my tail. Put in the missing numbers (Fig. 9.3).

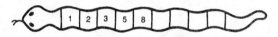

Fig. 9.3

5. See Fig. 9.4. What number does ▲ =? What number does ● =?

Fig. 9.4

6. A child is asked to think of a number from 1 to 20. Other children ask questions of this child and try to find this number. The answers to these questions may be only 'yes' or 'no'. The children may develop useful strategies if they have enough experience of this game. They could look for the fewest number of questions in order to find any number without guessing.

   This activity could be extended by increasing the range of numbers from 1 to 50, or 1 to 100.

9.2.8 Darts (2 L2; 3 L3, 4)

1. David throws two darts at the board shown in Fig. 9.5. They both score. What total scores are possible? Record them and arrange them in order of size. (2, 4, 6, 8 and 10)

Fig. 9.5

   Suppose, instead, he threw three darts at this board and they all scored. What could the total scores be now? Record them, and arrange them in order, least to greatest. (3, 5, 7, 9, 11, 13 and 15)

2. What different scores could be obtained by throwing three darts at the board shown in Fig. 9.6? They all score. List the totals. (6, 7, 8, 9, ..., 14, 15)

3. Mary threw two darts at the board shown in Fig. 9.7. Both scored different numbers. What could the total scores be? List them, in order. (14, 16, 18, 20, 22)

   Suppose she threw three darts and they all scored. What could the total scores be now? (18, 20, 22, ... 32, 34, 36)

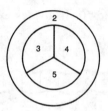

Fig. 9.6

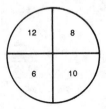

Fig. 9.7

4. Three darts are thrown at the board shown in Fig. 9.8. They all score and their total is 12. What may each of the darts have scored? (Note—scoring a 2, a 3 and a 5 is considered to be the same as scoring a 5, a 2 and a 3.) Can you find nine different ways?

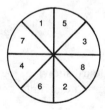

Fig. 9.8

9.2.9 What's Missing? (2 L1; 2, 3 L2; 3 L3)

These questions could be given to individual children, or groups of two or three children. In each case the task is to find the missing symbol or number (Fig. 9.9).

If $(4,2) \rightarrow 6$	If $(2,4) \rightarrow 8$	If $(2,1) \rightarrow 5$
$(3,4) \rightarrow 7$	$(5,2) \rightarrow 10$	$(3,1) \rightarrow 7$
$(1,7) \rightarrow 8$	$(4,4) \rightarrow 16$	$(4,2) \rightarrow 10$
$(2,5) \rightarrow ?$	$(2,7) \rightarrow ?$	$(1,4) \rightarrow ?$

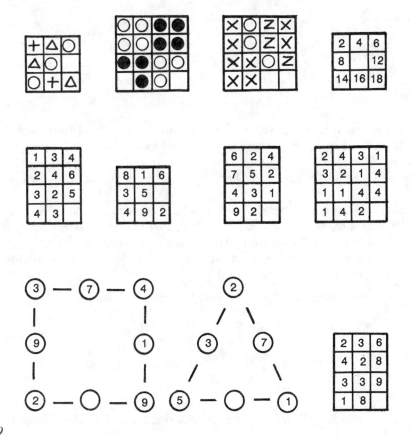

Fig. 9.9

9.2.10 How Many of Each? (2, 3, 12 L2; 3 L3, 4)

Some kind of representation, either concrete or pictorial, could be used to assist in the finding of solutions to these questions. The teacher could provide, with each, a set of cards on which are drawings of the items concerned, e.g. car and bicycle cards clearly showing wheels, or ant and spider cards clearly showing legs. Toy plastic animals or metal cars and lorries may be available. Gummed paper cut-outs of children, dogs, cats and rabbits might also be used. Pennies could be used or pretend 'sweets' with price labels on them. Children could sometimes make drawings of items with wheels or legs on them which may be counted.

Children should be encouraged to use systematic approaches and recordings of the steps involved. For example, suppose some rabbits and chickens have 16 legs altogether. How many are there of each? One approach is to consider one rabbit, two rabbits, three rabbits, etc. and find the number of chickens to put with each of them. Rabbit and chicken cards could be used.

Put out one rabbit card, then chicken cards, one at a time, counting legs until 16 is reached. (4, 6, 8, 10, 12, 14, 16.) We reach 16 when one rabbit and six chicken cards are on the table. Record this in a list (Fig. 9.10).

No. of rabbits	No. of chickens
1	6
2	4
3	
4	

Fig. 9.10

Put out two rabbit cards, then chicken cards, counting legs until 16 is obtained. (8, 10, 12, 14, 16.) We attain 16 when two rabbit cards and four chicken cards are on the table. Enter this in the list.

This procedure is continued with three rabbit cards, then four, until the question is completed.

Some children could use a more detailed method of recording but still use apparatus to deal with some of the calculation. For example, solving '8 legs, how many chickens?' could be done by putting 8 cubes into twos. Others may do calculations mentally. Each step is included in the list, and working entered row by row until all possibilities have been examined (Fig. 9.11).

Number of rabbits	Number of legs	Number of legs left	Number of chickens
1	4	$16 - 4 = 12$	6
2	8	$16 - 8 = 8$	4
3	12	$16 - 12 = 4$	2
4	16	xxxxx	xx

Fig. 9.11

Methods of working, similar to those just described, may be used in the following:

1. Chairs and three-legged stools have 10 legs altogether. How many chairs and stools are there? (1 chair, 2 stools.) Consider 1 chair, 2 chairs, 3 chairs, in turn.
2. Fruities cost 2p each and Minties cost 4p each. I bought only one kind of these sweets and spent 10p. What did I buy? (5 Fruities.) Another day I bought some of each kind and spent 10p. What may I have bought? (1F and 2M or 3F and 1M.) Consider buying 1 Fruitie, 2 Fruities, 3 Fruities, etc. in turn.
3. Some cars and bicycles are in the parking space. Altogether there are 12 wheels touching the ground. How many cars and bicycles were there? (1C and 4B or 2C and 2B.) Consider 1 car, 2 cars, 3 cars, etc. in turn.
4. In the park I see tricycles and bicycles. Altogether they have 14 wheels. How many of each were there? (1B and 4T or 4B and 2T.) Consider 1 bicycle, 2 bicycles, 3 bicycles, etc. in turn.
5. Lollies cost 2p each and Chews cost 3p each. Altogether I spent 13p and bought some of each. How many of each could I have bought? (2L and 3C or 5L and 1C.) Try 1, 2, 3, 4, etc. Chews, in turn.
6. A tin contains 2-hole and 4-hole buttons. I pick out some of each. Altogether they have 18 holes. What may I have picked? (1FH and 7TH, 2FH and 5TH, 3FH and 3TH, 4FH and 1TH.) Consider 1, 2, 3, 4, etc. four-hole buttons, in turn.
7. Ants and spiders: altogether they have 42 legs. How many of each? (3 ants and 3 spiders)

8. I see some children and dogs in the park. Altogether I count 4 heads and 12 legs. How many dogs are there? 4 heads indicate there are either 3 children and 1 dog, 2 children and 2 dogs or 1 child and 3 dogs. Test all these possibilities and enter necessary calculations in a table (Fig. 9.12).

Number of dogs	Number of dog's legs	Number of children	Number of children's legs	Total number of legs
1	4	3	6	10
2	8	2	4	12
3	12	1	2	14

There were 2 dogs and 2 children in the park.

Fig. 9.12

9. A farmer has chickens and rabbits. He counts 5 heads and 14 legs. How many rabbits were there? (2 rabbits)
10. Scooters and tricycles: altogether there are 7 machines and 17 wheels. How many scooters are there? (4 scooters)
11. Cats and girls: altogether there are 8 heads and 26 legs. How many cats were there? (5 cats)
12. Six-wheeler and four-wheeler lorries: there are 9 vehicles altogether and 44 wheels touching the ground. How many four-wheelers were there? (5 four-wheelers)
13. Ants and spiders: 9 creatures altogether with 62 legs. How many ants and spiders were there? (5 ants and 4 spiders)

9.2.11 Patterns and Predictions (2, 3, 12 L2; 3, 5 L3)

Some activities we set could involve the observation of patterns and then acting on these observations. Counting is needed, followed by comparisons of the numbers involved and then some further calculation.

For example, show three or four children the groupings of red and white plastic counters, Unifix or Cuisenaire rods, as seen in Figure 9.13.

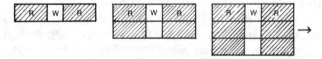

Fig. 9.13

Talk about the shapes getting larger. Ask a child to make the next bigger shape and encourage the children to join in and talk about it. Ask another child to make the next shape but before she starts she must say how many white counters she intends to pick up. She completes the shape perhaps with interjections of help from other children. Ask another child to make the next one but this time indicate the number of red counters she will need. In turn she completes the shape. Ask if anyone can tell how many whites and how many reds will be needed for the next shape before we make it. The children may then be able to predict how many reds will be needed for one of the later shapes in the series. Some recording is necessary for this in order to continue the pattern 2, 4, 6, 8, 10, ... (An able group of 6-year-olds were able to predict the 38 counters needed for the 19th shape, with confidence.)

Other examples which could be done individually, or by children working in twos or threes, are now suggested. Further activities are also included in Chapter 8 'Shape and Space', Section 8.6.5, *Geometrical Work Involving Number Patterns*.

1. Two or three children working together could use Cuisenaire rods, twos and threes only, to find the number of different ways of arranging 1 green and 1 red, 2 green and 1 red, 3 green and 1 red, or 4 green and 1 red in a row, end to end. They display the arrangements with the number of ways alongside (Fig. 9.14).

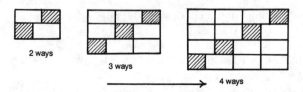

Fig. 9.14

What happens next? Suppose there are 10 rods (9 green and 1 red), what would be the number of ways of arranging them? (10) How many ways of arranging 18 green and 1 red? (19) Suppose the number of arrangements were 24. Describe the number, and colour, of the rods.

3. Use straws, or matchsticks, to make rows of triangles (Fig. 9.15), and make the next two shapes. How many triangles in each shape? (1, 2, 3, 4, 5) How many would there be in the 8th and 12th shapes?

Fig. 9.15

How does the number of straws in the perimeters grow? (3, 4, 5, 6, 7) How many would be in the perimeters of the 11th and 15th shapes?

How does the number of straws in the shapes grow? (3, 5, 7, 9, 11) How many would be in the 13th shape? Which shape would have 19 straws in it?

How many straws to make ten triangles? For this we need perhaps to record, and extend the data in Figure 9.16. On discussion some children may notice that the bottom number is always 'twice the top number, add one'. So for 10 small triangles the number of straws is 10 + 10 + 1, or 21.

No. of triangles	1	2	3	4	5
No. of straws	3	5	7	9	11

Fig. 9.16

4. Using wooden cubes, or Multilink, of different colours, make the shapes shown in Fig. 9.17, then make the next two shapes. Look at them from *one direction only* as shown. How many faces can be seen in each set of cubes? (3, 5, 7, 9, 11) How many

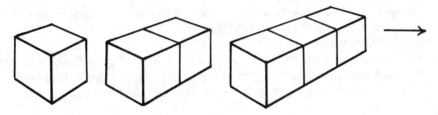

Fig. 9.17

could be seen in the 8th set? If you see 15 faces, how many cubes would there be?
5. Make shapes as shown in Fig. 9.17, and the next two shapes, but this time walk around the shapes and count the number of faces seen in each set of cubes. (5, 8, 11, 14, 17) How many faces could be seen in the 10th set? If 26 faces are seen, how many cubes would be joined?
6. Prepare a work card. Use dot lattice triangular paper or hexagonal-grid paper with shapes coloured in as shown in Fig. 9.18. On the same kind of paper a child draws and colours these shapes followed by the next two shapes. How do the perimeters grow? (6, 10, 14, 18, 22) How long would the perimeter be if 8 hexagons were joined? What about 12?

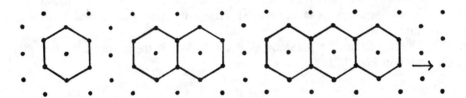

Fig. 9.18

Suppose instead these hexagonal patterns were made with matchsticks. How would the number of matchsticks grow? (6, 11, 16, 21, 26) How many matchsticks would make 9 hexagons joined together? If there were 56 matchsticks, how many hexagons would be joined together?
7. On squared paper copy the shapes shown in Fig. 9.19 and then draw the next two shapes.

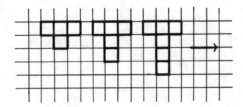

Fig. 9.19

Write down the number of small squares in these five diagrams. (4, 5, 6, 7, 8) How many small squares in the 8th and 11th shapes?

Suppose the shapes were made of matchsticks. What series describes how the number of matchsticks grows? (13, 16, 19, 22, 25) Predict the number of matchsticks in the 9th and 12th shapes.

How many matchsticks in the perimeters of these shapes? (10, 12, 14, 16, 18) How many matchsticks in the perimeters of the 9th and the 12th shapes?

8. Copy the shapes shown in Fig. 9.20 and draw the next two shapes.

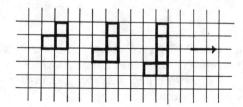

Fig. 9.20

Write down, for these five shapes, the number series which describe:

a) how the number of small squares grows (3, 4, 5, 6, 7)

b) how the number of matchsticks in the perimeters grows (8, 10, 12, 14, 16) and

c) how the number of matchsticks in each shape grows. (10, 13, 16, 19, 22)

Use these growth patterns to describe the 8th and 12th shapes: e.g. the 8th shape has 10 small squares, is made with 31 matchsticks and has 22 matchsticks in its perimeter.

9. Do as indicated in the previous question **8**, but with reference to the shapes illustrated in Fig. 9.21.

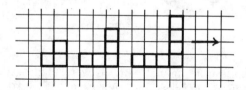

Fig. 9.21

10. Do as indicated in question **8**, but with reference to the shapes illustrated in Fig. 9.22.

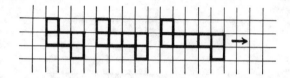

Fig. 9.22

11. For use in a group activity session with the teacher. The group requires eight paper strips of different colours, about 2 m long and 2 cm wide, and 25 cardboard circles about 8 cm in diameter. Talk with the children about roads which cross and illustrate this, on the floor, with two of the paper strips. Encourage the children to

talk about the traffic movement where the roads cross. Children have suggested to the writer the use of a bridge, traffic lights and a roundabout. Accepting these solutions, concentrate on the use of the roundabout and place a circle where the roads cross to represent one. The problem is to consider the number of round-abouts needed by the inclusion of more roads in order to relieve traffic on all other roads. At each roundabout we do not want more than two roads crossing and each new road needs to cross all the others. Children then put extra roads into the system, one at a time (Fig. 9.23). Each time a new road is included the number of roads and the number of roundabouts is recorded. One child can write numbers, with a felt pen, in a table previously prepared on a large sheet of paper (Fig. 9.24).

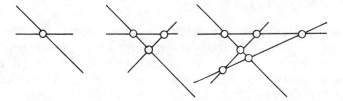

Fig. 9.23

As each new road is introduced talk about the number of extra roundabouts needed. The children in the group look for a pattern and try to predict the number of roundabouts for further roads. After six, or fewer, roads have been placed on the floor the pattern is usually discovered. This enables predictions to be made about further roads without the use of paper strips. The children could extend the table and find the number of roundabouts needed for ten roads, or twelve roads.

No. of roads	2	3	4	5	6	
No. of roundabouts	1	3	6	10	15	→

Fig. 9.24

12. For use in a group activity session with the teacher. The problem is to find how many handshakes would be needed if eight children are all to shake hands, just once, with each other. The teacher organizes the group into pairs, then threes, then fours, then fives. A child records in a table, written on a large piece of paper, the number of handshakes needed for each number of children (Fig. 9.25).

Number of children	2	3	4	5	
Number of handshakes	1	3	6	10	→

Fig. 9.25

The number of handshakes becomes harder to find as the number in the group increases but if the children are well organized the counting, or recording and adding, should not prove too difficult. Let one child shake hands with the others and then stand aside. Then another child shakes hands with the remainder of the group and then stands aside. If this procedure is continued the group gets smaller by one each time, until one child remains, and no child should have shaken hands more than once with each person.

When the table has been completed for up to five children, and the series 1, 3, 6, 10 has emerged, the number of handshakes for eight children may be predicted. (28)

A group of eight children could check this, if required, using the procedure outlined earlier and recording handshakes each time a member stands aside. (7 + 6 + 5 + 4 + 3 + 2 + 1 = 28)

9.3 MONEY (2, 8, 12 L2; 3 L3, 4)

Money activities often occupy a considerable amount of time in schools because the use of money is a common feature of everyday life. Shopping is generally the focus for many activities, these being presented to individual children rather than to a group. Questions often involve the use of number so they must be carefully allocated to children. The calculations required within the tasks must be within the skill levels of the children concerned. The use of coins is necessary, particularly in the early stages, and they need to be carefully introduced and integrated within the number work as it is developed. As children acquire number facts and skills the need to use coins becomes less.

Activities often centre around the total amount of money to be paid for purchases and the change required from the appropriate coin or note. There is clearly a need for grading questions ranging from the buying of a single item which costs little to others where several items, including multiples, are bought and the total cost involves pounds and pence. Further details about this can be found in Chapter 2, 'Money'. Calculations involving money, arising within everyday situations, are also included in Chapter 2, Section 2.13.

Younger children can often tackle questions, without using sophisticated methods, if they are encouraged to work methodically and write results down in lists or tables. The teacher needs to talk with children about the method of working to be used and the form of recording to accommodate it.

For example, some children bought sweets in a shop. They bought chews for 3p each and gobstoppers for 5p each. The same number of chews and gobstoppers were bought and the lot cost 96p. What did they buy? This could be set to two children working together. (Further examples like this could be devised with particular children in mind by adjusting the price of each sweet and/or the total spent.)

It could be suggested that information is entered in a list, as the working proceeds (Fig. 9.26) starting with 1 of each sweet, then 2, then 3, etc. until the required total is achieved.

Number of each	Chews (3p)	Gobstoppers (5p)	Total
1	3p	5p	8p
2	6p	10p	16p
3	9p	15p	24p
4	12p	20p	32p
11	33p	55p	88p
12	36p	60p	96p

Fig. 9.26

So they bought 12 chews and 12 gobstoppers.

A supplement to this question could be to ask how many children there might have been if they all bought the same. This involves sharing equally 12 chews and 12 gobstoppers. (12 red and 12 green cubes could be used to represent sweets.) Again, a form of recording and a systematic way of working could be discussed and then followed. For example, could they have 1 of each? 2 of each? 3 of each? etc. Solutions could be entered in a list as each possibility is explored (Fig. 9.27).

Number of chews	Number of gobstoppers	Number of children
1	1	12
2	2	6
3	3	4
4	4	3
5	5	xxx
6	6	2

Fig. 9.27

The question is now completed because two children is the smallest group we can have.

Money questions often ask what might be bought for a given amount, or they involve finding different ways of paying prescribed amounts, and some of these have already been included in Chapter 2, Sections 2.7, 2.8 and 2.9. Further questions of a similar nature are given below, sometimes with a few hints about strategies which may be pursued:

1. a) Chews cost 2p and fruities 3p each. I buy some of each and spend 10p. What did I buy? (Use pennies. Buy 1 chew. Put 2 pennies aside. Can the remaining pennies be arranged in threes? (No.) Buy 2 chews instead. Put out 2 pennies and 2 pennies. Can the remaining pennies be arranged in threes? (Yes—3 and 3.) So 2 fruities and 2 chews could be bought. Proceed farther, as above, buying 3 chews and 4 chews. No more solutions are found.)

    Children at a higher level could use wrapped 'sweets' with 2p and 3p labels on them, and investigate the buying of 1, 2, 3, 4 twopenny sweets, in turn, together with 3p sweets.
   b) Apples cost 4p each and pears cost 6p. Diane bought some of each and spent 22p. What could she have bought? (1 apple, 3 pears or 4 apples, 1 pear.)
2. a) A chocolate bar costs 10p. Find three ways of paying for it. If this is achieved the child could be challenged to find more ways. (Try 1 tenpence; 2 fivepences; 1 fivepence and other coins; 5 twopences, 4 twopences, 3 twopences, 2 twopences and 1 twopence, with pennies. Eleven possible ways.) Rubber coin stamps or gummed paper money could be used to record the answers.
   b) Find different ways of paying 8p. (Try 1 fivepence with other coins; 4 twopences, 3 twopences, 2 twopences and 1 twopence, with pennies. Seven possible ways.)
   c) Find different ways of paying 9p. (Eight ways.)
   d) Find ten different ways of paying 18p. Answers could be entered in a table, for those children who are ready (Fig. 9.28).

1p	2p	5p	10p	TOTAL
8			1	18p
	4		1	
3		1	1	
1	1	1	1	

Fig. 9.28

    e) Find eight ways of paying 24p.

3. a) Pay 8p using five coins.
    b) Pay 15p using six coins. Find three ways.
    c) Pay 16p using four coins. Find two ways.
    d) Pay 18p using seven coins. Find two ways.
    (At first put out the required amount using the smallest number of coins and count them. Increase their number, if necessary, by exchanging 2 pennies for 1 twopence, 1 penny and 2 twopences for each fivepence, 5 pennies for each fivepence, and so on, counting coins each time.)

4. Use a price list or go to the classroom shop. What could be bought costing no more than 20p? List the items. (Look for single items; then two together; then three together, etc.)

5. Frank has 1 penny, 1 twopence, 1 fivepence and 1 tenpence. What amounts could he pay exactly using one or more of these coins? (Use 1 coin; 2 coins; 3 coins; 4 coins. Record the number and type of coins used and their totals. Arrange the totals in order. Amounts of 4p, 9p, 14p, 19p or more, cannot be paid.)

6. Graham has three trouser pockets. He has 1 coin in each. All are different and less than 50p. What is the most he could have? What is the least? Can you find four more possible amounts he might have? (Most: 35p; least: 8p.)

7. Roy has two trouser and two jacket pockets. He has 1 coin in each pocket. All are different and less than £1. What is the least amount he could have? What is the most? Can you find six more possible amounts he might have? (Least: 18p, most: 85p.)

8. Helen has five coins (one 50p, two 20p, one 10p and one 5p) in her purse. She buys an item for 72p. What coins could she use to pay with and what change would she obtain? Give details of each way. (She could use 50p, 20p, 10p and receive change 8p; 50p, 20p, 5p and receive change 3p; 50p, 20p, 20p and receive change 18p.)

9. Jill has thirteen coins (one 50p, one 20p, three 10p, one 5p, four 2p and three 1p) in her purse. She buys sweets costing 46p and pays this money exactly. What coins could she have used? Can you find four different ways? What is the least number of coins that she could use? What is the greatest number? Give details of each way. (5 coins is least—20, 10, 10, 5, 1; 11 coins is the greatest number—10, 10, 10, 5, 2, 2, 2, 2, 1, 1, 1.)

10. You have plenty of 3p, 4p and 5p stamps. Select some to post a letter costing 15p. Can you find four different ways? List them.
    Suppose instead the letter to be posted costs 20p. What stamps could now be used? Can you find five different ways?

11. You have plenty of 2p, 3p, 4p and 5p stamps. Select some to post a letter costing 15p. Can you find ten or more different selections? List each set of stamps in order, such as (2, 3, 5, 5). This will help to avoid repeating answers.

9.4 SHAPE AND SPACE

9.4.1 Finding Triangles and Rectangles (2, 10, 11 L1; 2, 10 L2; 10 L3)

For each of these questions the teacher needs to prepare a recording sheet. This would contain the diagram drawn enough times for a full solution together with two or three spare diagrams. The child colours in a triangle (rectangle) on each diagram until all different triangles (or rectangles) are displayed.

Solution hints—find first the smallest triangles (or rectangles). Then find larger triangles (or rectangles) made by two adjoining regions. Then even larger triangles (or rectangles) made by three adjoining regions.

1. How many different triangles in each of the diagrams in Fig. 9.29?

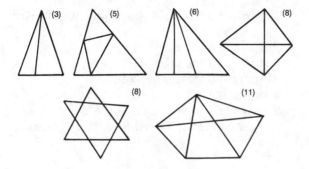

Fig. 9.29

2. How many different rectangles in each of the diagrams in Fig. 9.30?

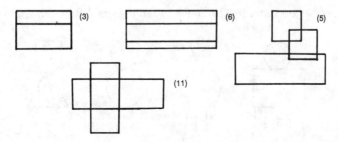

Fig. 9.30

3. How many different triangles? How many different four-sided shapes? (Fig. 9.31).

Fig. 9.31

9.4.2 Removing Straws (2, 3 L1; 10 L2)

These questions each need to be put on a work card.

1. Make this shape (Fig. 9.32) with 9 straws of the same length. Take away:

2 straws and leave 3 triangles;
3 straws and leave 1 triangle;
3 straws and leave 2 triangles;
2 straws so that 2 triangles remain (different sizes).

Fig. 9.32

2. Make this shape (Fig. 9.33) with 12 straws of equal length. Remove:

2 straws and leave 3 squares;
4 straws and leave 1 square;
4 straws and leave 2 squares;
5 straws and leave 2 squares;
2 straws and leave 2 squares (different sizes);
1 straw and leave 3 squares (different sizes).

Fig. 9.33

9.4.3 How Many Legs? (2 L1; 3, 10 L2)

How many legs do you think the Triangleman in Fig. 9.34 should have? Give reasons.

Fig. 9.34

9.4.4 Different Routes (2, 11 L1)

Each of these questions could be done by a small group of children provided with a large sheet of paper on which there is a drawing of the park or road system. A 'people sort' walking child could be used to walk, or a model car to drive, along the paths taken. Routes could be marked with different colours of wool or tape stretching from start to finish to record various paths taken. In the questions about finding ways to school different roads must always be used on any journey.

1. This park has two gates (Fig. 9.35). How many different ways are there of going into and coming out again from the park? (Using the gates) (4 ways.)

Fig. 9.35

2. How many different ways to school? (Fig. 9.36). (4 ways.)

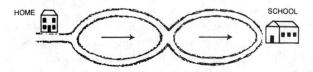

Fig. 9.36

3. How many different ways to school? (Fig. 9.37). (6 ways.)

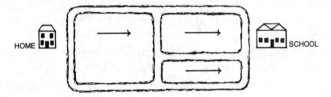

Fig. 9.37

4. How many different ways to school? (Fig. 9.38). (5 ways.)

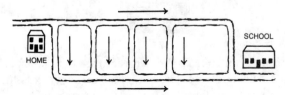

Fig. 9.38

5. Find the number of different ways of walking from home to school (Fig. 9.39). (4 ways.)

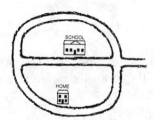

Fig. 9.39

9.4.5 Arrangements with Stamps (2, 11 L1; 11 L2)

These questions concern arrangements with stamps. Coloured cards could represent
stamps or squares drawn in on squared paper. If coloured cards or franked stamps are
used the various arrangements can be displayed, beneath one another, on the table. If
squared paper is used the child can see those arrangements which have already been
found. It is important for the child to have previous arrangements on display because
they assist the finding of new arrangements. Thus, a lot of coloured cards or used stamps
are needed. Looking at previous arrangements aids the thinking process and enables
strategies to be formed and then followed through.

1. How many different ways can you arrange three fourpenny stamps (blue) and one
   threepenny stamp (red) in a row on an envelope? Display or draw the arrangements.
   (4 ways—move the 3p stamp from left to right one place at a time.)
2. How many different ways can three stamps (one 10p (orange), one 3p (red) and one
   2p (green)) be arranged in a row on an envelope? Display or draw the arrangements.
   (6 ways—put a different colour of stamp on the extreme left in turn.)
3. Find different ways of sticking two tenpenny stamps (orange) and two twopenny
   stamps (green) in a row on an envelope. Display or draw the arrangements. (6
   ways—put the orange stamps next to each other, then with one stamp between and
   then with two stamps between.)
4. Two 10p stamps (orange) and two 2p stamps (green) are to be stuck in a square
   pattern on an envelope (Fig. 9.40). How many different arrangements for these
   stamps? Draw them. (6 ways—put the orange stamps side by side, above each other,
   and diagonally.)

Fig. 9.40

5. Four 10p stamps (orange) and one 2p stamp (green) are to be stuck on a small packet
   in a 'domino 5' pattern (Fig. 9.41). Draw possible arrangements for these stamps.
   How many different ways are there? (5 ways—put an orange stamp in the middle,
   then a green one.)

Fig. 9.41

6. Three 10p stamps (orange) and two 2p stamps (green) are to be stuck on a letter in a
   'domino 5' pattern (Fig. 9.41). Draw the different possible arrangements for these
   stamps. How many different ways are there? (10 ways—put an orange stamp in the
   middle and then a green one.)
7. You go to the Post Office to buy two 10p stamps. The postmistress tears them from a
   sheet. How many different ways could the stamps be arranged when sold to you?

Note—show some stamps torn from a sheet to illustrate the difference when two stamps are joined. (3 ways—separated and 2 ways if they are joined.)

Suppose, on another occasion, you buy three 10p stamps. How many different ways could these be arranged when sold to you? Draw these ways on squared paper. (9 ways—separated and 2 ways if two are joined and 6 more ways if all three are joined.)

9.4.6 Flags and Shields (2, 11 L1; 2 L2)

Many children find difficulty when drawing shields and flags a number of times to keep them the same size and make orderly arrangements. They also often take a considerable time drawing them. For these colouring activities, therefore, the teacher needs to prepare worksheets with shields or flags drawn on them. There should be enough drawings to cater for full solutions with two or three extra.

Find, in the following problems, how many different ways there are of colouring in the shields or flags. All regions next to each other must be coloured differently, unless otherwise stated.

1. Colour the shield in Fig. 9.42 red and green. (2 ways)

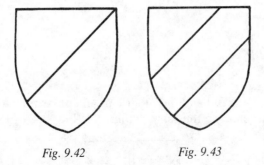

Fig. 9.42   *Fig. 9.43*

2. Colour the shield in Fig. 9.43 red, green and blue. (6 ways—make the central stripe red, green and blue, in turn, taking into account the remaining colours each time.)
3. Use two of the colours red, green and blue to colour the shield in Fig. 9.44. (6 ways—make the central stripe red, green and blue in turn, and take into account the remaining colours each time.)

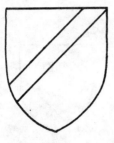

Fig. 9.44

4. Colour the shield in Fig. 9.45 red, green and yellow. (6 ways—make the central circle red, then green, then yellow.)

Fig. 9.45

5. Colour the flag in Fig. 9.46 red, white and green. (6 ways—make the region near the pole red, then green, then white.)

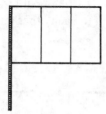

Fig. 9.46

6. Colour half of the flag red and the other half green, keeping to the lines. Regions next to each other may be the same colour. See Fig. 9.47. (6 ways.)

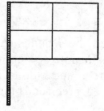

Fig. 9.47

Fig. 9.48

7. Use red, green and blue to colour the shield in Fig. 9.48. Colour in those shields only which have a red circle. Then predict how many different ways there would be of colouring in the shields altogether. Do not colour more shields. (18 ways—6 with a red circle, 6 with a green circle and 6 with a blue circle.)

9.4.7 Arrangements (2, 11 L1; 2 L2)

1. John has a blue pullover and a red pullover. He has grey trousers and green trousers. In how many different ways could he dress himself? Draw these ways. (4 ways.)
2. Mary has a red cardigan and a yellow cardigan, a grey skirt and a blue skirt, black shoes and brown shoes. In how many different ways could she dress? (8 ways) Draw the different outfits. The teacher prepares a worksheet with twelve drawings of Mary on it for the child to colour in.
3. Teddy bears are either brown, blue or yellow with red or green bows around their necks. Draw all the different colours of teddy bears. (6 different bears) The teacher prepares a recording sheet with nine bears, each with a bow tie, on it.
4. Grandma had one apple, one pear, one orange and one banana in her fruit bowl. She said I could have two of them to eat. What possible selections could I have made? (6 different selections) Draw them. Gummed paper cut-outs could be used instead.
5. Mother has two flower pots, one brown and one green. She has one red, one blue and one white hyacinth bulb but she does not know which colour of flower any bulb will give. She plants two of the bulbs, one in each pot. Draw what might happen when both the hyacinths are in flower. (6 possible colour arrangements) The teacher prepares a recording sheet with nine flowers, in pots, to be coloured in.
6. A shop sells white short socks with two different coloured bands around their tops. These bands are either blue, green or yellow, and the shopkeeper has all the different colour arrangements in stock. How many different kinds of socks were there? (6 different kinds) Draw them. The teacher prepares a recording sheet with ten socks on it for children to colour in.
7. Peter's sports clothes consist of shorts, a shirt and socks. The colours available to buy all these items are green, red and yellow. His outfit must involve two colours only. How many different outfits did Peter have to choose from? The teacher prepares a worksheet with ten drawings of Peter on it for the children to colour in.

   A child may find it tedious to find all 18 different outfits for himself. This problem, therefore, could be done by three children working together. One could deal with green and yellow clothes, another with red and yellow and another with red and green.

9.4.8 Folding Shapes (2 L1; 10 L2, 3)

For the following activities the children will need congruent paper circles, triangles, rectangles, regular hexagons and regular octagons. These could be produced by drawing around cardboard templates and cutting out the shapes produced. Templates needed are a rectangle about 10 cm long and 7 cm wide; a circle 8–10 cm in diameter; a triangle with sides 7–10 cm long; and a regular hexagon and a regular octagon with sides about 3 cm long.

Some of the more demanding tasks, questions **3–7**, could be done by two or three children working together.

1. Congruent triangles needed. Fold a triangle once, open it out, colour in the two parts and describe each part. Find different ways of dividing the triangle. (It can be divided into two triangles, or one triangle and one four-sided shape.)
2. Congruent rectangles needed. Fold a rectangle once, open it out and colour in the shapes obtained. Divide a rectangle into each of the following: 2 triangles, 2 equal rectangles, 2 unequal rectangles, 2 four-sided shapes (not rectangles), 1 triangle and 1 pentagon. Display these ways.
3. Use paper circles. Fold a circle once and open it out: fold it again and open it out; fold it again and open it out. Line in the creases. How many parts is the circle divided into? What is the least number of parts? (4) What is the greatest number? (7) Display the various results. (A circle can be divided into 4, 5, 6 and 7 parts.)
4. Congruent regular hexagons needed. Fold a hexagon once, open it out and colour in the two shapes. Count the sides in each shape and write them down. (3, 5) could be suggested as a means of recording that it was divided into a triangle and a pentagon. Display the various ways a hexagon can be folded: (3, 5), (3, 7), (4, 4), (4, 5), (4, 6) and (5, 5).
5. Use congruent regular octagons. Do as requested in question **4**. An octagon can be folded into (3, 7), (3, 9), (4, 6), (4, 8), (5, 5), (5, 6), (5, 7) and (6, 6).
6. Congruent triangles needed. Fold a triangle once and open it out, fold it again and open it out. Colour in the shapes obtained. Write down the number of sides in each shape, in order. For example, if the triangle was divided into two triangles and two four-sided shapes, this could be recorded as (3, 3, 4, 4). Exhibit different ways of dividing the triangles on a wall display: (3, 3, 3), (3, 3, 4), (3, 4, 4), (3, 3, 3, 4), (3, 3, 4, 4), (3, 4, 4, 4) and (3, 3, 4, 5).
7. Congruent paper rectangles needed. Fold the oblong once and open it out; fold it again and open it out. Colour in the shapes obtained. Write down the number of sides in each shape as in Question 6, above. Prepare a wall display to show the various ways of dividing the rectangle: (3, 3, 3), (3, 3, 4), (3, 3, 5), (3, 3, 6), (3, 4, 4), (4, 4, 4), (3, 3, 3, 3), (3, 4, 4, 4), (3, 4, 4, 5), (3, 3, 4, 4), (3, 3, 5, 5) and (4, 4, 4, 4).

9.4.9 Making Triangles (8 L1; 2, 10, 11 L2; 11 L3)

1. Use a set of geostrips to make triangles with three equal sides, two equal sides and all sides of different lengths.
2. Use straws 8, 10, 12 and 14 cm long, four of each. Pick three straws of different lengths and lay them, ends touching, on the table to form a triangle. How many different triangles can be made? Display them and also record their side lengths, e.g. (8, 10, 12). There are four different triangles: (8, 10, 12), (8, 10, 14), (10, 12, 14) and (8, 12, 14).
3. Use straws 8, 10 and 12 cm long, six of each. Pick three of these straws and put them on the table, ends touching, to make different triangles. Each triangle is to have two equal sides. Display the triangles and also record their side lengths, e.g. (8, 8, 10).

There are six different triangles: (8, 8, 10), (8, 8, 12), (10, 10, 8), (10, 10, 12), (12, 12, 8) and (12, 12, 10).

9.4.10 Making Shapes (8 L1; 2, 10, 11 L2; 11 L3)

1. On centimetre-squared paper draw eight rectangles, 8 cm long and 6 cm wide. Draw a diagonal in each rectangle, cut them out, and then cut each rectangle into two square-cornered triangles. Put equal sides of two triangles together, and touching, to make 4-sided shapes. Stick these shapes on a piece of paper. Can you make six different shapes?
2. Draw on centimetre-squared paper an 8 cm square and an oblong 8 cm long and 6 cm wide. Draw one diagonal of the oblong. Cut out the square, and oblong, then cut the oblong diagonally into two triangles. You should now have one square and two square-cornered triangles. (More shapes like these will need to be cut.) Put the three shapes (one square and two triangles) with equal sides coinciding and touching to make another larger shape. Repeat this making different shapes and sticking them on paper. Can you make eight different shapes?

9.4.11 Shapes in a Dot Lattice (2, 8 L1; 10, 11 L2; 11 L3)

Use square dot lattice paper. Within a 3 by 3 dot square draw as many different sized triangles as possible (Fig. 9.49). Each triangle must have a dot at each corner. (There are 8.)

•   •   •

•   •   •

•   •   •

Fig. 9.49

How many different 4-sided shapes can you draw within the 3 by 3 dot square? Can you find ten?

How many different pentagons can you make? How many different hexagons?

9.4.12 Halving Squares (2, 3, 8, 11 L2; 11 L3)

1. Draw, on centimetre-squared paper, a square of side 3 cm (Fig. 9.50). Divide the

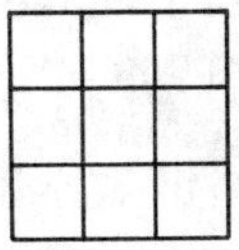

Fig. 9.50

square into two parts of equal area, by joining squares and half squares. (The only half squares that may be used are those obtained by cutting small squares diagonally.) No rotations or flip-overs are allowed. Can you find seven different ways?

2. Draw, on centimetre-squared paper, a square of side 4 cm (Fig. 9.51). Keeping to the lines, divide the square into two parts of equal area. Draw the different ways. Can you find seven ways? No rotations or flip-overs are allowed.

Fig. 9.51

9.4.13 Using Coloured Straws (2 L1; 2, 10, 11 L2; 11 L3)

1. Cut some red, blue and white straws into 8–10 cm equal lengths, 15 of each. Select three straws and form a triangle with them on the table. How many different colours of triangle can be made? Display them. Rotations and flip-overs are not allowed. (Pick three straws of the same colour, then two of the same colour; then all of different colours. Ten triangles can be made.)

2. Fifteen red and fifteen blue straws are needed of the same length. Select any four straws and form a square with them on the table. Display the different colours of square which can be made. Rotations and flip-overs are not allowed. (Pick four straws the same colour, then three the same colour, then two the same colour. Six different squares can be made.)

3. Use green, red, white and blue straws of equal length, twelve of each. Select three straws and form triangles with them on the table, each triangle having two sides of the same colour. Display different triangles. Rotations and flip-overs are not allowed. (Pick two red, then two green, then two white and then two blue straws. Twelve triangles can be made.)

9.4.14 How Many of Each? (2 L1; 2, 10, 11 L2; 11 L3)

These questions involving shapes concern number rather than geometry. Children could use plastic shapes to assist their thinking, and find solutions, but some recording is necessary in order to show what has been, or is being, done. The need to record becomes more evident as the number of steps involved increases. Children, initially, often tackle these questions in a haphazard way and the teacher needs to encourage them to use systematic methods and suitable ways of recording the steps. Some questions have more than one solution and in order to find them all there is a need to explore all possibilities in an orderly manner.

For example, some triangles and squares have 14 sides in all. How many are there of each? This could be explored by putting out triangles (or squares) 1, 2, 3, 4, etc. of each, in turn, and finding the number of squares (or triangles) to go with each of them. A more formal approach would be to enter the working in a table (Fig. 9.52). Calculations could still be assisted by using shapes, particularly in the last step of each stage for which squares could be put out and sides counted, to see if the remaining number of sides is a multiple of four. A calculator, however, could be used instead.

Number of triangles	Number of sides	Number of sides left	Number of squares
1	3	14 − 3 = 11	–
2	6	14 − 6 = 8	2
3	9	14 − 9 = 5	–
4	12	14 − 12 = 2	–
5	15	–	

Fig. 9.52

Individual children, or children working in twos or threes, could be given the following questions:

1. Bill takes some triangles and squares from a box. Altogether they have 17 sides. What did he pick up? (3 triangles and 2 squares—put out 1, 2, 3, 4, 5, 6 triangles, in turn, and put squares with each of them.)
2. Mary has some triangles and squares. Altogether they have 16 sides. How many of each did she have? (4 triangles and 1 square)
3. Susan has some circles and squares. They have 16 sides altogether. How many of each shape? (4c and 3s or 8c and 2s or 12c and 1s—put out 1, 2, 3, 4 squares, in turn, and put circles with each of them.)
4. Barry has some triangles and circles. Altogether they have 15 sides. What could he have? (1t and 12c, 2t and 9c, 3t and 6c or 4t and 3c—put out 1, 2, 3, 4 triangles, in turn, and put circles with each of them.)
5. A box contains triangles, squares and pentagons. I pick out some of two kinds of these shapes only. They have 14 sides altogether. What may I have chosen? (2t and 2s; 3t and 1p, 1s and 2p. Choose squares and triangles, then squares and pentagons and then triangles and pentagons.)
6. Elizabeth has some circles, triangles and squares. They have 13 sides altogether. What shapes may she have? (1s and 2t and 3c; 1s and 1t and 6c; or 2s and 1t and 2c—put out 1, 2, 3 squares, in turn, and put triangles and circles with each of them.)
7. A box contains circles, triangles and squares. I pick some shapes from this box. They have 8 sides altogether. What may I have picked? (8c, 2s, 1s and 4c, 2t and 2c, 1t and 5c, 1s and 1c and 1t—pick one shape only, then two shapes only and then all three shapes.)

9.4.15 Where Are They? (11 L2, 3)

1. Marie invites Jean, Lisa and Jenny to her party. They sit at a round table. Jean sits opposite Marie. Lisa sits next to Marie on her right. Draw a picture to show where the children sit.
   This could be given to four children. They could use their own names if all different. Give them seating instructions. The children arrange themselves at a table.

2. A blue counter, a yellow counter and a red counter are placed in a row on the table. The red counter is to the left of the blue one and next to it. The yellow counter is to the right of the red counter. Arrange the counters in order. (Use plastic counters or coloured cards and move them around on the table—red, blue, yellow.)
3. A black counter, a blue counter and a red counter are placed in a row on the table. The red counter is to the left of the black counter. The blue counter is at the end of the row but is not next to the black counter. Arrange the counters in order. (Use plastic counters or coloured cards—blue, red, black.)
4. Four houses coloured red, white, green and blue are side by side in a terrace. The red house is to the left of the blue one. The green house is to the right of the white one. The blue house is next to the green one, but not at the end of the row. Arrange the houses in order. (Use cut-outs of houses or appropriately coloured cards. Put the houses on the table in stages as the question is read through, statement by statement—red, white, blue, green.)

9.5 PUZZLES

9.5.1 Comparisons (2, 8 L2)

Each of the following questions needs to be written on a separate work card. They could be attempted by children individually or working in pairs. Solution hints—express all statements as taller than, older than or heavier than, and record each with an arrow diagram. Then combine the diagrams into one (Fig. 9.53). For example, George is older than Harry and Mary is younger than George. Who is the youngest?

Fig. 9.53

From Fig. 9.53 we see that George is older than both Mary and Harry. We cannot say, however, who is the younger of Harry and Mary.

1. John is taller than Peter. Peter is taller than Mary. Who is tallest? Who is shortest? (John, Mary)
2. Mary is taller than Janet but shorter than Christine. What is the tallest girl called? (Christine)
3. Mary is older than Bill but younger than Elizabeth. What is the name of the youngest person? (Bill)
4. Susan is taller than Mary. Bill is shorter than Mary. Who is tallest? Who is shortest? (Susan, Bill)
5. Ian, John and Susan are three children. Ian is shorter than John. The girl is the shortest. Who is the tallest child? (John)
6. David is taller than Peter. Mary is shorter than David. Who is the tallest? Who is shortest? (David, cannot say)

7. Mary is heavier than Jane. Diane is lighter than Mary. Jane is not the lightest. Who is the lightest? (Diane)
8. John is older than Betty and older than Kevin. What is the youngest person called? (Cannot say; either Betty or Kevin)
9. Alison, George and Michael are aged 14, 12 and 9. Alison is younger than Michael but older than George. How old is Alison? How old is George? (12, 9)

9.5.2 Who's Who?

These questions require some form of concrete representation to aid the children's thinking. For this, cards could be used, some of which have drawings of animals on them and others with their given names on them. Some questions will need four cards, others six. These cards could be placed on the table with animal cards in one set and name cards in another. As the problem is read through the cards are gradually paired off. Usually one pair can easily be united, leaving two pairs to be manipulated and identified. Each question needs to be written on a separate work card and could be done by individual, or pairs of, children.

1. Two animals, a cat and a dog, are called Blackie and Rover. Rover is not the cat. What animal is Blackie? (cat)
2. Farmer Giles has a pig, a horse and a cow. The animals are called Bluebell, Princess and Ben. Bluebell moos. Ben grunts. What is the horse's name? (Princess)
3. Thumper, Tigger and Ben are a cat, a rabbit and a dog. Thumper has a fluffy tail. Ben is bigger than Tigger. What is each animal's name? (Thumper the rabbit; Tigger the cat; Ben the dog)
4. Prince, Flash and Chester are the names of a horse, a cat and a dog. Flash is the tallest animal and Prince can bark. What is the cat called? (Chester)
5. Jane, Amanda and Peter each have a pet. The pets are a dog, a rabbit and a budgie. Peter has the heaviest animal. Jane's pet has two legs. What animal does each child have? (Jane, a budgie; Peter, a dog; Amanda, a rabbit)
6. An elephant, a horse and a cat are called Princess, Blackie and Beauty. Beauty has a trunk. Prince is not the smallest animal. What is the cat called? What is the elephant's name? (Blackie, Beauty)
7. Ann, Elizabeth and William each have one pet. The pets are a goldfish, a hamster and a cat. Elizabeth's pet has no legs. Ann's pet is the smallest furry animal. Which animal does each child have? (Ann, a hamster; Elizabeth, a goldfish; William, a cat)
8. Emma and Jane have the surnames Evans and Jones but the initial letters of their names are different. What are the people called? (Jane Evans; Emma Jones)
9. Mary, Judith, David and Peter are two sets of twins, aged 8 and 6. Mary is much older than Judith and David is much younger than Peter. Which twins are aged 8? (Mary and Peter)
10. Linda, Anne, Bill and David belong to two different families. Bill is not David's brother. Linda is David's only sister. What children are in each family? (Bill and Anne; David and Linda)

9.5.3 Crossing the River

Three children, Ann, Peter and Mary, need to cross a river in a small rowing boat. The boat will only hold two children at a time. They can all row a boat but none of them can swim. How do they all get across? None gets wet and the boat is rowed across each time.

This activity is for one or two children. The river could be drawn on a sheet of paper and placed on the table. The three children, plastic People Sorts, could be put on one river bank and a tin lid used for the boat. The procedure is then carried through. They could tell, or show, teacher how it is done.

9.5.4 Leapfrog

Exchange the set of black counters for the set of white counters in the Leapfrog puzzle (Fig. 9.54). The black counters move to the right and the whites to the left. A counter may only move by going into a neighbouring empty space or by leapfrogging a counter of the other colour into a free space. What is the least number of moves needed? (8 moves)

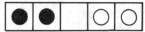

Fig. 9.54

If this is successfully completed a child could try to do the same with three counters of each colour (Fig. 9.55). What is the least number of moves required? (This is harder and takes 15 moves, at least.)

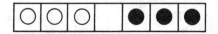

Fig. 9.55

9.5.5 The Tower of Hanoi

A child could attempt the Tower of Hanoi puzzle (Fig. 9.56). Three rings, of different diameters, form a tower on spike A. The task is to remove the tower from spike A and rebuild it on spike B, using these rules:

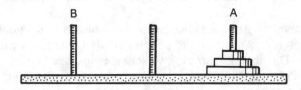

Fig. 9.56

Only one ring may be moved at a time from one spike to another.

A ring may be moved to an empty spike.
A ring may be placed on another larger ring on any spike.
What is the least number of moves needed? (7)

Some children could attempt the same thing using a four ring tower instead. The least number of moves in this case is 15.

9.6 CHILDREN'S LITERATURE

Children's literature is often a useful basis for cross-curricular work. The mathematics involved may sometimes be suggested by the author who presents it in terms of difficult situations to be overcome. Authors, such as Ronda and David Armitage, include such features in their books, *The Lighthousekeeper's Lunch* and *The Lighthousekeeper's Catastrophe*, published by André Deutsch. The children listening to the story could be asked to consider what Mr and Mrs Grinling could do in order to overcome the various difficulties as they are met. The children often enjoy the book with the author's solutions after making their own suggestions. They may also take the author's solution and try out some aspects of it for themselves.

In *The Lighthousekeeper's Catastrophe*, Mrs Grinling makes a collection of things which together weigh the same as Mr Grinling in order to test her solution for getting into the lighthouse after the key is locked inside. The children may try to produce a collection of things whose weight is equivalent to one of themselves.

Mrs Grinling gave Mr Grinling some lovely lunches. Sometimes she made sand-wiches. Some of these could be said to consist of yellow cheese, red tomatoes and green lettuce, in three layers between two slices of bread. The children have to find the number of different sandwiches which could be made by looking at the different ways of arranging these layers. The children could be provided with a page of drawings of sandwiches to colour in (Fig. 9.57).

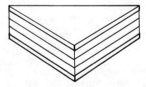

Fig. 9.57

The author's experiences have been that some children start to colour in the sand-wiches in a haphazard way. Their attention could be drawn to the work of other children who have started in a systematic way. The idea of remembering what has been done, and what still needs to be done, could be discussed. They may in the end be satisfied with the six different sandwiches they found by colouring. Some children, on the other hand, may point out that some of the sandwiches are the same as others should they be turned over. If we allow turning over, how many different sandwiches would there be?

Another activity could be related to Hamish the cat being placed in the basket on the ropeway to the lighthouse. Mr Grinling is polishing the reflector on the lighthouse and sees the basket, which has the word HAMISH written on its side, coming towards him.

Children could investigate whether he could read the word HAMISH in the polished surface. What did he see? (HƧIMAH) They could further investigate which capital letters could be read in the mirror. The teacher would need to provide large cut-out capital letters and a large metal mirror. The letters could be provided on a strip of durable paper. Finally the children could be challenged to make up a name for the cat which could be read by Mr Grinling in the reflector. (They may not be very exciting names but something like TOT, TOOT, VIV or MIM could be chosen.)

When he is at the top of the lighthouse Mr Grinling is able to lean over the rail and look at the sailing boats, each of which has a number on it. He uses these numbers as a basis for the selection of teams on his football coupon. The teams on the coupon are numbered from 1 to 58 and he needs to choose eight of these team numbers. He finds these numbers using one or more of the numbers on the sails (Fig. 9.58). The children could find eight numbers which he might use. For example, 8, 43, 7 (4 + 3), 35 (13 × 3 − 4), are but a few.

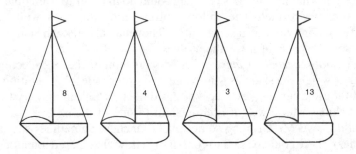

Fig. 9.58

In the book illustrations of Mr Grinling he wears a checked handkerchief on his head similar to that shown in diagram A of Fig. 9.59. A discussion could take place about how many squares there are of one colour and how many of the other. It may be seen that these numbers of squares are not the same and so there is not the same amount of handkerchief in one colour as the other. Given some squared paper and crayons, the children could be asked to design other handkerchiefs for Mr Grinling making sure there are equal amounts of each of two colours. At first they could use a '4-square' handkerchief and by colouring whole and/or half squares produce patterns similar to those of B, C and D in Fig. 9.59. They might also repeat this activity on a '16-square' handkerchief, but only colouring whole squares. For an example, see diagram E in Fig.

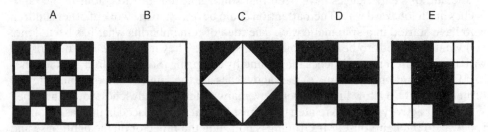

Fig. 9.59

9.59. During these activities some discussion could take place about rotations and turn-overs producing the same handkerchief.

The basket in which Mrs Grinling packs the lunch is unsuitable. In one story the gulls are able to remove the tablecloth from it and get at the sandwiches. In the other story the gulls are able to set it in motion so that it rolls down the cliff into the sea. The children could investigate boxes to see which of them rolled and which could not be rolled. In another investigation the children could put sets of six plastic squares together and make hexominoes. They could then select some of these, draw them on squared paper, cut out and fold them, to find those which make cubes (Fig. 9.60). This may be

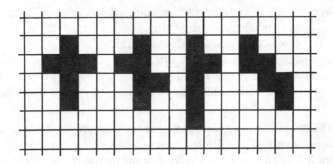

Fig. 9.60

followed by giving the children a net of an open box which has been drawn on large-squared paper (Fig. 9.61). The net is cut out and pasted on to thin card. The card is cut to the net and the net is folded and its sides Sellotaped to make a box. In order to make this box suitable for a lunch box it must be impregnable to seagulls and so must have a lid. The children are then invited to use the same net as before but this time to draw a square or oblong onto that net in order to form a lid. Cutting out and folding take place to test whether the lid has been correctly placed and is of the right size.

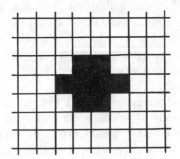

Fig. 9.61

Mrs Grinling tries to give Mr Grinling things he likes to eat. He is thrilled when he finds she has popped a bar of his favourite chocolate in his lunch box. The children could suggest what they think this could be. The teacher could set up a chocolate taste test and the children could record and communicate the results. Alternatively the children could each supply a wrapper from their favourite chocolate bar and use them to create a graph which shows which kind is most popular. Perhaps Mr Grinling also likes that one?

Activities could also stem from *The Jolly Postman* by Janet and Allan Ahlberg, published by Heinemann. Children could work on:

1. The making of a 'spell-proof' tent, a life-size newt and a 'giant' for the classroom.
2. The shapes of the various nets needed to make different envelopes.
3. The amount of paper it takes to make an envelope.
4. The making of an envelope to take a specified size of card.
5. A variety of questions relating to the purchase of stamps.
6. The number of ways of putting a set of stamps, in a row, on an envelope.
7. Destination zones and the cost of posting.
8. Questions involving collection and delivery times.
9. The location of post boxes and post offices.
10. Distances involved in a postal round.
11. Questions concerned with weighing and the cost of posting parcels.

There could be at least four activities relating to 'Sing a Song of Sixpence'. Children could find some, if not all, of the different ways of making 6p. They could also consider the number of radial cuts needed to cut slices from a circular pie for different numbers of people, e.g. 1 piece needs 2 cuts, 2 pieces need 3 cuts, 3 pieces need 4 cuts, and so on. How many cuts for 7 pieces? Hanging clothes on a line suggests an arrangement problem. For example, find different ways of arranging a pair of trousers, a pullover and a pair of socks on the clothes line. Finally, could four-and-twenty blackbirds fly into two trees so that there are the same number of birds in each tree? What about three trees or five trees? Other numbers could also be considered.

In the *Frog and Toad Tales*, by Arnold Lobel, published by World's Work Ltd., there is a tale of 'A Lost Button' in which a description of Toad's lost button is given. A task, which could be tackled by some children, is to find Toad's button, the teacher having placed a button of this description into a pot containing many other different buttons.

The book *Titch*, by Pat Hutchins, published by Puffin, provides an opportunity to find some, or all, of the different coloured sets of clothes which it is possible for Titch to wear. Titch originally had a complete outfit in red, green and blue. The children could tackle this activity using coloured gummed paper cut-outs of Titch's jumpers, trousers and socks. Alternatively the teacher could prepare a worksheet with drawings of Titch on it for children to colour in.

Note—If the children find the number of different ways of colouring Titch when he is wearing a red pullover, they could *calculate* the total number of ways he could dress. Colouring in all 27 different outfits would prove tiresome and difficult and is not necessary. See Section 9.4.7, *Arrangements*, for other examples of this type.

Other books which lend themselves to the use of mathematics are:

Icecream for Rosie	Ronda and David Armitage	Hippo Books
Jim and the Beanstalk	Raymond Briggs	Hamish Hamilton
Python's Party	Brian Wildsmith	OUP
Rosie's Walk	Pat Hutchins	Picture Puffin
Shopping Basket	John Burningham	Picture Puffin

9.7 INTEGRATED PROJECTS

Applications, including some of those already indicated, may arise from work within a cross-curricular project. Some of these demand an investigative approach since there may be no readily available data which could lead directly to an immediate solution. The approach to be used and the data to be collected may be recorded in some form which will allow patterns or trends to be perceived and conclusions drawn. Some activities of this kind, arising in the project *Ourselves*, have already been indicated in other parts of this book. See the *Introduction* and Sections 1.15, 1.16, 1.18, 2.13, 3.19, 3.21, 4.5, 4.6, 4.7, 5.10, 5.12 and 6.19.

In the project *Our School* the children could look at the work of *People Who Help Us*, other than the teachers. The work of the school clerk involves collecting and banking money, purchasing postage stamps and totalling registers. She may also be engaged in collecting monies, of differing amounts, for the various sized photographs from the school photographer.

If attention is focused on school dinners, not only is there the number of children having dinners and the payments, but also the planning which has to be made by the school cook. In one school the cook was interviewed and outlined her plans to the children. She had to work out when to put the meat joint in the oven on 'roast dinner day'. This was her information.

The children eat at 12 noon. The meat must be cooled before carving and this cooling takes 20 minutes. The carving takes 10 minutes. The meat must stay in the oven, at the right temperature, a sufficient time for it to cook. It needs 20 minutes of cooking time for each pound of meat and an additional 20 minutes. Taking this information into account, and being told how heavy the joint was, the children in this school calculated when cook had to put the joint in the oven.

The project *Our Families* includes many applications of mathematics which occur within the field of the children's experience. For example, we may wish to know if a video tape is of sufficient duration to tape a programme from the television. The tape we have has room for 180 minutes of programmes. The programme we wish to tape starts, according to *Radio Times*, at 8.20 p.m. and ends at 10.45 p.m. Are we able to get all of this programme on the tape?

Again, within this project, we may have occasion to look at water shortages in the region and the ways in which we use water. We may need to find the amount of water wasted by a dripping tap. Attention may be drawn to the amount of water used when a toilet is flushed. The children, with the help of the teacher, could find that it takes a bucket of water to refill it, and then find out how much water is used by the class in a day. The children could also find the amount of water used by their families, for particular purposes, during the day.

Work related to the *Supermarket* or *Our Families* includes looking at check-out bills and the family shopping basket. Work could be based upon milk products only, or the buying of 'necessities'. This then might include costs of items, total costs and the change required. Some tasks may concern the buying of small or larger amounts. For example, a small tin of baked beans costs 22p for 225 g whilst a larger tin of the same brand costs 26p for 450 g. A 100-g jar of coffee costs £1.55 whilst a 200-g jar of the same brand costs £2.87. The children could give reasons for which they might buy. Sometimes there may be reasons why the larger quantity might not be purchased, even if it is comparatively cheaper.

Parents are just now being offered the opportunity to buy E.C. milk for their children to drink at school. The children could find out how much milk to order for their class each week, and how long it would take for their own milkman to deliver this amount of milk to their home and what this would cost. They might also find out how much E.C. milk could be bought for what they pay for the family milk each week.

A project on *Birds* could lead the children to work with some of the data given in *Birds and Mathematics* published by the RSPB. Information is included about bird counting and feeding, bird sizes, making a nesting box, and distances travelled with the times taken by different species. Work on population growth (*Birds and Mathematics*, page 7) could be included with that of Section 9.2.11, *Patterns and Predictions*. For example, a pair of blue tits often raise a brood of six young, male and female in equal numbers. If they all survive to breed amongst themselves once a year, but the parents die, how many birds will be produced the following year? What about the year after, and so on, if the same conditions hold? Find the total number of birds at the end of each year for the first five years. (Use a calculator, if necessary.) See Fig. 9.62. Discussion could take place about the reasons for the blue tit population not really growing at this rate.

End of	1st Year	2nd Year	3rd Year	4th Year	5th Year
Number of birds	6	18	54	162	486

Fig. 9.62

Some projects may be based upon the environment and these could include local industry. This may involve the setting up of a model industrial project within the school. The authors were involved with a school which set up a 'company' to make ginger beer which was then sold to the children in the rest of the school at break times. The profits were donated to charity. Basic commodities and equipment were needed so these costs were taken from a 'starter' fund and met eventually from the receipts of sales. Calculations of costs and quantities of product had to be made if the 'company' was not to fall into 'debt'. At one point falling sales caused concern and it was decided to offer two for the price of one to try to increase sales. At a later stage, and temporarily, it was decided to change the product. The children solved the difficulties involved to the extent that they were, after a term's trading, able to donate £250 to cancer research.

In another environmental project the children were engaged in recording the flow of traffic at a cross-roads near the school. The flow was controlled by traffic lights and it was noticed that 'build-ups' occurred at certain times. Questions emerged about the length of time for which the lights should be set to green. This was discussed and, after a variety of suggestions, it was proposed to link the length of the green signal with the data on 'traffic density' which the children had collected. When this solution was communicated to the Borough Engineer the reply to the children indicated that their solution was, with little modification, the one that he himself had used.

Investigations, such as the previous one, depend upon the collecting of data which are perceived to be relevant. Opportunities for investigations of this type present themselves in many of the projects in which children become engaged.

In the project *'Ourselves'* the teacher could suggest to a suitable group that she believes that most families take their holidays abroad. She might do this in order to promote discussion about the truth of this statement. After hearing their immediate responses she might discuss with them the kind of information which would be needed in order to find out. The children could then collect the necessary information and arrange it in such a form as will enable them to ask further questions and to draw conclusions. The findings of the group could then be communicated to the rest of the class.

In the same project the statement that *'Children are not interested in serious TV programmes but only like watching children's programmes, quiz shows and films'* could be made. This could be investigated and contributory information could be sought, perhaps by means of a questionnaire produced by the children. The assertion that *'Children watch at least 2 hours of TV a day'* should have the desired effect of producing some hot discussion and the desire to give a reasonable response.

Children who are engaged in a project on *'Colour and Light'*, in which there is much science, could as part of the project turn their attention to camouflage and to colours that are easier to see in poor light. Associated with this could be a statement that *'Yellow is not a popular colour for cars'*. A consideration of information gained from parents, a road traffic survey and manufacturer's statistics, could make children aware of one of the factors in road accidents.

Other statements which could be used to promote discussion and generate the perceived need to collect and analyse relevant information could be:

Most people use gas to heat their homes.
The wind rarely blows from the North.
It's generally sunny in June.
Most families have a pet of some kind.
Monday is washing day for most families.
More tea is drunk than coffee.
More people eat brown bread than white.
People eat more margarine than butter.
Girls are able to spell better than boys.
Most children go to bed before 8 o'clock.
Most people eat two or more apples a week.
Most people drink more than five cups of liquid a day.
Most people have a first name with six or more letters in it.
After dogs and cats, budgerigars are the next most popular pet.

Appendix

EQUIPMENT

Names and suppliers, for some of the equipment mentioned in this book, are:

E. J. Arnold, Parkside Lane, Dewsbury Road, Leeds LS11 5TD
James Galt, Brookfield Road, Cheadle Hulme, Cheshire SK8 2PN
Invicta Plastics, Oadby, Leicester LE2 4LB
Philip and Tacey, North Way, Andover, Hampshire SP10 5BA
Taskmaster Ltd., Morris Road, Leicester LE2 6BR
Osmiroid Ltd., Fareham Road, Gosport, Hampshire PO13 0AL

Brief details about the items and names of suppliers are listed below:

Abacus or counting tablets These 2.5 cm plastic squares can be used in number work and as covering units for finding areas. These can be obtained from Invicta Plastics.

Area measuring grids Clear plastic grids ruled in 1-cm squares, sizes 25 cm × 25 cm and 9 cm × 9 cm, can be obtained from E. J. Arnold.

Aspirators 9-litre and 4.5-litre polythene aspirator bottles, with taps, can be obtained from Griffin and George, Bishop Meadow Road, Loughborough, Leicestershire LE11 0RG. *Note*— ensure that the aspirator is made from 'see-through' polythene.

Attribute blocks These sorting shapes (squares, oblongs, circles, triangles and hexagons) are manufactured by Invicta Plastics.

Bank notes Token bank notes of value £5, £10 and £20 are supplied by E. J. Arnold.

Blank dice Cubical dice with plain faces, which can be marked as required with a spirit marker, are supplied by E. J. Arnold.

Brass cylindrical masses 10-g, 20-g, 50-g and 100-g masses, which can be stacked, are supplied by E. J. Arnold.

Brass masses 1-g, 2-g, 5-g, 10-g, 20-g and 50-g masses can be obtained from Taskmaster.

Cardboard coins 1p, 2p, 5p, 10p, 20p, 50p and £1 coins are supplied by E. J. Arnold.

Centicubes Plastic interlocking cubes of side 1 cm and mass 1 g are supplied by Osmiroid.

Clixi A construction set for investigating 3-D geometrical shapes and their nets. Supplied by E. J. Arnold.

Clock face stamps Philip and Tacey supply rubber stamp clock faces, either numbered or blank. The blank clock-face stamp could be adapted to make 'timer' cards.

Clock with geared hands A model clock-face with synchronized hands is sold by Philip and Tacey.

Common balances Tough plastic balances, ranges 0–500 g and 0–1 kg, from Osmiroid; tough plastic, 0–2 kg, and cast iron, 0–1 kg, from E. J. Arnold; metal scales, two-pan and one-pan, from J. Galt.

Compression balances 0–500 g, 0–1 kg, 0–5 kg, 0–10 kg from E. J. Arnold: 0–750 g from Philip and Tacey.

Count down/count up timer A combined timer and clock with 6-digit display showing hours, minutes and seconds. Will count up to, or down from, 24 hours in seconds. Obtainable from Taskmaster.

Counting Toys An assortment of miniature plastic toys which are useful for sorting activities and number work. Manufactured by E. J. Arnold.

Cuisenaire rods Used in number work and volume activities. Obtainable from E. J. Arnold.

Decimal set Wooden blocks, flats, longs and units, based on 1-cm unit cubes, used for notation and number operations, are supplied by Taskmaster.

Dienes Aloblocs These desk-size and giant-size squares, oblongs, triangles and circles, used for sorting and logic work, are obtained from E. J. Arnold.

Dienes wooden multibase based on 10-mm cubes. These blocks, flats, longs and units are used in the teaching of notation and number operations. Supplied by E. J. Arnold.

Digital stop-watch Has a 6-digit display, minutes and seconds. Timing range of 59 min 59.99 sec. Obtainable from Philip and Tacey.

Egg-timer A 3–4 minute sand-glass is available from E. J. Arnold.

Geometrical models Sets of 15, and 30, plastic 3-D shapes, are manufactured by Taskmaster. (Prisms, pyramids, etc.)

Geometrical strips Geo Strips can be joined to make two-dimensional shapes and are supplied by Taskmaster.

Geometric shapes Sets of 16 different 2-D shapes, 10 of each, based on 50-mm or 75-mm modules, suitable for work on sorting, shape, tessellation and area, are supplied by E. J. Arnold and J. Galt.

Gridsheets Square, triangular and hexagonal grid papers, also square and triangular dot lattice papers, can be obtained from Excitement in Learning, 88 Mint Street, London SE1 1QX.

Gummed paper shapes A set of useful shapes, Shirley shapes, includes boy and girl cut-outs, and can be used for preparing work cards on number and building up pictograms. Supplied by Philip and Tacey.

Gummed printed coins Gummed 'push-out' coins are useful when compiling work cards. Obtained from E. J. Arnold.

Iron masses 100-g, 200-g, ½-kg and 1-kg iron masses, hexagonal in shape, with and without ring handles, can be obtained from Philip and Tacey. 50-g, 100-g, 200-g, 500-g, 1-kg, 2-kg, 5-kg, and 10-kg masses can be obtained from Griffin and George, Bishop Meadow Road, Loughborough, Leicestershire.

Lab timer or 'buzzer' A one-hour timer, graduated in minutes, is available from E. J. Arnold.

Large 3-D models Ten hollow plastic prisms and pyramids, 15 cm tall, which can be filled with water. Supplied by Taskmaster.

Logic block set A 60-piece set including circles, triangles, squares, oblongs and hexagons, useful for sorting and logic work, is supplied by E. J. Arnold.

Multilink Plastic interlocking cubes of side 2 cm. Useful for making solids for work with symmetry, volume and number patterns. From E. J. Arnold.

Number lines Plastic, washable, number lines for wall or table-top use, blank or numbered from 0–100, supplied by Taskmaster. Card number lines 0–10 and 0–20, for table-top use, can be obtained from Philip and Tacey.

Number line stamps Rubber-stamp number lines 0–10 and 11–20 are supplied by Philip and Tacey.

Pegboards Plastic pegboards, 16 cm × 16 cm, holding 10 rows of 10 pegs, can be obtained from Invicta Plastics. Wooden pegboards, 16.5 cm square, holding 10 rows of 10 pegs, holes 13 mm apart, from J. Galt. Plastic 15-cm square pegboards holding 100 pegs, also from J. Galt.

Personal scales Graduated in kg and ½ kg. Range 0–125 kg. Supplied by Taskmaster.

Plastic coins 1p, 2p, 5p, 10p, 20p, 50p and £1 token coins are supplied by E. J. Arnold.

Plastic cubes Cubes of side 2.5 cm and 5 cm are manufactured by Philip and Tacey.

Plastic shapes Shapes such as circles, squares, oblongs, equilateral and isosceles triangles, trapezia, rhombuses, parallelograms, regular pentagons, regular hexagons, regular octagons, in 50-mm and 75-mm module sizes, are supplied by E. J. Arnold and J. Galt. Useful for sorting, tessellation, area work.

Plastic squares 2.5-cm plastic squares, Abacus tablets, can be obtained from Invicta Plastics, as well as 28-mm squares. 5-cm and 7.5-cm squares from E. J. Arnold or J. Galt.

Poleidoblocs G This set of wooden shapes, consisting of various prisms and pyramids, is supplied by E. J. Arnold.

Polydron Construction set for building 3-D shapes. Supplied by E. J. Arnold and Taskmaster.

Sand timer 1 minute, 3 minute and 5 minute sand-glasses are available from Osmiroid.

Seconds timer or stopclock This clock has a hand which revolves once each minute over a dial graduated in seconds and can be obtained from Taskmaster or J. Galt.

Spring balances 0–250 g, 0–500 g, 0–1 kg, 0–2 kg, 0–3 kg and 0–5 kg instruments can be obtained from E. J. Arnold.

Stacking masses Brass cylindrical masses, 10 g, 20 g, 50 g (half-hecs) and 100 g (hectograms), which can be stacked, are supplied by E. J. Arnold. Square plastic stacking masses, 5 g, 10 g and 20 g, from E. J. Arnold. Plastic circular stacking masses, 1 g, 2 g, 5 g, 10 g and 20 g, from Philip and Tacey.

Steel springs 220 mm long, 6 mm diameter and 80 mm long, 8 mm diameter springs can be obtained from Griffin and George, Bishop Meadow Road, Loughborough, Leicestershire. (Extensions 1.2 cm and 1.8 cm for 25 g, respectively.)

Stern apparatus Cubes, blocks, pattern boards, number cases, number tracks, etc. are supplied by E. J. Arnold.

Tower of Hanoi This logical puzzle can be obtained from Tarquin Publications, Stradbrooke, Diss, Norfolk IP21 5JP.

Trundle wheel A wheel, 1 metre in circumference, either plastic or wooden, fitted with a clicking device, can be obtained from E. J. Arnold.

Unifix material This is supplied by Philip and Tacey.

Volume relation models Hollow plastic prisms and pyramids, 10 cm tall, are sold by E. J. Arnold. Water can be poured from one to the other to show that the volume of a pyramid equals one-third of the volume of a prism having the same base and height.

Wooden building blocks Sets of playbricks consisting of cylinders, rectangular prisms, triangular prisms, arches, etc. can be obtained from J. Galt and E. J. Arnold.

Wooden cubes Cubes of 2.5-cm side are supplied by E. J. Arnold, J. Galt and Taskmaster.

Wooden solid shapes A 14-piece set of various prisms, pyramids, etc., 10 cm tall, supplied by Taskmaster.

BIBLIOGRAPHY

Brissenden, T. (1988) *Talking about Mathematics*. Oxford: Basil Blackwell.

Burton, L. (1984) *Thinking Things Through: Problem–Solving in Mathematics*. Oxford: Basil Blackwell.

Cockcroft, W. *et al.* (1982) *Mathematics Counts*. London: HMSO.

Denvir, B., Stolz, C. and Brown, M. (1982) *Low Attainers in Mathematics 5–16*. **Working Paper 72**. Schools Council.

Department of Education and Science (1985) *Curriculum Matters: Mathematics from 5 to 16*. London: HMSO.

Donaldson, M. (1984) *Children's Minds*. Flamingo.

Fisher, R. (ed.) (1987) *Problem-Solving in Schools*. Oxford: Basil Blackwell.

Hatch, G. (1984) *Bounce to It*. Manchester: Manchester Polytechnic.

Haylock, D. and Cockburn, A. (1989) *Understanding Early Years Mathematics*. London: Paul Chapman.

Hughes, M. (1986) *Children and Number*. Oxford: Basil Blackwell.

Mason, J., Burton, L. and Stacey, K. (1982) *Thinking Mathematically*. Wokingham: Addison-Wesley.

Merttens, R. (1988) *Teaching Primary Maths*. Sevenoaks: Edward Arnold.

Shuard, H. (1986) *Primary Mathematics—Today and Tomorrow*. Harlow: Longman.

Walsh, A. (ed.) (1989) *Help Your Child with Maths*. London: BBC Publications.

Williams, E. M. and Shuard, H. (1982) *Primary Mathematics Today*, 3rd Edition. Harlow: Longman.

Womack, D. (1988) *Developing Mathematical and Scientific Thinking in Young Children*. London: Cassell.

Woodman, A. and Albany, E. (1989) *Mathematics through Art and Design*. London: Unwin Hyman.

Index